*Flavours
of the Riviera*

Also by COLMAN ANDREWS
Catalan Cuisine

FLAVOURS OF THE RIVIERA

Discovering the Real
Mediterranean Cooking of
France and Italy

COLMAN ANDREWS

GRUB STREET • LONDON

FOR
CLAUDE CASPER-JORDAN
(1906–1994)

Published by
Grub Street
The Basement
10 Chivalry Road
London SW11 1HT

British Library Cataloguing in Publication Data
Andrews, Colman
  Flavours of the Riviera
  1. Cookery, Mediterranean
  I. Title
  641.5'91822

ISBN 1-902304-21-7

Printed and bound in Great Britain
by Biddles Ltd, Guildford and King's Lynn

❖ --- ❖

The handmade pottery in the
photographs was kindly loaned by
Baglady at Northcote Road Market,
Battersea, London SW11.
Contact: bagladydesign@hotmail.com

❖ --- ❖

Contents

Acknowledgements

It's hard to know where to begin in thanking the many people, in Italy, France, the United States, and elsewhere, who generously assisted me, in so many ways, in my research for this book – but I suppose I might well start in California, where I lived when I undertook this project: wine and food merchant (and legendary expert) Darrell Corti, whose roots are Genoese, gave me advice, encouragement, and practical assistance of all kinds, including introductions to members of his family in Genoa and frequent assistance with my fumbling translations from Niçois and Genoese – and then, in reading my manuscript from start to finish, saved me from half a hundred little errors. Mauro Vincenti and Piero Selvaggio gave me counsel both general and specific, and helped keep me nourished, and inspired gastronomically, in a splendid Italian style in the early days of this project (in their flagship restaurants in Los Angeles – Rex Il Ristorante and Valentino, respectively). Food and language scholar Charles Perry provided most of the etymological information in these pages, and answered many questions on both language and culinary history. Paula Wolfert was, as usual, more than generous with her time and knowledge. From elsewhere in America, Steven Wagner and Karen Kelly Miller – both of Italian derivation and fluent in that language despite their Anglo-Saxon names – offered further information and more help with translations.

In Liguria, I must begin by thanking Giorgio Bergami and wife, Maria Deidda, for introducing me to their complex and fascinating (and, in travel writer jargon, "greatly underrated") city and to several of its more erudite citizens, for helping give me a sense of direction in my research, for the trip to "Sardinia" in the hills above Genoa, and, not least, for a number of fine and instructive home-cooked meals. I owe a great debt, too, to Carlo Arcolao, who organized complex schedules for me (with, as he once proudly noted "quasi-Swiss efficiency"), made helpful introductions all along the Ligurian coast, and was a charming and informative dinner companion on numerous occasions.

Diego Moreno of the Pôle Ethno-Botanique et Histoire in the Modern and Contemporary History Department of the University of Genoa – both a serious food lover and respected agricultural historian – provided me with documentary material, introduced me to his friends and colleagues, and in general helped me understand the relationship between the vineyards, farms, and kitchen gardens of the Ligurian interior and the tables of the coast. His university colleague Giovanni Rebora gave me an overview of Genoese food history, and fed me anecdote and lore. Linda and Benito Belforte and their sons, Renato and Gianni, answered my endless questions and guided me around Genoa both literally and figuratively. Franco and Melly Solari of Ca' Peo in Leivi offered their hospitality, their recipes, and unlimited access to their superb little library of Ligurian cookbooks and historical material. (I doubt that there is any "library" in the world where one eats and drinks better.)

Sandro and Erica Oddo were my keys to Triora and the Valle Argentina, and – with the kind assistance of Adriana and Anna Saldo, Sandro's mother and aunt, respectively – taught me how to make torte the old-fashioned way. Don Sandro Lagomarsini welcomed me to his isolated, beautiful corner of Liguria, the Val di Vara. Silvio Torre was more than generous with his books, his erudition, and his time. Romolo Giordano introduced me to rare dishes I might not otherwise have found. Paolo and Barbara Masieri offered me recipes and advice on techniques. Francesca Bornato and Umberto Bornato taught me much about Ligurian olives and their oil.

I owe a special debt to Francisca Pallares, former director of the Istituto Internazionale di Studi Liguri in Bordighera; to Istituto scholar Bruna De Paoli; and especially to Ines Pastorello, who welcomed me so often to the Istituto's superb, jewel-like little Museo Bicknell library – where I spent many of my most profitable Ligurian hours (and found many of the books and periodicals cited in the following pages).

In Nice, I owe a huge debt of gratitude to Franck and Véronique Cerutti, who fed me, provided recipes, and introduced me to the markets, food shops, and culinary culture of Nice. My sincere thanks, too, to Fritz and Denise Gerbert for their hospitality, to Jean and Christiane Giusti for their kindness (and recipes), and, in the Niçois backcountry, to Marie-Madeleine Fulconis and the Association des Stéphanois in St. Étienne-de-Tinée.

For recipes, recommendations, facts and figures, and/or practical assistance, I must gratefully acknowledge Alberto and Marina Bisagno, Mara Allavena, Maria Benvenuto, Giuseppina Poggi, Pino Sola, Piero Sattanino, Delio Viale, Gianni Franzi, Angela Maria Zucchetto, Andrea Rossi, Pietro Attilio Uslengo, Aristo Ciruzzi, Giuseppe Robatto, Salvatore Marchese, Tania d'Ambra, Lucia Solaro, Marco and Maurizio Profumo, and Piero Zali, all in Liguria; Catherine-Hélène Barale and Ginette Touati in Nice and its region; and, in various other parts of Europe and in America, Burton Anderson, Diane Kochilas, Gian Paolo Orlandi, Dr. Kjell Grønn, Peter Gati, Azita Nosrati, Amy Albert, Jonathan White, and Paul Rayton.

Among the many winemakers of Liguria and the Niçois region who welcomed me and let me taste copiously of their wares, I must first of all thank Marco

Romagnoli, who was a veritable fount of information, and of wine (and olive oil). Thanks, too, to Alberto Forlini and Germana Cappellini, Riccardo Arrigoni, Giobatta Cane, Claudio and Paolo Rondelli, Pippo Viale, Tommasso and Angelo Lupi, Riccardo Bruna, Bice and Agostino (Pippo) Parodi, Domenico Boiga, Vladimiro Galluzzo, Innocenzo Turco, Maria Rosa Moretti, Piero Lugano, Fabio Lambruschi, Pieralberto and Francesco Ferro, Cécile Sassi, Ghislain de Charnacé, Jean Massa, and Ludovic Cambillau.

Finally, sincere thanks to Kelly Kochendorfer and Cathy Young for testing some of the more initially vexing recipes herein, to Christopher Hirsheimer for both culinary and photographic (not to mention moral) support, to Christy Hobart and Belle Holahan for helping with the research in their spare time, and to Bette and Sid for understanding; to my agent, Barbara Lowenstein, and my editor, Fran McCullough, for their guidance and, above all, their patience; to Tim Johnston, Jonathan Waxman, and Reed Hearon – hearty souls (and gullets) who travelled from Paris, New York, and San Francisco, respectively, to share meals and bottles with me along the Riviera; and to Paula, just because.

Needless to say, any errors, misinterpretations, or mistranslations in the pages that follow are my own, and occur despite the best efforts of those named above.

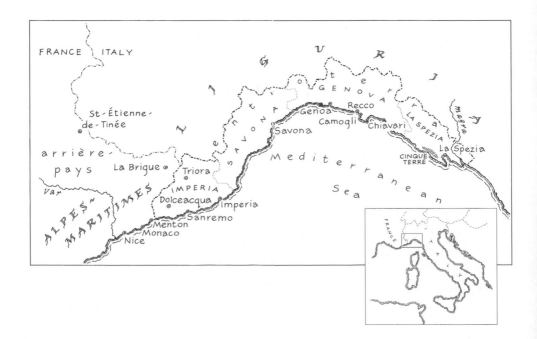

Author's Note

It is not much of an exaggeration to say that this book grew out of a casual after-dinner conversation. I was dining with friends, eight or nine years ago, at Da Puny, on the Piazza Martiri dell'Olivetta in Portofino – a town widely considered to be the jewel of the Italian Riviera. Da Puny occupies a privileged position on this most picturesque of squares, and every night is filled with the *gente internazionale* who have made Portofino one of their capitals – blond Tuscan goddesses, pewter-skinned Milanese plutocrats, sun-bronzed yachtsmen from Nice and Málaga and Jersey, chipper Americans on their way to see Great Art in Rome or Florence – all dining and drinking happily (and expensively) while proprietor Luigi "Puny" Miroli himself, with his perfect pale blue cashmere sweater knotted around the collar of his ivory-coloured polo shirt, scutters nervously between the tables, dancing attendance on his affluent charges.

The casual observer might be forgiven for assuming that Da Puny is just another of the many glitzy tourist traps that thrive along the Mediterranean littoral. But there are two surprises here: First, the food, though undeniably pricey, is surprisingly unpretentious and largely regional in character – homemade pappardelle noodles in pesto corto, or short pesto (a delicious half-and-half mixture of pesto and fresh tomato sauce), spaghetti in an exquisitely salty-sharp sauce of anchovies and arugula, an impeccable fritto misto of baby seafood, whole orata (gilthead bream) baked in a crust of salt and still tasting of the sea, and so on.

And second, once the goddesses and yachtsmen have cleared out for the evening and you get Miroli (who opened his restaurant only in 1980, but whose grandmother ran a trattoria in Portofino a century earlier) talking about the cooking of his native region, the harried restaurateur vanishes and in his place appears a passionate and knowledgeable scholar, and defender, of real Ligurian cuisine.

I found this out by accident. Sitting around over grappa after our meal, my friends and I were talking about a famous local dish we had sampled at another restaurant earlier in the day, a veritable emblem of Ligurian cuisine called cappon magro, or fast-day capon – which isn't capon at all but an elaborate salad composed of fish and assorted raw and cooked vegetables arranged over pieces of hardtack or sea biscuit.

Miroli overheard us – he knew we were journalists – and interrupted. "You can't make cappon magro in a fancy restaurant," he declared. Why not? one of us asked. "Because," he replied, "it's a dish of leftovers. You need a week to make it.

You must take potatoes from one day, beans from the next, turnips from the next, and so on. You have people who make up cappon magro like a fresh salad, and then load lobster and shrimp and mussels on it. No! This is absolutely wrong! Ligurian food is poor food. . . ."

He was by now gesturing dramatically, occasionally stepping forward to rap his knuckles on our table for emphasis. "Do you know how the farmers cook porcini mushrooms here?" he continued. "Porcini are expensive, so they alternate layers of porcini and layers of potatoes in a baking dish with oil, parsley, and garlic, then seal it with oiled paper – like butchers use, you know? Then they cook it in the oven for a long time, very slowly, until the potatoes soak up the flavour of the mushrooms and you can't tell them apart. That way, you see, they've doubled the quantity of mushrooms.

"Or the sauce you've had tonight, pesto corto – well, it was probably invented because somebody had eight people to feed but only enough tomato sauce for four and enough pesto for four. The Ligurian cook is always improvising, always looking for ways to stretch out the ingredients so that more people can enjoy them. Do you get the idea?"

Miroli paused to catch his breath. "I'll give you one more example," he said. "Do you know what the most perfect pasta sauce in the world is? You have to cook it on a boat: You catch some sardines, then you grill them right on deck. Then you put oil, capers, and garlic in a pan – that's all – and throw in the sardines. Put that on some pasta and you simply don't need anything else. It's the best."

He stepped back and looked at us sceptically, as if uncertain whether we'd grasped what he was saying. "People don't understand food like this anymore," he added. "They don't appreciate it." We do, I protested. "Then write about it!" he exhorted. "Write about it!"

Ecco, Signor Miroli. . . .

– C. A.

To read a book about a country's cuisine isn't simply to go looking for "good things"; it is also to better know – by means of the recipes – the customs and the richness or poverty of a place, and the spirit of those who inhabit it. It is, above all, to participate in the symbolic celebration of the shared repast.

– GINETTE OLIVESI-LORENZI,
LA CUISINE MENTONNAISE

Defining Some Terms

A Note on Authenticity

*You can export all the ingredients, and even
the cook, but you cannot seal in a tin the shining of
the sun or the blue of the sky and the sea, and pour
it into a saucepan.*

> – How to Eat in Genoa:
> A Gastronomical Itinerary,
> quoted by Joseph Wechsberg
> in Blue Trout and Black
> Truffles

By definition, authenticity resists accessibility.

> – John Thorne and Matt Lewis
> Thorne, Cookbook,
> January/February 1993

Authenticity in cuisine is a will-o'-the-wisp, elusive and impossible to define – or, rather, all too easy to define, except that everybody defines it differently. If there were a single, canonical recipe for every dish in a given culture's culinary repertoire, then any variation on that recipe – especially one that introduced new ingredients or techniques or that simplified or lightened the result – would be, by definition, inauthentic. But traditional cuisine isn't made from recipes; it is born out of necessity, availability, and intuition, and it is codified not in books but in individual recollection or in common wisdom. Traditional cuisine is folklore, inspired by the world in which its creators live, imbued with lessons about that world, and passed down by a people among themselves, with infinite variation and frequent adaptation.

A few years ago at a gastronomic conference in Spain I incurred the wrath of several champions of traditional Spanish cooking (among them a Cuban-American and a couple of English women) by daring to suggest that contemporary French and Italian influences perhaps had a place in modern Spanish kitchens. That I would approve such culinary pollution made their blood boil, one of the women told me. Yet, earlier, these same defenders of the purity and integrity of Spanish cuisine had been talking about how it had been shaped in the first place by Phoenicians, Greeks, Romans, Moors, and Goths. With the best esprit de l'escalier, it later occurred to me that what I should have asked them in reply was when it was, exactly, that food in Spain had died and become fossilized. At what point did some authority say, All right, that's enough foreign stuff; we're on our own from here on out?

But it doesn't work like that, of course. Cuisine, like language, changes as long as it's alive – and admits as potential influences anything it comes across. Academies may attempt to protect both language and cuisine, but in the long run, both language and cuisine do what they want to do – or, more correctly, what the people who use them want them to do. We can't stop the process; we can only record, remember, and, if appropriate, appreciate the way they used to be.

In asking how authentic the rendering of a traditional dish is, there are other factors that ought to be considered. To begin with, not all traditional dishes are terribly old. Pesto, for instance, isn't mentioned in print until 1848. Salade niçoise as we know it today almost certainly doesn't predate the turn of the century, since raw tomatoes, one of its key ingredients, weren't eaten in Nice until around that time. The famous focaccia col formaggio of Recco, though its origins may well date back to antiquity, wasn't revived in popular cooking until around World War I. When somebody says that a certain dish has "always" been made in a certain way, then, they might just mean that that's how their mothers or grandmothers made it. If a dish is traditionally that recent, who can gainsay an honest change made in it today or tomorrow?

Even if we're able to convincingly reproduce food that seems genuinely ancient, it can't possibly mean to us what it meant to those who ate it centuries ago. The signal dishes of Niçois and Ligurian cuisine were born out of imperatives of poverty and rigorous seasonality, religious regulation, and social attitudes. We can make a torta pasqualina (a sort of savoury Swiss chard pie) or follow an elaborate recipe for ravioli today, and if we're careful and at least reasonably adept, the food we produce will taste delicious. But it isn't likely that we'll make these dishes, or enjoy them, for the same reasons their inventors did – as an exultation, a largesse, a symbolic (and sometimes literal) expenditure of precious resources. By the same token, we can eat a soup of reconstituted dried chestnuts in hot milk (a common winter meal in the poverty-stricken Ligurian backcountry) if we want to, but it would be sort of silly, except as a lark or an academic experiment. People didn't eat food like that for pleasure; they ate it to survive. Why would we eat it today when we could almost as easily have the torta pasqualina – or, for that matter, go out for a burger?

The point is that we can probably never really duplicate authentic traditional cuisine, from the Riviera or anywhere else, unless we're part of the tradition to which it is authentic. Even if we have the same raw materials and understand all the appropriate techniques, we aren't the same people. We're dilettantes by definition. We'll always be cooking someone else's food.

Take that plate of ravioli, for instance: The old-fashioned Genoese recipe for this popular dish includes, in the filling, not only lean veal, sweetbreads, and calf's brains but also spinal marrow and heifer's udder. Now, if we leave out these specific ingredients (the last of which is considered particularly important to the flavour and texture of the dish in Genoa), we are obviously not being authentic. But let's say, for the sake of argument, that we are able to find calf's spinal marrow and heifer's udder – the latter, at least, is sold in this country, in various kinds of ethnic markets, but is hardly common – and do include them in the dish. Sorry, but we're *still* not being authentic. Why? Because these are, for us, speciality ingredients, unfamiliar, even exotic; the whole point of ravioli is that it uses bits and pieces of commonly available raw materials, which udder and spinal marrow are, or at least were, to the Genoese. If we track them down and use them, we might echo the flavour of the original – but we will alter its whole spirit.

Does this mean we shouldn't try to make Genoese ravioli? Of course not. We just have to adapt the recipe to our own circumstances – just as a Genoese cook would do if he or she were suddenly set down in a kitchen in Blackburn or Brighton and invited to prepare the dish. Adapting doesn't mean making it with minced turkey and low-fat ricotta, but it might mean leaving a few things out, or making a few educated substitutions.

Knowing what to leave out or what to substitute, of course, is the trick – and the way to start to gain that knowledge is to come at food from, as it were, the inside, trying to understand how and why the dishes we want to cook developed the way they did, and who developed them. The more we know about the people who created a cuisine, in fact – the more we understand their motives and their personalities, and the cultural and historical context in which they operated – the better our approximations of their cooking will be. It may never be authentic, but it will be an honest try – and all the more savoury for that.

The Myth of the
Mediterranean Diet

*[T]he media have proclaimed far and wide . . . the
advantages of a simple, tasty and at the same time
healthy diet which has been the norm all along
Mediterranean shores since ancient times.*

– María-José Sevilla,
Spain Gourmetour,
January–April 1995

According to a romantic notion now current in gastronomic circles, the people
of southern Europe, northern Africa, and the western shores of the Middle East
have fed themselves for centuries through an admirable, time-honoured nutritional
system known as the Mediterranean Diet – which goes something like this: whole
gardens full of vegetables, glorious fruit straight from the tree, copious quantities
of grains and legumes, very little meat or animal fat, an abundance of just-caught
seafood (simply grilled or roasted, then dressed in delicate olive oil and scattered
with fresh herbs), a bit of crusty home made bread, perhaps a little wine –
everything fresh and bright and perfect, and in commendable moderation.

That's a very attractive idea, but in truth it sounds more the way people eat at
Chez Panisse than the way they eat, and have traditionally eaten, around the
Mediterranean – or at least that portion of it that encompasses Liguria and Nice.

These regions have always been poor at heart. The single most important source
of nourishment in the mountains was probably – and you could win a bet on this
with most self-styled Mediterranean specialists in the UK today – the chestnut.
The favoured seafood, for those who could afford it, was stockfish, which was
long-lasting air-dried cod – a little of which went a long way – imported from
Norway. Much of the food consumed in the region, in fact, even by the wealthy,
has always been preserved – dried fish, dried pasta, olives and vegetables pickled
or marinated in oil, cured ham and sausages.

Moderation was imposed here, as in many other parts of the Mediterranean, by
insufficiency, and by the dietary laws of the Catholic Church – which mandated
periods of fasting and of abstinence from meat and other animal products. It was
not elected as a secular moral or nutritional choice. (The first study per se of what
we now call the Mediterranean Diet was undertaken on the island of Crete after
World War II by epidemiologist Leland Allbaugh. In his findings, published in

1953, he reported that, while fish, meat, and dairy products provided only 7 percent of the energy in the Cretan diet, some 72 percent of the families he surveyed identified meat as their favourite food, and that Cretans overall listed meat as the element they most desired more of to improve the way they ate.) Throughout the region, pork products, offal meats, cheese, and eggs were all used enthusiastically when they could be obtained (and were permitted). Those who could afford it were gourmands; the ideal in nineteenth-century Nice, for instance, was to be able to "manjà à crèpa pansa" – eat until one's belly burst. On major holidays, even poor families gorged themselves on multi-course meals that seemed to go on all day. ("Quande a Zena vegn' Natale," says a Genoese proverb, "ciaschedün mangia pè duì" – "When Christmas comes to Genoa, everyone eats for two." Easter was scarcely more restrained.)

Historically, in Liguria and Nice, fresh seafood was rare, and the preferred varieties – sea bass, say, as opposed to lowly anchovies – were more expensive than meat. This was partly because the Ligurian Sea is notorious for its winds and eddies, and thus difficult for small fishing boats to sail – but also simply because, as Fernand Braudel points out, the Mediterranean is comparatively poor in fish. It is a deep sea, with a floor that drops off suddenly from the shoreline, leaving few shallow shelves for fish to congregate and feed. In addition, its ancient waters have long been biologically fatigued – and they grew even feebler with the opening of the Aswan Dam in Egypt in 1960, which stemmed a major flow of nutrients into the Mediterranean. As long ago as 1642, James Howell cited a proverb, inspired by Dante, which maintained that "There are in Genoa mountains without wood, seas without fish, women without shame, and men without conscience."

Liguria is also, in general, poor farming country. Because of its geographical configuration – the precipitousness with which its mountains rise behind its shoreline, the narrow steepness of its river valleys – it offers little arable soil. The most fertile land, on the valley floors, was often flooded. In higher elevations, relatively minor changes in temperature or rainfall could destroy whole crops, meaning starvation for those who raised them. Perhaps this is why, today, only about 7 percent of the workforce in Liguria is involved in agriculture – the lowest proportion in Italy; and more than half that number works in the floriculture industry.

Even olive oil, the very fuel of Mediterranean life, has been used only sparingly in these parts. True, it has been produced in ample quantity here, at least at times. But it was a precious resource, often sold rather than used locally. This is suggested by a proverb from Oneglia, centre of the Ligurian olive trade, which warns, "I panè i nu son uive, e uive i nu son öiu, e l'öiu u nu l'è sodi" – "The first blossom isn't yet its olive, the olive isn't yet its oil, and the oil isn't yet money." For centuries the favoured cooking fat in the region wasn't olive oil at all but lard or fatback – in other words, pork fat. There was even a variety of pistou made in the mountains behind Nice by crushing little pieces of soft salt pork with basil and garlic. Is this what the media mean by the Mediterranean Diet? Probably not.

It seems to me that the varied, low-fat, robustly healthful way of eating I described rhetorically above is more a platonic ideal than a functioning nutritional system. That doesn't mean that we can't try to emulate that ideal diet – it sounds quite wonderful – but I think it does mean that we probably shouldn't try to lend such a diet a cultural, historical, or geographical validity it may not have.

I also think we ought to remember that at least some of the reported health benefits of the Mediterranean Diet are almost certainly due to the conditions under which food is eaten. I'm convinced that long, dedicated mealtimes, the sharing of dishes with family and friends, the savoury nature of the dishes themselves, even the after-lunch siesta all contribute to whatever salutary properties all those grains and greens and such might possess in themselves.

That said, it must be stressed that Liguria and Nice are rich with light, healthful, delicious dishes, capable of inducing gustatory pleasure and inspiring conviviality without raising anyone's cholesterol. Greens and grains and legumes indeed are common, and fresh fruit and vegetables are appreciated – perhaps all the more so because of their comparative rarity in the past. Good fish (local and otherwise) is available throughout the area today at acceptable if not exactly bargain prices, and is often cooked with admirable simplicity. If desserts remain minimal, I suspect it's at least partially because once you taste a perfect apple from Finale or a fistful of pigeon-heart cherries from Nice, a sugary cake or rum-drenched pudding tastes faintly vulgar. It may not be quite what the media have in mind, but this corner of the Mediterranean is full of delicious food in great variety – and that's no myth at all.

About the Recipes

In the pages that follow, I've tried to represent the cuisine of Liguria and Nice as accurately as possible. I've included a small number of difficult dishes that, frankly, will probably never attain great popularity here – because omitting them would be false to that cuisine. But most of what I've offered is accessible and, I think, attractive food – delicate and hearty both. A number of the dishes may already be familiar to the reader, if sometimes in slightly different form; but at least some will come, I hope, as a pleasant surprise.

The recipes come from several sources: Some were given to me by professional chefs or home cooks; some are borrowed from historical sources, and even occasionally from poetry, or from contemporary cookbooks published in Italy or France. The majority, though, are amalgams; in these cases, I had in mind an ideal version of a certain dish, and through repeated testing, and with the help of various sources, developed a formula that closely reproduced it. Where recipes have a single source, I have of course given their provenance; those without attribution are my own adaptations – though certainly not my own creations.

Though most of the dishes I've given recipes for are traditional, even if the tradition is a fairly recent one, I have also offered a handful of unapologetically contemporary ones – based on the products, techniques, and above all the spirit of the cooking of Liguria or Nice, but with a refinement or a twist. There's a lot of imitation-regional cuisine in the area today, especially around Nice; it's all too easy for a chef to scatter olives, garlic, and basil over everything and call it Niçois. On the other hand, modern-minded chefs like Franck Cerutti in Nice, Paolo Masieri in Sanremo, and Melly Solari in Leivi – all of them brought up on the traditional cooking of their respective areas, and all of them passionate about it – seem to me to be enriching and nourishing their native cuisines by the very act of updating them. Thus there are recipes from all three, and from a handful of their worthy colleagues, included here.

In specifying ingredients in these recipes, I've tried to keep substitutions to a minimum. Most of the raw materials on which the cooking of Liguria and Nice is based are now readily available here. Twenty years ago, it was common for cookbooks published here to transmute fava beans into lima beans (which resemble each other in colour and shape, but unfortunately not in flavour or texture); happily this is no longer necessary, as fresh favas have become more generally available, at least in season. So have baby artichokes, Swiss chard, small aubergines, fresh basil, and other Mediterranean basics. Stockfish still takes some looking for in many parts of the country, but that's no excuse for confusing it with salt cod – which, again, cookbooks used to do. Prescinsêua, a fresh sort of cheese that is one of the secret ingredients of real Ligurian cooking, on the other hand, is difficult to find even in Genoa. In this case, I have offered a recipe for creating an approximation of it, and offered an alternate suggestion if that fails.

A Note on Language

That curious, mysterious, awful, and
attractive Ligurian dialect, which has been heard
across all the seas . . .

– Amy A. Bernardy, *Liguria*

We don't know much about the language of the first inhabitants of Liguria and Nice, but the region's indigenous medieval tongues, Niçois (or Nissart) and Genoese (or Zeneise), are still actively spoken – especially in rural areas and in such specialized urban milieus as marketplaces and ports. Both are derived from Latin: Niçois is a dialect or subgroup of Provençal (or, more broadly, of Occitan). Genoese is less a dialect of Italian than one of its cousins. Both appear first in the twelfth century.

If Tobias Smollett ever heard Genoese on his brief journey across Liguria to Rome, he doesn't mention it. But he heard plenty of Niçois, and abhorred it. "Almost every word . . . ," he wrote, "may be found in the Italian, Spanish, and French languages, with a small change in the pronunciation. . . . To express, *what a slop is here!* they say *acco fa lac aqui,* which is a sentence composed of two Italian words, one French, and one Spanish." That Niçois – like Genoese – might actually be older than Italian, French, or Spanish apparently didn't occur to the contentious Scot.

Niçois is spoken high up into the mountains above the city, with some local adaptations. The dialects of Menton and Monaco betray a closer intimacy with Genoese. On the Italian side of the border, it is said that the Genoese spoken in central Liguria – not just in Genoa itself but from about Savona to Chiavari – is fundamentally homogenous and comparatively modern, while that spoken on the western and eastern peripheries of the region is more closely allied to the Genoese of the thirteenth and fourteenth centuries. There is plenty of lexicological variation within Liguria, though. In the region of Varese Ligure, inland from Sestri Levante, for instance, some farmers grow the shrub-borne berry called, in Italian, mirtillo – a fruit widely appreciated in Europe for tarts and preserves. (This is not *Myrtus communis,* which we call myrtle, but *Vaccinium myrtillus,* known in English as whortleberry or bilberry.) According to a locally published study of peasant life in the region, no fewer than six different names for this berry are used within an area of 70 or 80 square miles – puèlle, pièle, pèlle, pèrpie, pèrcive, and pèllétte. I asked the chef at the Albergo degli Amici in Varese one evening if this were true, and showed him the six words. "Well, I don't know about that," he said, "but here we call it 'perceue.' "

Restaurant menus in Liguria and Nice are almost always written in French or Italian, with perhaps a few of the more traditional local names scattered in; this is true to such an extent that establishments that are profligate with alternate forms (rendering cima as çimma, for instance, or tourte de blettes as torta dé bléa) are to be suspected of touristically inspired folklorism. For this reason, and because the orthography of the region's native tongues is so inconsisent (credible sources sometimes disagree on exact spellings and diacritical marks even for Genoese as spoken in Genoa itself), I have usually given French or Italian names – with English translations appended – to the dishes in the pages that follow. The few exceptions are either those known primarily by their regional name (tomaxelle, mandilli de sæae, and sbïri in Liguria, say, or socca, merda de can, and estocificada in Nice) or, in rare cases, and without apology, dishes whose regional name I find instructive or just irresistible. The traditional mixed-herb-and-walnut sauce of the Castelnuovo Magra region in far eastern Liguria, for instance, appears here as pisto kastarnoésa, not pesto alla Castelnuovo – because I think the former name helps suggest the region's individuality and symbolic distance from Genoa. On the other hand, I don't see the point of identifying salade niçoise as salada nissarda.

Introduction

Seduced and Astonished

[T]he spoiled and petted Riviera has been the scene
of almost continuous disturbance and bloodshed for
the substantial period of some seventeen hundred
years, and . . . has now become a Garden of Peace,
calmed by a kind of agreeable dream-haunted stupor
such as may befall a convulsed man who has been
put asleep by cocaine.

– SIR FREDERICK TREVES, THE
RIVIERA OF THE CORNICHE
ROAD

The Riviera—On ev'ry street a gay casino / Where
continentals sip their vino / And leave their
fortunes to chance.

– "THE RIVIERA," MUSIC BY CY
COLEMAN, LYRICS BY JOSEPH
ALLAN MCCARTHY

I first saw the Riviera – that fabled stretch of Mediterranean coastline that begins somewhere on the shores of Provence and reaches all the way to Tuscany – in 1979, when I got off the overnight Train Bleu from Paris to Nice and walked out into the morning sunshine along the Boulevard Jean Médecin, toward the Place Masséna and the sea.

Long before that, though, the Riviera had seduced me. I'd read *Tender Is the Night* and seen *To Catch a Thief;* I'd clipped travel magazine paeans to idyllic Portofino and the rugged Cinque Terre. I'd constructed a romantic Riviera in my mind, part literary, part cinematic, wholly glamorous. My Riviera was suave rogues in dinner jackets and knockout countesses in pastel silk and diamonds. It was baccarat, sleek yachts, fast convertibles, gated villas cloaked in bougainvillea. It was also Shelley drowned near Lerici ("the fish which came / To worship the delusive flame"), Pound obfuscating from Rapallo, Coward vamping at marvellous parties in Cap Ferrat. It was Bardot topless.

My initial attraction to the Riviera, in other words, was not exactly gastronomic. Once I got to the Riviera, though, it didn't take me long to figure out that – whatever its other charms might be (and they were ultimately both more and less than I had imagined) – it could also be a wonderful place to eat.

I discovered, to begin with, the cooking of Nice. This happened all at once, in a single evening, at an eccentric restaurant called Barale, near the city's Vieux Port. Here, in a dining room crowded with old farming implements, kitchen tools, and music boxes, proprietor Catherine-Hélène Barale offered me (and sixty or seventy other diners) her immutable fixed-price menu – which turned out to be practically an encyclopedia of Niçois cuisine: a wedge of crisp-crusted pissaladière, a pizza-like tart topped with anchovy purée, thin-sliced onions, and a scattering of salty, purple-black Niçois olives; a piece of socca, or chickpea-flour crêpe, creamy in the middle and slightly charred around the edges; a salade niçoise – the real thing – with tomatoes, radishes, spring onions, hard-boiled eggs, anchovies, and good tuna, but no lettuce, and no green beans or potatoes or anything else cooked; a healthy helping of ravioli filled with Swiss chard (the defining vegetable of Nice) and ricotta cheese and moistened with daube de boeuf; herb-stuffed veal birds with a little mesclun salad on the side; and a thick slab of tourte de blettes, a sweet tart of chard with raisins, pine nuts, and apples, covered with a sugar-dusted crust.

That first dinner chez Barale – I have since returned many times, even partially memorizing the words to Menica Rondelly's nineteenth-century civic anthem "Nissa la Bella," which Barale makes everybody sing after they've eaten – was a revelation. I'd had salade niçoise before, of course, and had certainly sampled (and even made) another dish claimed by Nice, ratatouille. But I had never before realized that Nice had its own unique cuisine, so immediately appealing and definitively Mediterranean. I was seduced anew.

I returned to Nice the following year, and this time pushed on into Liguria, wandering around Ventimiglia and Sanremo, seeing the sights in Genoa, and finally installing myself for a few days in the pretty little fishing town of Camogli. Not far from there, in the hills above Rapallo, I trumped my meal at Barale. This time, the restaurant was called A Çighêugna – local dialect for La Cicogna, the Stork. I'd read about this place (now disappeared, alas) in an Italian restaurant guide, and it sounded irresistible. Open only for dinner on Saturdays and lunch on Sundays, and nearly impossible to find (my hotel clerk was incredulous when I told him I was going there), it was the preserve of a woman named Maria Asinaro, who cooked by herself, using almost entirely products that various members of her family had grown or made. Even the wine came from an uncle in Piedmont.

Again, the repertoire was encyclopedic. It was also much more exotic to me than even Barale's had been. Among the endless courses, I remember wedges of polpettone di patate (a kind of thin mashed-potato gratin) and crunchy rice tart, plump rectangles of herb-scented focaccia, slices of cima alla genovese (a sort of Ligurian ballottine of veal innards and vegetables), plates heaped with ravioli stuffed with bitter herbs and tossed with butter and sage, pansotti (pot-bellied ravioli) in walnut sauce, and trenette (the local form of linguine) with pesto, big chunks of rabbit cooked with white wine and herbs. . . . There was certainly more, but I vaguely recall waving away whatever came after the rabbit.

Again, though, I was astonished and impressed. Everything seemed so honest, so direct – so much of the region, and confident in its regional identity. And everything tasted wonderful. This was real food, and not food I was likely to encounter anywhere else in the world. The rogues and poets and Bardots were all very well and good, but this was a more delicious Riviera than I had ever imagined.

What the Riviera Is

The early history of this brilliant country is very dim.

> – SIR FREDERICK TREVES, *THE*
> *RIVIERA OF THE CORNICHE*
> *ROAD*

The Italian Riviera is easy to define: It is simply the coastline of Liguria, one of Italy's twenty administrative regions. Between the Tuscan border and Genoa, this coastline is known officially as the Riviera di Levante (of the East); from Genoa to the French border, it's the Riviera di Ponente (of the West) – with a further subdivision identifying the coast between Cervo and the frontier, quasi-officially at least, as the Riviera dei Fiori, or Riviera of the Flowers. (The flowers, unfortunately, are found more in the warehouse-dull greenhouses that cover the hills than blooming wild in plain sight; this region is the floriculture capital of Italy.)

In France, "Riviera" is more a *nom de fantaisie* than a geographical distinction. This Riviera begins at the Italian border, where the Riviera di Ponente leaves off – but just how far it extends into France can be debated. Some would have it range all the way to Marseilles. Others consider its western boundary to be the demarcation between the départements of the Var and the Bouches-du-Rhône, about halfway between Bandol and Cassis. In terms of recent social history, St. Tropez would seem to be about far enough. For culinary and cultural purposes, however, I'd say that the Riviera stops at the Var River, on the western flank of Nice – geographically the farthest extent of the Ligurian littoral and historically the dividing line between Provence (and later France) and the Comté de Nice. Nice is not Provence, it must be stressed – and from the east bank of the Var, both the gastronomic and the physical landscape stretch not toward Aix or Avignon but into Liguria, to Genoa and beyond.

The Riviera divides not just geopolitically, into its French and Italian (formerly Niçois and Genoese) halves, but also – and this is the more dramatic division – culturally and topographically, on both sides of the border, between sea coast and mountainous interior. Called the *entroterra* (literally "interior land") in Italy and the *arrière-pays* ("backcountry") in France, this interior, though contiguous with the coastal regions, remains vividly different from the resort towns and ports of the littoral – with its own dialects, legends, and concerns, and most definitely its own dishes, often unknown even a few miles closer to the sea. (Ingredients that are rare on the Mediterranean shoreline – mushrooms, snails, wild game, cornmeal, chestnuts, and the like – are all but essential to Ligurian and Niçois mountain cooking; fresh fish, on the other hand, rarely seems to make it even three or four miles inland.)

Archaeologists believe that Liguria – in the broadest sense, encompassing what is now the French Riviera – was one of the first parts of the Italian peninsula (and its extensions) to be inhabited. According to one theory, Celtic hunters from the north came down the Rhône Valley in search of large mammals, then continued eastward along the sea. (In prehistoric times, the Mediterranean was lower than it is now, and the region thus had much broader beaches, which served as a route of transit.) Richly furnished tombs discovered in the nineteenth century, in caves at the foot of the dramatic, iron-rich red cliffs of Balzi Rossi, a few steps over the border from France, date back as much as 30,000 years.

Liguria is named for its first settlers, the Ligurii, a group of tribes who battled fiercely among themselves and later fought constantly with Rome. Their dominions once reached from Catalonia to Ticino, the Italian-speaking portion of eastern Switzerland. The true identity of the Ligurii is a matter of some dispute. Were they in fact a distinct ethnic group – or did the Romans simply apply the name to anybody who happened to be passing through the region at the time? Waverley Root, in *The Food of Italy*, quotes the French historian Pierre Belperron as having called the Ligurians "a primitive aboriginal substratum which it is preferable not to try to identify, under pain of being shot down in flames by the ethnologists."

Modern-day Liguria, as a region of Italy, is a boomerang-shaped curve of landscape, about 200 miles long, averaging only about 30 miles in width, hemmed in by mountains (portions of the Alps and then the Apennines, which meet about midway through the region) and cleft by narrow river valleys running perpendicular to the sea. Divided into four provinces – Imperia, Savona, Genoa, and La Spezia, from west to east – it is the second-smallest Italian region in area, after the Valle d'Aosta, with a total population of not quite two million. About a third of this number lives in Liguria's capital, the great maritime city of Genoa – which calls itself La Superba, the Proud, and whose economic power and cultural influence in the Mediterranean once rivalled that of Venice.

The word *riviera,* which simply means sea coast or shoreline in Italian, has been applied to this stretch of coastline with a capital R for hundreds of years. I found the term used casually in a book published in Genoa in 1602 (*Del conservar la sanità, et del vivere de genovese* by Bartolomeo Paschetti); other sources trace it back at least as far as the late fifteenth century. The term *Côte d'Azur,* which applies to the French part of the Riviera, is considerably more recent, incidentally; it was coined by the Burgundian poet Stéphen Liégeard, as the title of a book of verse published in 1887.

The Riviera in the mythic sense was, of course, an invention of the British and to a lesser extent the Americans. One of the first northern Europeans to write about Nice and parts of Liguria was Tobias Smollett, who lived in Nice with his wife from 1763 to 1765 (though his view of his host city was so jaundiced that, it was later said, "if he were to go again thither the Nissards would certainly knock him on the head"). By the 1820s, there was already a small winter colony of British on the Côte d'Azur, and the publication in Edinburgh in 1855 of *Doctor Antonio* – a romantic novel set in Bordighera, written in English by an expatriate Italian named Giovanni Ruffini – drew literally thousands of Britons to western Liguria. By the beginning of World War II, the Riviera, French and Italian both, had become a year-round international playground.

The subject of my book is the cooking of Liguria and the region of Nice. If I identify the area broadly not by those names but as the Riviera, it isn't the international playground I seek to evoke. The diet of the denizens of my fantasy Riviera might sometimes have been – or still be – quite appealing, but it is not my present concern. I use the term instead because it has a largely forgotten historical validity, and because it applies equally to two contiguous and intricately related regions – and thus helps to suggest the cultural, and by extension culinary, kinship between them.

La Superba and La Bella

*Genoa in the distance, all crowned with lights, is exquisite
beyond description. . . . [But it] is no tourist city. . . .
It is a devil-town; a seaman's whore.*

— SEAN O'FAOLAIN,
A SUMMER IN ITALY

*For all the brightness of its sun and the brilliant blue
of the Mediterranean in the Baie des Anges,
Nice is a city of secrets.*

— MARY BLUME, *CÔTE D'AZUR*

The Riviera – French and Italian, inland and coastal – has its messy urban
sprawl and its tacky resort communities, but it is also full of handsome towns and
rustic villages, many of them with culinary specialities of their own. In the pages
that follow, we will meet a good many of these towns and villages, as we
encounter the food for which they're famous. As an introduction to the region and
its cooking, though, it seems appropriate to say a few words about the Riviera's
two most important cities.

Genoa is the capital of Liguria and, historically and gastronomically, of the
Riviera as a whole. Nice is the capital of the Côte d'Azur and of the département
of the Alpes-Maritimes. Though the cities are only about 125 miles apart and
share elements of a common historical, cultural, and culinary legacy, they are very
different places. Nice is the easier of the two to enjoy; its most attractive quarters
are contiguous, it opens itself to the sea for pleasure's sake, it has an infectiously
lazy air about it, and its citizens have a raffish and sometimes dangerous charm.
Genoa is larger, more serious, more difficult to get around; its people, though they
can be witty and quietly stylish, seem business-like and often dour – and it treats
the sea, as it has always done, as strictly business.

Genoa may be the least visited of Italy's major cities. Tourists go to the
picturesque resort towns of the Riviera on either side of the capital but rarely stop
in Genoa itself. If they do, it's for a few hours of sightseeing and perhaps a meal at
one of the city's better-known restaurants – none of which, incidentally, serves
much in the way of Ligurian cuisine. This is a pity, because Genoa can be an
extremely appealing city for anyone who takes the time to discover it.

Greater Genoa – the city absorbed nineteen surrounding communes in 1926 –

stretches from Voltri in the west to Nervi in the east, along nearly 20 miles of coastline, and reaches about a dozen miles inland into the Val di Polcevera. But the heart of the city is its old quarter, between the Piazza Corvetto (an elegant, tree-lined space, part Paris and part Madrid in feeling, fed by eight or ten busy streets approaching from various elevations) and the port. Within this area are squares both grand and jewel-like (the handsome, rather than beautiful, Piazza de' Ferrari is particularly notable), dazzling palaces, magnificent churches, richly furnished museums, and a mysterious, fascinating warren of *carrugi* – ancient, narrow streets – filled with shops, bars, and little houses. As the city's official tourist periodical, *Genovagando*, once put it memorably in an English-language note, "Genova is a puzzle of noises and colours under a cheeky sun."

Of the carrugi between the city's famous port, one guidebook says, "[E]fforts to gentrify this area have encountered serious difficulties, so that when the sun sets the ingenuous visitor may worry about unpleasant encounters." There's a better reason than that to visit the area in the daytime: The shops will be open. A number of these, between the port and the city's heart, have to do with gastronomy – speciality greengrocers and rice-and-flour merchants (Armanino under the arches on the Via Sottoripa deserves a look), wine merchants, herbalists, old-fashioned take-out shops selling farinata (the Genoese socca) and vegetable-filled tortas (Andrea on the Via Sottoripa is a local favourite), delicatessens (like the Salumeria di Micheli on the Via Macelli di Soziglia, whose cappon magro is constructed as a kind of coarse vegetable terrine bound with bread, promiscuously stained by beetroot juice), specialists in things dried and pickled (for instance, Serafina Astrea on the Vicolo Canneto il Curto), even a tripe shop (on the Vico della Casana), in which tripe broth is brewed over wood fires in big copper cauldrons. If the flavour of old Genoese cooking is still anywhere out in public these days, it's in places like these.

Genoa, apparently named for a Ligurian tribe called the Genuates, was first dubbed La Superba by Petrarch, after he visited the city in 1358. The Genoese have traditionally translated the term as the Proud, but it might be noted that the word can also mean grand – or arrogant. All three adjectives have certainly been applicable at various times in Genoa's history. Alternately a thriving port and a quiet fishing village for its first fifteen hundred years or so, which began back in early Roman times, Genoa began to redevelop as a commercial and maritime centre in the tenth century A.D. – and by the late eleventh century had become a powerful commune, with the beginnings of an overseas policy and a budding rivalry with Pisa and Venice. By the twelfth century, it had transformed itself into an independent republic with a population of 100,000 (today it's a bit more than 800,000), and by the thirteenth, into a major capital of banking and trade. In his

classic *La Mediterranée et le monde méditerranéen à l'époque de Philippe II,*
Fernand Braudel calls the city's Casa di San Giorgio, a fifteenth-century
agglomeration of lending institutions, the most sophisticated credit operation of
the Middle Ages.

After a period of decline, the city's fortunes revived in the sixteenth century
under the great admiral Andrea Doria, and in 1541, with the defeat of Savona,
Genoa became master of Liguria, controlling both the eastern and western rivieras.
The government established by Doria remained more or less unchanged until the
outbreak of the French Revolution, but Genoa subsequently fell again into French
hands and, after the defeat of Napoleon in 1815, was attached to the Kingdom of
Sardinia. Following the unification of Italy in 1860, Genoa reestablished its
position as a major Mediterranean port – and has remained such, to a greater or
lesser degree, ever since.

Genoa's commercial influence was by no means restricted to the Mediterranean.
In the fourteenth and fifteenth centuries, Genoese ships made frequent voyages to
England, Germany, and the Netherlands, and the city established trade colonies on
the Black Sea, in the Crimea and Turkey. (The story is told of a sailor caught
stealing figs from a Turk's orchard in Anatolia. "What navy are you from?" he is
asked. "Genovese," he replies. "Then eat freely, son," answers the Turk, "from the
tree your father has planted.") Braudel even mentions a Genoese colony in Brazil
in the sixteenth century. It is little wonder that a medieval proverb said,
"Genuensis ergo mercator" – Genoese, therefore a trader – and that an English
joke of the period described Genoa as "More market-place than nation."

Much of Genoa's trade was agricultural. As Genoese historian Giovanni Rebora
has pointed out, La Superba was perhaps the only medieval city of any importance
that was only and exclusively a city – a city without a countryside. When you left
Genoa by land, you didn't find yourself amid pastures, orchards, and vineyards;
you found yourself instead facing steep mountains that were all but barren. There
were a few vines, olive trees, and kitchen gardens on the slopes of nearby valleys –
but hardly enough to supply 100,000 people. Thus the city had to seek food
elsewhere, as far afield as its mighty ships could travel.

One of the most important commodities Genoa traded was wheat. Liguria grew
almost none of its own but had need for great quantities of flour for its
commercial pasta industry (even then) as well as for home use. This it obtained
from Russia and Asia, through the Crimea, and from southern Italy and northern
Africa. "Grain . . . ," writes Paolo Lingua in his definitive *La cucina dei genovesi,*
"was one of the political and economic keystones of the republic." Braudel notes
that an entire book could be written on Genoa's grain policies alone. In the

sixteenth century, he adds, it was common for the Genoese navy to seize grain ships flying under other flags, confiscate the cargo, and negotiate payment later.

The first recipe identified in print as Genoese was published in 1520 – a formula for torta alla genovese (a sort of pie filled with apples, dates, raisins, and pulverized almonds, hazelnuts, and pine nuts) appearing not in an Italian text but in the *Libre del coch,* the seminal Catalan-language cookbook by Mestre Robert (also called Rupert de Nola), who was probably chef to the king of Naples.

In the centuries that followed, Genoa's culinary sophistication grew. Though some important Ligurian dishes and sauces can be traced to other parts of the region – testaroli (pasta disks that suggest a cross between a tortilla and a pancake) come from the Lunigiana in far eastern Liguria, for instance, and salsa marò, the extraordinary "pesto" of raw fava beans and mint, is a speciality of Sanremo – the majority of the definitive dishes of the region's kitchen were either invented by the Genoese or perfected and disseminated by them. Among these are cima, minestrone, ravioli, pesto, cappon magro, farinata, pansotti, polpettone di verdura, buridda (fish stew), ciuppin (fish soup), stoccafisso alla genovese (stockfish with olives and potatoes), lattughe ripiene (meat-stuffed lettuce in light stock), sbïra (tripe stew with toasted country bread), tomaxelle (stuffed veal rolls), and pandolce (the Genoese panettone) – essentials of this region's cooking. The entroterra and the coastal fishing towns had raw materials (however meagre) and individual dishes; Genoa wove them into a cuisine.

Nice is another story altogether. It was never the seat of an important Mediterranean power. It had no merchant fleet to speak of, and certainly no far-flung colonies. Its port is tiny, its streets all but innocent of grand palaces and stylish squares. And its cuisine, though well-developed and with strong accents of its own, is frankly less original than Genoa's – for the simple reason that much of it derives from there. On the other hand, Nice is an immensely appealing city, warm and sensual, full of art and myth (Joyce once claimed that the idea for *Finnegans Wake* came to him in Nice), and patently proud of both its culture – culinary and otherwise – and the sheer magnificence of its physical situation. If Genoa is La Superba, Nice is content to call itself La Bella – the Beautiful.

Bordered in the west by the Var River and in the east by a string of little mountains running inland from the sea, Nice curves gracefully around the Baie des Anges, or Bay of the Angels. Today the fifth-largest city in France, with a population approaching 400,000, the city grew out of two pre-Christian settlements, one Greek and one Roman. The former, founded in the fourth century B.C. by Phocean Greeks from Marseilles, was called Nikaia, after the goddess of victory – and this ultimately gave Nice its name.

Nice was a part of the kingdom of Provence for more than four hundred years, until it cast its lot with the Savoyards in 1388 – maintaining its own identity as a comté, or county, when it did. (The borders of the Comté de Nice ranged far beyond the city, at one time corresponding almost exactly to the modern-day boundaries of the département of the Alpes-Maritimes and for a brief time, beginning in 1855, extending as far east as Oneglia.) Throughout its Savoyard period, Nice was besieged repeatedly and occasionally occupied by the French – and was even annexed to France by Napoleon in 1792. It reverted to the Savoyards in 1814, and then voluntarily became part of France again in a plebiscite held in 1860 – the year that Italy was united into a modern nation. Nice was never really "Italian," then, in the sense of being part of Italy. But Italian was the city's official language from 1561 until the union with France, and Garibaldi – who is said to have remained inconsolable over the results of the Niçois plebiscite until his death in 1882 – once said, "To deny the Italianness of Nice is like denying the light of the sun." He would perhaps be at least faintly mollified to know that an Italianate flavour remains palpable in the city to this day.

This is especially obvious in the historic and sentimental heart of the city, the portion of its southeastern quarter that encompasses the port, the little streets and squares of Vieux Nice, and the neighbourhood around the jaunty Cours Saleya. Here the architecture is Baroque, the language has an Italian accent, and family names seem to end in stressed vowels more often than not. Indeed, Vieux Nice resembles an Italian hill town more than a French village. The streets curve almost imperceptibly, overhung with narrow wrought-iron balconies, open shutters, flower boxes, strings of laundry. The colours of the buildings are earthy but distilled into memorable hues – most notably that saturated terra-cotta red called *rouge sarde,* Sardinian red. Little shops sell not just souvenirs and local crafts but fish, meat, cheese, pasta, coffee, bread, ice cream. As late as the 1960s, Waverley Root also noticed horsemeat vendors, "displaying entire carcasses of fat horses with artificial roses running down their spines and ribbons fluttering from their flanks" – but these are now gone.

Between Vieux Nice and the sea runs the Cours Saleya – a tile-paved promenade lined with cafés, restaurants, and shops. The businesses on the seaward side are housed in buildings two stories high, surmounted with broad terraces. Now inaccessible, these terraces – one built in 1780, the other in 1844 – were once the social centre of Nice. Here, on a kind of elevated esplanade overlooking the sea – but at a safe distance from it – tout Nice gazed and gossiped and ladies displayed their latest frocks from Paris. The local British colony preferred to stroll along the sea itself, and in 1820 constructed a broad path immediately above the beach, which evolved into the modern-day Promenade des Anglais.

Today, the Cours Saleya itself is a different kind of social centre. Six mornings a week, beneath awnings striped in red, green, blue, and orange, one of the best and liveliest flower and produce markets in France sets up here. (On the seventh day, Monday, a flea market takes over the promenade.) The tenor of the market, of course, depends on the season. In early February, there are pears and apples, lemons and oranges, lettuces and cabbages, a few long-stemmed leaf-wrapped baby artichokes and fava beans (from Spain or Italy, and expensive), and lacy clumps of frisée, their yellow-white interiors improbably bright. By early May, there are favas everywhere, artichokes galore, fat carrots, shiny onions, braids of long-stem garlic, deep green courgettes with brilliant orange flowers attached, asparagus in green, white, and deep, inky purple. By midsummer, the market is in full flower, bursting with a surfeit of cherries, peaches, melons, nectarines, tomatoes, peppers, garlic, asparagus, courgettes, even cascades of early mushrooms. In the autumn, the mushrooms have multiplied – cèpes, girolles, pieds-de-mouton, pleurottes – and there are pears and apples again, and heaps of onions, and cabbages and all their cousins. And always, all year round, there are herbs and cheeses and, above all, olives – the famous little local ones and also an extravagance of imports, from other parts of France and from Italy, Spain, and Greece – black, green, purple, almost grey, almost red, and spicy, fleshy, sour, mild. Their perfume overwhelms even that of the tuberoses and the basil.

Despite the Genoese origins of many of its signal dishes, Nice can indeed be said to have its own cuisine; it is one of the few cities in France (Lyons is another) of which that is true. The ancient epic dish of this cuisine is estocaficada – an earthy, hearty ragout of slightly chewy stockfish (dried cod) with tomatoes, onions, potatoes, garlic, and olives. Nationalist poets wrote odes to estocaficada in the nineteenth century ("Gloria a tu, stocafic divin," begins one); even today, it is said that natives of Nice forced to live in Paris or elsewhere in France often fly home when they can just for a fix of the stuff.

Other essential Niçois dishes – besides the pissaladière, socca, salade niçoise, chard-filled ravioli, herb-stuffed veal birds, mesclun salad, and tourte de blettes mentioned earlier – include minestrone-like soupe au pistou (pistou being the local name for pesto), colourful farcis à la niçoise or petits farcis (assorted stuffed vegetables), meltingly tender tripe cooked with onions and tomatoes, beignets (fritters) of every kind, and the world-renowned vegetable mélange called ratatouille.

Lovers of the local cuisine fear that it is on the verge of dying out. They cite as the villains "le fast-food," the homogenizing influence of television, and just simply changing times – which mostly means that the grandmothers who used to take the time to make this food are disappearing and that their daughters, and certainly their granddaughters (and grandsons), have other things on their mind. For now, though, especially in Vieux Nice and around the Cours Saleya and the port, it is still possible to discover the true flavours of Nice.

How the Riviera Eats

[Ligurian] cuisine is healthy and light. . . .
The flavours, simple and elementary, come directly from
the vegetable garden. . . . The dishes are the fruit of
centuries of experience, of authentic self-denial.

– PADRE FRANCESCO
FERRAIRONI, *CULTURA E*
TRADIZIONI IN ALTA VALLE
ARGENTINA

The indigenous traditional cuisine of the Riviera – as opposed to hotel and fancy restaurant fare and more contemporary refinements – is based on ingenuity, conservation, and reuse. It has been called "la cucina della misura," the cuisine of moderation, and also "la cucina di ricupero," the cuisine of salvage – which is to say, of leftovers. It is a cuisine that wastes nothing, and that labours mightily to transform even the most pedestrian ingredients into something savoury and satisfying.

As noted, for much of its history, the Riviera – particularly inland – has been tragically poor. The nineteenth-century French ethnographer Chabrol de Volvic observed in his *Statistique des provinces de Savone, d'Oneille et d'Acqui* that "in the upper valleys and the mountains [of western Liguria] . . . [i]nhabitants harvest grain only to sell. Their diet consists of smoke-dried chestnuts, vegetables, and polenta; they eat meat only on holidays; the bread is made with a mixture of rye and wheat flour, and they don't eat much of it." In many areas, there wasn't even pasta. Instead, peasants ate little clots of rye or chestnut flour cooked in milk or in weak stock, or simply pieces of fried leftover bread dough seasoned with salt or honey. Rye flour was also roasted and used to make a kind of coffee, since the real thing would have been unthinkably expensive.

The situation was no better in the Comté de Nice. Tobias Smollett claimed to have known a local peasant who fed his family with the skins of boiled beans. There are records into this century of a poor Niçois soup called boudroira, made with assorted dried legumes, chard ribs, and squash peels – and old-timers in the

Tinée Valley, high above Nice, remember when it was the custom to conserve the water in which pasta was cooked and eat it after the noodles as a kind of soup, with the remnants of the sauce stirred in – so as not to waste even a trace of life-sustaining starch.

The very poverty of the region's cuisine mandated a certain rustic inventiveness, a culinary creativity grown not out of artistic inspiration but out of the sheer need to survive. Vegetables could be doubled in size by stuffing them with their own scooped-out flesh mixed with wild greens gathered in the fields and the crumbs of hardened bread. Fried squash or courgette blossoms, originally made with the flowers that fell from the plants without setting fruit, were a way of bringing even aborted vegetables to life. A few hundred grams of wheat flour could be stretched into a thin tourte or torta shell and filled with chard or courgettes from the garden – bound with a bit of cheese and a few eggs – to feed half a dozen people. The lowly chickpea could be processed into flour of its own and used to make the thick crêpe-like socca or farinata or the long, thin beignets known as panisses or paniccie. Small quantities of dried or salted fish, cured meat, or dried mushrooms could flavour huge pots of soup or sauce; herbs, which grew abundantly and spontaneously, could enliven (and add nourishment to) almost any dish.

Not all of the region's dishes were born in the poverty-stricken mountains, of course. Things were better on the coast. Ligurians – and above all the Genoese – have always been sailors and specialists in the long haul, and the exigencies of seafaring affected the development of the local cuisine in at least two ways: First, Ligurian merchants traded with most of Europe and the Middle East, even beyond the Mediterranean, and brought home a wealth of imported ingredients to enrich their kitchens. (One example: Ligurians are the only Italians who use walnuts regularly in savoury dishes, a habit they might well have imported from their trade colonies on the Black Sea.) Second, sailors who travel long distances need to carry food products that will last a long time; thus they developed a host of recipes using dried fava beans and other legumes and air-dried cod (stockfish). They also used dried, as opposed to fresh, pasta much more than, say, their Piedmontese neighbours did.

Waverley Root suggests that maritime traditions might have influenced Genoese cooking in still another way: "[W]hen the sailor returned, after months or years of absence, to his family . . . ," he writes, "[n]o pains were too great to be taken to please the wayfarer, so that Genoese cooking is distinguished by patience . . . [and] became elaborate." Thus, Genoa developed such dishes as cappon magro, which grew from a simple, thrown-together peasant dish into a composed salad of baroque complexity; or the famous torta pasqualina or

Eastertide torte, traditionally made not with two but with thirty-three layers of dough (one for every year of Christ's life). Dishes like these have an almost ritualistic dimension, both in preparation and consumption. And they seem wonderfully anachronistic – edible links to the past.

Another Genoese creation, of course, is pesto – probably the most famous of all Italian sauces. And Genoa takes credit for such hearty, homey, universally appreciated dishes as focaccia, minestrone, and ravioli; their origins may be disputed, but the region's cooks are undeniably masters of their preparation.

The Niçois are masters of ravioli, too, and they also make (and devour) gnocchi, fettuccine-like noodles (often called simply pâtes fraîches), and other pasta dishes with great enthusiasm. There are more similarities with Genoa. Nice's socca is virtually identical to farinata; its pistou is, in essence, pesto; its stuffed vegetables and beignets are barely distinguishable from those of Liguria. And if Genoa has its cappon magro, Nice has its salade niçoise, admittedly less elaborate, but clearly related. There is sometimes, inevitably, a touch of Gallic refinement about some Niçois cooking that sets it apart from its counterpart on the other side of the border. But the two sides of the Riviera share so many products and dishes and basic ideas about food that the culinary kinship between the two is intimate – and that border is certainly more political than gastronomic. I can't imagine writing about one without the other.

Duelling Cookbooks

The first Genoese cookbook, published in Genoa in 1864 by the firm of Fratelli Pagano, was *La cuciniera genovese; ossia la vera maniera di cucinare alla genovese* (The Genoese Cookbook, or the Real Way to Cook Genoese-Style). *La cuciniera* was a compilation of nearly 200 recipes from various sources, including virtually all the essential classics of Genoese cuisine, from buridda and cappon magro to ravioli and torte. The author, whose name wasn't revealed until the book's third edition in 1865, was G. B. Ratto – the former proprietor of a Genoese printing firm, who had apparently assembled the book originally as a gift for friends.

In 1865 or 1866, across the Tuscan border from Liguria in Livorno, there appeared a markedly similar volume, containing many recipes that were all but identical to Ratto's – though there were 128 more of them. (The date is uncertain because no copies of the first edition are known to exist today.) This one, called *La vera cuciniera genovese facile ed economica, ossia maniera di preparare e cuocere ogni sorta di vivande all'usanze di Genova* (The Real Genoese Cookbook, Easy and Economical, or How to Prepare and Cook Every Kind of Dish in the Manner of Genoa), bore the name of an historian named Emanuele Rossi. Rossi advised his readers in his introduction that Ratto's book was "too succinct to be utilized by those who are less than knowledgeable about the secrets of the kitchen" – and announced, in a rather brazen apologia for plagiarism, that "These [readers] are the ones I wanted to pay more attention to, and to this end I have used what was good and useful in *[La cuciniera genovese]*, as well as my own experience and the suggestions of Genoese cooks practised and skilled in their art."

Fratelli Pagano denounced Rossi's book, but no legal action was ever taken – and, as Silvio Torre puts it in *Il grande libro della cucina ligure,* "the two 'cuciniere,' often confused with one another, continued to be published through the nineteenth century." (He might well have added the twentieth century, since facsimile editions of both books are still in print.) Taken together, Torre adds, the books were "the two milestones, for over one hundred years, of Genoese cuisine – and not only that but an outline, a portrait, of a way of life, of our habits, our customs at the table, of our taste, of a mentality, of the way we were."

Dickens Dines in Genoa

While visiting Genoa in 1844, Charles Dickens reports in his *Pictures from Italy,* he encountered "a fair specimen of a real Genoese tavern, where the visitor may derive good entertainment from real Genoese dishes, such as Tagliarini; Ravioli; German sausages, strong of garlic, sliced and eaten with fresh green figs; cocks' combs and sheep-kidneys, chopped up with mutton chops and liver; small pieces of some unknown part of a calf, twisted into small shreds, fried, and served up in a great dish like whitebait; and other curiosities of that kind." The calf parts, he might have been interested to learn, were most probably the intestines of milk-fed baby animals – a dish still served today in the entroterra, often under the name *mazzetti,* or little bundles (*massetti* in Genoese).

The Port

When Nathaniel Hawthorne visited Genoa in 1859, he, like so many visitors, got his first view of it from the deck of a steamer. "We saw the city," he wrote, "lying at the foot of a range of hills, and stretching a little way up their slopes, the hills sweeping round it in the segment of a circle, and looking like an island rising abruptly out of the sea; for no connection with the mainland was visible on either side."

Seen from this direction, Genoa is a marvel, a gigantic amphitheatre glowing in the Mediterranean light. If you can't approach Genoa by sea, the next best thing is to visit the port – which is Italy's largest, berthing more than 200 ships at a time and employing more than 20 percent of the city's inhabitants directly or indirectly – and look back inland from one of the jetties.

I did this myself one mid-December morning. The port is a fascinating place, its architecture a jumble of styles, periods, and sensibilities.
I found a perch on the Banchina Molo Vecchio, in 70-degree air, beneath a clear blue sky tufted with cotton-wool clouds, and looked around. In one direction was the monumental fortified gate known popularly as the Porta Siberia. Some Genoese will tell you that it's called that because it looks cold and forbidding; the truth is that the name is a corruption of Ciberia, from the Latin word *cibus,* food – because all comestibles imported to the city were supposed to pass through this portal.

In another direction, I saw two structures designed by the Genoese architect Renzo Piano for the Columbus quincentennial celebrations here in 1992. One was a sculptural fantasy inspired by the cargo booms that bristle around the docks: seven thick white needles soaring into the air at various angles, with an observation car suspended from one of them. The other, an open-air theatre, suggested the bleached carapace of a gigantic squill. Behind the theatre, across the road from the port, stood the freshly painted, delicately hued painted facade of the Palazzo San Giorgio, former headquarters of the Genoese bank that all but ruled medieval trade.

In the background, hills formed a ring of dusty green, out of which rose buildings old and new, mostly in pink, ochre, and smoke-darkened white or cream. Here and there, the crown of a medieval tower or the slender dome or tall, thin belfry of a church would rise. I thought how sensible and self-contained the city looked – how proud.

The Bounty of Nice

In his letters of September 2 and October 4, 1764, Tobias Smollett, who otherwise had little good to say about Nice – or about anything he ate while in the city – enthused about the quality and variety of the food products available there:

"Autumn and winter are the seasons for game; hares, partridges, quails, wild-pigeons, woodcocks, snipes, thrushes, beccaficas [buntings], and ortolans. Wild-boar is sometimes found in the mountains: it has a delicious taste, not unlike that of the wild hog in Jamaica; and would make an excellent barbecue. . . . The hares are large, plump, and juicy. The partridges are generally of the red sort; large as pullets, and of a good flavour. . . .

"Nice is not without variety of fish; though they are not counted so good in their kinds as those of the ocean. Soals, and flat-fish in general, are scarce. Here are some mullets, both grey and red. We sometimes see the dory, which is called *St. Pierre;* with rock-fish, bonita, and mackarel. The gurnard appears pretty often; and there is plenty of a kind of large whiting, which eats pretty well. . . . One of the best fish of this country, is called *le loup,* about two or three pounds in weight; white, firm, and well-flavoured. Another, no-way inferior to it, is the *moustel,* about the same size, of a dark-grey colour. . . . We have abundance of the *sæpie,* or cuttle-fish, of which the people in this country make a delicate ragout; as also of the *polype de mer* [octopus] . . . [which] are stewed with onions. . . . The market sometimes affords the *ecrivisse de mer,* which is a lobster without claws, of a sweetish taste. . . .

"I shall now take notice of the vegetables of Nice. In the winter, we have green pease, asparagus, artichoaks,

cauliflower, beans, French beans, celery, and endive; cabbage, coleworts, radishes, turnips, carrots, betteraves, sorrel, lettuce, onions, garlic, and chalot. We have potatoes from the mountains, mushrooms, champignons, and truffles. . . .
The fruits of the season are pickled olives, oranges, lemons, citrons, citronelles, dried figs, grapes, apples, pears, almonds, chestnuts, walnuts, filberts, medlars, pomegranates, and a fruit called azerolles [another sort of medlar]. . . . In summer we have all those vegetables in perfection. There is also a kind of small courge, or gourd, of which the people of the country make a very savoury ragout, with the help of eggs, cheese, and fresh anchovies. Another is made of the badenjean, which the Spaniards call berengena [aubergine]. . . .

"In May we have strawberries . . . of a good flavour. . . . In the beginning of June, and even sooner, the cherries begin to be ripe. They are a kind of bleeding hearts; large, fleshy, and high flavoured, though rather too luscious. . . . The cherries are succeeded by the apricots and peaches, which are all standards, and of consequence better flavoured than what we call wall-fruit."

Carnaval

*[Carnival in Nice] has developed now with the
advancing ugliness of the times. . . . The humble village
fête has become a means of making money and an
opportunity for clamour, licence and display.*

– Sir Frederic Treves,
*The Riviera of the
Corniche Road* (1921)

Nice has celebrated the pre-Lenten season with a carnival –
Carnaval – for more than seven hundred years. Charles II,
Count of Provence and Duc d'Anjou, for instance, writes of
passing happy days at such an event in the city in 1294. But
Carnaval began in earnest as a civic festival after Nice attached
itself to France in 1860. Parades became more elaborate,
battles fought with bouquets of flowers were joined, and
townspeople – many of them in costume or at least wearing
masks – roamed the streets, tossing dried favas, rice, juniper
berries, or eggshells filled with soot or flour at passersby.
Today, unfortunately, carnival-goers seem more partial to
plastic string – a kind of gummy filament in Day-Glo colours,
squirted out of aerosol cans.

I visited Nice during Carnaval in 1994. To prepare myself for
the event, I stopped in at the Musée Alexis et Gustav-Adolf
Mossa on the Quai des États-Unis, which is dedicated to the
works of a father-son team of artists (1844–1926 and
1883–1971, respectively) who created countless Carnaval
floats, drew fantastical images of Carnaval, and in general, between them, embodied its visual spirit for at least a century.

Carnaval was traditionally associated with feasting (the

word comes from the early Italian *carnelevare,* removal of meat, indicating that it was the last day, before the forty days of Lent, on which animal products could be eaten by good Catholics), and a number of the floats depicted in the Mossas' works have gastronomic themes. One, from 1950, was entitled "Lucullus Soupe Chez Lucullus" ("Lucullus Dines with Lucullus"), and was laden with vessels marked "stocaficada," "pissaladiera," "pissala" (fermented anchovy sauce), "amploua" (anchovies), "trule" (blood sausage), and "vinum belletum" (Bellet wine). Another, dubbed "Les Merveilles de la Cuisine Niçoise" and dating from 1960, contrasted feasting and fasting menus: On one side of the float was a gigantic mortar filled with pistou, along with such dishes as pissaladiera, soupa au pistou, cantarea (snails) de Canteron (a village in the arrière-pays), and tourta de bléa, plus a bottle of Bellet 1860. On the other side were nothing but dishes made of fresh or dried cod, with a flagon of aigua de Vesubia (water from the Vésubie River), vintage 1960.

Later that day, I paid 50 francs to get into the Place Masséna, which had been closed off for Carnaval, and have a close-up look at the year's floats before they rolled out for one of the corsos or parades. These included works by the usual crew of single-named Nice-based celebrity artists – Ben, Arman, and César – all very bright and cartoony. I wandered around for a while, as the Gipsy Kings blared over a tinny sound system and children in department-store costumes begged their parents for pistachio nuts and Cokes. I found it all rather forced, and not very much fun, and decided not to stay.

Part 1

From the Farms and Gardens of the Riviera

VEGETABLES, HERBS AND FRUIT

*The flavours [of Ligurian cooking], simple
and elemental, come directly from the
market-gardens.*

– PADRE FRANCESCO
FERRAIRONI, *CULTURA E
TRADIZIONI IN ALTA VALLE
ARGENTINA*

*Ogni frûto a sô stagion, chi vêu mangiâlo
matûro e bôn. (Every fruit in its season, if
you want to eat it ripe and good.)*

– GENOESE PROVERB

The Riviera is neither salad bowl nor bread-basket. Agribusiness mostly does its business elsewhere. Grain grows in ripples rather than in amber waves. There are rarely enough cows in any one place to be called cattle. Farms are small, and olive groves and vineyards tend to climb up steep hills, or sprout on narrow terraces behind dry stone walls, instead of sprawling across broad panoramic landscapes.

But the fruit and vegetables that do grow in the region can be of extraordinary quality, and have traditionally been used ingeniously and well. Precisely because farmland is sparse and quantities of produce are small, what does grow here seems special; it is cossetted while growing and treated with intelligence and respect when harvested.

Wild mushrooms and wild greens (both salad leaves and herbs, with the distinction between the two sometimes blurred) are an important part of the indigenous diet. The most important cultivated vegetables on the Riviera, however – other than chestnuts, if you consider them vegetables – have always been legumes, and above all favas and chickpeas.

Favas – which are related to both lima beans and soy beans, though not much like either – originated either in Persia or Africa, and have been known in the Mediterranean basin for at least 3,000 years. In *Cuisine traditionnelle en pays niçois*, Bernard Duplessy quotes one Abbé Expilly as having written, in 1781, that "Favas are the principal resource [of the Niçois]. They live on them for six months out of the year." He presumably meant dried favas, which show up in all manner of Niçois soups and stews to this day. In spring and summer, though, the Niçois happily eat favas fresh (and even raw) in salads or even just as a snack by themselves. In Genoa, where fresh favas are known by the curious name of *bazann-e* (a bazann-a is also an altercation or a scrimmage) and dried ones are called *bacilli* (related to the Italian word *baccelli,* meaning legumes), the beans were an essential constituent of many soups and stockfish dishes until they began to be replaced by the potato in the early nineteenth century. Chickpeas show up in soups, too, and in the classic soupy Ligurian vegetable stew called zimino di ceci or ceci in zimino, and, as noted, are also turned into flour for use in farinata (socca) and panizzie (panisses). In *Mandili de sæa,* his book of traditional Genoese recipes, however, Franco Accame estimates that 90 percent of today's young Ligurians have never tasted chickpeas!

Turnips were an important food in some mountain regions, and salsify *(Tragopogon sassefrica;* scorzonera in Italian, scorsonëa in Genoese) is particularly favoured around Genoa. Liguria is also one of the few parts of Europe where the spring onion, called scarzöi in Genoese (the "öi" sound resembles the "eu" in French), is used frequently – in frittelle (fritters) and to flavour farinata in certain neighbourhoods, for instance. Fennel and cardoons are popular as well. And, of course, there are the Riviera's famous artichokes, which are arguably the most delicious in the world – especially the small, spiny, purple-green variety. Those of Genoa were particularly prized by Antoine-Auguste Parmentier, the great populizer of the potato, who dubbed them "sucré de Gênes" – "sugared of Genoa" – for their sweetness. Lettuce, cabbages, spinach, and various kinds of chicory have long been grown and eaten along the Riviera, too. The definitive leafy green of the region, however, is Swiss chard, in both its red- and white-stemmed versions. Called bietola in Italian, giæa in Genoese, blette or bette in French, and bléa in Nissart, this deliciously earthy vegetable – it conveys the flavours suggested by another of its English names, beet-spinach – is absolutely vital to a wide range of dishes on both sides of the border.

The standard "Mediterranean" vegetables – tomatoes, peppers, and courgettes and related squashes – as well as white beans and potatoes are relative newcomers to the kitchens of the Riviera. They were absolutely unknown, of course, before that son of Genoa, Columbus, made his voyages. But even after he and his successors first imported these foodstuffs to Europe, it took a long time for most of them to gain widespread acceptance. The potato, for instance, was introduced to Italy as early as 1560 – but only as an ornamental plant. It was first mentioned in print in Liguria as a potential foodstuff only in 1773. Even at that, though, Liguria was the first region on the Italian peninsula to adopt the potato enthusiastically. Paolo Lingua suggests that it was Napoleon's soldiers, marching through the region in the early nineteenth century, who first popularized it.

(Whole potatoes roasted in the embers of cooking fires were common French military fare by that time; see page 51.) In any case, potatoes quickly replaced dried favas and chickpeas in soups and as an accompaniment to stockfish, and were adapted for gnocchi, turned into a filling for torte, and even cooked in the same pot with pasta destined to be dressed with pesto.

Tomatoes, like potatoes, had to wait for acceptance. The first published recipe for pasta with tomato sauce in Italy (under the name "Viermicielli co le pommadoro") appeared in Naples only in 1839. Around the same time, the Niçois started cooking tomatoes – but they didn't use them raw until the beginning of the twentieth century. Tomato recipes appeared in several Genoese cookbooks in the latter half of the nineteenth century, but scholar Paolo Lingua says that Genoa didn't really take to tomatoes, even in cooked form, until the early 1900s – and when it did, it was largely due to the commercialization and promotion of "conservati" or tinned tomatoes. The Genoese still sometimes tell you that tomatoes, especially with fish, are too acidic and alter the natural flavour of the other ingredients in a dish.

Beans of American origin, including the plump fagioli bianchi or white beans so prized today in Liguria, were probably the earliest New World crops to win favour in Italy – perhaps because they were not entirely dissimilar from varieties of native European beans already well known and liked on the peninsula (favas, for instance). Cultivated in the early sixteenth century in the Veneto, they were being eaten in Liguria by the early seventeenth. Bell peppers took a bit more time to get integrated into the cooking of the region, but still predated the tomato, reaching the kitchens of Genoa and Nice by the mid-1800s.

When people think of the herbs used on the Riviera, they think first and most of all of basil. Basil is the region's heraldic leaf; there are even those who suggest, not entirely in jest, that basil should adorn the civic flag of Genoa. But basil, curiously enough, has but one use in Liguria: in pesto. An occasional anomalous improvisation aside, it simply does not appear in other forms. A herb which might be termed more important to Ligurian cooking, if far less obvious because of the way it is used, is borraggine (boraxa in Genoese) – borage. A leafy, subtly earthy, bright green herb, with attractive pale blue blossoms (also edible), borage is a hidden ingredient in ravioli and torta fillings, fish and vegetable soups, pasta dough, rice dishes, and more, all along the Riviera. It is also used in frittelle, alone or mixed with other ingredients; in the town of Pieve di Teco, in the entroterra, it is mixed into farinata dough; its leaves are sometimes eaten steamed or sautéed as vegetables.

In mountain regions, nettles – the first edible green to appear every spring as the snow melts – are also highly esteemed. They're cooked into soup in the region of Triora, above Sanremo, for instance, where they are considered a specific for anaemia, senility, and other ailments – and they're used in soups and pasta fillings around St. Étienne-de-Tinée, in the mountains northwest of Nice. Other popular herbs along the Riviera are rosemary, marjoram (which the Genoese call erba persa, or Persian herb), oregano, thyme, bay leaves, wild fennel, sage, mint, savoury (especially in the arrière-pays, where it is known as pebre d'aë, or donkey's pepper), and the lemony melissa (erba çitruninn'a in Genoese).

Almost nobody in the region cooks with those dried, mixed herbs so popular in Provence. Jacques Médecin calls them "the aromatics which dreadful cooks without talent use to murder all flavours, including those of the herbs themselves." On the other hand, old-fashioned Niçois cooking sometimes employs a kind of bouquet garni of fresh herbs – typically borage, purslane, dandelion greens, and sow thistle – called refrescat, to "refresh" a soup or stew. These are tied in a bundle, added to the pot, and then discarded when the dish is done.

Fruit is ample, though not always in commercial quantity, along the Riviera, and certain towns along the Ligurian coast are particularly famous for certain varieties. The villages of the Cinque Terre, for instance, are renowned for their table grapes as well as grapes for wine. The pears of Camogli and the peaches of Savona are highly regarded, as are the figs – especially when dried – of Chiavari. (Figs are also common in the entroterra, and there was even flour made from them in earlier times.) Finale Ligure has been known for its Carli apples since at least the eighteenth century, when Smollett encountered them and called them "the most agreeable I have ever tasted." Persimmons grow in many corners of the region and were traditionally food for the extremely poor; when there was nothing else to eat, there was often a fruit-laden persimmon tree nearby.

The most famous fruits of the Riviera, however, are citrus. In Liguria, lemons and oranges are grown mostly on the Riviera di Ponente and around Genoa, with some groves around Monterosso in the Cinque Terre as well. Nervi, now a suburb of Genoa, was once famous for its lemons, and did a brisk business in them in the city's port. Where there were sailors, there was always great demand for citrus fruit, and at Nervi, lemons were cut on the stem, not picked, while the skin had a slight rosy hue. This way, it is said, they'd last for years, growing hard and a burnt yellow on the outside but with the juice intact within – perfect for long sea voyages.

The Riviera town best known for citrus growing, however, is French: Menton, the first town over the border from Italy. Legend has it that when Adam and Eve were expelled from the Garden of Eden, Eve stole a lemon and carried it away with her, cupped in her hands. She and Adam roamed the earth looking for another paradise, and when they found it on the strip of warm, protected coastline that was to become Menton, Eve planted the lemon there. In fact, it is likely that lemons were first brought to the region during the Crusades, between the eleventh and thirteenth centuries, probably from Palestine or Egypt. Archival records show that as early as 1495, citrus fruits were being exported from Menton to northern Europe, and in 1671 the city established the office of Magistrat des Citrons, a council of eighteen members named each year by the prince, charged with regulating citrus commerce. (After the French Revolution, the name of the body was changed to a more democratic-sounding Comité des Citrons.) When a nineteenth-century British visitor asked why Menton and neighbouring Roquebrune had voted, in 1860 – by a majority of 833 to 54 – to attach themselves to France rather than Italy, he was told "Citroni!" In other words, the union with France was expected to improve the citrus market.

There are now only eleven full-time commercial *agrumiculteurs* (citrus farmers) – or, as they are known locally, *limounaïres* – in the Menton region, growing lemons (mostly of the kind called citron des quatres saisons), and seven varieties of oranges, kumquats, and grapefruit, and harvesting their fruit twice a year. The most famous of Menton's fruit is the orange amère, or bitter orange. It was perhaps these oranges, which are small and firm, often with greenish markings, that the nineteenth-century English cleric and naturalist Clarence Bicknell encountered. He disliked the oranges of the Niçois region (where the fruit is called portugale) intensely, he wrote. "When more leathery than usual," he continued, "they may be utilized as cricket balls; but I cannot honestly recommend them for this or any other purpose."

La Fête du Citron

Unlike Nice, Menton doesn't have an annual springtime Carnaval. Instead, it has its Fête du Citron – Lemon Festival. The event, originally called the Carnaval des Fruits d'Or or simply the Carnaval de Menton, was launched in 1876. At first, it was a more or less conventional pre-Lenten celebration, with a citrus-themed exhibition attached. In 1934, though, it was baptized with its present name, and began to take on its present form.

The festivities today include art exhibitions, concerts, fireworks, a communal dinner, and an orchid show – but the main events are an elaborate night-time parade, held on Shrove Tuesday evening, featuring floats constructed not of flowers but of oranges and lemons, and a static exhibition at the Jardins Biovès, in which oranges and lemons are fashioned into monumental sculptures according to an annual theme. One year recently, it was "Féeries Marines," "Enchantments of the Sea," and exhibitors as diverse as the city of Cannes, the mountain town of Ste. Agnès, a local produce company called Primatour Menton, and the German spa capital of Baden-Baden contributed citrus-covered pieces, depicting everything from King Neptune and his court to a trio of goofy-looking dolphins jumping through hoops.

The Fête uses close to 300,000 pounds of lemons and oranges annually. When it's over, any fruit still in good condition is sold inexpensively, in bulk, for the manufacture of vin d'orange (see page 306) and vin du citron.

You Are What You Eat

In the Niçois backcountry, jocular dialect nicknames are sometimes awarded to the inhabitants of various towns according to what is perceived to be their favourite foodstuff. In an article called "Le Folklore niçois," appearing in *Les Annales du Comté de Nice* in 1936, Paul Canastrier recounts some of these: The people of Aspremont, he writes, are known as "mangia-chourrous" (fava eaters); those of Lantosque "cougourdiés" (gourdies); those of Châteauneuf and nearby villages "limassiés" (snailies); those of Lucéram "panissiés" (panissies); those of Roquebillières, "meoûs" (honeys); those of Contes "mangia-faioû" (bean eaters) and also "trempa-oli" (oil dousers). The people of Nice, in honour of their heroic consumption of a certain leafy green, are known as "cagabléa" – chard shitters.

No Spice, Please, We're Genoese

If herbs are fundamental to the cuisine of Liguria and the region of Nice, spices – with the exception of black pepper and, to a lesser extent, nutmeg (common in meat-based fillings) – are not. Cloves, allspice, cinnamon, vanilla, and other aromatics may occasionally be used in desserts and conserves in the region, but the spice box is, in general, almost wholly absent from local kitchens. This is especially curious considering that Genoa was a major player in the medieval spice trade.

The usual theory is a predictable one: that spices were too valuable for the thrifty Genoese to waste on themselves when there was serious profit to be made by selling them. But it is the virtue of spices that a little bit goes a long way, and surely the ingenious Genoese could have found a way of saving a bit of imported pungency for themselves if they'd wanted to. Waverley Root proposes another theory altogether. Because, he writes in *The Food of Italy,* "the Genoese were deep-sea sailors," they quickly grew tired of the pungent odours of the spices they transported long distances – "pepper from India, cloves from Zanzibar, cinnamon from Ceylon, pimento from the West Indies" – and by the time they docked, "the last thing in the world they wanted was more spice." He cites a single tantalizing exception: Ginger, he says, was consumed on shipboard to ward off scurvy, though it never found a place in land-bound kitchens. Maddeningly, he gives no source for this information, and I have never found a Genoese recipe – ancient or modern – in which ginger figures.

Stewed Chickpeas
Ceci in Zimino

Since this dish is widely considered to be one of the basics of Genoese cooking, it's curious how much disagreement there is about how it is made. In its simplest form, it's simply a soupy dish of reconstituted dried chickpeas stewed with onions, celery, and other vegetables. Some recipes, though, call for pork – either pieces of meat or sausages. Others suggest tomatoes and/or dried mushrooms. Some cooks add pasta, others don't.

There is even disagreement about the name of the thing: Is it ceci in zimino (çeixai co-o zemin in Genoese) or zimino di ceci? And what does the apparently untranslatable term *zimino*, also spelled *zemino*, mean? (The term is also used for salt cod or cuttlefish cooked similarly – and in Corsica, a *ziminu* or *aziminu* is a kind of fish stew.) I have no clue as to its etymology – scholar Charles Perry is unconvinced by Genoese attempts to give it an Arabic derivation – but I do like the dish in its simplest form, without pork or pasta.

to serve 6

450 g/1 lb	dried chickpeas
1	small onion, finely chopped
1	small celery stalk, finely chopped
1	garlic clove, finely chopped
2	flat-leaf parsley sprigs, finely chopped
4	leaves Swiss chard, with ribs, finely chopped
	Extra-virgin olive oil
150 g/5 oz	crushed tinned tomatoes
	Salt
6	slices grilled or toasted country bread
	Freshly grated Parmigiano-Reggiano

Place chickpeas in a large bowl with water to cover at room temperature, and let soak overnight (10–12 hours).

Drain chickpeas and rinse thoroughly, then place in a large saucepan with water to cover, bring to a boil, then cover saucepan loosely, reduce heat to low, and simmer for about 2 hours. Add more hot water if necessary during cooking, to keep chickpeas barely submerged.

Meanwhile, in a heavy sauté pan, cook onion, celery, garlic, parsley, and chard slowly in olive oil for 30–40 minutes, stirring frequently. Stir in tomatoes and cook for 10 minutes longer. Set soffritto aside until chickpeas have cooked for 2 hours, then add it to the saucepan. Let chickpea mixture cook for another hour, uncovered, then salt to taste.

To serve, place a slice of bread in each of 6 wide soup plates or bowls, ladle in chickpeas, and sprinkle Parmigiano on top.

Chickpea and Pasta Soup
Pasta e Ceci

The town of Quiliano, in the hills west of Savona, is known for its Granaccia – an uncharacteristically dark and hearty (for Liguria) red wine, made from the Grenache grape. On our way to visit a few of Quiliano's handful of wine producers, the heroically proportioned Savonese gastronome (and tourist official) Giuseppe Robatto took me to lunch at the town's Da Tina trattoria. Here we tucked into a robustly satisfying chickpea soup – basically ceci in zimino but with pork, tomatoes, mushrooms, and pasta added. It pleased me so much I had to ask for the recipe, and it was freely given. This is my slight adaptation of it.

to serve 6

450 g/1 lb	dried chickpeas
1	small onion, finely chopped
1	small carrot, finely chopped
1	small celery stalk, finely chopped
1	garlic clove, finely chopped
2	flat-leaf parsley sprigs, finely chopped
	Extra-virgin olive oil
225 g/8 oz	pork skin or 115 g/4 oz pancetta, cut into 6 pieces
4	leaves Swiss chard, with ribs, finely chopped
	Salt
15 g/½ oz	dried porcini mushrooms
150 g/5 oz	cup crushed tinned tomatoes
2	small potatoes, peeled and thinly sliced
115 g/4 oz	short pasta (tubetti)

Soak chickpeas overnight and begin to cook as in previous recipe.

Meanwhile, when chickpeas have started to simmer, cook onion, carrot, celery, garlic, and parsley in olive oil as in previous recipe.

As vegetables cook, place pork skin or pancetta in one saucepan and chard in another, both with water to cover. Bring both to a boil and cook both for about 15 minutes, then drain and set aside separately. Add salt to the chard.

Soak mushrooms in 3 changes of warm (not hot) water, for a total of about 15 minutes. Drain, chop, and add to vegetables, along with the reserved chard.

When vegetables have cooked 30–40 minutes, add tomatoes and cook for 10 minutes longer, then stir vegetables into chickpeas. Add reserved pork skin or pancetta to saucepan. Stir in raw potatoes and pasta, and continue cooking, uncovered, until both are cooked through, about 15–20 minutes.

Fava Bean "Pesto"

Salsa Marò

I think this pungent, addictive sauce – in effect a "pesto" of raw fava beans – is one of the best things I discovered in my many months in Liguria. Though Paolo Masieri, at the innovative Paolo e Barbara in Sanremo – the city that claims the sauce as its own – uses a particularly minty version of salsa marò on his gnocchi-like trofie (with sweet little red shrimp added), it is not traditionally considered a pasta sauce at all. Instead, it accompanies roasted meats, or is spread on toasted country bread. One popular etymology for the word *marò* links it with *maraq,* the Arabic word for broth or soup, and it is said that Moors on this coastline were fond of eating roast goat or mutton with a kind of green sauce that probably included mint, if not necessarily favas. Again, Charles Perry thinks this derivation is unlikely. Whatever the name means, the sauce is quite wonderful.

to make about 225 ml/8 fl oz

40–45	shelled fresh fava beans (about 450 g/1 lb in pod)
1	garlic clove, minced
6	fresh mint leaves
2	anchovy fillets
2	heaping tablespoons finely grated Pecorino Sardo or Parmigiano-Reggiano
	Extra-virgin olive oil

Shell favas, then blanch beans by dropping them in boiling water for 30 seconds. Drain and rinse well in cold water. Slip beans out of their skins by grasping each one by its grooved end and squeezing gently so that it pops out. Discard skins and set beans aside.

Crush garlic and mint leaves into a paste with a mortar and pestle, then work in anchovy fillets, continuing to crush until mixture is well amalgamated. Add about ⅓ of the favas to the mortar and begin crushing them. (If they are too slippery, sprinkle in a bit of the cheese to give the pestle a better purchase.) Continue adding favas until all are crushed into a paste with garlic, mint, and anchovies.

Work in cheese a little at a time, then drizzle in enough oil, working it into the fava mixture, to form a smooth paste, about the consistency of pesto.

Serve with roasted lamb, goat, or beef, or on toasted country bread.

Fried Favas

Fèves Frites

This simple, unusual recipe is adapted from *La Cuisine mentonnaise*, published by the Societé d'Art et d'Histoire du Mentonnais, and was supplied originally by a Menton housewife named Brigitte Bertolino. (Dried chickpeas may be similarly prepared.)

to serve 6–8

900 g/2 lb	dried favas
	Extra-virgin olive oil
	Salt and freshly ground black pepper

Soak the favas in a large bowl or pot in at least 4.5 litres/8 pints water for 48 hours, changing water 4 times. Skins should loosen and favas soften somewhat.

Drain favas, slip off the skins, and separate each one into two pieces. Spread fava halves out on a large tea towel and blot dry *very thoroughly* with another tea towel.

Heat about 4 cm/1½ inches of olive oil in a large frying pan until hot but not smoking, then fry favas in small batches for 3–4 minutes or until deep golden-brown. Remove with slotted spoon as done and drain on paper towels.

Season generously with salt and pepper and serve with aperitifs.

Vegetables with Anchovy Sauce
Bagna Càuda

This dish of raw vegetables in a "hot bath" of oil and butter spiked with anchovies and garlic is of Piedmontese origin but has been enthusiastically adopted in Nice and vicinity – where the anchovy is practically the regional mascot, both for its flavour and its fecundity (its very name in Niçois, *amploua,* seems to promise amplitude). One could theoretically dip almost any vegetable, raw or cooked, into this sauce, but it seems to have a special affinity for a small number of items with a vague, earthy similarity of flavour. Serving a bagna càuda with too many vegetables – I have one recipe that calls for nineteen! – seems gastronomically confusing, and not at all in the Niçois spirit. Cardoons are frequently a part of this dish, and in Nice are eaten raw. The variety available here, however, must be cooked; raw, it is inedibly bitter.

to serve 6

12	baby artichokes
2–3	tender cardoon stalks (optional)
	Salt (if using cardoons)
2	bulbs fennel, cut into thin lengthways strips
12	white inner celery stalks, with leaves
12	baby carrots, scrubbed, with leaves attached
125 ml/4 fl oz	extra-virgin olive oil
8–10	large oil-packed anchovy fillets
4	garlic cloves, crushed
115 g/4 oz	unsalted butter
1 tablespoon	red wine vinegar (optional)

Cut stems off artichokes. Pull off tough outer leaves by hand and trim a few more layers of leaves with a sharp knife. Slice off tops, then cut artichokes into halves or quarters lengthways.

Strip stringy parts off cardoon stalks (if using) and trim both ends, then cut into pieces about 7.5 cm/3 inches long. Cook in boiling, salted water for 30–40 minutes, then drain and cool.

Arrange all vegetables on a platter and refrigerate.

Heat oil in a pan, then add anchovies and mash with a fork until they begin to disintegrate. Continue stirring them into the oil with fork or a wooden spoon until they are well amalgamated. Stir in garlic cloves and let oil cook over lowest possible heat for about 5 minutes. Remove pan from heat and whisk in butter. Stir in vinegar if desired.

To serve, pour anchovy sauce into a small fondue pot or chafing pot or place in the top portion of a small bain-marie with boiling water in the lower portion. The sauce should remain warm. Serve alongside platter of vegetables as a dipping sauce. Sop up any sauce remaining after vegetables are finished with crusty French or Italian country-style bread.

Asparagus and Leeks in Olive Oil Emulsion
Asperges et Poireaux en Bouillon d'Huile d'Olive

The market on the Cours Saleya may be the most attractive and romantic place in Nice to buy fruit and vegetables, but the *best* place, from the professional chef's point of view, is the local M.I.N. Located on the road that leads up the east bank of the Var toward Grenoble and officially known as the Marché d'Intérêt National/Produits Alimentaires, the Niçois M.I.N. is one of eighteen such markets in France (another is the famed Rungis market just outside Paris), all jointly financed by the French Ministry of Agriculture and various regional governments.

Open to the trade only, the M.I.N. offers a dazzling array of produce and other foodstuffs, from factory-farms and tiny growers alike. Peasant farmers from France and Italy (and even sometimes from Spain) come here to sell their wares on Mondays, Wednesdays, and especially Fridays – and it was at 6 A.M. on a chilly Friday morning in February that I visited the place with Niçois chef Franck Cerutti, proprietor of the excellent little Don Camillo and also sous-chef to Alain Ducasse at the three-star Louis XV in Monte Carlo.

The M.I.N. is an immense open pavilion with a row of offices and permanent stalls along one side. In the middle of the pavilion, at little tables or just around stacks of wooden crates, farmers had gathered in clumps around flaming braziers or propane tank heaters, sipping coffee and rubbing their hands against the cold. The crates displayed late winter's bounty: long bunches of celery ending in an exuberance of leaves, thorny little egg-shaped artichokes dwarfed by their stems and almost concealed by their tropical-frond leaves, the season's first few trays of favas (some of them positively minuscule, and scattered with their fragrant leaves), luminescent yellow-green broccoli stalks standing straight up, bushy sprays of parsley and other herbs, wide fans of baby chard with faint pink ribs fading to ivory, radishes packed like Christmas candy under cellophane. . . .

Cerutti bantered and bartered, placed orders, took a few flats with him and arranged for others to be delivered, then stopped in the accounting office on the way out to pay. Then he drove me back to Nice and went on to his restaurant, while I went back to bed. That evening, he prepared this dish for me, using two of the prizes he had purchased – tender violet-green asparagus stalks and sweet little leeks not much thicker than spring onions. When I asked him for the recipe later, he warned me that this dish is "simple but difficult," because the moment of emulsification of the liquid can be tricky. He added that it was hard to prepare for more than one or two people at a time, but that, if all goes well, the final stage of cooking shouldn't take more than about three minutes.

to serve 2

10	medium-thick spears green asparagus
	Salt
2.3 litres/4 pints	chicken stock
10	baby leeks, trimmed to retain about 8 cm/3 inches of green leaves*
125 ml/4 fl oz	extra-virgin olive oil
115 g/4 oz	unsalted butter
	Freshly ground black pepper
	A dash of red wine vinegar

Peel asparagus spears with a sharp knife, then plunge them into boiling salted water to blanch for 2–3 minutes, depending on thickness. Drain and set aside.

Meanwhile, salt chicken stock and bring it to a boil in a large saucepan, then add leeks. Reduce heat to medium and cook for about 10 minutes. Drain leeks, reserving stock. Set leeks aside, and measure out about 150 ml/5 fl oz of stock, keeping the rest for another use.

Place oil and butter in a large sauté pan over high heat and add about 75 ml/3 fl oz stock. Add asparagus and leeks and, shaking pan constantly so that they don't stick to the bottom, let the oil, butter, and stock come to a boil and emulsify. (Add a bit more stock if necessary.) Quickly season to taste with salt and pepper, add vinegar, and serve at once.

*Choose leeks no more than 2.5 cm/1 inch thick, usually available only in early spring, and bend them gently first to make sure they don't have pithy cores. After trimming, separate remaining green leaves gently with your fingers and rinse thoroughly to remove any hidden sand or dirt.

Crustless Green Bean Tart

Polpettone di Fagiolini

Polpetta is Italian for croquette, and a polpettone is thus a large croquette – though it might be more accurate to say it's a large, flattened-out one, baked and not fried. In Genoese slang, however, a porpetton (which is the same word) is something boring, and frankly I can see how polpettone might be considered less than exciting by some. This is not dazzle-your-guests party fodder or Mediterranean exotica. It's home-cooking, kitchen-table fare – as undemandingly reassuring to a Genoese as pappa al pomodoro is to a Tuscan or mashed potatoes and gravy might be to us. A classic example of Ligurian culinary ingenuity, it is basically a way of turning vegetables into a main dish, or at least a hearty appetizer, by adding little more than miscellaneous odds and ends. I find it quite delicious.

to serve 4

900 g/2 lb	fresh green beans, trimmed*
	Salt
½	onion, finely chopped
1	garlic clove, minced
	Extra-virgin olive oil
4	flat-leaf parsley sprigs, finely chopped
	Leaves from 3–4 sprigs marjoram or oregano
75 g/3 oz	Parmigiano-Reggiano or pecorino Sardo, grated
4	large eggs, lightly beaten
75 g/3 oz	prescinsêua (see page 124) or ricotta
	Freshly ground black pepper
25 g/1 oz	breadcrumbs

Preheat oven to 150°C/300°F/Gas Mark 2.

Cook beans for 10–12 minutes in a saucepan of boiling, salted water. Cook onion and garlic in olive oil over low heat for about the same amount of time. Drain beans, rinse under cold water, and set aside. Add parsley and marjoram to onion and continue cooking for 10 minutes more.

*This dish can also be made with haricots verts – more expensive but worth it if you can find good ones – or with long yellow beans. Other kinds of green vegetables – including Swiss chard, spinach, artichokes, and courgettes – are also turned into polpettone, and a very good one can be made by substituting 900 g/2 lb of sliced, boiled potatoes for the beans in the recipe above, or using 450 g/1 lb each of potatoes and beans.

Meanwhile, cut beans into 2.5 cm/1 inch lengths. Remove onion mixture from heat and stir in beans, followed by about half the Parmigiano, the eggs, and the prescinsêua. Season the mixture with salt and pepper and make sure it is very well amalgamated.

Lightly oil a round baking dish, large pie tin, or small paella pan, then pack the mixture lightly into it, smoothing down the top with a palette knife. Mix the remaining cheese with the breadcrumbs and salt and pepper to taste and sprinkle it evenly over the bean mixture. Drizzle a bit of oil over the top of the polpettone, then bake for 1 hour.

Serve in wedges, warm or at room temperature.

Swiss Chard Frittata

Trouchia

In the region of Nice, as in Provence and in Catalonia, an omelette is a trout. In all three areas, that is, the same word is used for both the fish and the egg dish – trouchia (or trucchia), troucho, and truita, respectively. I've never heard a convincing explanation of this identity of terminology, but I suspect that what we have here is another example of what might be called the Welsh rabbit phenomenon – the ironic naming of a dish for the thing it might substitute for. Thus, a Welshman who can't shoot or snare (or afford to buy) a rabbit for dinner might have to settle for melted cheese on toast, and call it rabbit; and a fisherman who comes home with an empty creel might have to break some eggs for supper. (In medieval and renaissance Florentine cooking, a French-style omelette is called a *pesce finto,* or fake fish.) This recipe comes from Franck Cerutti, who serves little squares of trouchia along with excellent Niçoise olives and little olive-studded fougasses (focaccias) as an hors d'oeuvre at his Don Camillo restaurant in Nice.

to serve 4–6

450 g/1 lb	Swiss chard*
½	onion, finely chopped
4	large eggs, lightly beaten
50 g/2 oz	Parmigiano-Reggiano, grated
6–8	basil leaves, cut in chiffonade
2–3	flat-leaf parsley sprigs, finely chopped
	Salt and freshly ground black pepper
	Extra-virgin olive oil
	Sea salt crystals (gros sel)

Preheat oven to 140°C/275°F/Gas Mark 1.

Remove stalks from chard and reserve for another use. Gently cut chard into a chiffonade. (Chopping it, says Cerutti, will release too much moisture and ruin the consistency of the trouchia.)

In a large bowl, mix chard thoroughly with onion, eggs, Parmigiano, basil, and parsley, and season with salt and pepper.

Lightly oil a 13 × 25 cm/5 × 10 inch rectangular baking pan, then pack the mixture gently into it, smoothing down the top with a palette knife. Bake for ½ hour, then remove from oven, drizzle a bit of oil down the sides of the pan (the trouchia should have come away from the sides slightly), and carefully reverse it onto a lightly oiled platter or small cutting board. Carefully slide upside-down trouchia back into baking dish, return to oven, and bake for 15 minutes longer.

To serve, allow to cool slightly or to room temperature, cut into squares, drizzle a little more oil on top of each piece, and scatter a few crystals of salt over each.

*In the unlikely event that you should encounter some wild asparagus, Cerutti counsels that it makes a superb trouchia, too, in place of the chard. Parboil and chop it before mixing it with the other ingredients.

Stuffed Lettuce Leaves in Broth
Lattughe Ripiene in Brodo

Leivi is a little village of about 200 inhabitants on a winding road above Chiavari, overlooking the Golfo Tigullio. It isn't isolated and picturesque; it seems more a hilltop suburb than a hamlet. But it is still small-farm country, with olive trees and grapevines here and there and patches of vegetables and herbs behind many of the houses. The Romans called the town Solaria, for its beneficial exposure to the sun – and it thus seems particularly fitting that Leivi is also the site of a converted farmhouse, now a restaurant called Ca' Peo, at which Franco Solari and his wife, Melly, serve some of the best food on the Riviera. Solari's father built the farmhouse, and Franco was born there; he is a child of Leivi through and through. He and Melly are also self-taught chefs – but their food is sophisticated in the best sense, strongly grounded in tradition but wonderfully individual, with a deft contemporary flair.

It's always difficult to know what to order at Ca' Peo, because everything is so seductive, but one of my favourite dishes is Ca' Peo's version of this quintessential Ligurian speciality, which has been traditional Genoese Easter fare since the sixteenth century. (An ancient Genoese proverb says, "Pe Pasqua nu ghe cuxin-a ca nu fasse a laituga pin-a" – "For Easter, there's no kitchen that doesn't make stuffed lettuce.") Though we're more used to stuffed cabbage than stuffed lettuce here, the latter, in this dish at least, has a mild sweetness that functions as a perfect link between the richness of the filling and the simplicity of the broth.

to serve 4

225 g/8 oz	veal sweetbreads
	Salt
25 g/1 oz	dried porcini mushrooms
4 tablespoons	unsalted butter
225 g/8 oz	lean ground veal
	1 bay leaf
25 g/1 oz	Parmigiano-Reggiano, grated
1	garlic clove, minced
1	pinch nutmeg
	Leaves from 3 sprigs fresh oregano or marjoram
3	flat-leaf parsley sprigs, finely chopped
1	large egg and 1 large egg yolk, lightly beaten together
	Freshly ground black pepper
20	leaves salad bowl or butter lettuce
1.7 litres/3 pints	strong beef or veal stock
3 tablespoons	tocco (Genoese meat sauce; see page 103), optional

Plunge sweetbreads into a small saucepan of boiling salted water, cook for about 2 minutes, then drain and place in a bowl of cold water. Carefully pick the skin off the sweetbreads and chop very finely. Place mushrooms in a bowl of warm (not hot) water.

Melt the butter in a heavy frying pan, then add ground veal and bay leaf and cook over medium heat, stirring frequently, until meat is cooked through. Remove meat with a slotted spoon and set aside, leaving bay leaf in pan. Add sweetbreads to pan and cook as you did the veal. Remove sweetbreads with a slotted spoon and add to veal. Discard bay leaf.

Place ground veal and sweetbreads in a bowl and mix in Parmigiano, garlic, nutmeg, oregano, parsley, and eggs. Season to taste with salt and pepper and set aside.

Plunge lettuce leaves into a large saucepan of boiling salted water and cook for 2 minutes, then drain and refresh with cool water. Dry thoroughly by pressing between two tea towels. Turn leaves concave side up and place 1–2 tablespoons veal mixture in the centre of each leaf. Carefully fold in the ends of each leaf and roll it to make a little bundle enclosing the filling. Wrap and tie each bundle with kitchen string.

Bring stock to a boil, then reduce heat, add lettuce bundles, and cook at a low boil for 5–6 minutes. To serve, lift bundles out of stock with a slotted spoon, cut and remove the string, and place 5 in each of 4 large soup plates. Stir tocco (if used) into stock; ladle stock over bundles.

Ratatouille

Probably the best known of the Riviera's many vegetable dishes, ratatouille is a definitively (post-Columbian) Mediterranean combination of onions, tomatoes, peppers, courgettes and aubergines cooked in olive oil with garlic. The origin of the name of the dish is a matter of some dispute. Some dictionaries suggest that it is a blend of the French verbs *ratouiller,* to shake, and *touiller,* to stir – though, as far as I know, the dish is not shaken in its preparation. The Genoese, who sometimes claim the dish for themselves, call their version rattatuïa – and point out that the same word in their language means "remains" or "residue," with a figurative meaning of something of little value. Paula Wolfert, meanwhile, tells me that she has heard Greeks maintain that the word derives from *tourlou* – a term used on Corfu to describe a similar mélange of tomatoes, potatoes, onions, courgettes, peppers, and parsley.

Just to confuse matters, in Menton there's a very similar dish, but with potatoes added, known as giambalaia. (The Louisiana Creole concoction known as jambalaya borrows its name from a similar Provençal word.) And, according to Jean and Danièle Lorenzi, in their book *Cuisine monégasque/Cüjina de Munégu,* the traditional name for ratatouille in Monaco is brandayun. This is doubly confusing: Not only does the word suggest the brandade of stockfish known in Liguria as brandacujun; it is also almost identical to the Monégasque word for Jerusalem artichoke – which is branduyun or brandugliun. The Lorenzis report that they've found one local cook who actually puts Jerusalem artichokes in her ratatouille – but they suspect she does so only because the similarity of names leads her to think she's supposed to.

"Contrary to what is generally believed," writes Jacques Médecin in *La Cuisine du comté de Nice,* "ratatouille is a dish requiring particularly long and difficult preparation." This is because – again, contrary to popular belief – all the vegetables should be cooked separately to begin with, before being married in the pot. The authoritative texts on Niçois cooking agree closely on how ratatouille should be made; this recipe is an amalgam of formulas from several of them, with Médecin's taken as the final word (except when he suggests dusting the sliced aubergines and courgettes lightly with flour, which seems unnecessary to me).

to serve 6 plus*

900 g/2 lb	long, slender aubergines, trimmed
900 g/2 lb	courgettes, trimmed
450 g/1 lb	green bell peppers, cores, seeds, and stalks removed
450 g/1 lb	red bell peppers, cores, seeds, and stalks removed
900 g/2 lb	onions
	Extra-virgin olive oil
	Salt
8	cloves garlic, finely chopped
1	small bunch flat-leaf parsley, finely chopped
20–25	basil leaves, roughly torn
	Leaves from 3 sprigs fresh thyme
1.5 kg/3 lb	ripe tomatoes, skinned, seeded, and coarsely chopped

Slice aubergines and courgettes into rounds about 12 mm/½ inch thick, then spread them out on paper towels and salt them very lightly.

Slice the bell peppers into 12 mm/½ inch rings, then cut the rings in half; set aside. Chop the onions into pieces approximately 2.5 cm/1 inch square.

Place 4 large frying pans on the stove and pour several tablespoons of olive oil into each one. Warm the oil over a medium-high flame for about 1 minute, then lightly fry the aubergines, courgettes, mixed green and red peppers, and onions, each in a different pan, in batches if necessary. When vegetables are cooked through and lightly browned but not overdone, remove them from their pans with a slotted spoon and drain on paper towels. Reserve any oil remaining in the pans.

In a large casserole or heavy saucepan, combine cooked vegetables, salt to taste, and cook, uncovered, over the lowest heat possible.

Meanwhile, pour oil from 3 of the vegetable pans into the remaining one, adding a little more if necessary, and cook the garlic, herbs, and tomatoes, uncovered, over low heat for about 20 minutes.

*This recipe should serve more than 6. In offering her own recipe for ratatouille in *Cuisine traditionnelle en pays niçois,* Mamé Clairette notes, "I give these quantities [of ingredients] not for the number of diners, but for what will be left over, to finish the next day with other friends."

Stir tomato sauce gently into vegetables with a wooden spoon, then drain excess oil from ratatouille in a colander. Return to casserole, adjust seasoning, and serve warm; set aside to serve at room temperature; or cool slightly and chill in the refrigerator for about 3 hours and serve cold.

Courgette Gratin
Tian de Courgettes

A tian is somewhere between polpettone (the flat, crustless Genoese vegetable tart) and an omelette (a trouchia). Like them, it turns a few vegetables into something hearty and presentable as a serious dish. In Bernard Duplessy's *Cuisine traditionnelle en pays niçois*, Mamé Clairette suggests that the cooking time of tians traditionally corresponded to the length of time it took to bake bread in a communal oven. The reason was simple: In earlier times, women prepared various dishes – tians, tourtes (or torte), stews, and such – at home and brought them to the local public oven or commercial bakery to be cooked. Real ovens were rare at home, for reasons of space, practicality, and safety (errant embers could burn down a house). Besides, this was a way to conserve resources. The bread had to be baked anyway, so the community could share the baker's fire for other purposes. But since the bread was more important in the grander scheme of things, and the baker couldn't keep opening the oven to pull out the tians, they had to be made in such a way that they would take exactly as long as the bread did to bake.

to serve 6

900 g/2 lb	small (not baby) courgettes
450 g/1 lb	Swiss chard
	Salt
1	garlic clove
	Olive oil
4–5	flat-leaf parsley sprigs, finely chopped
	Nutmeg
	Black pepper
50-75 g/2-3 oz	Parmigiano-Reggiano or pecorino Sardo, grated
5	large eggs
250 ml/9 fl oz	full-fat milk
2 tablespoons	crème fraîche
40 g/1½ oz	fine breadcrumbs

Preheat oven to 180°C/350°F/Gas Mark 4.

Cut courgettes in half lengthways and scrape out seeds, if any, with a spoon. Cut stems from chard and reserve for another use. Shred courgettes on the large holes of a four-sided grater and drain on paper towels in a colander. Cut chard leaves into a chiffonade, then blanch 5–6 minutes in boiling salted water, drain, dry thoroughly, and mix with shredded courgettes.

Rub the bottom and sides of a round 30 to 35 cm/12 to 14 inch glass or earthenware baking dish with garlic clove, then discard or save for another use. Lightly oil dish, then cover the bottom with a thin layer of courgette mixture. Scatter top of layer lightly with parsley, then season with a little nutmeg, black pepper, and salt. Scatter grated Parmigiano on top. Repeat the process until all the mixture is used. (There will probably be 3 layers, but 2 or 4 work just as well.)

Beat the eggs with milk and crème fraîche, until well mixed, then pour the mixture evenly over the top of the chard layers. Dust the top of the tian lightly with breadcrumbs and bake for 20 minutes. Raise heat to brown the breadcrumbs lightly.

Serve hot or at room temperature.

Stuffed Squash Blossoms
Fiori di Zucca Ripieni

Fried courgette or zucca (squash) blossoms are a Niçois staple, but I found this unusual treatment of the latter mentioned in *Un paese di pietra (Apricale),* Claudio Nobbio's little book on Apricale, a town in the western Ligurian entroterra.

to serve 4

450 g/1 lb	potatoes, sliced
450 g/1 lb	green beans, trimmed and cut into 5 cm/2 inch lengths
1	onion, finely chopped
	Salt
16–20	squash or pumpkin blossoms (or about twice as many courgette blossoms)
	Milk
2	large eggs, lightly beaten
175 g/6 oz	Parmigiano-Reggiano, grated
	Freshly ground black pepper
	Extra-virgin olive oil

Cook potatoes, green beans, and onion together in boiling salted water for about 30 minutes, then drain and set aside.

Meanwhile, gently open blossoms and remove pistils, then wash carefully, inside and out, and place in a bowl large enough to hold them all. Fill the bowl with enough milk to cover them.

Preheat oven to 200°C/400°F/Gas Mark 6.

When cooked vegetables have partially cooled, purée them in a blender or food processor or with a food mill. Stir in eggs and Parmigiano, and season with salt and pepper. Remove blossoms from milk and pat dry with paper towels, then fill each one with a tablespoon or so of the vegetable mixture and gently pinch them closed.

Lightly oil a large rectangular baking dish and place blossoms in it in a single layer. Bake for 20 minutes and serve hot.

Coaraze-Style Stuffed Vegetables
Légumes Farcis Coaraziens

Coaraze, officially designated as one of "Les Plus Beaux Villages de France," is a pretty little medieval hill town in the arrière-pays, not quite 20 miles north of Nice. Tradition has it that its rather curious name is a contraction of *cauda rasa* or *coa rasa* – local dialect for *queue rasée,* meaning shaved or razed tail – either for a variety of tailless lizard found nearby or in commemoration of the time villagers tried to catch the devil by gluing down his tail, only to have him escape by leaving the appendage behind. Tourists sometimes find their way to Coaraze to see the sixteenth-century frescoes in its Chapelle St. Sébastian and the twentieth-century ones in its Chapelle Bleue. The village, proud of its sunny exposures, also boasts six sundials – four on the facade of the town hall and two on the Place du Parlement – done in 1961 by six artists, the best known of them being Jean Cocteau (whose design features lizards without tails).

There are, to the best of my knowledge, no uniquely Coarzien gastronomic specialities, but the surrounding area is still largely agricultural and produces good-quality olives and olive oil – there is an annual Fête de l'Olivier in August – as well as goat cheese, honey, and chestnuts (honoured by a festival of their own in October). And the village is the site each year, also in August, of a particularly appealing, very homey little culinary celebration called La Manjiuca – which means something like "the Fodder" or "the Chow." La Manjiuca is a town-wide pot-luck supper: Four or five long communal tables and a little bandstand are set up on the Place Ste. Catherine, and maybe 100 of the village's 500 or so inhabitants participate, each bringing something on a platter or in a pot or a terrine. There are huge mixed salads, bowls of gnocchi in tomato sauce, pâtés and home-made sausages, vegetable-stuffed tourtes, and more. Food is passed, shared, sampled, complimented; recipes are asked for and given. An accordionist performs; songs are sung (some in French, some in Niçois, even some in Piedmontese); a little orchestra appears and plays old-fashioned dance tunes into the early hours of the morning.

Among the dishes always served at La Manjiuca are several interpretations of farcis niçois, or stuffed vegetables. Farcis – called ripieni in Liguria (and pinn-e in Genoese) – are eaten all along the Riviera, and especially between Genoa and Nice, and perhaps no class of dishes better demonstrates the frugality and ingenuity of the local populace. Based almost entirely on ingredients grown or processed locally – vegetables, herbs, eggs, cheese, sometimes a bit of meat (usually in the form of salt pork or sausage), sometimes wild mushrooms – they can be quite elaborate: Jacques Médecin, for instance, gives a different filling for each of six vegetables in his Niçois cookbook. They can also be very simple, sometimes made with little more than the scooped-out flesh of the vegetables themselves, with herbs, cheese, and breadcrumbs added. The version that follows, which occupies a sort of middle ground, was given to me by Ginette Touati, president of the Coaraze tourist office.

to serve 6–8

4	small aubergines
6	small or 3 large green bell peppers
8	small onions, peeled
4	small courgettes
3	medium tomatoes
8	large white or brown mushrooms
	Extra-virgin olive oil
125 g/4 oz	cooked ham, finely diced
125 g/4 oz	Italian sausage
225 g/8 oz	lean beef, finely diced
125 g/4 oz	lean salt pork or pancetta, finely diced
2	garlic cloves, minced
	Salt and freshly ground black pepper
2	large eggs, lightly beaten
125 g/4 oz	Parmigiano-Reggiano, grated
40 g/1½ oz	breadcrumbs

Preheat oven to 190°C/375°F/Gas Mark 5.

Cut aubergines in half lengthways and scoop pulp from them with a spoon, leaving about 12 mm/½ inch of shell. Cut tops from small peppers or halve large peppers lengthways and remove ribs and seeds.

Blanch onions for 10 minutes in a large saucepan of salted water, then drain and cool. Halve them crosswise and remove centres, leaving a shell of about 3 layers. Roughly chop centres and set aside. Halve courgettes lengthways and scoop out pulp, leaving ½ inch shell. Cut tomatoes in half lengthways, and gently squeeze out juice and seeds. Scoop out pulp and mix with chopped onion, and courgettes and aubergine pulp.

Remove stalks from mushrooms and finely chop stalks. Mix pulp of all vegetables, including mushroom stalks, together and cook in olive oil in a large sauté pan over low heat for about 5 minutes, stirring frequently. Add ham, sausage, beef, salt pork and garlic. Season with salt and pepper, and continue cooking for about 15 minutes longer, stirring occasionally. Remove pan from heat, allow to cool slightly, then stir in eggs.

Arrange vegetable shells on one or more oiled baking trays. Fill each one with stuffing, but don't pack them too tightly. Mix cheese and breadcrumbs, then scatter on tops of vegetables; drizzle with olive oil, and bake for 30–40 minutes or until all vegetables are tender. Serve hot or at room temperature.

Potatoes in Their Jackets

Patake en da Burnisa

This is probably the oldest potato recipe in Italy. Though Napoleon's soldiers are said to have cooked and eaten potatoes in this manner, the technique was known even earlier in eastern Liguria – especially in the areas of Castelnuovo Magra and the Lunigiana, where peasants roasted potatoes in the fields during the cold fall and winter days of the olive harvest. This recipe is adapted from Gianfranco Cricca's *Antiche ricette di Castelnuovo Magra*. The only simpler potato recipe I can imagine is one given in *Manjar coumo en viage a Sant Esteve,* a collection of recipes from St. Étienne-de-Tinée, in the far backcountry of Nice, a few miles from the Piedmontese border. This one, called triflos mé la sal "pelo-manjo" (potatoes with salt "peel and eat") reads as follows: "Cook the potatoes in water in their skins. Then everyone peels his potato, salts it, and eats it." These latter potatoes figured in an old pre-Lenten tradition in the region: The day before

Mardi Gras, local conscripts would march through St. Étienne dressed in white garments with red sashes, wearing forage caps and carrying empty flour sacks and baskets. Singing to the beat of a drum, they would beg at all the houses and cafés for a bit of flour for the sack and for potatoes, eggs, wine, or bread for the basket. Then they'd return to their homes and have lunch with their families, the pièce de résistance typically being the potatoes cooked in this most basic way.

to serve 4

8 medium-small baking potatoes, unpeeled
Extra-virgin olive oil
Salt
1 small onion, finely chopped (optional)

Wash potatoes thoroughly and pat dry, then place directly in the embers of a wood or charcoal fire, heaping the glowing embers around them. Cook until done: It is impossible to estimate the time this will take, as it depends on the size and variety of the potatoes and the heat and number of the embers. It should take at least an hour, however, and could take two. To check if cooked, insert a thin metal skewer into the potatoes.

When cooked, remove potatoes from embers and carefully brush off any loose charred pieces. Potatoes should be lightly burned but not ashy. Place 2 potatoes on each plate and roughly crush them, with their peels, with a wooden spoon. Drizzle olive oil over them and salt them generously. Sprinkle with chopped onion if desired.

Triorese Potato Casserole

Patate int'a Föglia

According to Sandro Oddo, whose speciality is the cuisine and customs of the Valle Argentina, which stretches inland from Sanremo in western Liguria, this dish – the name literally means potatoes in the baking pan – is one of the basics of the region's traditional cooking. It resembles a French potato gratin but is richer – being bound with flour and loaded with cheese. The use of butter and milk is typical of the Valle Argentina – one of the few parts of Liguria where dairy products are consumed in any quantity.

to serve 4

900 g/2 lb	potatoes, peeled and thinly sliced
3 tablespoons	flour
350 ml/12 fl oz	milk
225 g/8 oz	Parmigiano-Reggiano or pecorino Sardo, grated
225 g/8 oz	fresh mozzarella, cut into 12 mm/½ inch cubes
½	onion, minced
	Extra-virgin olive oil
	Salt
25 g/1 oz	unsalted butter, in very thin slices

Preheat oven to 160°C/325°F/Gas Mark 3.

Place potatoes, flour, milk, 175 g/16 oz of the Parmigiano, mozzarella, onion, 2 tablespoons olive oil, and salt to taste in a large bowl, then gently mix together with your hands.

Oil a shallow baking dish, deep enough to hold ingredients, then pour potato mixture into it. Place butter slices at even intervals on top and sprinkle with remaining cheese.

Bake for 1 hour or until potatoes are cooked and top is golden-brown.

Potato and Pine Nut Croquettes
Cuculli di Patatte

Cuculli (also spelled cucculli and coccôlli) is Genoese slang for little darlings or chubby little ones – and, by extension, for someone credulous or dim – but it also means a certain kind of fritter. Cuculli are usually made from chickpea flour, in a form not dissimilar to panizzie or panisses (see page 189) – except that cuculli are leavened and thus lighter on the palate. The potato version is by no means unknown in traditional Genoese cooking, however. Bohun Lynch describes it perfectly in *The Italian Riviera* (1928), though not by name, when he notes that, at a hotel in Albissola Capo, he sampled "little croquettes of mashed potato [which] were in the first place the most inviting things of their kind to look at that I can remember. The surface of them was crisply and evenly fried a golden brown; there was a hint in them – no more – of egg and cheese.

They were very wonderful." And wonderful they are. This recipe is adapted from a formula published in 1867 under the name *"Galletti (cuculli) di patate"* in Emanuele Rossi's *La vera cuciniera genovese*.

to serve 4

900 g/2 lb	floury potatoes, unpeeled
50 g/2 oz	pine nuts
3	large eggs, separated
50 g/2 oz	unsalted butter
	Leaves from 2 sprigs marjoram or oregano
75 g/3 oz	freshly grated pecorino Sardo or Parmigiano-Reggiano
	Salt
115 g/4 oz	dried breadcrumbs
	Corn or peanut oil

Boil the potatoes in their jackets until done, 30–40 minutes.

Meanwhile, crush the pine nuts lightly with a mortar and pestle and set aside, then lightly beat the eggs' yolks and whites in separate bowls.

When potatoes are cooked, peel them and purée them with a mortar and pestle (if you have a mortar large enough) or in a bowl with a potato masher. Stir in pine nuts, egg yolks, butter, marjoram, grated cheese, and salt to taste.

Form potato mixture into rounded cylinders about the size and shape of large walnuts. Dip in egg whites, roll in bread crumbs, and fry in batches in hot oil until golden-brown, turning if necessary. Drain on paper towels, season with additional salt if desired, and serve hot.

SOME CLASSIC HERB AND VEGETABLE DISHES

Pesto and Its Pastas

*[Pesto] is a famous sauce rarely met outside
of Genoa.*

– ADA BONI, *ITALIAN REGIONAL
COOKING* (1969)

According to the bylaws of the Confraternità del Pesto – an organization founded in Genoa in 1992 to foster the appreciation (and safeguard the integrity) of this celebrated but often misinterpreted green sauce – pesto is a "typical and ancient Ligurian condiment . . . synonymous with 'Genoese-ness' for all the Ligurians scattered around the world, who find in it the nostalgic memory of their land."

In reality, pesto became the defining symbol of Liguria only in the late nineteenth century. The earliest published recipe for the sauce as we know it today apparently appeared in an anonymous cookbook called *Cuciniere italiano ovvero l'amico dei ghiotti,* published in Florence in 1848. Martin Piaggio, the food-obsessed nineteenth-century Genoese poet, who celebrated most of his city's great dishes in verse, never mentions it. The intrepid English gastronomic traveller Lieut.-Col. Newnham-Davis, on a visit to Genoa in the early 1900s, encountered pesto – which he defines as "a paste in which pounded basil, garlic, Sardinia cheese, and olive oil are used" – only as a flavouring for minestrone, not as a pasta sauce.

Today, of course, pesto *is* Liguria – and has also become probably the most famous of Italian sauces. However limited its range may have been when Ada Boni wrote her book on the regional cooking of Italy almost thirty years ago, it is everywhere today, a standard in Italian restaurants and Italian recipe books in every corner of the universe. Rumor has it that Franco Malerba, the first Italian astronaut, even smuggled pesto into space.

We've all had pesto, and quite possibly even made it ourselves. I think it's safe to say, however, that anyone who has never tasted pesto in or near Genoa has probably never really experienced it. At its best, Genoese pesto is an absolutely memorable culinary triumph – a remarkable, well-balanced mix of fragrance and flavour, a bit salty, a bit sweet, a bit earthy, and unmistakably redolent of its defining herb.

Ada Boni exaggerates only slightly when she writes that "there is one element that pervades the whole [Genoese port] area, as well as the whole of Greater Genoa from Arenzano to Sestri Levante – a characteristic odour that rises above the sharp, pungent smell of sea brine. This is the aroma of *pesto* . . . as penetrating and evocative as Bavarian sauerkraut or the perfume of cognac in a cellar in south-west France." Basil, it has been said, is the perfume of Genoa and the soul of pesto, and one unmistakable characteristic of good pesto, as it is served in these parts, is that you can quite literally smell it across the room – and what you're smelling, I hasten to add, is always the basil, never the garlic.

At least a bit of garlic (which Braudel calls "the spice of the poor") is essential to pesto, of course. A Genoese proverb says, "O mortâ o sa sempre d'aggio" – "The mortar always smells of garlic." Olive oil and pine nuts – or, in some regions, walnuts (or even a combination of both) – are basic to the sauce as well. Long, thin Mediterranean pine nuts, which are not as oily as the more common tear-drop-shaped Chinese variety – and which cost twice as much – are preferred by connoisseurs. Cheese is apparently a more recent addition, and its inclusion is usually forbidden in any pesto or pistou destined to be stirred into the soup. On the other hand, Ligurian culinary historians like to trace the origins of pesto back to a popular Roman condiment called *moretum,* made from aged sheep's cheese pounded in a mortar with garlic, olive oil, vinegar, and not basil but celery leaves, rue, and coriander. (Virgil describes eating such a paste spread on bread as a morning meal in the *Georgics.*) And some scholars believe that the original pesto "cheese" might have been thick yoghurt imported by the Genoese from their colonies on the Black Sea in the fourteenth or fifteenth century. To this day, prescinsêua – the Genoese speciality, not dissimilar in character to thick yoghurt – is sometimes stirred into pesto on the Riviera di Levante.

The other cheese long associated with pesto is pecorino Sardo, Sardinian sheep's-milk cheese. Sardinia has been a leading exporter of cheese since the sixteenth century, and Genoa has a long historical and commercial association with that island. It is hardly surprising, then, that the Ligurians – who produce little cheese of their own – should be such good customers for the product. Sardo, often made in Liguria itself today by transplanted Sardinian shepherds, is now widely used in pesto, often in half-and-half combination with Parmigiano. It is slightly sweeter than the latter, and it really does seem to add something to the mix.

As the Genoese will gladly tell you, there is only one way to make pesto correctly: in a mortar, with a pestle – as pesto's very name suggests. (It derives from the Genoese verb *pestâ,* to pound or beat. An early Italian synonym for pesto was *battuto,* which means something beaten.) A marble mortar with a wooden pestle, its business end roughened for better crushing power, is considered ideal. A blender simply isn't possible.

This isn't just culinary romanticism, say the Genoese. Cutting rather than crushing basil, they maintain, stops up the capillaries in the leaves, so that fewer of the basil's odour and flavour components are released. Purists even claim that the heat produced by the blender blades causes aromas to evaporate, and that the centrifugal action of the blender causes the basil's pulp and juice to separate, thus enervating the herb's character.

I'm frankly not sure whether any of this is true, but, having made pesto both ways (and a third way – simply hacking everything up together with a large knife on a big cutting board), I must say that the mortar-and-pestle stuff does seem to be the best. It is indeed more aromatic, and also seems slightly less bitter. Anyway, I find the process of crushing the ingredients together, standing over the mortar as they release their seductive odours, immensely satisfying. That said, I must add that one of Liguria's best chef-restaurateurs confessed to me one evening that he always starts pesto in a mortar but then transfers it to a blender to obtain a smooth consistency, difficult with the traditional method.

The Genoese also have definite ideas about how pesto should be used. Other than being stirred into minestrone and an occasional other soup, it is specifically a sauce for a few certain types of pasta – most notably trenette (the local version of linguine), trofie (a kind of gnocchi – little twisted cylindrical bits of pasta hand-made with white, or sometimes chestnut, flour), mandilli de sæa ("silk handkerchiefs," thin lasagna-type sheets tossed with the sauce), corzetti (pasta discs stamped with family initials and other designs, or, in some regions, flat figure-eight-shaped pasta pieces), and testaroli (more or less pasta-dough pancakes). Pesto on spaghetti? Marginal. With ravioli? Only as an experiment. In risotto? Are you kidding? As a sauce for fish or chicken? You *are* kidding. This isn't ketchup we're dealing with here. This is Genoese-ness itself.

Basil Under Glass

One autumn morning, Pietro Uslengo and I trudge up a steep path above the A-10 autostrada in Prà, just west of Genoa. On both sides of us, on narrow terraced ledges, are long, low-slung commercial *serre,* or greenhouses – not glittering high-tech horticultural palaces but something more like elongated garden sheds, with rust-flecked metal frames and cloudy glass panes veined here and there with time-worn cracks. I've come with Uslengo, a founding member of the Confraternità del Pesto, to see how Liguria's defining herb, sweet basil, is grown.

Basil, which was apparently first cultivated in India, exists in many sub-varieties, with varying degrees of pungency and dramatic differences in flavour. A relative of mint, it was long considered to be a sacred or at least noble plant. The Copts used it to sprinkle holy water; a legend claimed that Saint Helena, mother of the Emperor Constantine, found the True Cross under a clump of it. In some European cultures, it could be cut only with a knife made of gold or silver, never of some baser metal. Its very name suggests its stature, deriving from the Greek word *basilikós,* meaning regal.

Sweet basil *(Ocymum basilicum),* the variety most often eaten on the Riviera and elsewhere in the western Mediterranean, is a hardy annual that thrives in warm climates. It is by definition a summer herb – though in the hot Italian south, "summer" might last six months or more. In earlier times, basil harvested in the warmer months was preserved in salt or oil, and doled out during the winter. Then came the greenhouses.

As early as the late eighteenth century, wealthy Genoese

families had greenhouses, heated only by the sun, in which they amused themselves by growing pineapples and other tropical plants. Around the same time, some farmers probably started using the same kind of structures for growing basil and other herbs – though because they were not artificially heated, the season extended probably only from about April through November. In the late 1920s, though, a botanist in Chiavari recorded in his diary, "For the first time in my life, I had basil in winter." This was from a stove-heated greenhouse. Today, serre – most of them growing flowers but a number of them devoted to basil and other herbs and vegetables – cover the hillsides outside Genoa and along that portion of the western Riviera called the Riviera dei Fiori. There are literally thousands of serre, and they pose an environmental problem, occupying valuable watershed and polluting the air (since they are usually heated with petrol-run generators; solar-powered serre exist but are rare). They have become, however, an indispensable part of the local culinary landscape.

As far as the Genoese are concerned, the only basil worth bothering with is that grown in one of the urbanized agricultural communities that surround their city – Prà, Pegli, Coronata, Palmaro, and Voltri. Soil, climate, and farming methods here are supposedly ideal for the herb. (One thing is certain: The best Genoese basil seeds, sown in, say, Southern California or New Jersey, yield nothing like the local version.)

What's grown here has been called "il unico vero basilico al mondo," and it is known for its immense fragrance and forthright flavour, coupled with an almost complete absence of the minty character basil so often has. Commercial producers in these areas have even awarded themselves an appellation: Their basil now comes to market bearing a tag reading "Basilico di Genova." Local connoisseurs consider basil from Albenga, on the western Riviera – another major source of the herb – an inferior product. And don't even get them started about that so-called basil – all pepper and mint – that grows in Sicily or Naples.

Pino Sacco, the owner of the greenhouse I've come to visit, is one of about 150 small growers in Prà alone. He meets us at the second greenhouse down from the crest of the hill, and, ushering us inside, offers me a crash course in indoor basil farming the Genoese way. Down the length of the greenhouse, on three levels, stretch long, unbroken strips of tiny bright green leaves, covering every inch of raised beds roughly 18.3 metres/60 feet long and about 2.4 metres/8 feet wide. The beds are filled with soil that is mixed with rice hulls for good drainage, fertilized, and irrigated regularly; the interior is thermostatically controlled, with sliding glass panels in the roof to let in fresh air and sunlight when appropriate. This helps maintain a constant temperature. (The larger the greenhouse, says Sacco, the easier the temperature is to regulate.)

Half a dozen men, stooping over the beds or crouched on planks stretched across them, are harvesting basil when we enter – not clipping it or plucking off the leaves but pulling up whole tiny plants, hardly more than sprouts, by their delicate roots. (Basil of this sort is sometimes called white basil – *baxaicò gianco* in Genoese – because it is so pale in colour.) "When the plants sprout four large leaves and two to four smaller ones," says Sacco, "the basil is ready to pick. This takes about thirty to thirty-five days, from seed, in winter, and maybe ten days less in warmer weather." For two months in full summer, when outdoor basil is abundant, the greenhouse soil is allowed to rest.

The harvesters gather the basil into *mazzi,* or bunches, of about half a dozen plants each. Later, I watch as two old women, working in a small room filled with smoke from the unventilated woodstove on which they're cooking their lunch, separate masses of damp excelsior-like shredded plastic – a by-product of the manufacture of milk cartons – and stuff it into individual plastic bags. Later, bundles of eight or ten *mazzi* of basil will be placed in each of these bags and sent to market. Packed this way, it will last for four or five days.

Each bundle – about enough for a family-size batch of pesto – sells in the better shops in Genoa for as much as 10,000 lire (about £4.00). This is expensive, but, then, good basil is essential to good pesto, and good pesto is essential – in Genoa at least – to a good life. When he travels outside of Liguria, Pietro Uslengo tells me as we head back to the city after our visit to Prà, the first thing he does when he comes home is to throw some pasta in a pot and make himself some of that fabled sauce. "It's a drug," he says.

Genoa's Other
Green Sauce

Salsa genovese is not pesto, but it might be called pesto's sharp-tongued cousin. Like pesto, it is a raw sauce, best made with a mortar and pestle – but it is based on parsley, not basil; is full of sourish, acidic elements; and is applied not to pasta or to soup but to cold fish dishes – most importantly the elaborate seafood and vegetable creation called cappon magro (see page 87). In effect, salsa genovese is an elaboration of the classic Italian salsa verde, or green sauce, traditional with boiled meats – a sauce that Silvio Torre quotes Spanish writer Alvaro Conqueiro as calling "the most Roman, the most Vatican of all sauces; that which most openly proclaims the supremacy of European flavours – garlic, parsley and vinegar – over the assorted spicery of the infidel East." To make approximately 450 ml/16 fl oz, drizzle enough good red wine vinegar over 25 g/1 oz of fresh breadcrumbs to moisten them lightly, then set them aside. Finely chop the leaves of a small bunch of flat-leaf parsley, then crush them in a mortar. When they've formed a paste, gradually work in the moistened breadcrumbs, about a tablespoon of pine nuts and another of capers, a small minced garlic clove, 10 or 12 small green olives (pitted), a hard-boiled egg yolk, and a couple of anchovy fillets. Adding a few drops of olive oil if necessary for consistency, crush them into a smooth paste. Salt the paste to taste, then dilute it with about 2 tablespoons additional vinegar and 4 tablespoons additional oil. (Since this is a much less delicate sauce than pesto, it could also be made in a blender or food processor. Soak the breadcrumbs as above, then add all ingredients to the work bowl and process.)

Pesto Genovese

Though pesto is a simple sauce, requiring only a handful of ingredients and a single technique of preparation, there are countless variations on the recipe. This one was inspired by a passage about making pesto (not a recipe, exactly) in Vito Elio Petrucci's excellent *Profumi e sapori di Liguria,* but has been adapted according to suggestions from several Ligurian chefs and my own experiences of making pesto at home.

Here are some additional pieces of pesto lore that may prove helpful: According to Renato Belforte, who runs the dining room at the Yacht Club in Genoa – and in contrast to what some cookbooks will tell you – pesto shouldn't be kept for very long. "Make it and use it," he suggests, "and it should never be more than two or three days old. As it ages, the basil loses flavour and the garlic becomes more pronounced, so the sauce loses its balance." Various authorities maintain that pesto destined to be used in soup should not contain pine nuts, or cheese, or even oil. Almost everyone agrees that neither cream nor butter should be added to any pesto – though Petrucci confesses that he does use a bit of the latter. (My Genoese friend Alberto Bisagno tells me that his grandfather, who was a chef, used to stir an egg yolk into his pesto, but this was surely just a chef's gloss.) One recipe I have for pistou calls for letting the basil leaves dry for 24 hours after they're washed; a related suggestion from one Italian source suggests adding a pinch of dried basil to the pesto after crushing the fresh leaves.

to serve 4

1	garlic clove, finely chopped
3 tablespoons	pine nuts
	Coarse salt
	A large handful of basil, leaves only*
50 g/2 oz	each Parmigiano-Reggiano and pecorino Sardo (or 50 g/2 oz Parmigiano)
125 ml/4 fl oz	extra-virgin olive oil, preferably Ligurian

Place garlic, pine nuts, and a pinch of salt in a large mortar, then crush them with a pestle, using smooth, regular motions, to make a smooth paste.

Add basil to mortar a little at a time. Crush to a coarse paste, grinding leaves against side of mortar with pestle. Add a pinch more salt and continue crushing, then gradually stir and crush in cheese.

*See note on page 64.

Drizzle in olive oil and continue working until pesto is very smooth and no large pieces of basil are visible. To serve, dilute with 1–2 tablespoons pasta cooking water and toss with trenette (see page 65), trofie (see page 67), or mandilli de sæa (see page 69), corzetti (see page 134), or testaroli (see page 158).

Castelnuovo-Style Pesto

Pisto Kastarnoésa

Since the region of Castelnuovo Magro is notoriously poor, even by Ligurian standards, the idea of mixing basil with other herbs might very well have developed here simply as a measure of economy. (Vito Elio Petrucci, a founding member of the Confraternità del Pesto, writes in *Profumi e sapori di Liguria* that when summer basil disappeared for the year and greenhouse basil began appearing in the markets at a higher price, his mother would exclaim, "Ahimemi! Son furti, son laddri!" – "Woe is me! They're thieves, they're robbers!" – and make pesto with parsley instead.) This recipe is adapted from Gianfranco Cricca's *Antiche ricette di Castelnuovo Magra;* "alternative" pestos like this one are all but unknown in Liguria today, in Castelnuovo or anywhere else, and are far more likely to be found in historical collections than on home or restaurant tables.

to serve 4

1	garlic clove, finely chopped
25 g/1 oz	chopped walnuts
	Coarse salt
	A small handful basil, leaves only*
	A small handful flat-leaf parsley, leaves only
1 tablespoon	fresh marjoram leaves
75 g/3 oz	grated Parmigiano-Reggiano or pecorino Sardo
6 tablespoons	extra-virgin olive oil, preferably Ligurian

Follow the instructions for pesto genovese on page 63, crushing parsley and then marjoram leaves into the mortar after the basil but before the cheese. Serve with the pastas mentioned in the previous recipe, or, more authentically, with tag'aín con faa ar pisto – taglierini with favas, potatoes, and Castelnuovo-style pesto (see page 66).

*Use the smallest (i.e., youngest) leaves possible. To avoid a greenish bitterness, trim off the stems so that literally just the leaves are used – and if the leaves are very large, cut out even the centre vein.

Pistou

Pistou is pesto's Niçois cousin. Was it borrowed from the Genoese? Probably, but the Niçois don't always believe that. Consider this charming exchange about pistou between Bernard Duplessy and Mamé Clairette, from *Cuisine traditionnelle en pays niçois:* "On dit qu'il est venu de Gênes, Mamé?" "On peut aussi dire qu'il est allé à Gênes!" ("They say that it comes from Genoa, Mamé?" "One could say also that it went to Genoa!") Apart from occasional uses on pasta – the pâtes au pistou at La Merenda in Nice is particularly famous – it almost always goes into a minestrone-style soup. The cheese used for pistou is almost always Parmigiano, incidentally, but Jean Giusti of La Merenda once confided to me that the secret of his particularly creamy pistou was shredded Emmentaler.

to serve 6

3	cloves garlic, finely chopped
10–12	large basil leaves
2 teaspoons	grated Parmigiano-Reggiano
3 tablespoons	extra-virgin olive oil

Crush the garlic in a mortar, then add basil leaves and crush to a paste. Stir in cheese with the tines of a fork, then work in the oil, also stirring with a fork. To serve, spoon into minestrone or other vegetable soup.

Trenette col Pesto

Trenette is the Genoese name for linguine, probably derived from *trenna,* a Genoese word meaning silk or cotton millinery trimming or ribbon. (*Fettuccia,* on which *fettuccine* is based, means approximately the same thing.) In earlier times, trenette was always *avvantaggiate* ("improved"), a mildly ironic term that means that it was made with whole wheat flour, or white flour with some bran mixed in. Today it is almost exclusively white.

Visitors to Liguria are often surprised when they first encounter trenette with pesto and find the pasta mixed with green beans and pieces of potato. But this is an old tradition. One theory is that it's a way to stretch the pasta – yet another expression of Genoese frugality, in which store-bought pasta is extended by stirring in something that can be grown at home. Another theory, espoused by Genoese restaurateur Pino Sola, is that "It's to balance the aggressiveness of the garlic and basil." Pesto is a raw sauce, he reminds us, made with three potentially pungent ingredients – basil, garlic, and (sometimes) sheep's-milk cheese. The comparative sweetness of the potatoes and beans, he believes, simply has an ameliorating effect.

to serve 4

	Salt
225 g/8 oz	thin green beans, trimmed
225 g/8 oz	small potatoes, peeled and cut into slices
450 g/1 lb	about 1 cm/⅓ inch thick
	trenette, linguine, or tagliatelle
	Pesto (see page 63)

Bring a large saucepan of salted water to a boil, then plunge in green beans. Cook at a boil for about 3 minutes, then remove with a slotted spoon, drain, and set aside.

Add potatoes to the same boiling water and cook for about 3 minutes.

Add more salt to boiling water if necessary, then add pasta and cook until just done, 8–10 minutes.

Just before pasta is done, remove 2 tablespoons cooking water and stir into pesto. Drain pasta and toss in a large bowl with pesto and green beans.

❖ ❖ ❖

Taglierini with Favas, Potatoes, and Castelnuovo-Style Pesto

Tag'aín con Faa ar Pisto

This variation on the traditional Genoese trenette al pesto is eaten in the region of Castelnuovo Magro. Again, the recipe is adapted from *Antiche ricette di Castelnuovo Magra* by Gianfranco Cricca.

to serve 4

40–45	shelled fresh fava beans (about 450 g/1 lb in pod)
	Salt
450 g/1 lb	potatoes, peeled and cut into 2.5 cm/1 inch cubes
450 g/1 lb	linguine or tagliatelle
	Pisto kastarnoésa (see page 64)
	Grated Parmigiano-Reggiano or pecorino Sardo

Blanch and peel fava beans (see pages 36-37). Bring a large saucepan of salted water to a boil, then add in favas, potatoes, and pasta. Cook until pasta is done, about 5–7 minutes.

Just before pasta is done, remove 2 tablespoons cooking water and stir into pisto kasternoésa. Drain pasta, favas, and potatoes, and toss in a large bowl with pisto. Before serving, top pasta with plenty of additional grated cheese.

Ligurian Gnocchi
Trofie

Trofie, also called troffie (and, diminuatively, troffiette) are small Ligurian gnocchi, found in Genoa and occasionally on the western Riviera, but a speciality of the Riviera di Levante, and specifically of the town of Recco. (In Genoese slang, it is said of a worthless sort of fellow that he "nu và 'na troffia" – isn't worth a little gnoccho.) Unlike the gnocchi often made in other parts of Italy, those from Recco are not plump little dumplings, nor do they contain potato – though according to one theory, their name is a corruption of *tartuffoli,* an early Genoese word for precisely that tuber (based on the potato's supposed kinship with truffles). There is a version of trofie made wholly or partially with chestnut flour, but in general, the recipe includes nothing more than white flour and water (egg pasta is not traditional in Liguria). Trofie are always made by hand; the machine has not yet been invented that can produce the real thing fresh (though there is some dried pasta sold under that name along the Riviera, not much like trofie at all).

I had the chance to see a masterful trofie-maker at work, quite by accident, when I visited the farm of Maria Benvenuto, in the hamlet of Arbora, in the hills above Recco. I met Benvenuto through ethno-botanist Giuseppina Poggi, who in turn discovered her through her research on the Ligurian greens mixture called preboggion (see page 140) – conducted for an EEC-funded project with the long-winded title "Les produits de terroir en Europe du Sud. Caractérisation ethnologique, sensorielle et socio-économique de leur typicité. Stratégies de valorisation." (There's no bureaucrat like a Eurocrat.) My initial interest in Benvenuto had to do with the fact that she is one of the few people who still makes prescinsêua (see page 124), in the traditional manner. But as we were talking about this ancient product, Poggi mentioned that Benvenuto was also famous for her trofie – and she immediately pulled out an old flour-dusted board and put a small pot of water to heat on the stove. She then scooped two bowls full of flour out of a large sack, forming two white mounds on the board. One she used for dusting, scattering some on the board and returning to it frequently in the moments that followed to keep both her hands and the board well coated. The other she indented slightly with her hand; then she poured hot (but not boiling) water over it and quickly worked the flour and water together to form a crumbly dough. This she kneaded for a minute or two, then formed into a tapered, sausage-shaped length. She next pulled a piece from the length and formed it into a smaller tapered sausage. Then came the truly amazing part: With her hands almost a blur, she pinched a tiny piece of dough from the smaller length, threw it on the floured surface, rolled it out gently but firmly with the flat of her hand, then rolled it back toward herself. The result was a perfect, corkscrew-like bit of pasta with two sharp ends. ("Well-made trofie always have two points," she said.) The practised fluidity with which she worked was amazing, as was her speed: No more than ten minutes after she had first pulled out her floured board, enough flawless hand-made trofie to feed two or three people were resting on one side of it.

to serve 6

---

350 g/12 oz	flour
	Salt

Place all but 50 g/2 oz flour in a mixing bowl and mix in about 1 teaspoon salt. Add about 450 ml/16 fl oz water gradually to the bowl, working it by hand to form first a crumbly dough and then a firm but pliant one. Add a little more water if necessary. (Dust your hands and work surface with a bit of the additional flour so that dough doesn't stick.) Allow dough to sit, covered with a clean tea towel, for about ½ hour.

Spread remaining flour out on a pastry board or other work surface. To make trofie as Maria Benvenuto does, take a piece of dough about the size of a small grape, place it on the floured surface, roll it away from yourself under your hand, then roll it back toward yourself with your hand, still flat, turned inward almost 45 degrees. This is a simple technique, but it takes time to master, and should be practised first. Alternately, roll a piece of dough of the same size between your hands (well-floured) to form a baton-like shape about 4 cm/1½ inches long. Grasping each end of the baton, give each one a quick twist in opposite directions. With either technique, scoot the finished trofie to one side of the floured surface. If they're well dusted with flour, the trofie can be placed on top of one another as you run out of room.

"Silk Handkerchiefs"
Mandilli de Sæa

There are two different dishes served in Liguria under the name lasagna al pesto. One, the less common, is literally lasagna in the sense that we know it – large, overlapping, layered sheets of pasta baked in the oven. The difference is that, instead of ricotta or other cheese between the layers and meat or tomato sauce on top, the filling – and topping – is pesto. This is pretty hardcore; you've got to really love pesto to find such a concentration and abundance of the sauce appealing. The other dish, more typically Genoese, consists of thin lasagna-like sheets of pasta draped beautifully in a pile with a dollop of pesto on top or gently stirred in. This preparation is traditionally called mandilli de sæa, Genoese for silk handkerchiefs – a reference to the size and thinness of the pasta. (The Genoese, who are fond of giving Arabic derivations for words in their language whenever possible, relate *mandilli* to the Arabic word for handkerchief, *mandil*. This is reasonable enough, except that *mandil* is itself a Romance loan word in Arabic, apparently from the Latin *mantele,* meaning towel or napkin.) In any case, mandilli de sæa is one style of Ligurian pasta that is usually made with eggs, simply to hold the dough together as it is rolled out to near translucency.

to serve 6–8

350 g/12 oz	flour
½ teaspoon	salt
5	large eggs
1 tablespoon	extra-virgin olive oil

Sift flour into a mixing bowl, mix in about 1 teaspoon salt, then break eggs into flour and work them in thoroughly with your hands. (Dust your hands and work surface with a little of the additional flour so that dough doesn't stick.) Divide dough into four balls, then roll each one out as thinly as possible. Roll each dough sheet through a pasta machine (cutting it to fit if necessary), through setting No. 6. Cut dough into sheets 10-12.5 cm/4-5 inches square. Set sheets aside on a floured surface, making sure they don't touch, then repeat the process until all the dough is used.

Cook sheets four at a time in plenty of boiling salted water to which olive oil has been added until just done – usually 3–4 minutes. To serve, toss gently with pesto (see page 63) or the Genoese meat sauce called tocco (see page 103).

"Crazy Little Lasagne" with Mortar-Made Pesto

Lasagnette Matte al Pesto di Mortaio

This is a variation on mandilli de sæa, created by Franco Solari at Ca' Peo restaurant in Leivi. The chestnut flour gives a faint sweetness to the pasta, offset nicely by the pungency of the pesto and the bitterness of the broccoli rabe.

to serve 4

300 g/11 oz	white flour
90 g/3½ oz	chestnut flour*
	Salt
4	large eggs
225 g/8 oz	new potatoes, scrubbed, peeled, and cut into 12 mm/½ inch slices
225 g/8 oz	broccoli rabe (broccoletti), trimmed
	Pesto Genovese (see page 63)

Sift white and chestnut flours together in a mixing bowl, then proceed as for mandilli de sæa on page 69, but cut rolled-out dough into strips measuring about 5 × 10 cm by 2 × 4 inches. Set sheets aside on a floured surface, making sure they don't touch.

Bring a large saucepan of salted water to a boil, then plunge in potatoes and broccoli rabe. Cook at a boil for about 5 minutes, or until potatoes are done, then remove potatoes and broccoli rabe with a slotted spoon, drain, and set aside.

Return the water to a boil, add pasta, and cook until just done, 4–5 minutes. When pasta is cooked, toss it gently in a bowl with potatoes, broccoli rabe, and abundant pesto.

*See page 240.

Minestrone

Aquéu bròdou vous di: Manji-mi!
This soup says to you: Eat me!

– NIÇOIS SAYING

Here, "minestrone" is just a fancy name for vegetable soup. We buy it in tins. We find it offered as the soup of the day in cafés – chicken noodle Thursday, tomato soup Friday, minestrone Saturday. For us, it isn't a dish, it's a cliché. In Italy, on the other hand, and especially in Liguria, it's not just a dish but an eagerly appreciated one – a celebration of the season.

The word *minestrone* means a large or particularly rich *minestra* – a word that derives from the Latin verb *ministro*, to serve, and that describes thick soups in general. (A *minestrina*, on the other hand, is a thin soup, a broth.) In Genoa and vicinity, a particularly well-made minestrone, with an abundance of ingredients – the kind one might make to honour a guest, for instance – is sometimes called "Signor Minestrone," or, in Genoese dialect, "Scignore Menestron." In local slang, a menestron is also a gourmet or connoisseur.

According to Franco Accame, minestrone was a great speciality of the port of Genoa and the nearby waters, where it was served up from *catrai,* a most curious brand of "inn." The catrai (the name might derive from the Genoese word *catran,* which means tar – substance, not sailor – with a secondary meaning of strong wine) were sea going soup kitchens. Set up on small boats that would pull alongside ships in or near the harbour, they'd sell sailors portions of pasta, fish soup, and, above all, minestrone – its abundance of vegetables particularly appreciated, notes Accame, after a long voyage with a diet of dried fish and ship's biscuits.

I'm sure that menestrons from Genoa and Nice alike would disagree, incidentally, but if there's any fundamental difference between minestrone alla genovese and soupe au pistou (other than the slight difference between pesto and pistou), I have not been able to discover it.

Fried Soup

Probably no Ligurian dish has so fascinated and eluded me as minestrone fritto – fried minestrone. The erudite Silvio Torre says that this curious-sounding dish comes from around Albenga, on the Riviera di Ponente, where it is eaten as a between-meals restorative, especially from November through March, during the region's long olive harvest. Vito Elio Petrucci includes it in his charmingly idiosyncratic *Cucini e santi,* describing it as perhaps "the simplest recipe in the world, but the most forgotten" – but offers no opinion as to its origins.

How can a soup be fried? It's simple: Minestrone is a thick soup, dense with vegetables. The idea is that any leftovers can be reused by passing the vegetables through a mouli-légurees, stirring in a little flour, forming the mass into patties or a single omelette-like shape, and then frying it in oil – much as leftover pasta or risotto in other parts of Italy is sometimes formed into croquettes, dusted with breadcrumbs, and fried for a next-day meal. According to my Genoese friend Giorgio Bergami, the vegetables shouldn't be over-cooked to begin with – and the mixture should definitely include pasta, preferably the short little noodles called bricchetti (matchstick) in Genoese, to provide added starch to help hold the mixture together. Of course, there is some disagreement on the matter. Someone else I asked informed me that minestrone destined to be fritto should never have pasta in it – and that the sustenance-level peasants who made it originally would never have used flour (which would have been too expensive) but would have thickened it with breadcrumbs.

I can't speak more authoritatively on the subject myself

Opposite: Chickpea and Pasta Soup

because I have been unable to find anyone with any trappings of authority in the matter to make the dish for me. Even if I had, though, I wouldn't quite be satisfied: I have also learned that, in Triora, in the hills above Sanremo, peasants used to make bernardun di minestrone – which was baked, not fried – and I'd have to try that as well.

Minestrone alla Genovese

There are vegetable soups by one name or another all over Italy, of course, but the two regions most famous for minestrone are Lombardy and Liguria – whose versions are often known as minestrone milanese and minestrone genovese, respectively. The differences between the two may be somewhat elusive today; cross-pollination has been intense. But traditionally, the Milanese added onion to the soup, while the Genoese did not – presumably because their version was always spiced with garlic-rich pesto. (The exception would have been winter minestrone in the old, pregreenhouse – and thus prepesto – days, when onions would have been used in the soffritto stirred into the soup.) The Milanese were also more likely to include pancetta and/or lardo (which is more or less Italian bacon), while the Genoese used only vegetables (or, at the most, stirred in tiny pieces of anchovy for flavouring). And, while Genoese minestrone almost always includes short noodles of some kind, the Milanese version is often bulked up with rice.

There is no canonical recipe for minestrone, at least in Genoa. Even those gastronomes who maintain that there is only one correct way to make, say, pesto or focaccia are likely to agree that minestrone is by definition changeable. The best formula is simply that which uses whatever vegetables are best at the time. The only constants, in Genoa at any rate, seem to be white beans, dried porcini, pasta, and of course (these days) pesto. And the Genoese *never* use meat or poultry stock for minestrone; there's no need to if you cook the soup long enough. There was once a custom, though, of putting a couple of crusts of Parmigiano-Reggiano in the soup as it cooked. (There is also a version of minestrone in which the vegetables are cooked whole for three or four hours, then mashed together into a kind of coarse purée.)

The only secret of a good minestrone, besides the quality and variety of the produce used, is the cooking time. Forget the present-day preference for lightly cooked vegetables; forget any romantic notions you may have of bright, quick, light Mediterranean cuisine. Minestrone must simmer for at least an hour to extract and marry the flavours of its constituent elements. Despite the fact that you should use only the best vegetables you can find in making this dish, what you should taste when you finally lift spoon to mouth is not vegetables at all, but soup.

to serve 4

	Salt
1	bunch spinach, coarsely chopped
1	bunch Swiss chard, coarsely chopped
2	small courgettes, in 6 mm/¼ inch slices
2	medium white potatoes, peeled, quartered lengthways, and cut into 12 mm/½ inch slices
2	small long, slender aubergines (about 225 g/8 oz total) in 2.5 cm/1 inch slices
25 g/1 oz	dried porcini mushrooms, soaked 20 minutes in warm water, then drained
2 tablespoons	extra-virgin olive oil
225 g/8 oz	(half 450 g/1 lb packet) tubetti or fideus pasta or square-cut spaghetti alla chitarra broken into lengths of approximately 4 cm/1½ inches
350 g/12 oz	cooked white beans
2	generous tablespoons pesto (see page 63)

Bring 2.3 litres/4 pints salted water to a boil in a large saucepan. Add spinach, chard, courgettes, potatoes, aubergines, mushrooms, and oil, then reduce heat to a simmer and cook, uncovered, for 1 hour.

Add pasta and cook for about 10 minutes longer, or until pasta is almost done. Add cooked beans and cook about 5 minutes more.

Remove saucepan from heat, and adjust seasoning. Allow to cool for about 10 minutes, then stir in pesto and serve. (Some Genoese prefer to eat the soup at room temperature.)

NOTE: Other vegetables frequently used in Genoese minestrone include green beans, peas, favas, escarole, kale, turnips, leeks, carrots, cauliflower, pumpkin or courgette blossoms, and many kinds of both summer and winter squash. Some cooks add pine nuts to the soup; some also add tomatoes, though this is frowned upon by most traditionalists.

Sanremo-Style Cold Minestrone

Minestrone Freddo Sanremasco

Paolo e Barbara in Sanremo is one of the best restaurants on the Riviera, and one of the very few that serves what might genuinely be called contemporary

Ligurian food. The restaurant is tiny, reservations are a must, and Barbara Masieri runs a crisply efficient dining room while her husband, Paolo, labours intensely at his stove. There is no glad-handing or celebrity-chef preening here; what there is is one of those maddening menus (like the one at Don Camillo in Nice) where everything sounds good and making choices is always difficult. In creating his specialities, Masieri uses only fish landed at Sanremo, meat from just across the mountains in Piedmont, and locally grown organic vegetables. He prepares several pure, classic Ligurian dishes – his cappon magro and brandacujun (a brandade of stockfish), for instance, are textbook-perfect. But it is when he improvises intelligently on regional themes that his cuisine becomes so irresistible – for instance, rabbit "prosciutto" with sweet-and-sour onions and black cherry preserves; fried red mullets and sage leaves in citrus sauce; strips of buckwheat-and-chestnut-flour testaroli (pasta discs; see page 158) with rabbit and olive sauce; roasted goat with sautéed asparagus and baby onions; or this elegant improvisation on minestrone.

The idea of cold vegetable soups, it should be noted, isn't contemporary. They were introduced in Genoa in the early nineteenth century by the little greengrocer shops called *bisagnine* – originally named for the region of Bisagno, from which many of the city's herb and vegetable merchants came. Made up early in the morning and sold to workers for lunch in terra-cotta cups, together with small loaves of dark, crusty bread, they were sometimes called "minestre usate" – used soups. Masieri's version, needless to say, is somewhat more sophisticated – and more al dente. (The following wealth of ingredients is optimum, but of course some may be omitted if unavailable, and substitutions may be made according to the season.)

to serve 4

1	medium-large or 2 small potatoes (about 175 g/6 oz), peeled
1	large carrot, peeled
1	celery stalk, trimmed
2	small courgettes, trimmed
1	onion
2	leeks, white parts only
150 g/5 oz	fresh green beans, haricots verts, or yellow wax beans, or a combination of these, trimmed

8	asparagus spears
6–8	courgettes or squash blossoms, trimmed
2–3	leaves Swiss chard, stalks removed
3	large basil leaves
6–8	borage leaves
2.3 litres/4 pints	chicken stock
	Extra-virgin olive oil
225 g/8 oz	fresh peas, shelled
225 g/8 oz	fresh fava beans, shelled
50 g/2 oz	cooked chickpeas
50 g/2 oz	cup cooked white beans
	Leaves from 3–4 sprigs fresh marjoram
	Salt and freshly ground black pepper
	Hot red pepper flakes

Keeping vegetables separate, cut potato(es), carrot, celery, and courgettes into cubes about 8 mm/⅓ inch square; finely chop onion; cut leeks into thin discs; cut green beans into 12 mm/½ inch lengths; and cut tips from asparagus spears, reserving the rest of the spears for another use. Cut courgette blossoms, chard, basil, and borage into a fine julienne, keeping courgette blossoms separate.

Heat chicken stock over medium heat. Meanwhile, in a large heavy saucepan, heat oil over medium heat, then add carrot, celery, onion, and leeks. Cook for about 1 minute, then add potatoes, green beans, asparagus tips, and peas. Cook for 4 minutes, then add courgettes, favas, chickpeas, and white beans. Cook for two minutes and add julienned chard, leaves and marjoram. Cook for 1 minute more, then add hot chicken stock. Season to taste with salt and pepper and a small quantity of hot red pepper flakes. Remove immediately from heat and allow to cool, uncovered, to room temperature. (Vegetables should remain al dente.) Refrigerate for at least 4 hours before serving.

NOTE: At Paolo e Barbara, morsels of steamed Mediterranean spiny lobster are added to the soup before serving.

Cappon Magro and Salade Niçoise

*Cappon magro is the most fantastical –
someone has said "monumental" – [salad]
in Italian cuisine.*

> – SALVATORE MARCHESE, *LA
> CUCINA LIGURE DI LEVANTE*

*[Salade niçoise] is the national dish of Nice;
one must respect it.*

> – MAMÉ CLAIRETTE, QUOTED IN
> *CUISINE TRADITIONNELLE EN
> PAYS NIÇOIS* BY BERNARD
> DUPLESSY

In my early days of tramping around Europe, eating fearlessly and dining foolishly but well, it quickly occurred to me that I always felt much healthier – much less often importuned by my digestive tract – in Italy than in France. That I was eating more olive oil and less cream and butter in the former country than the latter probably had something to do with it, but I've always believed that another factor must have been all the salad I've always consumed in Italy.

Sure, the French sometimes eat one of those little plates full of butter lettuce drizzled with mustardy vinaigrette, but my theory is that they don't really like salad, don't really consider it *food*, unless it involves foie gras and haricots verts, or at least baked goat cheese. The Italians, on the other hand, seem scarcely able to imagine a meal without it. The typical Italian insalata mista, found in restaurants all over the country, includes lettuce, some variety of chicory (often radicchio), shredded carrots, a few wedges of ripe tomato (in season), and maybe some very thin rounds of radish, all tossed tableside by a waiter (even in trattorias that make you pour your own wine) with too much oil, too much vinegar, and too much salt – sublime!

I don't know that it's particularly Ligurian, but I encountered a nice refinement on this basic salad several years ago at one of Liguria's more celebrated restaurants, Manuelina in Recco. This one was made of nothing more than lamb's lettuce (mâche in French, valerianella in Italian, servetto or serzetto in Genoese) and shredded courgette, in addition to the usual shredded carrots and tomato wedges, all dressed with, well, too much oil, too much vinegar, and too much salt.

The definitive salad of Ligurian cuisine, an arrangement of fish and vegetables called cappon magro, is considerably more elaborate than that. Magro literally means lean or meagre, but in food terms always carries the sense of religiously inspired meatlessness; a magro dish is one suitable for consumption on a day when the Catholic Church requires (or rather required) its adherents to abstain from eating animal products (including fowl). The cappon in the story, according to some sources, is the fish of that name – capone in Italian, gunard in English – which might be used in the salad. More likely, since a gunard would be magro by definition, the word refers to capon the bird, and the dish name is thus more irony, on the model of the aforementioned trouchia.

It is also possible, however, that cappon refers to the gallette marinare or ship's biscuits (hardtack) around which the dish is literally built; similar "croutons" are called *chapons* in France. Gallette – the most famous in Liguria come from the towns of Rapallo and San Rocco di Camogli – are small rounds of bread that are baked and then dried in a very slow oven, so that their moisture evaporates and they can be stored without spoiling almost indefinitely. They have been used by seafarers all over the Mediterranean at least since the Byzantine era.

Whether it's named for them or not, the fact that cappon magro is literally built on ship's biscuits suggests that it was a sailor's dish to begin with. Nada Boccalatte Bagnasco and Renzo Bagnasco, in *La tavola ligure,* propose that it descends from a meal fashioned by galley oarsmen from their rations of gallette, olive oil, favas (dried), chestnuts, and salt cod. It is also easy to imagine a fisherman, home from a day on the water, combining gallette with a few piscatorial odds and ends and some vegetables from his garden to create a hearty one-dish meal. It is even easier to imagine that the vegetables would have been – as Luigi Miroli at Da Puny in Portofino insists – leftovers of varying ages that had to be used before they spoiled.

Today, the dish has grown into a complex set piece, usually constructed with great care and occasionally graced with true artistry. Sometimes it is even formed into the shape of a fish, on an oval platter – a refinement dating, Paolo Lingua believes, from the eighteenth century. Some gastronomes consider cappon magro to be a refutation of Liguria's reputation for "poor" cuisine – and it is clearly a "rich" dish, magro or not, both in its variety of ingredients and the complexity of their arrangement.

As with minestrone, the vegetables used in cappon magro vary with the season – though olives, capers, and mushrooms preserved in oil are all but essential. Waverley Root, who made a serious study of the dish, observed that scorzonera – salsify – was found in a good many versions. Green beans, potatoes, carrots, celery, and beetroot are probably the other key vegetal elements. It is also common to include anchovies and/or thin slices of mosciame (dried tuna) or bottarga (dried, pressed tuna roe; see page 209 for more on both).

Whether the salad should also include luxurious ingredients is another question. The celebrated chef Nino Bergese (who was not Ligurian), in his book *Mangiare da re,* offers a recipe for cappon magro for 12 that includes a 1.5 kg/3 lb lobster, a dozen large shrimp, a dozen oysters, and a hake weighing 675 g/1½ lb, besides a veritable cornucopia of vegetables. (Paolo Lingua notes that some cappon magros are "adorned with the trophies" of lobster, crayfish, shrimp, etc. – which is a nice way to put it.) Other recipes, in contrast, call for little more than anchovies or mosciame and a few small pieces of hake or something similar by way of seafood. I take a middle view myself: The best cappon magros I've sampled have involved a good assortment of elements but have not been unduly tarted up.

Capponada (also called capponata and cappon di galera – galley cappon) is in effect a more modest version of cappon magro, with fewer and less expensive ingredients involved – a cappon magro closer to its roots, it might be said. A related salad is the array of vegetables called condiggion or cundiggiun in Genoa and cundigliùn or condiglione along the Riviera di Ponente. The names seem to derive from the verb *condire,* which means to season in both Latin and Italian – and in its purest form, condiggion is nothing more than a few ingredients (tomatoes, peppers, onions, cucumber, garlic, and olives are standard) in a simple dressing. In the Valle Argentina above Sanremo, for instance, farmers used to carry oil and vinegar with them into the fields, to drizzle over just-picked vegetables and greens for a lunchtime cundigliùn. More complex versions might include celery, spring onions, green beans, chard, cardoons, or artichokes – some of them cooked – as well as anchovies and tinned tuna.

Condiggion, for obvious reasons, has been called the Genovese salade niçoise. Salade niçoise itself – a dramatic exception to my remarks earlier about the French attitude toward salad (but then the Niçois don't necessarily consider themselves French) – is one of those universally popular dishes, like paella or fettuccine Alfredo, made all over the world in versions that usually bear no resemblance at all to their original form.

Salade niçoise as it is found here, for instance, even in credible French restaurants, tends to be an arrangement of baby lettuces with cooked potatoes and green beans, a few olives and pieces of hard-boiled egg, a couple of anchovy fillets, and some chunks of tinned tuna, all drizzled with vinaigrette. In restaurants of a certain class, the tinned tuna is replaced with fresh grilled tuna.

In Nice, it is quite a different story. Though some authorities will accept some lettuce – usually hearts of romaine – all serious scholars of the subject (chief among them Jacques Médecin; see box page 82) tend to agree on four points: The salad should contain no cooked vegetables; the tomatoes should be salted three times (to help them lose excess moisture); there should be no vinegar added (it is widely believed around the Mediterranean that tomatoes and vinegar don't go together); and there should be either anchovies *or* tuna included, but never both – with the former more common and the latter considered mostly a show-off addition for special occasions. Waverley Root claims that the tomatoes must be cut into quarters: "[I]f they are sliced," he says, "it's not a salade niçoise; the local population is adamant on this point." Jacques Médecin's recipe (see page 93) does indeed call for quartered tomatoes, but he does not apply his customary adamancy to the matter.

Oh, and as for the grilled tuna: The Niçois consider the idea idiotic. Fresh tuna is fine to eat on its own, they say, but tuna preserved in oil has been a staple of the Mediterranean diet at least since medieval times, and is highly regarded in its own right – top-quality olive-oil-packed tuna is indeed superb – and salade niçoise is a dish flavoured with *preserved* fish, tuna or otherwise. Substituting fresh tuna for tinned in the salad would be sort of like, I don't know, maybe serving an appetizer of figs with pork chops instead of with thinly sliced cured ham.

The Mayor Makes a Salad

The definitive book on Niçois cooking is *La Cuisine du comté de Nice* by Jacques Médecin, first published in France in 1972. (An English-language version, called *Cuisine Niçoise: Recipes from a Mediterranean Kitchen,* appeared in 1983, but is now out of print.) Encyclopedic and authoritative, it offers more than 300 recipes, many with brief but informative introductions and all bearing the same subtext, stated or implied: This is the way it's done, period, and I oughta know.

Médecin sets the tone in his introduction, invoking the spirit of his "sweet grandmother," who left behind a book of "centuries-old" recipes, which she had learned in turn from one Tanta (Aunt) Mietta, a peasant in the arrière-pays. He is writing his own book for several reasons, Médecin continues, among them the fact that his generation seems to be the last repository of the region's ancestral traditions, and that, "with the exception of two or three restaurants in Nice, one can no longer eat, outside the parlors of the Niçois, the authentic cuisine niçoise." He is also writing, he adds, because "all over the world, horrified, I have seen the remains of other peoples' meals being served under the name 'salade niçoise.' "

Médecin is a legend in Nice, and not just for his defense of local dishes. Médecin's father, Jean, was mayor of the city from 1928 to 1945 and again from 1947 to 1965 (with an enforced two-year break in between for his support of the Vichy government during World War II). Médecin *fils* – "Jacquou," as he is affectionately known to the many locals who worship him, even now, as a saviour – succeeded him immediately. He also became president of the regional council for the département of the Alpes-Maritimes. In Nice, the Médecins were a dynasty.

It was something of a shock, then, to Nice and to the rest of France, when Médecin left the city on what was supposed to be an official visit to Japan in 1990 and turned up a few days later in self-imposed exile in Argentina – later moving on to the Côte d'Azur-ish beach resort of Punta del Este in Uruguay. "He is my god," one local restaurateur told reporters when the news hit. "I worship him. We owe him everything."

What Médecin owed was several million dollars in back taxes. He was subsequently implicated in the misappropriation of tens of millions of francs meant for specific civic purposes, and accused of taking kickbacks from large government-funded construction projects in the region. There were even rumours, never substantiated, of his involvement in the disappearance of a potential business rival and the death of a former business associate in California.

Médecin claimed political persecution: He was a supporter of Jean-Marie Le Pen, head of the extreme right-wing Front National party (which is particularly popular in Nice), and had been accused of making anti-Semitic remarks in public on more than one occasion, and he had few friends in the then-Socialist French government. A court in Grenoble, apparently unimpressed by his contentions, found him guilty of fraud in 1992 and sentenced him to a year in prison in absentia and a fine of 2.5 million francs, and banned him from holding political office for the rest of his life. In 1994, Uruguay extradited him to France, where he stood trial in person, and was again convicted, and sentenced to an additional two years in prison. (He was released early, and chose to return to Uruguay, where he now resides – perhaps permanently.) Médecin's transgressions, cracked the Parisian press, were presumably an example of "salade niçoise."

The Monks' Mixture

Mesclun, the *other* famous Niçois salad, takes its name from the Niçois verb *mescla,* to mix. Tradition credits Franciscan monks from the monastery in the hills of Cimiez with its invention. It is said that these holy men, who depended on the charity of their neighbours for their livelihood, gathered baby greens each spring and presented them, tied into bouquets, to their benefactors. Ideally, the greens would be a combination of sweet and bitter leaves, in equal parts – and were considered symbolic of the season, an expression of the renewal of life. According to one tradition, the monks' mesclun (the word is pronounced mes-CLOON in Niçois) included twelve different kinds of leaves, one for each of the Apostles. Jacques Médecin names riquéta (Nissart for roquette or rocket), dents-de-lion (wild dandelion greens), and young lettuce as the essential ingredients, while Bernard Duplessy suggests that hyssop, basil, and trévise (a kind of radicchio) might also be included. Today in France, mesclun typically contains young lettuce of the type known as sucrine (a name that suggests its sweetness), as well as oakleaf lettuce, chicory, rocket, a little chervil, frisée (curly endive), escarole, and sometimes purslane.

Here, the term *mesclun* has come to mean any mélange of young edible leaves, including those of Asian derivation (tat-soi, mizuna, and the like), and even amaranth and edible flowers – and from a miscellany of little-regarded wild greens harvested for free from the fields, mesclun has become the most expensive and refined of salad fixings, often sold for as much as £6 or £8 a pound.

Spontaneous Grasses

The Cinque Terre, or Five Lands, is a collection of five villages stretching out along the coast west of La Spezia, between Levanto and Portovenere. Their rather extravagant name, which dates from 1537, seems to have been applied to the villages not because they had any great political or economic importance, but simply because of their splendid isolation. Four of them – Riomaggiore, Manarola, Vernazza (the jewel of the bunch, a postcard-perfect village built around a pretty little harbour), and Monterosso al Mare – are wedged into seaside clefts in steep hills that drop off straight into the Mediterranean. A fifth, Corniglia, is perched in those hills. Inhabited for at least 5,000 years, the Cinque Terre remained accessible only by boat or on foot until the late nineteenth century.

There is no one culinary speciality associated exclusively with the Cinque Terre, but there is a famous local collection of greens called gerbi – a term that apparently derives from the Spanish yierbas, meaning herbs, and dates only from the nineteenth century, after emigration to South America from this part of Liguria, and particularly from Monterosso, had become common. "Gerbi aren't a gastronomic delicacy or a folkloric dish," explains Vito Elio Petrucci in *Profumi e sapori di Liguria*. "They're a way of living – almost vanished – from that which nature gives." Gerbi are bundles of assorted wild plants (erbe spontanee is the evocative Italian term), which grow, Petrucci continues, in the hills of the Cinque Terre, "in the meagre earth that the wind and the water have deposited on the walls of the amphitheatres that the Ligurians of yesterday constructed without mortar."

Among the greens that might constitute these bundles are spinach, lo screpolo (literally "the crack" – a relative of spinach with shorter, fatter leaves), sow thistle, rattalegoa (which is possibly Reichardia picroides [L.] Roth, called grattalingna or caccialepre – hare-catcher – in Italian, and better known in Liguria as talegua), gagginn-e grasse (another variety of thistle), loffi (which might be *Silene vulgaris,* called silene or maiden's tear in English), bavaratta (perhaps a kind of poppy), salsify leaves, pastemaghe (apparently a kind of wild celery or dill), l'erbiera (this term is used generically to mean various minor herbs, but no one could give me a specific identification), leek leaves, bassiggia (wild fennel), escarole, catalogna (a variety of long, dentate chicory), borage, various lettuces, tiny Swiss chard leaves, mallow sprouts, and even the very tips of potato and fava plants.

Traditionally in the region, and especially around Manarola, women go out to gather these plants, wrap them in oversized handkerchiefs, and carry them home on their heads. There, Petrucci reports, they are washed thoroughly, boiled, wrung dry in a towel, and then eaten with potatoes and green beans or with green beans only, for lunch and even breakfast, in a dressing of olive oil and salt – plus lemon juice, he adds, if there are no potatoes.

Cappon Magro

Cappon magro takes entirely too much time and trouble to prepare in small quantities – and requires almost as much work to make for two as it does for a dozen or more. Anyway, it's a party dish by nature – a showpiece, a slightly silly (but delicious) excess. The preparation of ingredients for cappon magro is only half the job, however; then comes combining them – which, as Waverley Root has pointed out, "is less the work of a cook than of an architect." Apart from the aforementioned cappon magros sculpted into the shape of a fish, the salad usually assumes the form of an oval-shaped mound or a sort of rounded-off pyramid. Use your imagination, though.

to serve 8–10

4–6	ship's biscuits (gallette marinare)
1	garlic clove
	Red wine vinegar
	Salt
3	plump carrots, trimmed and peeled
1	white celery heart, trimmed
1	small cauliflower, trimmed
2	medium potatoes, peeled
225 g/8 oz	green beans, trimmed
8	large leaves Swiss chard, stalks discarded, leaves coarsely chopped
225 g/8 oz	fresh shelled peas (optional)
3	salsify roots (optional)
	Juice of 1 lemon (if using salsify)
4	beetroots, peeled
900 g/2 lb	fresh cod, hake, or other firm-fleshed white fish
12	medium fresh prawns or scampi (saltwater crayfish)
3	hard-boiled eggs
50 g/2 oz	bottarga (see page 209), very thinly sliced, or 12 anchovy fillets
350 ml/12 fl oz	salsa genovese (see page 62)
	Extra-virgin olive oil
12	black or green olives, pitted
12	large Italian or Spanish capers
12	baby artichoke hearts or 12 small mushrooms, packed in oil

Split the gallette in half with a knife (it doesn't matter if they fragment or crumble a bit), then rub the cut surfaces with the garlic clove. Drizzle vinegar over them to moisten them slightly, then arrange them on the plate or platter on which you plan to construct the salad. Set the plate or platter aside.

In a large pot, bring salted water to a boil and separately cook carrots, celery, cauliflower, potatoes, green beans, Swiss chard, and peas (if desired) until each is tender but still firm, removing each with a slotted spoon when done and setting aside to cool. Peel salsify roots (if desired) and immediately rub them thoroughly with lemon juice to prevent browning, then cut them into pieces and cook them in boiling salted water, too. Cook beetroots last.

Poach the cod or other fish and prawns together in salted water, removing prawns with a slotted spoon after about 4 minutes and setting them aside. Carefully peel prawns when cool enough to handle. Continue cooking cod until done, 12–15 minutes, then drain and set aside.

Cut the carrots, celery, cauliflower, potatoes, salsify (if using), and beetroots into slices about 6 mm/¼ inch thick. Cut green beans into 4-cm/1½-inch lengths. Thinly slice hard-boiled eggs, then cut cod into 4 cm/1½ inch slices.

To assemble cappon magro, top the gallette with half the bottarga or anchovies. If using anchovies, crush them lightly, pressing them into the gallette with a fork. Using the gallette as a foundation, build the salad, using alternate layers of various vegetables (only one kind per layer) and fish. (There should be enough fish for 3 layers, though 2 or 4 would be all right, too. Do not end with fish, however.) Spread a thin film of salsa genovese over the first layer. Drizzle vinegar and olive oil over the second layer and salt it lightly. Spread salsa genovese over the next layer, and then alternate between salsa genovese and the vinegar, olive oil, and salt combination until all ingredients are used up. When the salad is approximately halfway finished, insert a layer of hard-boiled egg slices.

After the cappon magro is completed, spread remaining salsa genovese lightly over the exterior (the colours of the vegetables should still show through), and garnish the top and sides of the salad with prawns, olives, capers, and marinated artichoke hearts or mushrooms. Fancy Genoese versions of the dish sometimes impale these last four items on small wooden *stecchi* or skewers and plant them in the cappon magro. If this is done skillfully, it accentuates the baroque appearance of the dish. Oysters on the half-shell are also a common garnish. Of the arrangement of the decorative elements, one Genovese restaurateur counsels that "it must be a little wild, or it will look like nouvelle cuisine."

Capponada

This poor relation of cappon magro was standard Genoese shipboard fare in earlier times. Some say it was a dish eaten especially during storms, when cooking hot food in the galley would have been too dangerous – and that, due to this unpleasant association, sailors avoided it like the plague when they were on dry land. Although the original capponada was almost certainly made only with preserved foods (tuna, anchovies, olives, capers, gallette, etc.), I think it is greatly improved by the addition of just a few fresh ingredients – and my opinion is widely shared in Liguria today. Many recipes for capponada add a few leaves of basil, incidentally, but I've replaced it here with fresh thyme – which is preferred in the La Spezia region, and which lends the dish an appealing earthiness.

to serve 6

2–3	ship's biscuits (gallette marinare)
	Red wine vinegar
	Extra-virgin olive oil
12	anchovy fillets
2 × 175 g/6 oz	tins best-quality olive oil-packed tinned tuna
20–25	small oil-packed olives, preferably Taggiasca or Niçoise
6–8	radishes, trimmed and quartered
4	spring onions, chopped
	Leaves from 3 sprigs thyme
3	small firm tomatoes, quartered (optional; see Note)
50 g/2 oz	bottarga, very thinly sliced (optional; see page 209)
	Salt
2	hard-boiled eggs, quartered

Cut or break the gallette into large chunks, then moisten them with vinegar, oil, and a few tablespoonfuls of water.

Place gallette chunks in a large bowl and add all remaining ingredients except eggs, including salt to taste. Toss salad gently with your hands, drizzle a little oil over it, and garnish with hard-boiled eggs.

NOTE: Contrary to popular opinion, and to British interpretations of Italian cuisine, in Italy, ripe tomatoes are used only for cooking; underripe, firm ones, often still slightly green, go into salads.

Condiggion

Louis Ravalin, the Mentonnais author who wrote under the name Marcel Firpo earlier this century, described the diet of a typical citizen of Menton this way: "[He] . . . is vegetarian par excellence, and eats meat only on Sundays and holidays. The rabbit and chicken that he raises are a special treat for him, and in his opinion there is no better bouillon than that made from an old chicken. Sometimes he consumes a good bit of fish, fresh or desalted, fried. [He eats] lots of raw vegetables, tomatoes, peppers, cucumbers, salad greens wild and cultivated, which he seasons with a sauce of crushed salted anchovies (maquet). He is a friend of whole salted anchovies, cured olives, and marinated herring. Garlic and onions figure in almost all his salads, especially those of tomatoes, peppers, cucumbers, and oil-packed tuna (coundian)."

Coundian is the Mentonnais name for condiggion, another of the famous salads of the Riviera, and one of the region's purest expressions of Mediterranean culinary simplicity. It isn't always clear where capponada leaves off and condiggion begins, but older sources indicate that the latter was primarily a salad of raw vegetables, eaten in the fields and orchards of the entroterra – and thus it doesn't seem to me to call for the capponada-ish preserved fish (i.e., oil-packed tuna) or ship's biscuits that some recipes include. This particular version is extrapolated (and slightly expanded) from a brief description of the dish as it was found in the mountains of the Triora region by Padre Francesco Ferraironi in the 1950s, recorded in his posthumously published *Cultura e tradizioni in alta Valle Argentina*.

to serve 4

4	baby artichokes
3	ripe tomatoes, sliced
1	small cucumber, peeled and sliced
4	small white celery stalks with leaves
1	small white onion, thinly sliced and separated into rings
4	spring onions, chopped
8–10	basil leaves, roughly torn
	Leaves from 3 sprigs oregano or marjoram
	Red wine vinegar
	Extra-virgin olive oil
	Salt

Cut stems off artichokes. Pull off tough outer leaves by hand, and trim a few more layers of leaves with a sharp knife. Scoop out the chokes and cut artichokes into quarters lengthways.

Arrange artichoke quarters, tomato and cucumber slices, celery stalks, and onion rings on a platter. Scatter with spring onions, basil, and oregano, drizzle with vinegar and oil, and salt to taste. Let salad sit for 15–20 minutes before serving.

"Salade Niçoise Sandwich"
Pan Bagnat

"If you ask a Mentonnais who is less than 60 what a 'pan bagna' is," writes Pierre Benini in La cuisine mentonnaise, "there are 99 chances in 100 that he will respond, 'It's a bit of bread with tomato, anchovy, olives, etc.' " This, he says, is not correct. In Menton (a dozen miles or so northeast of Nice at the Italian border), writes Benini, pan bagna – without the "t" the Niçois give it – is "a bread soup, fashionable in earlier times." This was made, he continues, simply with water or stock, the crusts of bread, salt, a clove of garlic, and a few drops of olive oil. He even cites a local saying: "Acò ès toutta soupa ou pan bagna," "This is all soup or pan bagna" – meaning something like "It's six of one, half dozen of another." To describe the salad-on-bread that the fourestié or foreigners are so fond of, he concludes, the correct term is "pan bagna de toumata."

Jacques Médecin makes no mention of Niçois pan bagnat (literally bathed or moistened bread) as a soup, but he does say that the original version of the dish was simply a salade niçoise arranged on top of stale bread, preferably coarsely crumbled. He calls the sandwich version "pan bagnat practique" (and curiously enough suggests moistening the bread with a few drops of vinegar – which he has earlier forbidden for salade niçoise on its own). Jean Giusti of La Merenda, on the other hand, says that pan bagnat was originally just dried-out bread sprinkled with water, then topped with olive oil, pissala, and tomatoes.

Today in Nice, pan bagnat is sold in sandwich form – a round, chewy little loaf of bread with salade niçoise inside – at stands all over the city. (If you've never been to Nice but have encountered the massive tuna-and-crudité sandwiches sold in Tunisian shops in Paris, you have the general idea.) Although pan bagnat makes a perfect lunch, the Niçois of an earlier time commonly ate it as a *merenda* or midmorning snack, around 9 A.M. – for instance, when they brought in their fishing boats.

to serve 4

4	small round loaves of crusty bread ("boules"), halved crosswise*
1	garlic clove, cut in half lengthways
6	medium firm tomatoes, 2 halved and 4 sliced
	Extra-virgin olive oil**
	Salt and freshly ground black pepper
	8 anchovy fillets *or* 1 × 175 g/6 oz tin best-quality olive oil-packed tinned tuna
1	cucumber, peeled and thinly sliced
1	green bell pepper, seeds and ribs removed, very thinly sliced
2	small onions, very thinly sliced
2	hard-boiled eggs, sliced
50 g/2 oz	Niçoise olives ***

Rub cut surfaces of loaves first with garlic pieces, then with halved tomato pieces, squeezing the juice onto the bread as you do so. Drizzle olive oil on cut surfaces and season generously with salt and pepper.

On the bottom half of each loaf, arrange tomato slices, anchovy fillets or pieces of tuna, and sliced cucumber, green peppers, onions, and eggs. Scatter olives over vegetables, *** close sandwiches, press together slightly, and let sit for about 1 hour before serving.

> *If small loaves are unavailable, pan bagnat can be made with a single large round loaf cut into quarters like a pie – but this is messy and less attractive, and should be done only as a last resort.

> **Colette Bourrier-Reynaud, in *Les Recettes de Réparate: la cuisine de tradition en pays niçois,* states firmly, "If you don't like olive oil, abstain from this dish. It cannot be made with another oil."

> ***In pan bagnat, as in salade niçoise, on pizza, with pasta, or in other uses, Niçoise olives are nearly always used unpitted. It would be a good idea to warn your guests of this fact, especially in the case of the sandwich. Alternately, you can pit the olives; this cannot be done neatly with olives so small and tender, but, then, nobody's likely to see them inside the sandwich.

The Real Salade Niçoise
La (Vraie) Salade Niçoise

"What crimes have been committed in the name of this pure, fresh salad . . . !" cries Jacques Médecin. Since I have no wish to be accused of any crimes myself, I hereby present an adaptation of Médecin's own recipe for the dish – adding only a few procedural notes and explications, and recasting the list of ingredients slightly for consistency's sake.

to serve 6

10	medium firm tomatoes, quartered
	Salt
12	anchovy fillets or 2 × 175 g/6 oz tins best-quality olive-oil-packed tinned tuna
225 g/8 oz	shelled baby fava beans (about 450 g/1 lb unshelled) or 12 baby artichokes*
1	garlic clove, cut in half lengthways
1	cucumber, peeled and thinly sliced
2	green bell peppers, seeds and ribs removed, very thinly sliced
6	small onions, very thinly sliced
3	hard-boiled eggs, quartered
100 g/3½ oz	Niçoise olives
6 tablespoons	extra-virgin olive oil
6	basil leaves, finely chopped
	Freshly ground black pepper

Place the tomatoes on a platter and lightly salt them. If using anchovies, cut each fillet into three or four pieces; if using tuna, shred it coarsely.

If using favas, blanch beans in boiling water for 30 seconds, then drain and rinse well in cold water. Slip beans out of their skins by grasping each one by its grooved end and squeezing gently so that it pops out. If using artichokes, cut stems off, pull off tough outer leaves by hand, and trim a few more layers of leaves with a sharp knife. Scoop out the chokes and cut artichokes into thin slices.

*Médecin allows that, if the season permits, both favas and artichokes may be used – but that it is also permissible to use one or the other, or neither.

Rub the bottom and sides of a large salad bowl with garlic pieces, then discard. Arrange anchovies or tuna, favas and/or artichokes (or neither), cucumber, green pepper, onion, eggs, and olives in the bowl. Drain the tomatoes, salt them again, and add them as well.

Make a dressing with olive oil, basil, salt, and pepper. Refrigerate both salad and dressing for about 1 hour before serving, then drizzle dressing over salad and serve.

Mentonnais Christmas Salad

Insarata de Natale

Besides the celery on which it is based, there are three parts to this simple, elegant, unexpected salad, which might be served in the more fortunate homes of the region for Christmas Day lunch: newly pressed olive oil because winter is the season of new oil on the Riviera, black truffles because it's Christmas and thus a time for luxury and indulgence, and anchovies because, well, it's Menton.

to serve 4

6–8   olive oil-packed anchovy fillets
Extra-virgin olive oil, preferably freshly bottled
Hearts, tender stalks, and interior leaves (i.e., all the "white" parts) from 6 bunches celery, finely chopped
As much fresh black truffle as you can afford

Crush the anchovies with a fork in about 2 tablespoons of oil in the bottom of a salad bowl, mashing them to form a medium-thick, liquid paste. Add celery and toss to coat well.

Divide salad between 4 plates and grate paper-thin slices of black truffle on top with a truffle grater, a small mandoline, or the slicing blade of a four-sided grater.

MEAT

Chi va de fûga no mangia bon rosto.
(He who goes too fast won't have a good
roast to eat.)

— GENOESE PROVERB

De vèspre, lou buhit es lourd.
(At night, the pot-au-feu is indigestible.)

— NIÇOIS PROVERB

Meat is hardly unknown on the Riviera. In the days when prehistoric hunters roamed the Mediterranean littoral, wild game was an important part of the local diet. In the medieval era, both game and domestically raised meat were eaten by the wealthy and aristocratic classes, especially in Genoa, and meat was favoured by the middle classes over fish – for the simple reason that, as noted earlier, good fish tended to be considerably more expensive.

Today, meat of all varieties is widely available in the region (even minced beef alla McDonald's, if you insist), as it is almost everywhere in Europe – and, to the dismay of nutritionists, forms an ever more important part of the Ligurian and Niçois diets. (According to some estimates, meat consumption in the Nice region has increased in the past 50 years from about 9 kg/20 lb per capita per annum to more than 90 kg/200 lb.)

Nonetheless, the traditional diet of the majority of the region's population has always been comparatively meat-poor. Even today, especially in rural regions, meat is a rarity, a special treat – something to be used for flavouring rather than as a centrepiece; something for Sundays and holidays, if even then.

To be sure, a bit of hooved game is still taken and enjoyed by hunters in the entroterra and the arrière-pays, but birds and rabbits are more frequently the prize. (Rabbit is also raised by many small farmers, and is immensely popular on the coast as well as in the interior.) There's a long history of appreciation around both Genoa and Nice for turkey as well – one of the earliest American imports to find favour in Liguria, as elsewhere in Italy. (Bartolomeo Scappi mentions it in 1570, not even a century after the first voyage of Columbus.) As in Britain, it is often part of the traditional Christmas menu. Goat is popular in the entroterra, and some lamb is eaten, more so on the French side of the border than the Italian – though in Liguria, the meat is sometimes cooked, to delicious effect, with artichokes and perhaps black olives. Veal seems to be appreciated mostly for its organs, and the beef used is typically a cheap cut, cooked long – in France as a stew-like daube and in Italy as a stew or brasato (a kind of pot roast preferably made with meat containing thick sinews, which turn gelatinous and dissolve into the sauce).

The Genoese meat sauce, tocco, might be based on a good chunk of veal or beef, but that chunk does double duty; the meat is cooked in a single piece with other ingredients, and then, with some of its flavour leached out, it is removed and put to another use. Other dishes extend good meat by stuffing it with cheaper meat and/or other ingredients. Liguria's tomaxelle, for instance, are meat "packets," shaped like plump little sausages, using only the thinnest slices of lean veal or beef as a wrapping, with a little minced veal and veal offal inside. Lou piech (or pietch) is Niçois veal breast stuffed with vegetables. In the case of the ancient, emblematic Genoese creation called stecchi (literally "stick"), the cheaper ingredients aren't put inside the lean meat but are alternated with it on skewers, forming a kind of exotic, sauce-coated, fried "shish kebab."

Steaks and chops are, for the most part, tourist (or businessman) fare on the Riviera. Whole roasts are for serious occasions, for showing off. There is a story that the lords of Diano Castello, in earlier times, used to offer their guests a large, succulent roast at the end of a full-scale banquet. The guests, already full, would inevitably refuse it – at which point, before their astonished eyes, it would be thrown to the dogs in the courtyard. The trick was that the "roast" was made of papier-mâché. With typical Ligurian frugality and ingenuity, the lords had found a way to make a display of their wealth at minimal cost.

I thought I had discovered at least one straightforward Ligurian beef dish with a traditional pedigree when I noticed references in several different places to something called bisteca sanremasca – Sanremo-style steak – but the name turned out to be more culinary irony: According to one source, bisteca sanremasca is a grilled mushroom cap; according to another, it's a sandwich – a small bread loaf split in two, rubbed with garlic, dosed with olive oil and salt, and filled with a ripe tomato, preferably of the kind called cuor di bue, or beef heart, a particularly delicious red-and-green variety with a deeply creviced surface. In neither case does it involve meat.

It is hardly surprising, considering the parsimonious nature of the Genoese and the Niçois alike, that offal of all kinds is greatly favoured in the region – from tripe and blood sausage to cow's udder and calf's spinal marrow (the last two of which, as noted earlier, are essential to traditional Genoese ravioli). Stewed tripe is practically a civic emblem of both Genoa and Nice. Blood sausage – called trulé in

Nice, trüli in Menton, beroudu in western Liguria, and berodo in Genoa – is nearly as popular. It usually includes pine nuts and sometimes onions, garlic, and other ingredients. (One recipe, from the Valle Argentina, calls for a litre of veal's blood, half a litre of milk, Swiss chard, and parsley, in addition to pine nuts, onions, garlic, and seasonings.) It is often served cut into crumbly slices and fried in oil with onions, and is quite good this way.

The most important of Genoese offal dishes, a preparation that seems positively medieval in both form and content – and that has traditionally been considered a speciality of celebratory, almost ceremonial importance – is cima, or çimma. This is a ballottine of finely ground organ meats inset with vegetables, wrapped in veal belly or some other similarly durable cut of meat, poached in broth (or sometimes roasted), thinly sliced, and served cold or at room temperature. The traditional Genoese recipe includes a formidable variety of calf and cow parts – brains, sweetbreads, testicles, udder, spinal marrow, etc. – in effect, the odds and ends of the slaughterhouse. In the country, away from commercial abbatoirs, the stuffing is more likely to contain a higher proportion of vegetables and eggs, and mortadella might take the place of at least some of the fresh meats. In either form, at its best, it can be extraordinarily delicate and flavourful – real Ligurian haute cuisine.

One Ligurian offal dish that I find somewhat less appealing, I must admit, is massetti (Genoese for "little bundles"). These are the uncleaned intestines of baby milk-fed lamb, cooked in oil with white wine, onions, garlic, various herbs, and bits of other lamb organs, heart, liver, and kidneys. I sampled the dish one spring at an excellent restaurant called Osteria del Portico, in Castelvittorio, not far from the western Ligurian wine town of Dolceacqua. I found the sauce and the other organ bits quite agreeable, but I simply couldn't manage more than three or four mouthfuls of the massetti. They were a little too, well, earthy for me.

A Counfetura Scounoushùa

In a collection of stories from the Menton region called *A Lambrusca de paigran (Grandfather's Wild Grapevine)*, Jean-Louis Caserio recounts a tale that neatly illustrates both the gastronomic unsophistication and the culinary value system of the arrière-pays.

The story is called "A Counfetura Scounoushùa," or "The Unknown Confiture." In it, Félix, the mayor of a backcountry town, invites his deputy, François, to accompany him to Nice for a conference. After their work is accomplished, the mayor suggests lunch at a local inn, assuring Félix (in Mentonesque) that, "Es a coumuna que paga" – "It's the commune that pays." The two order plates of blood sausage and a bottle of Bellet, and begin eating happily. Then François notices that some customers at another table are eating their sausage with a creamy yellow "confiture" (i.e., mustard) served in little pots. "What's that?" he asks Félix. "I don't know," the mayor replies, "but it must be very expensive because they use just a little bit at a time." François answers, "But for us, it doesn't matter if it's expensive, because today it's the commune that pays." Félix agrees, and tells his deputy to go and ask the kitchen for a pot of the stuff.

François returns with the pot, takes a big spoonful of it, and "as if it were soupe au pistou," swallows it down. He makes a terrible grimace, closes his eyes, turns red, and weeps huge tears. "Noun stà piourà coum' acò [Don't cry like that]," Félix says comfortingly to his friend. . . . "Es a coumuna que paga!"

Pig Tales (1.)

According to English historian J. Theodore Bent in his book *Genoa: How the Republic Rose and Fell* (1881), Genoa suffered from a veritable plague of pigs in the eighteenth century. It seems that the Lerinensian monks of St. Anthony, at their Genoese monastery, kept far more pigs than they had sties for – and the homeless ones roamed the streets of the city. "In 1751," says Bent, "a pig upset a senator in the street and an edict was passed calling them a public nuisance. Anyone who could catch a pig had the right to slay and eat it."

Pig Tales (2.)

In the days before World War II, according to Jean and Danièle Lorenzi in their *Cuisine monégasque/Cüjina de Munégu,* a couple of sausage makers from Germany, a husband-and-wife team, set up shop in Monte Carlo and quickly gained a loyal following for their delicious charcuterie. "It was their habit," the Lorenzis continue, "to close every Wednesday, in the style of the Rhenish, to make their sausages. Because some locals might not have known that this was an ancient tradition where they came from, they had a neighbour, who was a painter, make up a magnificent little sign for them to put in their shop window each Wednesday. It read "M. et Mme. X . . . Sont au sous-sol en train de faire des cochonneries jusqu'à demain." The hapless couple apparently meant *cochonnailles,* meaning charcuterie, not *cochonneries.* What their sign actually said was "M. and Mme. X . . . Are in the basement doing dirty things until tomorrow."

Daube de Boeuf

Virtually every authority on traditional cooking on the French Riviera will give you the same two pieces of advice regarding daube: It is almost impossible to overcook, and it is best made in large quantities. In their *Cuisine monégasque/Cüjina de Munégu,* for instance, Jean and Danièle Lorenzi note that one of their grandmothers insisted that it simmer for four hours, while one of their aunts cooked it for five to six. ("If you're eating the daube for lunch," they add, "the wife or the husband-who-cooks *[mari-qui-cuisine]* must get up early.") As for quantity, daube is certainly a dish more appropriate to a party of eight or ten than to an intimate supper for two. But if you make too much, don't worry: It only improves after a day or two in the refrigerator – and it can also be used as a pasta sauce, and as both a sauce and a filling for ravioli.

As might be expected with such a basic, old-fashioned dish, there are many variations on the recipe. Some versions call for veal bones (for flavour) or calf's feet (for flavour and texture) in addition to the basic beef. Some specify white wine in place of red. Some omit the tomatoes. Some toss in a whole gardenful of herbs. One particularly elaborate recipe, offered in *Cuisine monégasque,* calls for larding the beef, marinating it for eight hours with herbs and spices, and then cooking it in a way that uses six different pans! This is a considerably simpler, purer recipe, from Franck Cerutti at Don Camillo in Nice.

to serve 8

	Salt
1.75 kg/4 lb	beef chuck, cut into 5 cm/2 inch pieces
2 tablespoons	unsalted butter
2 tablespoons	extra-virgin olive oil
2	onions, chopped
3	carrots, peeled and chopped
3	cloves garlic, finely chopped
2	large, ripe tomatoes, skinned, seeded, and coarsely chopped
2	celery stalks, diced
850 ml/1½ pints	dry red wine
	Bouquet garni of 1 bay leaf and 2 sprigs each flat-leaf parsley and thyme, tied in a bundle with kitchen string
2 tablespoons	flour
25 g/1 oz	dried porcini mushrooms
	Freshly ground black pepper
1 tablespoon	jus de veau (optional; see page 102)

Salt meat generously, then heat butter and oil together in a large, heavy saucepan or casserole and brown meat evenly in small batches over medium-high heat. As meat is browned, transfer it to a platter and set aside.

Lower heat and pour off most of the butter and oil. Add onions, carrots, garlic, tomatoes, and celery to the pan, and mix well, scraping brown bits from the bottom of the pan.

Return meat to pan and add 1.2 litres/1¼ pints of the wine and the bouquet garni. Mix flour and remaining wine together smoothly in a bowl, so that no lumps remain. Add flour mixture to pan and stir in well. Cover and simmer daube for 2–3 hours.

Soak mushrooms in 3 changes of warm (not hot) water, for a total of about 15 minutes. Drain and add to casserole, then continue to simmer another hour. Remove bouquet garni and season to taste with salt and pepper. Stir in 1 tablespoon jus de veau if desired. Serve with polenta, panisses (see page 189), or egg noodles tossed with butter.

Veal Concentrate

Jus de Veau

This flavourful concentrate is more haute cuisine than traditional Riviera cooking, but it is an extremely useful "secret ingredient," capable of adding instant authority to soups, stews, pasta sauces, and other dishes. Franck Cerutti uses it, in place of the more classic glace de viande, in his daubes.

to make about 1.2 litres/1¼ pints

1.5 kg/3 lb	boneless veal breast*
	Salt
50 g/2 oz	unsalted butter
4 tablespoons	extra-virgin olive oil

Cut veal breast into pieces about 5 cm/2 inches square and salt generously, turning so that all surfaces of the meat are lightly coated.

Melt butter with olive oil in a large, heavy saucepan, and cook meat over low heat for 1½ hours, stirring occasionally, until it is well browned on all sides.

*Ask your butcher to bone the veal breast for you, and save the bones for stock.

Pour off about ¾ of the fat and juices, add 2.3 litres/4 pints water, and cook at a slow boil, uncovered, for 2 hours or until liquid is reduced by about half. Push the meat with its liquid through a chinois or fine strainer. Refrigerate the resulting liquid until the fat solidifies on top, then scrape off and discard fat. Store refrigerated or in the freezer.

Genoese Meat Sauce

Tocco

The nineteenth-century Genoese poet Martin Piaggio wrote a number of poems in praise of local dishes, among them not one but two about ravioli: a 179-line epic called simply "I raviêu" ("Ravioli") and a shorter one called "Riçetta per fâ i raviêu," or "Recipe for Making Ravioli" – which is just that. The latter begins with the words "Reçipe ûn bœllo pesso de vitella, / Da mette a rosto per fâ ûn bon tocchetto" – "Take a lovely piece of veal, / Put it to roast to make a good little sauce." *Tocchetto* is the diminuative of *tocco*, the definitive Genoese meat sauce. Tocco is widely cited in Ligurian culinary lore as a metaphor for patience; it was traditionally left to cook all day on a smouldering fire, in a terra-cotta pot, for use at the evening meal. In their *La tradizione gastronomica italiana: Liguria,* Paola Arvo and Gabriella Viganego note that "Once, it was not unusual for those who woke up late . . . to enter the kitchen and sip their coffee in a cloud of aromas from a tocco." Tocco might also be seen as symbolic of Genoese culinary thrift, since the meat that flavours the sauce does not ultimately become part of it but is reserved for another use – for instance, as filling for ravioli (the same ravioli the tocco will moisten).

to serve 4–6

2 tablespoons	unsalted butter
	Extra-virgin olive oil
1	medium onion, finely chopped
1	celery stalk, finely chopped
1	carrot, finely chopped
450 g/1 lb	boneless veal, in 1 or 2 pieces
	Flour
450 ml/16 fl oz	dry red wine
15 g/½ oz	dried porcini mushrooms
225 ml/8 fl oz	crushed tinned or fresh chopped tomatoes
	Salt

Melt butter with a tablespoon or two of olive oil in a large pan with a cover. Cook onion, celery, and carrot over low heat for about 20 minutes, until soft, then remove with a slotted spoon and set aside.

Add a little more oil to the same pan and increase heat to medium. Lightly flour the veal, then brown it on all sides in the oil. Reduce heat to low again, return vegetables to pan, and deglaze with red wine. Continue cooking over low heat, uncovered.

Meanwhile, soak mushrooms in 3 changes of warm (not hot) water, for a total of about 15 minutes. Remove mushrooms from water, reserving the liquid, and chop them. When wine has almost evaporated from meat and vegetables, add mushrooms, about 225 ml/8 fl oz of their soaking water, strained, and tomatoes. Salt to taste, cover very tightly, and cook for at least 3 hours. Check every hour, adding a bit more water if necessary.

Remove meat and serve sliced as a main dish with puréed potatoes, or use for stuffing vegetables or ravioli or other pasta.

Rabbit with Anchovies and White Wine
Lapin à l'Anchoïade et au Vin Blanc

Rabbit is much prized in the entroterra and the arrière-pays, where it is usually simply roasted or sautéed with olives. Of this particular recipe, however, I know nothing. I've never had the dish on the Riviera, and I don't know whether it is traditional or not. It appears, without credit, in *La Cuisine mentonnaise,* published by the Societé d'Art et d'Histoire du Mentonnais, and it simply looked so good (and, once you got the rabbit in the requisite condition, easy) that I couldn't resist making it. Having made it, it tasted so good that I can't resist adapting it here.

to serve 4

1	1.25 kg/2½ lb rabbit, completely boned but whole*
24	anchovy fillets
50 g/2 oz	Parmigiano-Reggiano, grated
175 g/6 oz	salt pork or thick-cut bacon, diced
20	pearl onions, skinned**
225 ml/8 fl oz	dry white wine
6	ripe tomatoes, halved and seeded

Opposite: "Silk Handkerchiefs"

Lay boned rabbit out flat on a work surface. Roughly chop half the anchovy fillets, then distribute them evenly over the surface of the rabbit. Sprinkle with the Parmigiano, then roll the rabbit up tightly lengthways and tie it, in the form of a sausage, with 5 or 6 pieces of kitchen string. Let it rest for 1 hour.

Blanch the salt pork or bacon for 3–4 minutes in boiling water. Drain, then cook it over low heat in a large heavy frying pan for 15–20 minutes, stirring occasionally, until it browns slightly and renders some of its fat. Remove it with a slotted spoon and drain it on paper towels.

Brown the rabbit lightly on all sides in the same pan at medium-low heat. Add onions, return salt pork or bacon to pan, and add white wine. Cover the pan and cook for 45 minutes, turning the rabbit several times.

Crush the remaining anchovies to a paste and add to the pan. Add the tomatoes, cover again, and cook for 30 minutes longer, again turning the rabbit several times.

To serve, remove twine and cut rabbit into slices. Spoon sauce and tomatoes on top.

*Unless you are very skilled at such things, try to convince your butcher to bone the rabbit for you.

**To peel pearl onions, plunge them into boiling water for about 90 seconds, drain, and cool. Slice the sprout end off each one, then grasp it by the root end and gently slip onion out of skin.

Goat with White Beans
Capra e Fagioli

"The orography of our valleys," Delio Viale, proprietor of Ristorante Gastone in Dolceacqua, noted when he sent me this recipe (he is famous for the dish), "doesn't permit the presence of large herds of cattle, and goats furnish instead to our families their milk, cheese, and pelts." They also furnish a variety of meat greatly prized in the kitchens of the entroterra – both for its flavour and for its nutritional value. Young goat (kid) is roasted; the grown animal is stewed. (Goat is said to be easily digestible, and was often specified, in earlier times, as an appropriate food for the ill and convalescing.)

For some reason we tend to be skittish about goat, unless our ethnic heritage has given us a patrimonial familiarity with it. I'm not sure why; it isn't particularly "gamy" (it is not inaccurate to describe it as tasting something like a cross between pork and lamb), and goats are certainly no cuter or pet-like than lambs, which we eat quite happily. Maybe it has something to do with all those cartoon images we've seen of goats devouring tins and rubber tyres – though the ones raised for food are more likely to feed on grass and grain. In any case, goat is available here in areas where there are Greek, Middle Eastern or Caribbean populations.

The happy combination of goat and white beans is typical of the western entroterra. This may have something to do with the fact that the best white beans on the Riviera – long, plump, sweet – come from this area, and particularly from Pigna, Badalucco, and Coneo. (Across the border in the arrière-pays, their quality is equaled by the "cocos" grown around the village of Figaret.) These are particularly good when they're fresh, in the early to late summer – depending on the region – but are also superb, and much easier to find, in dried form. (Whenever possible, however, try to find dried beans no more than a year old; they cook faster and taste better.) According to Delio Viale, the peasants in his region used to save the skins from dried beans to fill rough mattresses they'd leave in their farm sheds, out in the fields. "These were perhaps a little uncomfortable," he adds, "but they were used only a few nights of the year."

to serve 6

450 g/1 lb	dried cannellini beans, "cocos," or other good-quality white beans (as fresh as possible)
	Salt
2.7 kg/6 lb	goat meat (on the bone), skinned and cut into pieces 5-7.5 cm/2-3 inches square*
	Extra-virgin olive oil
2	onions, finely chopped
5	cloves garlic, finely chopped
1	carrot, diced
¼ teaspoon	dry red pepper flakes
1	bay leaf
6–8	sage leaves
3–4	sprigs thyme
1	sprig rosemary
1	bottle Ligurian Vermentino or other dry white wine
	Freshly ground black pepper

*Ask the butcher to skin and cut up the goat for you if you're not handy with such things.

Soak beans overnight in 6–8 litres/12-16 pints water. Drain and transfer to a large saucepan. Add 6-8 litres/12-16 pints fresh water, bring to a boil, then reduce heat and simmer, covered, for 1–2 hours or until beans are tender but not disintegrating. Drain and set aside.

Salt the goat meat liberally, then cook it in olive oil in a large heavy saucepan over low heat, turning frequently until meat is lightly browned on all sides. While meat is cooking, cook onions, garlic, carrot, and pepper flakes together in olive oil in another saucepan over low heat until onions are soft and translucent, 15–20 minutes. When onion mixture is done and goat meat is browned, combine them in the large saucepan.

Tie bay leaf, sage, thyme, and rosemary together with kitchen string and add to the saucepan, then add wine. Raise heat briefly and scrape burned bits off bottom of pan, then reduce heat to simmer, cover, and cook for 3 hours. Stir occasionally, and add a little hot water if sauce reduces too much. (It should be thick but still liquid when the cooking is finished.)

Season to taste with salt and pepper, then stir in white beans. Cook for about 10 minutes longer, then serve.

"Sturgeon-Style" Turkey

Tacchino alla Storiona

The Magra River, it is said, once teemed with sturgeon, and in the seventeenth century, the Genoese – surprisingly but undeniably – exported caviar all over Europe. (They presumably obtained their appreciation for both the fish and its roe in their trade colonies on the Black Sea.) Sturgeon has now vanished from local waters; the curious name and preparation of this turkey dish are said by modern gastronomic writers to be proof of, as one of them puts it, an "atavistic nostalgia" for the now-forgotten flavour of the sturgeon's delicious flesh. If this is true, it's a nice reversal of the preparation known as tonno di coniglio (or thon de lapin) – "tuna" made of rabbit – occasionally found in western Liguria and Nice, in which the meat is prepared to resemble (tinned) fish. A question about the identification of this dish with sturgeon is raised only by Emanuele Rossi's *La vera cuciniera genovese facile ed economica* (1865), in which it is described as tacchino detto alla stiriana – which suggests that it is prepared not in the style of sturgeon at all but in the style of Styria, a region in southeastern Austria, which might make more sense. In any case, tacchino alla storiona (bibbin a-a storionn-a in Genoese) was once de rigueur at fancy Christmas Day banquets – an elegant entrée to be served just before the roast. ("A Natale, o grosso o piccin, tûtti portan in tôa o sô bibbin," says a Genoese proverb – "At Christmas, there's a turkey, large or small, on every table.") Since it's served cold, however, and has a refreshing, spice-haunted flavour, it's also an excellent summer dish. This recipe is adapted from Rossi's "Styrian" version.

to serve 6

1	1.5-1.75 kg/3-4 lb turkey breast, boned, with skin removed
1 teaspoon	ground nutmeg
	Salt
4	very thin lemon slices
4	bay leaves
3–4	slices prosciutto di Parma
2	cloves
1	onion
2	flat-leaf parsley sprigs
1	carrot, scrubbed
1	celery stalk
2	fresh calf's or pig's feet
1	bottle Ligurian Vermentino or other dry white wine
	Whites of 3 large eggs, beaten to form peaks
6	very thin slices orange

Season top of turkey breast with nutmeg and salt to taste, then arrange lemon slices and bay leaves on top of it and cover them with overlapping layers of prosciutto.

Wrap and tie turkey breast in several thicknesses of muslin and place in a large saucepan. Stick cloves into peeled onion and add to pan, along with parsley, carrot, celery, and calf's or pig's feet. Add wine, enough water to cover all ingredients, and salt to taste. Cover and bring to a boil, then immediately reduce heat and simmer, partially covered, for 1½ hours.

Let turkey cool in broth to room temperature, then remove it from pan, reserving and refrigerating broth. Unwrap muslin and remove and discard lemon slices, bay leaves, and prosciutto. Place turkey in a terrine large enough to hold it with about 2.5 cm/1 inch of space on all sides. Cut a piece of thick cardboard to just fit terrine, wrap it in aluminium foil, and place it on top of turkey. Weight turkey with two or more tins of soup or vegetables and refrigerate for at least 12 hours.

Before serving, skim any fat off surface of refrigerated broth, then reduce broth over medium heat until about 1 litre/1¾ pints remain. Next, clarify broth by stirring in egg whites and returning it to a boil. Reduce heat, stir once or twice, then filter broth through several thicknesses of muslin. Allow to cool slightly, then pour over turkey. Cool to room temperature, and then refrigerate until gelatin solidifies thoroughly.

Before serving, dip terrine in warm water and unmould. Garnish top of unmoulded terrine with orange slices. Slice with a thin, sharp knife and serve like pâté.

Lamb with Olives and Artichokes
Agnello con Olive e Carciofi

Lamb is basic to the cooking of Provence, somewhat less basic in the region of Nice, and positively marginal in Liguria. That is not to say that lamb is not enjoyed – just that there isn't a whole lot of it. (The reason is the usual: lack of ample grazing land.) The one lamb dish that shows up in most Ligurian cookbooks is a fricassée of the meat in white wine, with artichokes. This is a spring dish, since both its main ingredients typically become available at about the same time, in March. Olives, though a fruit of the fall and winter, have a connection with the season, too, since they are often cured for several months before eating – which might well put them on tables in March or so. This is my interpretation of a dish I enjoyed at Ca' Ertè, a farmhouse in San Bernardino, above Sestri Levante, which serves meals to groups as a part of Italy's Agriturismo programme.

to serve 4

12	baby artichokes or 4 large ones
	Juice of 2 lemons
675 g/1½ lb	lamb shoulder chops, each cut into 2 or 3 pieces
	Extra-virgin olive oil
2	flat-leaf parsley sprigs, finely chopped
2	cloves garlic, finely chopped
225 ml/8 fl oz	Ligurian Vermentino or other dry white wine
30–40	Niçoise or Taggiasca olives*
	Salt and freshly ground black pepper

Pull tough outer leaves off artichokes, trim the stems and tops, cut in half lengthways, and cut or scrape out the chokes. Quickly dip cut sides of artichokes into lemon juice to prevent blackening, then set them aside.

Cook lamb pieces in a large heavy saucepan, in batches, in olive oil over medium heat. Turn frequently so that lamb is well browned on all sides. As lamb pieces are done, remove and set aside.

When all lamb is cooked, add parsley and garlic to the same pan, adding a little more oil if necessary, and cook over very low heat for about 5 minutes. Deglaze pan with wine over high heat, then reduce heat to low and cover pan.

If using baby artichokes, cut them crosswise into slices about 12 mm/½ inch thick and immediately add them to pan. If using large artichokes, first cut halves in half again lengthways, then cut into slices as above and add to pan. Cook artichokes, covered, for 15–20 minutes, or until tender.

Return lamb to pan, add olives, and season to taste with salt and pepper. Raise heat to medium-high and cook for 2–3 minutes, stirring constantly, to warm meat through.

*See third note, page 92.

Ligurian Veal Rolls
Tomaxelle

Though tomaxelle (pronounced approximately tuma-ZHEL-lay) is a dish of thin veal scallops rolled around a meat-and-cheese filling, its name apparently derives from *tomaculum* or *tomaclum,* a late Latin term, mentioned by Juvenal and Martial, for a kind of cooked sausage. Tomaxelle is often cited as a prime example of Ligurian "cucina di ricupero," cuisine of leftovers, since it was often made by Genoese stewards the day after a banquet, with the remains of roasted or boiled meat. In giving this recipe, several Ligurian cookbooks make the same comment, to the effect that this is one of the most appetizing dishes of Genoese cuisine but one that is increasingly difficult to find in restaurants. One restaurant that does serve it regularly is Franco and Melly Solari's superb Ca' Peo in Leivi. This is their recipe (except that I have omitted one of his key ingredients – that pesky old cow's udder again).

to serve 4

115 g/4 oz	sweetbreads
225 g/8 oz	lean veal, finely chopped (not minced)
1	bay leaf
	Extra-virgin olive oil
50 g/2 oz	pine nuts
2	cloves garlic
6	flat-leaf parsley sprigs
	Leaves from 3 sprigs marjoram or oregano
1	slice Italian- or French-style country bread
225 ml/8 fl oz	beef stock
115 g/4 oz	Parmigiano-Reggiano, grated
5	large eggs
	Salt and freshly ground black pepper
12	very thin slices veal, approximately 7.5 × 10cm/ 3 × 4 inches (225-350 g/8-12 oz total)

Plunge sweetbreads into a small saucepan of boiling water, cook for about 2 minutes, then drain and place in a bowl of cold water. Carefully pick the skin off the sweetbreads and finely chop.

Cook sweetbreads, veal, and bay leaf together in olive oil over medium heat, stirring until meats are lightly browned on all sides.

While meats are cooking, finely mince pine nuts, garlic, parsley, and marjoram together, then add to meats for the last 2–3 minutes of cooking.

Soak bread (including crusts) in beef stock, then gently squeeze out excess liquid. Chop soaked bread and add to meat mixture. Remove bay leaf, then mince mixture in a meat grinder or food processor until smooth and well mixed.

Place minced meat mixture in a bowl and stir in Parmigiano and eggs. Season generously with salt and pepper.

Divide mixture into 12 mounds of approximately equal size on a work surface. Place 1 mound about 2.5 cm/1 inch from the near edge of each slice of veal, then smooth it out so that it extends to within about 2 cm/¾ inch of the edges on each side. Roll each piece of veal to cover the mixture, then secure each end of the roll with a toothpick, inserted just beyond the filling.

Sauté the veal rolls in a large frying pan in olive oil over high heat, turning frequently so that they are lightly browned on all sides. Franco Solari recommends serving tomaxelle with puréed potatoes and steamed greens.

Genoese Skewers

Stecchi

Linda Belforte, the longtime chef at Genoa's Yacht Club Italiano – now retired – was describing to me some of the classic Genoese dishes she used to cook, one sunny afternoon on the terrace of the seaside caffè then run by her sons Renato (now director of the Yacht Club dining room) and Gianni (who holds a similar post at the venerable Circolo Artistico Tunnell on the Via Garibaldi). She offered her opinions on pesto, trofie, cappon magro – and then she started talking about a particularly elaborate speciality that involved veal organs, chicken, courgettes, and artichokes, among other things, strung onto skewers, coated in salsa besciamella (i.e., béchamel), and . . . At that point I interrupted and said, "And then you dip the skewers in an egg wash, dredge them in breadcrumbs, and fry them?" "Yes, exactly," she replied, somewhat surprised. "These are what we call stecchi."

Well, maybe so – but what she had also been describing, almost exactly, was a genre of classical French preparations known as *attereaux*. (In France, the dipping sauce is traditionally the more elaborate villeroi, not béchamel, but otherwise the technique is identical.) Both the *Larousse Gastronomique* and Escoffier's *Le Guide culinaire* give recipes for several versions of the thing. An attereau is a metal skewer; stecchi means skewers, too, and stecchi are considered to be one of the definitive dishes of Genoese alta cucina – in a class with cappon magro and cima. Given the rather unusual method of their preparation, it seems unlikely that stecchi and attereaux could have developed independently. Were they, then, a French invention that was adopted by the Genoese? Or did they originate in Genoa and travel to France, where they were elaborated and diversified? Escoffier appends the word *genevoise* to one of his attereau recipes, and it occurred to me to wonder if that might have been a misprint for *génoise*. Apparently not. But the *Larousse Gastronomique* notes that the sauce once called génoise was at some point renamed genevoise to avoid possible confusion with the sponge cake called génoise – so perhaps the same thing happened to the attereaux. Attereaux à la genevoise, that is, might originally have been attereaux à la génoise, which would at least suggest the possibility that the recipe might have come originally from Genoa. In any case, classic Genoese stecchi are flavourful and unusual. The basic ingredients are similar enough in colour and texture that, once they're encased in their rich, crisp coating, they acquire an element of delicious surprise. This is Signora Belforte's stecchi recipe.

to serve 4

½	fresh calf's brain*
115 g/4 oz	sweetbreads
	Extra-virgin olive oil
225 g/8 oz	lean veal, cut into 8 pieces
2	carrots
	Salt
2	small courgettes
8	baby artichokes
8	small, firm, thick-stemmed white mushrooms, cleaned
1.1 litres/2 pints	plus 1 tablespoon whole milk
115 g/4 oz	unsalted butter
	Flour
	Freshly ground black pepper
	Pinch of nutmeg
	Breadcrumbs
4	large eggs

Cook *calf's brain* for about 10 seconds per side in oil over medium heat, then remove from pan and set aside to cool. In the same pan, cook sweetbreads for 8–10 minutes, browning well on all sides. Remove from pan and set aside to cool. In the same pan, adding more oil if necessary, lightly brown veal pieces on all sides, cooking for 3–4 minutes in all. Remove and set aside.

Cook carrots in boiling salted water for about 5 minutes. Add courgettes to same pot and continue cooking for about 3 minutes longer, then drain vegetables and set aside to cool.

Meanwhile, cut stems off artichokes. Pull off tough outer leaves by hand, and trim a few more layers of leaves with a sharp knife. Blanch artichokes for 2–3 minutes in water to cover.

Trim carrots and courgettes and cut each one into 4 pieces of approximately equal size, to make 8 carrot and 8 courgettes pieces in all.

Cut calf's brain and sweetbreads into 8 pieces each.

Thread ingredients onto 8 metal or wooden skewers, 20-25 cm/8-10 inches long, beginning with artichokes and ending with mushrooms, so that there is one piece of each ingredient on each skewer. Set skewers aside on a board.

* Do not use frozen calf's brains, as they have a very unpleasant consistency. If fresh brains are unavailable, double or triple the quantity of sweetbreads called for.

Heat 50 g/2 oz milk over medium heat in a saucepan to just below boiling (do not boil). Melt butter over low heat in another saucepan, then gradually whisk in about 50 g/2 oz flour, stirring until it forms a thick roux. Slowly whisk in hot milk and, while continuing to stir, season lightly with salt and pepper and add nutmeg. Continue cooking and stirring for 3–4 minutes, or until sauce is thick and smooth.

Place besciamella in a wide, flat bowl to cool to room temperature. Dip skewers in sauce, covering all items thoroughly.

Sprinkle 180-300 g/9-11 oz flour and 115-150 g/4-6 oz breadcrumbs on different parts of a large work surface. Beat eggs lightly with tablespoon milk and a pinch of salt. Roll coated skewers in flour, dip in eggs, and dredge in breadcrumbs. Fry in about 2.5 cm/1 inch of hot oil in a very wide pan (a paella pan or flameproof earthenware casserole is perfect), turning once, for 2–3 minutes per side or until golden brown. Drain on paper towels, salt to taste, and allow to rest for 4–5 minutes before serving.

Tripes à la Niçoise

A few steps off the Cours Saleya in Nice is a little jewel of a place called La Merenda, opened in the 1950s by Jean and Christiane Giusti, with him in the tiny kitchen and her running the dining room. La Merenda is the kind of place other restaurateurs – even famous chefs, with Michelin stars – envy. The blackboard in the window warning "Pas de chèques, pas de cartes de crédit, pas de téléphone"; the Giustis' schedule (lunch and dinner only four days a week, Tuesday through Friday, with February and August off); the sign on the door reading "C'est fini" as soon as the tables filled up – who wouldn't dream of having a restaurant on those terms?

The Giustis are now threatening to retire, and have tentatively arranged to sell the restaurant to a long-time customer who has vowed not to change a thing. On my most recent visit to the place, however, Jean Giusti was still saying "Well, nothing is definite." If the ownership does change, I hope that through some miracle everything will remain the same. If not, I still have vivid memories of the food that La Merenda used to serve – the estocaficada (see page 237), a veritable ode to stockfish; the squash-blossom beignets, which the Gault Millau guide once called the best in France (see page 197); the classic daube; the politely pungent pâtes au pistou (with that "secret ingredient" of Emmentaler cheese in place of Parmigiano); and, ah, the tripes à la niçoise – so succulent and subtly flavoured that it could convert even tripe haters. This is Jean Giusti's recipe.

to serve 4

---

900 g/2 lb	honeycomb beef tripe, cut into 2.5-cm/1-inch pieces
125 ml/4 fl oz	white wine vinegar
125 ml/4 fl oz	extra-virgin olive oil
450 ml/16 fl oz	dry white wine
4	tomatoes, skinned, seeded, and roughly chopped
4	cloves garlic, minced
2	onions, thinly sliced
1	bouquet garni (1 bay leaf and 1 sprig each of flat-leaf parsley and thyme, tied together with kitchen string)
	Salt and freshly ground black pepper
	Freshly grated Parmigiano-Reggiano

Rinse tripe in several changes of cold water, then bring a large saucepan of water to a boil over high heat. Add vinegar, and when water returns to a boil, blanch tripe for 30 seconds, then drain.

Heat oil in a heavy sauté pan over medium heat. Add tripe and cook for about 2 minutes, stirring frequently to coat all pieces with oil. Add wine, tomatoes, garlic, onions, and bouquet garni, and season generously with salt and pepper.

Cover pan, reduce heat to lowest possible setting, and simmer for 8 hours. Serve with Parmigiano-Reggiano, to be stirred in by each diner according to taste. At La Merenda, this dish was always accompanied by panisses, chickpea flour "fries" (see page 189); it's also good with polenta.

Genoese Tripe Soup

Sbïra

"The tripe of Genoa," wrote the intrepid Lieut.-Col. Newnham-Davis in the early years of this century, "is as celebrated as that of Caen. . . ." Tripe shops used to be a fixture of the city's old quarter, though as far as I can tell, there is only one left – an apparently unnamed tripperia on the Vico della Casana, filled with copper cauldrons in which tripe broth, a popular hangover remedy, steams. Newnham-Davis most likely encountered tripe in a sit-down restaurant, however, which would have been more his style – and the Genoese tripe dish he sampled was probably the broth called sbïra, served over slabs of toasted bread. Sbïra is hardly fancy fare. It was a typical policeman's ration, its name deriving from *sbirro* – an impolite Genoese term for cops. (It also means a blockhead or dolt.) Sbïra is also an old dish, known in Genoa as early as the fifteenth century. Columbus might well have eaten it as a young man, they say – though without, of course, the potatoes.

to serve 4

900 g/2 lb	honeycomb beef tripe, cut into pieces about 5 × 2.5 cm/2 × 1 inches
125 ml/4 fl oz	white wine vinegar
115 g/4 oz	unsalted butter
	Extra-virgin olive oil
3–4	flat-leaf parsley sprigs, finely chopped
	Leaves from 3–4 sprigs thyme
	Leaves from 3–4 sprigs marjoram or oregano
115 g/4 oz	beef marrow*
4 tablespoons	tomato purée
2 litres/3½ pints	strong beef stock
900 g/2 lb	potatoes, peeled and cut into 12 mm/½ inch slices
	Salt and freshly ground black pepper
4	large, thick slices country-style bread, toasted
	Freshly grated Parmigiano-Reggiano

Prepare tripe as in previous recipe.

Melt butter with a little oil in a deep, heavy pan over low heat, then add parsley, thyme, marjoram or oregano, and marrow, and cook together, stirring as marrow melts, for about 5 minutes. Add tomato purée and half beef stock, stirring well so that tomato purée melts into mixture.

Add tripe, cover pan, and cook over low heat for 2½ hours. Add remaining beef stock and potatoes, and season to taste with salt and pepper. Continue cooking, covered, for 40 minutes more.

To serve, place 1 piece of toast in each of 4 large bowls and ladle tripe and broth over it. Serve with Parmigiano-Reggiano, to be stirred in by each diner according to taste.

*Ask your butcher to split 2 long beef shinbones for you, then scoop out the marrow with a demitasse spoon.

Genoese Veal Ballottine

Cima alla Genovese

One of the definitive classics (and unabashed showpieces) of Genoese cuisine, this dish was traditionally made with paunch, or pancetta, of veal – not the cured, bacon-like pancetta, but the same cut of meat in its natural state. *La vera cuciniera genovese* suggests that paunch or shoulder of lamb or goat may also be employed. Today in Liguria, however, breast of veal is commonly used – and that's a much easier cut of meat to find here.

As noted earlier, some versions of cima – the name literally means "summit," perhaps for the cima's monolithic form or perhaps because it is considered a peak of gastronomy – are made with fewer offal meats and more vegetables. I have a book of traditional recipes from the Oneglia region, for instance, that includes a cima stuffed mostly with chard; and food scholar Silvio Torre says that there is one version filled with practically nothing but artichokes. Vegetables are an accent only in this version of cima, based on the very good one served by Pino Sola at his Sola Enoteca Cucina e Vino in Genoa. It is a lot of work to make, but ultimately well worth it.

to serve 6–8

	Salt
225 g/8 oz	sweetbreads
1	fresh calf's brain*
	Extra-virgin olive oil
450 g/1 lb	lean minced veal
6	large eggs
75 g/3 oz	Parmigiano-Reggiano, grated
	Leaves from 6–8 sprigs marjoram or oregano, very finely chopped
2	cloves garlic, very finely chopped
115 g/4 oz	fresh shelled peas
1½-1¾ kg/3-4 lb	boned veal breast, with a pocket cut into it**
	Bones from veal breast***
1	onion, cut into quarters
1	celery stalk, halved
1	carrot, halved
3	sprigs flat-leaf parsley

Bring 2 small pans of salted water to a boil. Plunge calf's brain into one and sweetbreads into the other. Cook brain for about 1 minute, sweetbreads for about 2 minutes, draining each and placing in separate bowls of cold water. Carefully pick the skin off the sweetbreads and finely chop; finely chop brain, then set both meats aside.

Heat olive oil in a large sauté pan, then add veal, sweetbreads, and brains, and cook over high heat until all meat foams then lightly browns on all sides.

Gently beat eggs in a large bowl, then slowly add Parmigiano and whisk in well. Add marjoram, garlic, meat mixture, peas, and salt to taste, and mix together thoroughly.

Stuff pocket in veal breast with filling, packing it in loosely with your hands (filling will expand as it cooks).*** Sew opening shut with a large needle and thin kitchen string. Puncture cima in 3 or 4 places with a skewer. Wrap cima in muslin and gently form it into the shape of an oversized cocktail sausage. Tie it in this shape with more kitchen string.

Add veal bones, onion, celery, carrot, parsley, and salt to a large saucepan of water. Bring to a boil and gently lower cima into pan. Reduce heat to low and simmer, lightly covered, for 2 hours, skimming if necessary.

Remove cima carefully from pan and place it, still wrapped, in a large baking dish or other vessel that will just hold it. Cut a piece of thick cardboard to just fit inside the top of the dish and wrap it in aluminium foil. Place it on top of the cima, then place 2 or 3 tins of soup or vegetables on top of cardboard to weigh down cima. Allow to cool for about 2 hours, then transfer it to the refrigerator, still weighted, and let set overnight or for at least 8 hours.

To serve, cut off exterior string and remove muslin. Slice thinly with a sharp knife and serve cold or at room temperature.

*See note, page 113.

**Ask the butcher to prepare the veal breast in this manner.

***Many cima recipes call for hard-cooked eggs to be set into the stuffing, as much for decoration as anything. If you wish to do this, insert only half the filling into the veal breast, then nestle 2 or 3 hard-cooked eggs end to end down the middle of it. Place the remainder of the stuffing over the eggs and proceed as above.

Fried Cima

Cima Fritta

Restaurants in Liguria sometimes serve cima, but this "reuse" of the dish is strictly home-style fare. Late-night supper is not a Ligurian habit – but if it were, I'll bet this would be one of the meal's standards.

to serve 1

2–3   slices leftover cima (see previous recipe)
1–2   large eggs, lightly beaten
      Breadcrumbs
      Salt
      Extra-virgin olive oil

Dip cima slices in beaten eggs, then dredge in breadcrumbs. Season to taste with salt and fry in oil over medium heat, turning once, until golden brown on both sides.

❖ ❖ ❖

CHEESE

O formaggio o no guasta i maccaroin.
(Cheese won't hurt the maccheroni.)

– Genoese proverb

Cheese figures prominently in the cooking of Liguria and Nice, but the region produces very little of it. In the mountains, on both sides of the border, there are inevitably a few goat and sheep cheeses (a superb Brebis de Tende from the arrière-pays can be found in the market on the Cours Saleya in Nice), but these are mostly artisanal efforts, not commercially distributed. Some Sardinian-style pecorino is made around Genoa, and a sweet and supple white cheese called formagetta, once considered essential to focaccia col formaggio (see page 173), is produced in tiny quantities near Recco. In general, though, the region has lost whatever cheesemaking tradition it may once have had. Fortunately, the major cheese-producing regions of Piedmont and Emilia-Romagna (whence comes Parmigiano) are right next door. Two typical cheeses of the region that are still produced, barely, are an extraneously flavoured one and one that isn't quite cheese at all. The former is brousse (or brous, broussa, or bruzza), a creation of the mountains, found in the Tinée Valley and the region of La Brigue and Tende, high above Nice, and in the hills all along the western entroterra, at least as far east as Pieve di Teco. The term always refers to a strong, fermented milk product, but there are variations: Sometimes brousse is made from leftover ricotta, mixed with grappa (marc) or other alcohol, salt, pepper, and sometimes other spices. But it can also be simply fermented ricotta, without additions. (Confusingly, the term brousse – a feminine form of brous – is used in the Nice region to mean a mild, fresh cheese, similar to ricotta but not pressed into a mould.)

The best bruzza, according to Angelamaria Zucchetto – who sells all the culinary treasures of the region in her wonderful little shop, La Bottega di Angelamaria, in Molini di Triora – isn't really cheese at all but a kind of fermented curd made from goat's milk, placed in wooden tubs, where it is agitated daily with wooden paddles as it ferments.

Zucchetto recommends eating bruzza with boiled potatoes or with pane d'orzo, which are hard little buckwheat-flour biscuits. A kind of hardtack, these are soaked in water and vinegar before being spread with brousse and topped with a slice of tomato, salt, and oil. Bruzza is also sometimes used as a kind of instant pasta sauce, stirred into bowls of just-cooked gnocchi – and the stronger varieties may be eaten as spreads on slices of toasted country bread. (Bruzza can be very strong indeed: Jacques Médecin reports that in the Tinée Valley, locals used to consider their bruzza properly aged only when maggots began to move within it.)

The cheese that isn't quite cheese is prescinsêua (pronounced something like pray-shin-SIR-yah), which recalls something your grandmother might have made – the curds of sour, clotted milk. Prescinsêua is indispensable in traditional recipes for walnut sauce, torta pasqualina, and ravioli, among other savoury specialities of the Genoese kitchen. It is available in Liguria today in supermarkets and market cheese stalls, commercially made and packaged in little plastic tubs as we might buy cream cheese. (The manufacturers of the Virtus brand recommend it on the label as a diet food, among other things.) This prescinsêua, which is approximately the consistency of creamed horseradish, is nicely sour and has a pleasant flavour – but it isn't quite the real thing.

To find prescinsêua made in the old style, I paid a visit to Maria Benvenuto, in the hinterland above Recco. Benvenuto has her own cows, ten of them, which graze on wild herbs and grasses in the adjacent hills. She puts about three litres at a time of their fresh, unpasteurized milk into a pot with a little piece of rennet made from dried calf's stomach (she used to make her own rennet, but can no longer get the appropriate portion of the calf's anatomy) and keeps it warm for two days. It thickens into a rich curd, as dense as cream cheese, with a complex, faintly grassy flavour and a wonderful bite of acidity. (Benvenuto also makes formagetta, "little cheese," from the same milk, moulding, salting, and briefly aging it. "In the old days," she recalls, "when there was no Parmigiano sold here, we used to make formagetta in May to last through the summer and winter." This is the kind of cheese preferred for that famous Recco speciality focaccia col formaggio – but virtually everybody now uses stracchino instead, she says, except on special occasions.)

Today, ricotta is often substituted for prescinsêua, but it is not at all the same thing; ricotta is, by definition, "cooked," and is heavier in both texture and flavour. Prescinsêua is delicate but with a faint bite. Concealed within a pastry or pasta wrapping and cooked, it dries and grows a bit sharper; placed in little clumps inside a torta pasqualina, for instance, it provides an unexpected and very pleasant contrast to the surrounding vegetables – much more interesting than a hard-boiled egg or a mass of rubbery ricotta.

Sardinia alla Genovese

The links between Genoa and Sardinia are old and strong, and based at least partially on tuna and cheese. Pecorino Sardo was exported from Sardinia to the Ligurian mainland as early as 1166, and by the sixteenth century, the trade had become institutionalized. Sardo preceded Parmigiano-Reggiano as a mainstay of Genoese cooking. The tuna connection is a bit more complex. In the eighteenth century, a Genoese tuna-fishing colony on the island of Tabarca, off the coast of Tunisia, was seized by the Tunisian bey. The king of Sardinia ransomed the fishermen and installed them on the deserted Sardinian island of San Pietro, near a good tuna run. They stayed – and to this day, the people of Carloforte, the island's main town, and of the neighbouring island of Sant Antioco, speak a Ligurian dialect that has been identified as that of eighteenth-century Prà. They don't fish for tuna anymore, though. As one observer has noted, "The able-bodied men all sail out of the marina with remarkable salaries, and the Japanese have come to take their place [as tuna fishermen]."

There are many Sardinians living in or near Genoa today, among them Maria Deidda, wife of Genoese photographer Giorgio Bergami. One evening, Giorgio and Maria took me up into the mountains behind the city, to the village of Creto, for dinner with her cousins, brothers Emilio and Carmine Deidda. A scant thirty minutes from the Piazza de' Ferrari, this is real country, a landscape of high, rolling, grass-covered hills that seem to reach up into the mountains of Piedmont and down almost to the sea, and the Deiddas' house is a small, nearly self-sufficient farm. Sitting at a long table in front of a wood-burning oven set into the wall, we drank home-made wine and ate carta di musica (crisp, paper-thin flatbread from Sardinia), home-made wild boar prosciutto, a salad of finely minced radicchio sprouts with raw onion, slow-roasted baby lamb, and home-made ricotta. It was all wonderful, but perhaps the most memorable part of the meal was the Deiddas' own pecorino, which came out with the prosciutto and stayed on the table throughout the meal. It was slightly sweet, slightly sour, and astonishingly pure in flavour. I bought a wheel of it to take home, and savoured it for weeks.

Prescinsêua

Ricotta, as noted, is not the same thing as prescinsêua at all, though it can be substituted for it in recipes if absolutely necessary. My Genoese friends Alberto and Marina Bisagno have come up with another substitution: They mix equal quantities of good ricotta and soured yoghurt ("about five days past its expiration date," counsels Alberto) to make a kind of instant quasi-prescinsêua. If you're ambitious, you can also try making prescinsêua yourself. Here is a method suggested by cheese maker Jonathan White of the Egg Farm Dairy in Peekskill, New York.

to make 1 litre/1¾ pints

1.1 litres/2 pints	plus 4 drops fresh whole milk
1 tablespoon	soured cream or buttermilk
2	drops single-strength rennet

Starting in the evening, heat 1.1 litres/2 pints milk in a very clean saucepan to a temperature of 75°C/160°F as measured by a kitchen thermometer. Reduce heat and maintain it at approximately that temperature (never allowing it to fall below 70°C/150°F) for 30 minutes.

Preheat oven to 100°C/200°F/Gas Mark ¼.

Remove milk from heat and allow to cool to 48°C/90°F. As it cools, heat 3.3 litres/8 pints water in a large saucepan with metal handles to 48°C/90°F. Meanwhile, wash two 600 ml/1 pint heatproof jars very thoroughly with boiling water.

Stir soured cream or buttermilk into 48°C/90°F milk, then transfer milk to jars and place them in saucepan of 48°C/90°C water. Water should come at least three-quarters of the way up the sides of the jars.

Place pan with jars carefully in oven for 3 minutes, then turn oven off and leave pan in oven for 1 hour. Stir 4 drops milk into 1 tablespoon lukewarm water, then swirl in rennet. Divide rennet mixture into two equal parts. Carefully remove pan with jars from oven. Stir milk in one jar to get it moving, then slowly add one part rennet mixture. When all is added, continue stirring for 30 seconds – no longer. Repeat the process with the other jar and remaining rennet mixture. Very gently return pan with jars to oven and let sit overnight. In the morning, drain cheese in a fine sieve for 2–3 hours, remove jars from water, allow to cool to room temperature, and then refrigerate. Will keep, covered and refrigerated, for at least 1 week.

Four Ways with Cheese

One of Franck Cerutti's inspirations in the early days of Don Camillo in Nice was to offer selected cheeses of the arrière-pays, and occasionally one of two Italian classics – Gorgonzola or Parmigiano-Reggiano – not on a conventional cheese tray, but served individually, with unlikely but, as it turned out, surprisingly appropriate seasonings or accents. He used to offer three or four such presentations daily; now, because interest in them wasn't all it might have been, it's usually just one or two. Here are three of his ideas:

(1.) With slices of Brebis de Tende, mildly sweet sheep's-milk cheese from the far northeastern corner of the Niçois region (substitute Sardinian Fior de Latte or a mild, firm sheep's cheese): a drizzle of delicate extra-virgin olive oil, a few little wisps of the white part of spring onions, very thinly sliced, and a scattering of lightly cooked, peeled baby fava beans.

(2.) With Carré de Mercantour, a low-key cow's-milk cheese from the meadows below the peaks of the roughly crescent-shaped Parc National de Mercantour, which curves around part of the upper arrière-pays (substitute Doux de Montagne): again a drizzle of oil, some threads of oil-packed sun-dried tomatoes, and an anchovy fillet cut in two lengthways.

(3.) With Chèvre de Massoins, a politely sour goat cheese from a town near the vineyards of Villars-sur-Var (substitute any fresh, unflavoured French or British chèvre): olive oil yet again, a few coarse grinds of black pepper, and a sprinkling of sel de Guérande or other flaked sea salt.

(4.) Another enhancement of cheese that I've encountered in several restaurants around Liguria – among them the excellent Piedmontese-flavoured St. Cyr in Genoa (worth visiting for its selection of northwestern Italian cheeses alone) – is simply some crumbly slices of Gorgonzola, for which there is no substitute, drizzled with a few drops of chestnut or maple honey. These flavours meld wonderfully.

....

Part 2
Flour
and Grain

....

PASTA

On mange les macaronis.
(We eat macaroni.)

– CAPTION ON A WORLD WAR
I–ERA PHOTO OF LOCAL
CITIZENS, MUSÉE DES
TRADITIONS, ST. ÉTIENNE-DE-
TINÉE

Pasta has, for centuries, been abundant on the Riviera, in shapes and sizes both universal and unique to the locale – abundantly eaten, abundantly manufactured, and even exported with abundant success. The Genoese didn't invent pasta – if anyone did around the Mediterranean, it was almost certainly the Greeks – but the earliest mentions of dried pasta in Italy are associated with the city. The most famous of these is an act signed by a Genoese notary in 1279, enumerating the effects left by a deceased soldier named Ponzio Bastone. Among these was "una barixella una plena di macharonis" – a basket full of maccheroni Another early mention of pasta may be found in the state archives of the Republic of Genoa, in a report noting that, on May 31, 1351, two *lasagnari* (who made not lasagna in the modern sense, but flat or rolled fresh pasta with eggs in the dough), Pietro Embriaco and Giovanni Bertolotto di Fegino by name, boarded the galley of the arms maker Paganino Doria, to produce their specialities for a banquet he was giving.

By the sixteenth century, the pasta makers of Genoa, the *fidelari* (who, in contrast to the lasagnari, made extruded pasta without eggs), had their own union and their own bylaws, and their product had begun to win acclaim. The menu for a dinner offered to the Duke of Terranova by Giovanni Andrea Doria in 1592 specifically mentions "paste di Genova" among the many courses. By the early eighteenth century, there were as many as 120 pasta shops in the city, and by the early nineteenth, Genoese noodles were being exported to France, England, Spain, Switzerland, Germany, Egypt, Cyprus, and America – and even to Tuscany, Lombardy, and Piedmont. (One of Italy's largest and best-known pasta companies Agnesi, was founded in the hills above Porto Maurizio in 1824 by a young olive farmer who acquired an old-fashioned grain mill in Pontedassio and, with the help of his fifteen children, built a veritable pasta dynasty from there.)

As noted earlier, Genoa imported some of its wheat from the Crimea. This wheat was *Triticum turgidum* – durum, or hard wheat, with a high gluten content

Unlike the soft wheat, *Triticum aestivum,* known earlier in western Europe, Crimean wheat did not have to be bound with eggs to form cohesive pasta. Thus it was not only cheaper but also far more durable. Once dried, this sort of pasta could literally last for years – and, unlike raw flour, which would soon dampen and rot, it could be carried on shipboard for many months at a time. It is not far-fetched to say that, along with ship's biscuits (hardtack) and stockfish, pasta literally fueled Genoa's great voyages of trade and discovery.

The Niçois consume nearly as much pasta as their Ligurian neighbours do – and are by no means convinced that they inherited the habit from Italy. According to Bernard Duplessy, in his *Cuisine traditionnelle en pays niçois,* a visitor to the valley of Ubaye in the arrière-pays in 1788 – one Achard by name – remarked that the people of the region ate "crozets, macarrons, lasagnes, taillerins . . ." and other fresh noodles, and concluded from this that pasta came not from Italy but from the Alps.

Two forms of pasta particularly popular in both Liguria and Nice are ravioli and gnocchi. Ravioli and their countless variations deserve a chapter of their own (see page 138). Gnocchi, though less various, do exist in several forms – and under several names. Both Jean-Noël Escudier and Mamé Clairette claim that the word gnocchi comes from the Niçois word *inhoc* or (in Clairette's spelling) *ignoc,* but neither suggests what the word might mean. The term *gnocchi* is used on both sides of the border (the French give it a final "s"), in any case, for little dumpling-like pasta forms, made from flour or a combination of flour and potatoes. Mamé Clairette, who seems quite sure that gnocchi(s) are a Niçois invention, also maintains that the idea of mixing potatoes into the flour was conceived in the region of Nice. Since flour had earlier been extended with the ground fruit of hawthorn bushes and bitter vetch, she notes, "You can imagine the progress and acceptance of the potato" when it first appeared.

In Recco and neighbouring towns, and as far east as the Cinque Terre, small gnocchi – sometimes made with chestnut flour, or a combination of chestnut and white flour – are called trofie, troffie, or trofiette (see page 67). These don't resemble the dumpling – like gnocchi made elsewhere in Italy – but are usually thin and spiral-shaped. In Nice, gnocchi of the conventional sort are sometimes flavoured with Swiss chard (see page 132). In the arrière-pays and the Ligurian region of Triora, just across the mountains, a kind of potatoless gnocchi (because they predate the potato) are known as sugelli or sugeli – or, in the Brigasque dialect, corpi de diu. I might have been tempted to translate this as "bodies of God" – but it actually means "blows of the finger" *(colpi di ditto* in Italian), describing the action with which the dumplings are hand-formed. Also in the

Triora region, there are trofie-like gnocchi made partially with chestnut flour, called cornetti (see page 133) – not to be confused with corzetti (see page 134).

Long, flat noodles are eaten in Nice under the generic name *pâtes*. In Liguria, depending on the region and the width of the pasta, they may be called trenette, taggiaèn, tag'ain, or landarin, among other things. A speciality of the Savona region are broad noodles, sometimes green with spinach or chard, called piccagge or picagge. One unusual version of this pasta (see page 135) includes finely minced sausage in the dough – a notion I've never encountered anywhere else in Italy.

A typically Ligurian pasta type not found in Nice is corzetti (or crosetti). There are two kinds, both of them thin and flat: Corzetti alla polceverasca (from the Val di Polcevera) are pulled out into a figure eight between the thumbs and index fingers; the other kind, called simply corzetti, or corzetti stampati, are round and about 5 cm/2 inches in diameter, and stamped with special wooden dies with a family seal or other motif. (To a Catholic boy like myself, they look disconcertingly like Hosts.) These corzetti are often served with pesto, or with a delicate dressing of butter, marjoram, and toasted pine nuts. The figure eights typically bathe in a tocco or other meat or mushroom sauce.

There are also two rather curious pasta dishes in the entroterra of western Liguria – curious because neither is cooked in water. Fidelanza, made with spaghetti or some other long, thin noodle, is placed raw into tomato sauce and simmered until done (see page 136); pasta alla defiçeira – its name deriving from the local dialect word *deficeu,* meaning an olive oil press – is short pasta, for instance penne rigate, cooked raw in white wine, then seasoned with olive oil and cheese (see page 137).

Pasta as Ritual

In his book *The Italian Riviera,* published in 1928, Bohun Lynch describes watching a cook make tagliatelle in the kitchen of a trattoria in Levanto:

"You take flour and pile it on a large table kept exclusively for the purpose. You then make a hole in the flour and break an egg into it, and work it with your fingers, aided by a little water, until it is as smooth as silk. The paste is then rolled out with a three-foot rolling pin until it is so thin that you can see the grain of the wood beneath it. This sheet of paste is then spread upon a cloth to dry for half an hour or so. It is then rolled up tightly by hand, as though it were music or drawing-paper, and cut into thin slices as though it were a sausage. These slices are then deftly separated with the fingers, with the resulting appearance of *spaghetti,* save that the threads are square-sided, and not round. These are then put into boiling salt water and cooked for ten minutes or so, drained, and served up with one of the customary sauces. It is a very excellent dish, but the closest possible ritual must be observed in order to get it at its best."

Swiss Chard Gnocchi
"Merda de Can"

It is a curiosity of southern European cooking that appetizing dishes or foods are sometimes given lewd or scatological names – the firm little goat cheeses that the French call crottins ("turds"), the squiggly pasta shapes known in Rome as cazzetti d'angeli ("little angels' penises"), and so on. In that genre are these rather murky-looking but thoroughly delicious Niçois gnocchi, whose name literally means "dog shit consistency" (a reference to their shape and colour).

to serve 6

900 g/2 lb	medium potatoes, scrubbed
	Salt
350 g/12 oz	Swiss chard
	Extra-virgin olive oil
250 g/9 oz	flour
2	large eggs, lightly beaten

Cook potatoes, unpeeled, in a large saucepan of boiling, salted water for 30–40 minutes (depending on size), until done. Remove and immediately (and carefully) squeeze skins open and scoop out potato pulp.

While potatoes are cooking, trim stalks from chard, reserving them for another use, then cut into a very fine chiffonade and blanch for 5 minutes in another saucepan of boiling, salted water. Drain and set aside.

Mash potatoes with 2 tablespoons oil until very smooth. Very finely chop chard, then mash into potatoes. Salt to taste. Sift flour into potatoes, then add eggs. Work the dough together gently but firmly with your hands until all ingredients are well amalgamated and dough is formed into a large ball.

Take a small handful of dough at a time and roll it between your hands into a long sausage shape, about 2 cm/¾ inch thick and 10-12 cm/4-5 inches long. Cut dough into pieces 2.5-4 cm/1-1½ inches long and press the tines of a fork into 1 side of each one to leave an indent.

Let gnocchi dry slightly, spread out, for about 15 minutes, then cook in a large saucepan of boiling salted water, with a little oil added, until done, which should be no more than 3–5 minutes. Drain and serve with olive oil and Parmigiano-Reggiano, or with tocco (see page 103), or with the juice from daube de boeuf (see page 101), or toss with Parmigiano and finely chopped fresh and very ripe tomatoes.

Chestnut Gnocchi with Pine Nut Sauce
Cornetti

Cornetti are a speciality of the Valle Argentina in the western entroterra. The simple pine nut sauce is a typical condiment in the interior, especially in winter, when – in the days before greenhouse basil, at least – it was a common substitute for pesto.

to serve 4

225 g/8 oz	chestnut flour
350 g/12 oz	white flour
	Salt
115 g/4 oz	pine nuts
	Extra-virgin olive oil
	Grated Parmigiano-Reggiano

Mix chestnut flour with all but about 50 g/2 oz white flour in a large bowl, then mix in about 1 teaspoon salt. Add about 450 ml/16 fl oz of water gradually to the bowl, first stirring it in with a whisk and then working it by hand to form a pliant but firm dough, adding a little more water if necessary. (Dust your hands and work surface with a little additional flour so that dough doesn't stick.) Allow dough to sit, covered with a clean tea towel, for about ½ hour.

Spread remaining flour out on a pastry board or other work surface. Working as quickly as you can, take a piece of dough about the size of a grape and roll it between your hands (still floured) to form a baton-like shape about 4 cm/1½ inches long. Grasping each end of the baton, give each one a quick twist, then scoot it over onto the floured surface. (As long as they're dusted with flour, the gnocchi can be placed on top of one another.) When all gnocchi are made, set them aside for about ½ hour.

Crush pine nuts coarsely with a mortar and pestle or in a food processor (but, in the latter case, do not process too much; they should not be a smooth paste). Pour in a thin stream of olive oil and stir vigorously to obtain a thick but fluid sauce. Add salt to taste, then work in about 2 tablespoons Parmigiano.

Cook gnocchi in plenty of boiling salted water until done, which should only take 4 or 5 minutes. Drain thoroughly, then toss gently but thoroughly with sauce and additional Parmigiano to taste. Serve immediately.

Pasta Discs or Figure Eights
Corzetti

Unless you're particularly handy with wood-carving tools and want to make your own, there's really no substitute for authentic Genoese corzetti stamps – which are two-part affairs, the top stamp, with a rounded handle, fitting down into a moulded base (itself sometimes used to cut the corzetti out of the pasta sheets). Because stamping the pasta is time-consuming busy work, the chore was traditionally left to children – who were also considered appropriate to the task because of their presumably light hand. Even in Genoa today, corzetti stamps are hard to find and expensive (when I tracked one down, it cost about £21, and was of no particular distinction), which argues in favour of shaping corzetti in the figure-eight Val di Polceverera style – though of course there's nothing wrong with serving unstamped pasta discs.

to serve 6

350 g/12 oz cups	flour
	Salt
	Yolks of 4 large eggs

Sift flour into a mixing bowl, mix in about 1 teaspoon salt, then break eggs into flour. Work eggs in thoroughly with your hands, after first dusting them and your work surface with a bit of additional flour so that dough doesn't stick.

To make round corzetti, divide dough into four balls, then roll out one at a time, as thinly as possible, on a floured surface, or use pasta machine to No. 5 setting. Cut out circles of dough with a round biscuit cutter or the rim of a glass about 5 cm/2 inches in diameter, setting finished rounds aside on a floured surface. Repeat process until all the dough is used up, then work remaining cut-out pieces of dough together into another ball, roll out, and repeat the process.

To make figure-eight corzetti, leave dough in one large ball. Pinch a piece of dough about the size of a shelled walnut between your fingers, then grasp ends between your thumbs and forefingers (the fingertips of both hands should touch) and gently flatten and twist dough, slightly extending it to form a figure-eight shape. Repeat the process until all the dough is used up, setting figure eights aside on a floured surface as made.

Allow corzetti to dry in the refrigerator, spread out and covered loosely with a damp tea towel, for 24 hours, then cook in a large saucepan of boiling salted water until done – about 10 minutes. Serve with pesto (see page 63), tocco (see page 103), simple fresh tomato sauce, or melted butter with pine nuts and marjoram leaves lightly crushed together with a mortar and pestle.

Broad Green Sausage Noodles
Picagge Verði

Picagge verdi can also be made without sausage and cheese, and even without the greens; the plain version, specific to fast days, is sometimes called picagge in bianco. This more elaborate interpretation, though, is unusual and satisfying. (Colette Bourrier-Reynaud gives a recipe for a related Niçois pasta called capounets verts in her *Les Recettes de Réparate*; this pasta, which contains chard, spinach, leek greens, a little onion, and a few ounces of finely chopped salt pork, is cooked in a light pork bouillon and served with garlic sauce.)

to serve 4–6

225 g/8 oz	each borage leaves and Swiss chard or 450 g/1 lb Swiss chard
	Salt
115 g/4 oz	mild Italian sausage
350 g/12 oz	flour
3	large eggs
15 g/½ oz	Parmigiano-Reggiano, grated (about 2 tablespoons)

Trim stalks from chard, reserving them for another use. Cut chard (and borage, if using) into a very fine chiffonade and blanch by dropping into a saucepan of boiling, salted water for 5 minutes. Drain, squeeze as dry as possible, and set aside.

Meanwhile, cook sausage in 1 piece in boiling salted water for about 5 minutes. Allow to cool, then strip off casing, crumble meat very finely, and drain.

Sift flour into a mixing bowl, mix in about 1 teaspoon salt, then break eggs into flour and work them in thoroughly with your hands, after dusting them and your work surface with a little of the additional flour so that dough doesn't stick. Add sausage and Parmigiano and amalgamate well.

Divide dough into two balls, then roll one out as thinly as possible. Fold dough sheets gently over onto themselves to a width of about 5 cm/2 inches, then cut into strips measuring about 12 mm/½ inch wide. Gently unroll noodles and spread out on a tea towel to dry for 15–20 minutes.

Cook picagge in a large saucepan of boiling salted water until done – 10–15 minutes. Serve with oil or butter and a generous amount of Parmigiano, or with tocco (see page 103) and Parmigiano.

Spaghetti Cooked in Tomato Sauce
Fidelanza

It is said that this unusual pasta dish was invented by farmers in the western entroterra, who had to cook and eat their own lunch in the fields. Potable water was not always available, and only a limited amount could be carried over long distances, so these workers developed the technique of simmering their pasta directly in a sauce of water and fresh tomatoes – which they might very well have plucked right from the vine for the purpose. Fidelanza is also reminiscent of the fideus of Catalan Spain, in which short lengths of spaghetti-thin pasta are first browned in oil and then cooked directly in rich fish stock flavoured with tomatoes and onions.

to serve 4–6

1	onion, finely chopped
2	cloves garlic, minced
75 g/3 oz	pancetta or salt pork, finely diced
	Extra-virgin olive oil
1.5 kg/3 lb	tomatoes, skinned, seeded, and finely chopped
	Salt and freshly ground black pepper
8–10	basil leaves, roughly torn (optional)
450 g/1 lb	spaghetti or linguine
	Freshly grated Parmigiano-Reggiano

In a large, heavy-bottomed sauté pan, cook onion, garlic, and pancetta or salt pork in oil over low heat for 20–30 minutes, or until onions are tender and translucent. Add tomatoes, salt and pepper to taste, and basil (if using). Stir well, cover, and cook for 20 minutes over low heat.

Add 450 ml/16 fl oz water, bring water to a boil, then stir in pasta. Cook for 3–4 minutes at a boil, then reduce heat to low and continue cooking, uncovered, stirring frequently so that pasta doesn't stick together. Add more water, 125 ml/ 4 fl oz at a time, if necessary. Pasta should take about 30 minutes to cook, and sauce should reduce to a thick emulsion.

Serve with Parmigiano.

Pasta Cooked in Wine

Pasta alla Defiçeira

In the olive-growing towns above Bordighera and Sanremo, this dish was traditionally eaten to celebrate the first pressing of the fruit each year, and was seasoned with oil straight from the press. It was said to bring good luck.

to serve 4–6

1⅓	bottles Ligurian Vermentino or other dry white wine
	Salt
450 g/1 lb	maccheroni or penne rigate
	Extra-virgin olive oil
	Freshly grated Parmigiano-Reggiano

Bring wine and about 225 ml/8 fl oz water to a boil in a large saucepan. Add salt, then pasta. Reduce heat to a simmer and let cook, uncovered, stirring frequently, until liquid is completely absorbed and pasta is cooked – 18–20 minutes.

Stir in oil and Parmigiano to taste, and add salt if necessary.

RAVIOLI AND ITS COUSINS

O Raviêu o l'è ûn piatto bon, / Delicôu,
appetittoso, / Salûtare, sostanzioso. (Ravioli
is a good dish / Delicious, appetizing /
Healthful, substantial.)

– MARTIN PIAGGIO, "I RAVIÊU"

Ravioli are tiny, meat-filled envelopes made
of dough, so valuable they ought to be
marked REGISTERED.

– JOSEPH WECHSBERG,
BLUE TROUT AND
BLACK TRUFFLES

Ravioli, one of the most famous of all Italian pastas, is a Genoese invention – at least according to the Genoese. One popular tale has it that the word *ravioli* itself derives from a Genoese term, *rabiole,* meaning "leftovers" – for the miscellaneous material with which ravioli might be filled. (For the record, there's nothing close to that word in my Genoese dictionary; the standard term for leftovers is *avanzi.*) The *Grande enciclopedia illustrata della gastronomia,* on the other hand, states unequivocally that the term first appears in 1243 in the Cremona region, in Lombardy – which doesn't even border Liguria – and that it derives ultimately from *rapa,* the Latin word for turnip, with which the earliest ravioli (says the encyclopedia) were filled. Still another story attributes both the name of the pasta and the invention of the thing itself to a twelfth-century family named Raviolo, who were innkeepers in Gavi Ligure – once part of Liguria but now in the neighbouring region of Piedmont, in the province of Alessandria. (An early Genoese name for ravioli, incidentally, was *lasagne cun u zembu,* hump-backed pasta sheets.)

The idea of ravioli – which are merely filled dumplings of various kinds – is an obvious and ancient one. Paolo Lingua points out that ancestors of ravioli were eaten in Babylonia, Egypt, Greece, and Rome. The steamed or fried dumplings of China and Japan bear a familial resemblance to ravioli as well.

There is a cult of ravioli in Liguria and Nice, where it is widely considered "the queen of all *minestre* [thick soups] in the world" – to quote G. B. and Gio Ratto in *La cuciniera genovese.* It is a definitive "party dish," indispensable on

Christmas Eve and New Year's Eve and – especially in Nice and western Liguria – for Carnival. As noted earlier, it has inspired poetry. It even figures in a twelfth-century miracle: Franco Accame, who considers ravioli an expression of the poetic, fanciful side of the Genoese character, reports that, in the course of the beatification proceedings for the Sicilian hermit Gugleilmo di Malavalle, it was affirmed that "when he happened to be served, one day, ravioli filled with lowly chaff, he blessed them and they changed into exquisite food." And after the Italian Futurist poet Marinetti denounced pasta in 1930 and banned it from the Futurist table, a group of his Ligurian acolytes published a spirited defense of ravioli in the Genoese newspaper *Il Lavoro* – citing the Rattos to prove that it was technically a minestra and not a pasta, and thus could continue to be consumed in good conscience in the Futurist camp.

Joseph Wechsberg to the contrary, ravioli are not necessarily filled with meat. The formal, celebratory Genoese version of the thing does indeed boast a meat and offal-meat interior, and in Nice a bit of daube may be included – but ravioli filled only with cheese and herbs or with greens are common, and there are even ravioli stuffed with fish. Until around the time of Boccaccio (1313–1375), incidentally, ravioli were apparently sweet. Boccaccio, though, describes a dish of ravioli in capon broth, rolled in a mountain of grated cheese.

Ravioli has several close cousins along the Riviera. The raviolos of St. Étienne-de-Tinée – made with egg dough; filled with Swiss chard, cabbage and potatoes, leeks and potatoes, or dandelion greens; and served with tomato sauce, the juice of a daube, a simple walnut sauce, or just garlic and grated cheese – are made in the form of (as they say in the local dialect) *en chapel de jendarmo,* an old-fashioned gendarme's hat, a sort of misshapen crescent swollen in the middle and peaked at the ends. The boursotou (or boussotou, or borsotti; the word may relate to *borsa,* Italian for purse or bag) of the eastern Niçois backcountry were traditionally student fare. It is said that there are ten ways to make them and one hundred occasions on which to eat them. Colette Bourrier-Reynaud gives a recipe calling for a filling of leeks, Swiss chard, spinach, rice, anchovies, and grated cheese wrapped ravioli style in egg-dough pasta, and then fried to a golden-brown in oil. She adds that in Breil-sur-Roya, where boursotou are particularly esteemed, they are served abundantly at the beginning of a meal and then left on the table throughout – to be, inevitably, gobbled up entirely by the time the meal is through.

More famous along the coast, especially in Nice and Menton, are barbajouan (literally "Uncle John"), which are more or less the same thing as boursotou. These are also fried ravioli, stuffed sometimes with pumpkin, sometimes with greens, sometimes with ricotta. On the far eastern end of Liguria, which is prime frying country, the attractive town of Levanto has its own version of chard-stuffed fried ravioli, called gattafin – a word of mysterious origin, also used to describe certain kinds of cake, apparently dating from the fourteenth century.

Pansotti (pansòuti in Genoese) are an appealing eastern Ligurian variation on ravioli, with plenty of lore attached. These plump, vaguely triangular little dumplings – their name derives from the Italian word *panciuto,* meaning corpulent or potbellied – are nearly always filled with mixed green herbs and graced with a walnut sauce. This sauce is sometimes said to have Persian origins, but it seems more likely that it may have been developed in the Genoese colonies on the Black Sea, where walnuts are an integral part of the indigenous cuisine.

The greens are traditionally a mixture known as preboggion. A colourful folk etymology links the name with that of a Genoese crusader, Goffredo di Buglione. According to the story, di Buglione, suffering in his tent in the Holy Land from an unspecified illness, was restored to health by herbs gathered from nearby fields. The herbs were said to have been "per Buglione," which evolved into "prebuggiun." A far more likely explanation is that the word – which first appears in print only in the mid-nineteenth century – derives from *per bollire,* meaning either "for boiling" or perhaps "par-boiling," because the mixture is always cooked in water. (The same word, incidentally, is used in the upper Val Graveglia as a synonym for minestrone.)

Around the Golfo di Tigullio, in the hills above Rapallo and Chiavari, the ritualistic recipe for preboggion – which is almost always gathered by women, and either pulled from the ground or cut with a kind of blunt grafting knife – is said to include seven herbs: cicerbita (sow thistle), pimpernel, borage, chard, flat-leaf parsley, and what are apparently two relatives of dandelion, called talegna or talegua (see page 86) and dente di cane, respectively. In her work for the EEC-funded Produits de terroir en Europe du Sud (etc.) project, Giuseppina Poggi of the University of Genoa has catalogued a dozen ingredients for the typical mixture in the hills behind Recco – among them dandelion, pimpernel, and cow thistle, but also miniature poppy, ranuncula, and balsam leaves.

Paganini's Ravioli

Nicolò Paganini (1782–1840), the famous Genoese-born virtuoso violinist and composer, had interests other than music. Among other things, he was a compulsive gambler (he lost a small fortune at one point on a scheme to establish a gambling casino with a concert-hall annex in Paris), a serious drinker, and a lover of good food. In the year of his death, living on the Rue de la Préfecture in Vieux Nice, he wrote down his recipe for one of his favourite dishes – ravioli. The Paganini expert Renato De Barbieri, also Genoese, discovered the recipe some years ago in a manuscript now in the Library of Congress in Washington, D.C. It reads approximately like this:

"The stuffing for ravioli: For [dough made from] a *libra* [about 300 g/11 oz] and a half of flour, two *libre* of good lean meat [is needed] to make the sauce. In a pan, put some butter and then a little onion, finely chopped, and fry it for a little while. Add the meat and cook it until it begins to colour. And to obtain a consistent sauce, take a few pinches of flour and slowly, slowly *[adagio, adagio]* scatter it over the sauce until it browns, too. Then take some conserved tomatoes, dissolve them in water, and stir this water into the flour in the pan and mix to dissolve it completely; finally add dried mushrooms, finely chopped and crushed with a pestle, and that makes the sauce.

"Now we come to the pasta: Stretch out the leaves of dough without eggs. A few grains salt with the pasta is useful to give it a uniform consistency.

"Now we come to the stuffing. In the same pan with the meat [sauce], put into the sauce to cook a half *libra* of lean veal, then remove it, chop it, and crush it well. Take a calf's brain and cook it in water, then remove the skin which covers the brain; chop and crush the brain separately; take four *soldi* worth of luganega sausage, remove the skin, and chop and crush it separately like the meat. Take a handful of borage, called 'Boraj' in Nice, boil it, squeeze it dry, and crush it as above.

"Take three eggs, which are sufficient for [dough made with] a *libra* and a half of flour. Beat the eggs and unite them with the ingredients mentioned above, crushing them together with them; in said eggs place a bit of Parmigiano. That makes the filling.

"One can serve capon in place of the veal, and sweetbreads in place of the brains, to obtain a more delicate stuffing. If the stuffing remains firm, add some sauce. For ravioli, the pasta should remain fairly soft. Leave it for an hour covered by a plate to obtain thin sheets."

Ravioli alla Genovese

Martin Piaggio's poem "Riçetta per fâ i raviêu" – a recipe in verse form – specifies a ravioli filling of cow's udder, calf's brains, sweetbreads, marrow, and spinal marrow, among other ingredients, as well as prescinsêua (see page 124). An elaboration of Piaggio's instructions in Emanuele Rossi's *La vera cuciniera genovese* calls for both calf's and lamb's brains. The idea in either case is to achieve a filling of quenelle-like texture, both rich and delicate. The following recipe is based largely on both Piaggio's and Rossi's – with adjustments made for the sake of clarity, consistency, and the realities of the modern market and the modern kitchen. This is a rich, complex, special-occasion ravioli, it might be noted – not the kind that uses up leftovers.

to serve 6–8

350 g/12 oz	flour
	Salt
7	large eggs and yolks from 2 large eggs
	Extra-virgin olive oil
450 g/1 lb	or escarole leaves, trimmed and cut into a chiffonade
225 g/8 oz	veal sweetbreads
225 g/8 oz	calf's brains
225 g/8 oz	beef marrow
225 g/8 oz	long-cooked lean veal (i.e., from tocco; see page 103)
75 g/3 oz	prescinsêua or ricotta (see page 124)
	Tocco (meat sauce; see page 103)
	Freshly grated Parmigiano-Reggiano or pecorino Sardo

Mix flour and 1 teaspoon salt together in a large bowl. In another bowl, beat 5 eggs and 3 tablespoons oil together. Make a well in centre of flour and add egg mixture, stirring it into flour with a fork until it holds together but is very crumbly. Turn out dough onto a lightly floured work surface, divide into 2 pieces, and knead for 2–3 minutes, until smooth. Cover dough with waxed paper and refrigerate for at least 1 hour.

Meanwhile, cook borage in boiling salted water for about 10 minutes, or until very tender. Drain and set aside.

Peel skin and membranes from sweetbreads, cut into 3 or 4 pieces, and blanch in boiling salted water for 10 minutes. Drain and set aside. Blanch calf's brains, in one piece, similarly, and again drain and set aside.

143

Place beef marrow in a small bowl of boiling water for 2 minutes. Drain and set aside.

Finely chop borage sweetbreads, calf's brains, marrow, and lean veal, then mix together well in a large bowl. Add remaining eggs and egg yolks and prescinsêua or ricotta and incorporate well. Season generously with salt, then pass mixture through a food mill to form a coarse purée.

Remove dough from refrigerator and cut into an even number of strips to fit a pasta machine. Roll each strip through machineon setting No. 6 to form

thin dough sheets. As each one is done, lay it out on a lightly floured work surface.

Place about ½ teaspoon of filling about 2.5 cm/1 inch in from 1 corner of 1 dough sheet. Flatten it very slightly with the back of a spoon, then repeat the process, leaving about 2.5 cm/1 inch of dough on all sides of each portion of filling. When 1 sheet is filled, place another sheet over it and lightly but firmly crimp the edges and press down the dough between the portions of filling. Cut the ravioli into squares with a pizza cutter or long knife. Repeat the process until all the filling is used up.

Heat tocco. Meanwhile, cook ravioli in a large saucepan of boiling salted water until they float to the top and are done, 3–4 minutes. Gently drain, place in a large, wide bowl, and pour tocco over them. Do not stir. Serve with Parmigiano on the side. (In place of tocco, you can also drizzle olive oil or melted butter over the ravioli and sprinkle generously with grated cheese before serving.)

Artichoke Ravioli with Thyme
Ravioli di Carciofi al Profumo di Timo

From the shaded terrace in front of Ristorante Gastone on the Piazza Garibaldi, the western Ligurian wine town of Dolceacqua ("Sweetwater") is very pretty. Visiting here in 1861, Augustus J. C. Hare described it thus: "[Dolceacqua] suddenly burst upon the view stretching across a valley, whose sides are covered with forests of olives and chesnuts [sic], and which is backed by fine snow-mountains. Through the town winds the deep blue stream of the Nervia, flowing under a tall bridge, which is like the Rialto of Venice, in its great span and height, and above frowns the huge palatial castle of the Dorias, perched upon a perpendicular cliff, with sunlight streaming through its long lines of glassless windows. . . ."

The view is scarcely less impressive today. Just across the road from Gastone runs the broad, rocky bed of the Nervia, now more a trickle than a deep blue stream. The bridge, of unusual gracefulness if not exactly another Rialto, is intact. Beyond it are simple but attractive houses in clean pastel shades or white or beige, all with shutters in various shades of green, and a perfect little medieval church. The hill above the river is cloaked in terraced vines, and on one crest, the dramatic ruined castle of the Dorias still stands.

Back on the terrace at Gastone, meanwhile, I am very likely eating this excellent interpretation of ravioli – not a traditional dish, as the restaurant's proprietor, Delio Viale, is quick to say, but one based on tradition, which uses three of the most famous products of the Dolceacqua area: artichokes, olive oil, and wild thyme. (Note that this ravioli dough is made without eggs – reflecting the comparative poverty of the entroterra as compared with Genoa or Nice – and hence will be lighter and more fragile than the dough in the previous recipes.)

to serve 4

275 g/10 oz	flour
	Salt
125 ml/4 fl oz	extra-virgin olive oil
10	medium artichokes
	Juice of 3 lemons
2	leeks, white parts only, sliced into thin rings
2 tablespoons	ricotta
	Freshly grated Parmigiano-Reggiano
3	large eggs, lightly beaten
	Freshly ground black pepper
115 g/4 oz	unsalted butter
	Leaves from 6–8 sprigs thyme
50 g/2 oz	pine nuts

Mix 275 g/10 oz flour and 1 teaspoon salt together in a large bowl with 3 tablespoons olive oil and enough warm water to form a firm but supple dough. Turn out dough onto a lightly floured work surface, divide into 2 pieces, and knead each briefly in turn. Cover dough with waxed paper and set aside in the refrigerator.

Meanwhile, cut stems off artichokes. Pull off tough outer leaves by hand, and trim off more layers of leaves with a sharp knife until only tender ones remain. Scoop out and discard the chokes, chop artichokes into small pieces, and place the pieces in a bowl large enough to hold them all. Cover them with water mixed with lemon juice.

Cook leeks in remaining olive oil over low heat for about 5 minutes, then add artichokes. Cover and continue cooking for 15–20 minutes longer or until artichokes are very tender. Put leeks and artichokes through a mirlis-legumes or food processor to obtain a smooth paste. Stir in ricotta, about 3 tablespoons Parmigiano, and eggs. Season generously with salt and pepper.

Remove dough from refrigerator and cut into an even number of strips to fit a pasta machine. Roll each strip through all settings in machine to form thin dough sheets. As each one is done, lay it out on a lightly floured work surface.

Place about ½ teaspoon of filling about 2.5 cm/1 inch in from 1 corner of 1 dough sheet. Flatten it very slightly with the back of a spoon, then repeat the process, leaving about 2.5 cm/1 inch of dough on all sides of each portion of filling. When 1 sheet is filled, place another sheet over it and lightly but firmly crimp the edges and press down the dough between the portions of filling. Cut the ravioli into squares with a pizza cutter or long knife. Repeat the process until all the filling is used up, then refrigerate the ravioli for 30 minutes to an hour on a floured board.

About 10 minutes before cooking ravioli, melt butter in a pan over low heat and add thyme leaves. Crush pine nuts coarsely with a mortar and pestle and stir them into butter.

Cook ravioli in a large saucepan of boiling salted water until they float to the top and are done, 3–4 minutes. Gently drain, then place in a large bowl and pour butter sauce over them. Season with salt and pepper and serve with additional Parmigiano.

Niçois Fried Ravioli

Barbajouan

How these addictive little packets of fried dough enclosing ricotta, greens, or puréed squash got their name is something of a mystery. It literally means "Uncle John" in Niçois, but nobody seems to know just who this particular uncle might have been, or why this speciality was named after him. It is entirely possible, in fact, that the name isn't a tribute to some avuncular personality at all but rather an insult of one variety or another, applied to the dish for some long-forgotten reason: Barbagianni or Barba Zanni was a character noted for his clumsiness in classic Commedia dell'Arte; in Genoese slang today, a barbaggion is a grumbler; and in earlier times in Nice, a barbajouan (or barbalùcou) was a simpleton. These less than complimentary associations aside, barbajouan are quite delicious. This recipe is from Franck Cerutti of Don Camillo in Nice.

to serve 4–6

350 g/12 oz	flour
	Salt
6	large eggs
	Extra-virgin olive oil
1	onion, very finely chopped
450 g/1 lb	ricotta
115 g/4 oz	prosciutto di Parma or other good-quality cured ham, julienned and chopped
50 g/2 oz	Parmigiano-Reggiano, grated
	Freshly ground black pepper
	Vegetable oil

Make ravioli dough with flour, 1 teaspoon salt, 5 eggs, and 3 tablespoons olive oil, according to step one in the recipe for Ravioli alla Genovese (page 143). Refrigerate for at least 3 hours.

To make barbajouan, cook onion in 2–3 tablespoons olive oil over low heat for 15–20 minutes or until soft and golden.

Place ricotta in a bowl, then mix in onion, prosciutto, Parmigiano, remaining egg, and salt and pepper to taste.

Remove dough from refrigerator and cut into an even number of strips to fit a pasta machine. Roll each strip through machine on setting No. 6 to form thin dough sheets. As each one is done, lay it out on a lightly floured work surface.

Place about ½ teaspoon of filling about 2.5 cm/1 inch in from 1 corner of 1 dough sheet. Flatten it very slightly with the back of a spoon, then repeat the process, leaving about 2.5 cm/1 inch of dough on all sides of each portion of filling. When 1 sheet is filled, place another sheet over it and lightly but firmly crimp the edges and press down the dough between the portions of filling. Cut the ravioli into squares with a pizza cutter or long knife. Repeat the process until all the filling is used up, then refrigerate the ravioli for 30 minutes to an hour on a floured board.

Fill a deep cast iron frying pan or other deep, heavy pan with about 5 cm/2 inches of vegetable oil and heat to about 190°C/375°F, or use a deep-fryer, and fry ravioli in small batches until light golden-brown. Alternately, bake for 4–5 minutes on a lightly greased baking tray in a preheated 190°C/375°F/Gas Mark 5 oven, until light brown. Serve immediately.

Raviolis à la Niçoise

This is another, far simpler interpretation of ravioli, adapted from a recipe offered by chef Franck Cerutti of Don Camillo in Nice. Unlike the Genoese ravioli on page 143, this version does depend on leftovers of a sort: It calls for some of both the meat and the juice of a daube – and nobody in the region would dream of making one specifically for the purpose.

to serve 4–6

175 g/7 oz	flour
	Salt
2	large eggs
	Extra-virgin olive oil
	Flour
900 g/2 lb	Swiss chard
450 g/1 lb	meat from daube (see page 101)
	Freshly grated Parmigiano-Reggiano
2	large egg yolks, lightly beaten
225 ml/8 fl oz	sauce from daube (see page 101)
	Freshly ground black pepper
	Balsamic vinegar

Mix flour and a pinch of salt together in a large bowl. In another bowl, beat whole eggs and 5 teaspoons oil together. Make a well in centre of flour and add egg mixture, stirring it into flour with a fork until it holds together but is very crumbly. Turn out dough onto a lightly floured work surface, divide into 2 pieces, and knead each briefly in turn. Cover dough with waxed paper and refrigerate for at least 1 hour.

Remove stalks and ribs from chard and reserve for another use. Steam chard leaves for about 15 minutes in a small quantity of salted water, then drain, cool under a cold tap, and squeeze out as much moisture as possible. Chop chard very finely and set aside.

Very finely chop meat from daube and mix into chard. Mix in 50 g/2 oz Parmigiano and egg yolks, then set mixture aside.

Remove dough from refrigerator and cut into an even number of strips to fit a pasta machine. Roll each strip through all settings in machine to form thin dough sheets. As each one is done, lay it out on a lightly floured work surface.

Place about ½ teaspoon of filling about 2.5 cm/1 inch in from 1 corner of 1 dough sheet. Flatten it very slightly with the back of a spoon, then repeat the process, leaving about 2.5 cm/1 inch of dough on all sides of each portion of filling. When 1 sheet is filled, place another sheet over it and lightly but firmly crimp the edges and press down the dough between the portions of filling. Cut the ravioli into circles with a 5 cm/2 inch biscuit cutter or the rim of a glass. (Leftover dough may be used for another purpose.) Repeat the process until all the filling is used up, then refrigerate the ravioli for 30 minutes to an hour on a floured board.

Heat daube sauce in a large saucepan. Meanwhile, cook ravioli in a large saucepan of boiling salted water until they float to the top and are done, 3–4 minutes. Gently drain, then add to pan with daube sauce, stirring to cover all ravioli with a thin glaze of sauce. Season with salt and pepper, then spoon onto plates. Before serving, drizzle ravioli lightly with balsamic vinegar and olive oil and dust lightly with Parmigiano.

Red Mullet Ravioli in Their Own Sauce

Ravioli di Triglia nel loro Sugo

With a handful of exceptions, Liguria doesn't really have a fish cuisine in the sense that, say, Provence or Catalonia does – and the idea of seafood ravioli is a comparatively recent one. It doesn't appear in either of the earliest purely Genoese cookbooks, *La cuciniera genovese* (1864) or *La vera cuciniera genovese facile ed economica* (1865 or 1866). On the other hand, three recipes for ravioli stuffed with puréed fish, mixed with various other ingredients, do appear in Gaspare Dellepiane's *La Cucina di strettissimo magro: senza carne, uova e latticini,* first published in 1880 – so it's obviously not a completely contemporary notion. Dellepiane, in fact, even gives recipes for ravioli stuffed with chopped-up oysters (combined with escarole, anchovies, garlic, parsley, and pine nuts) and even with caviar (plus escarole and pine nuts, but thankfully no anchovies or garlic in this case) – neither of which, frankly, sounds very good.

What does sound good, and *is* good, is ravioli filled with red mullet – a dish found with increasing frequency on the Riviera di Levante today. Often, this ravioli is served with simple tomato sauce, but this version, which Franco and Melly Solari offer at Ca' Peo in Leivi, has mullet inside and out.

to serve 4

675 g/1½ lb	whole red mullets, or sea bass
125 ml/4 fl oz	dry white wine
1	carrot
1	onion
4	flat-leaf parsley sprigs, minced
	Bouquet garni of 2 sprigs marjoram, 2 sprigs mint, 1 leafy interior celery stalk, and 1 bay leaf, tied together with kitchen string
50 g/2 oz	unsalted butter
3	large eggs
175 g/6 oz	ricotta
25 g/1 oz	Parmigiano-Reggiano, grated
	Salt and freshly ground black pepper
275 g/10 oz	flour
2	garlic cloves, minced
4	plum tomatoes, skinned, seeded, and chopped

Scale, fillet, and bone the fish, reserving heads and bones. Place these in a pot with wine, carrot, onion, ½ the parsley, and bouquet garni. Add enough water to barely cover ingredients, bring to a boil, reduce heat, then let simmer for about 1 hour.

Meanwhile, set aside about ½ of the fish. Cook the rest in half the butter over low heat until done, 4–5 minutes, then crush it to a paste with a mortar and pestle. Mix in 1 egg, ricotta, and Parmigiano, and season generously with salt and pepper. Set aside.

Mix flour and a pinch of salt together in a large bowl. Make a well in centre of flour and add remaining eggs, stirring them into flour with a fork until it holds together but is very crumbly. Turn out dough onto a lightly floured work surface, divide into 2 pieces, and knead each briefly in turn. Cover dough with waxed paper and refrigerate for 30 minutes, then remove dough from refrigerator and cut into an even number of strips to fit a pasta machine. Roll each strip through machine on setting No. 6 to form thin dough sheets. As each one is done, lay it out on a lightly floured work surface.

Place about ½ teaspoon of filling about 2 cm/¾ inch in from 1 corner of 1 dough sheet. Flatten it very slightly with the back of a spoon, then repeat the process, leaving about 2 cm/¾ inch of dough on all sides of each portion of filling. When 1 sheet is filled, place another sheet over it and lightly but firmly crimp the edges and press down the dough between the portions of filling. Cut the ravioli into squares with a pizza cutter or long knife. Repeat the process until all the filling is used up, then refrigerate the ravioli for 30 minutes to an hour on a floured board.

Cook garlic in remaining butter over low heat for about 5 minutes, then add tomatoes. Strain fish fumet into the pan, and add reserved fish. Raise heat and cook at a slow boil for 10–15 minutes, or until liquid reduces and sauce thickens. Reduce heat to very low, break up fish with a fork, add salt and pepper to taste, and add remaining parsley.

Cook ravioli in a large saucepan of boiling salted water until they float to the top and are done, 3–4 minutes. Transfer to a serving bowl and spoon fish sauce over them.

"Potbellied" Ravioli with Walnut Sauce
Pansotti con Salsa di Noci

Though pansotti are traditionally filled with the herb-and-green mixture called preboggion, such exotic leaves as pimpernel and sow thistle are not essential to the dish. The important thing is that the ravioli should be filled with a combination of greens, at least some of which are mildly bitter and have a bit of pungency – to provide a contrast with the rich, almost unctuous walnut sauce. Chard, spinach, and/or borage are a good place to start, but some member of the chicory family is always a good addition, and parsley never hurts. A handful of miscellaneous mesclun greens (see page 84) would be in the right spirit, too.

to serve 6

350 g/12 oz	flour
	Salt
7	large eggs
	Extra-virgin olive oil
450 g/1 lb	Swiss chard
450 g/1 lb	spinach (or 225 g/8 oz each spinach and borage leaves), julienned

1	small head radicchio, julienned
4	sprigs flat-leaf parsley, minced
225 g/8 oz	other assorted greens (curly endive, escarole, dandelion greens, mustard greens, etc.), julienned
350 g/12 oz	ricotta or prescinsêua (see page 124)
	Pinch of nutmeg
3 tablespoons	pine nuts
225 g/8 oz	shelled walnuts, very finely chopped
1	garlic clove
	Leaves from 4–5 sprigs marjoram

Make ravioli dough with flour, 1 teaspoon salt, 5 eggs, and 3 tablespoons oil, according to step one in the recipe for Ravioli alla Genovese (page 143).

Trim stalks from chard, reserving them for another use, then cut leaves into a very fine chiffonade and blanch for 5 minutes in a saucepan of boiling, salted water. Add julienned spinach, radicchio, parsley, and other greens to chard and continue cooking for about 3 minutes. Drain thoroughly and transfer to a large bowl. Allow to cool to room temperature, then lightly beat remaining 2 eggs and add to vegetables. Mix thoroughly and add 225 g/8 oz of ricotta or prescinsêua, nutmeg, and salt to taste.

Remove dough from refrigerator and cut into an even number of strips to fit a pasta machine. Roll each strip through machine to form thin dough sheets. As each one is done, lay it out on a lightly floured work surface.

With your hands, form filling into small spheres slightly smaller than Ping-Pong balls. Place 1 sphere about 5 cm/2 inches in from 1 corner of 1 dough sheet. Repeat the process, leaving about 5 cm/2 inches of dough on all sides of each sphere. When 1 sheet is filled, place another sheet over it and lightly but firmly crimp the edges and press down the dough between the portions of filling. Cut the ravioli into triangles with a pizza cutter or long knife. Repeat the process until all the filling is used up, then refrigerate ravioli on a floured board.

Toast pine nuts lightly by placing them in a small, heavy, dry frying pan over high heat and shaking pan until they start to colour. Transfer them immediately to a paper towel to cool.

Place walnuts, pine nuts, garlic, marjoram, and a pinch or two of salt in a large mortar and grind to a paste. When nuts are thoroughly crushed, work in remaining ricotta or prescinsêua, then drizzle in 6-8 tablespoons olive oil and continue working until mixture is thick and creamy. Thin slightly by working in 1 or 2 tablespoons warm water.

Cook pansotti in a large saucepan of boiling salted water until they float to the top and are done, 3–4 minutes. Gently drain, transfer to a serving bowl, and carefully stir in sauce.

PROTOPASTA

A tæra neigra a fa bon gran.
(Dark earth yields good wheat.)
— GENOESE PROVERB

In eating my way around the Riviera, I have encountered three particularly unusual, obviously ancient dishes, which I think of as protopasta – ancestors of the noodle preparations we know so well. Two of these are made not from flour-based noodles but from unmilled wheat, or one of its relatives. A third, though it involves a flour-and-water dough, seems more an intermediate step between flatbread and pasta than pasta itself.

The most celebrated of these dishes is mescciuà or mesc-ciua, from the city of La Spezia, on the southeastern end of Liguria. La Spezia, with a population of just over 100,000, is the second-largest city in Liguria, Italy's most important naval base, and a major commercial port and industrial centre. Napoleon once called it "the most beautiful port in the universe," though that may have had to do with the ease with which it can be defended: It sits at the head of a long, comparatively narrow bay.

The port is, in any case, considerably less imposing than that of Genoa, and more accessible to its city's population. After dinner at a moored barge-restaurant on the Molo Italia one evening, I walked farther out on the pier, past a veritable fleet of sleeping fishing trawlers, some of them draped with drying nets. In the distance was the huge, yellow-lit container section of the port, but at the end of the pier, near a squat cartoon-red lighthouse, a man sat hopefully in a battered old Fiat coupe, with the motor running, watching three fishing poles he'd propped up against the rail. And walking back toward terra firma, I realized that other dark cars I'd passed along the way, parked along the edges of the pier, were almost all occupied by couples – talking, smoking, occasionally kissing. Couples do not go out alone at night on the piers of the port of Genoa.

Its importance as a port aside, La Spezia is also the easternmost gastronomic outpost of Liguria. Its very name apparently derives from *spezie,* meaning spices; as the closest Genoese port to the eastern Mediterranean, it was the logical place for these precious commodities to be unloaded. Today, the local cuisine is hearty and surprisingly varied, and known primarily for three things: fried foods, ranging from delicate fragments of fried dough to substantial salt cod fritters; mussels, which have been grown commercially here since the late nineteenth century; and mescciuà.

Mescciuà – whose name, pronounced approximately "mess-chewu-A," is derived from the Genoese verb *mescciâ,* to mix or blend – is simply a hearty, starchy assemblage of chickpeas, white beans, and either wheat, buckwheat, or spelt (farro in Italian, färo in Genoese – an old variety of summer wheat, now enjoying something of a comeback in Europe), seasoned with olive oil and black pepper. Tradition holds that mescciuà was invented by impoverished local stevedores who scoured the port picking up odds and ends of grains and legumes that had fallen out of sacks being unloaded from ships, combining them to make a filling and nutritious meal.

Genoese author Vito Elio Petrucci doesn't buy this story. He says that chickpeas were already grown in the region; that white beans were also grown there, and that if they had been imported, they would most likely have come overland from adjacent Tuscany; and that every house, however poor, was apt to own a sack of grain. He opines that the dish was born, as he puts it, not of *polvere* (dust) but of *povertà* (poverty). Of course, it would have been poverty that inspired the foraging for "dust" – and the sacks in question might have been outbound rather than incoming.

However its constituent elements were first collected, mescciuà is just the sort of thing that might have been assembled by the thrifty, crafty La Spezians when there was not quite enough grain to grind for bread, and not quite enough beans for a fagiolata – a popular local dish of beans cooked with pork. In any case, warns Ligurian food expert Franco Accame, mescciuà is a dish in which "the poverty of the raw materials . . . is inversely proportionate to the ability and experience necessary for its honest preparation" – which of course might be said of much Ligurian cuisine.

A dish obviously much older than mescciuà – white beans are post-Columbian – is gran pistau, a name that literally means "grain crushed with a pestle." This is a speciality of the western entroterra, and especially the Val di Nervia, in which whole wheat berries are soaked in water, worked vigorously in a mortar or large wooden bowl with a pestle for at least half an hour (or, say traditionalists, for

300 blows), and then sifted to separate out the now-detached glume or chaff. Next, it is cooked for many hours (at least four and as many as twelve), and finally mixed with a soffritto based on leeks, perhaps with pork added. Bordighera restaurateur and food historian Romolo Giordano (La Via Romana) says that fatty lamb meat was sometimes used in place of pork in earlier times. He has also seen versions using sausage, potatoes, and/or assorted herbs. "In the old days," he explains, "every family had its own version of gran pistau."

A dish very much like gran pistau, he adds, was eaten by the Greeks and the Romans. Indeed, Greek food expert Diane Kochilas tells me that the people of Samos, Chios, and Lesbos still eat festive dishes known as keskeki, in which exactly the same kind of wheatberries are crushed in large mortars and cooked over low fires overnight, then combined with meat, chestnuts, raisins, and, just as in Liguria, leeks.

Testaroli (testaieu in Genovese) are a bit more sophisticated. Claimed by the Lunigiani as a local invention, and seldom found west of Genoa, these are pancake-like rounds of pasta dough less than a 6 mm/¼ inch thick – they suggest something between blinis and tortillas – traditionally cooked in a highly specialized way. They take their name from *testelli,* which are shallow, unglazed ceramic bowls about 15 cm/6 inches in diameter, made from a rare kind of diathermic clay. To cook testaroli, the empty testelli are heated over a fire or in an oven, then each one is filled with raw dough; the testelli are then stacked on top of one another, with chestnut leaves separating them, and the testaroli are left to bake in the radiated heat. The more modern method is to cook them on a griddle or in cast-iron pans, like the pancakes (etc.) they resemble – but this is frowned upon by purists. (Testaroli are usually fairly small, perhaps 15 cm/6 inches or so in diameter, and served whole; sometimes, however, they are made on a larger scale, perhaps 28-30 cm/15-16 inches across, and cut into wedges for serving.)

According to the Genoese agricultural historian Diego Moreno, testelli have been found in archaeological sites dating back at least to the Iron Age (their name comes from the Latin *testa,* pottery shard) – suggesting that something like testaroli might have been eaten that long ago. Testaroli are usually made with white flour, but sometimes chestnut or a mix of chestnut and white flour is used – and Moreno says he has encountered corn-flour testaroli, which must seem very much like tortillas indeed. (I've also heard about, though never encountered, a kind of Ligurian quesadilla, if you will, in which ricotta is sandwiched between two chestnut-flour testaroli; this is reportedly a speciality of the upper Val di Magra.)

Many sources recommend allowing the testaroli to dry somewhat and then cutting them into strips and boiling them in water before tossing them with a sauce. When I first sampled them, however, at the farmhouse restaurant called Ca' Ertà in San Bernardino, above Sestri Levante, they were served whole, and smeared with pesto or scattered with cheese. There is a variation on testaroli called panigacci or panigazzi; these are virtually the same thing but are made with about a third less flour, and are thus even thinner than testaroli.

Mescciuà

Some traditionalists maintain that mescciuà should be made with buckwheat instead of regular wheat; others hold out for spelt. There is also a version of mescciuà, from the Val Graveglia, made with no grain at all – its place taken by dried favas, probably reflecting the scarceness of wheat in the region. (The problem with dried favas is that they turn the dish a muddy black.) The most common version of the dish today, however, is made with wheatberries.

Some recipes call for all three principal ingredients to be soaked and cooked separately; some combine the grain and chickpeas for both soaking and cooking, or at least for the latter. Almost everyone agrees that, once the ingredients are mixed, they should be seasoned only with olive oil, salt, and plenty of black pepper; a sprinkling of grated cheese adds complexity to the dish but is widely considered heretical. Mescciuà is admittedly an acquired taste; it is not a subtle dish, but some people find it a bland one. I find it wonderfully restorative myself, especially with good bread on the side, and especially in cold weather.

This recipe comes from an audiotape entitled "Il Segreto della Mescciuà/La Farinata," released by the Accademia Lunigianese di Scienze Giovanni Capellini in La Spezia. On it, two authoritative-sounding women of the city, identified only as Nella and Pietrina, describe the process of making the dish approximately like this.

to serve 6

350 g/12 oz	dried chickpeas
115 g/4 oz	raw wheatberries or spelt
225 g/8 oz	dried white beans (preferably cannellini or fagioli di Spagna)
	Coarse salt
	Extra-virgin olive oil
	Freshly ground black pepper

The night before making mescciuà, place chickpeas, wheatberries and white beans in three separate large bowls. Cover them all with an ample quantity of warm water, and stir 2 pinches of salt into the chickpeas and the wheatberries.

The next day, drain all three ingredients. Place the chickpeas and wheatberries or spelt in a large saucepan and cover them with cold water. Bring to a boil, then reduce heat and cook, uncovered, for 3 hours.

Meanwhile, place the white beans in another saucepan, also covered with ample cold water, and cook them for 1–2 hours, or until done. When the chickpeas are tender enough that a fork will pierce them, transfer the white beans to their pan with a slotted spoon or sieve. Continue cooking for several minutes longer. Mescciuà should be densely soupy. If it has too much liquid, drain some off.

Transfer to individual bowls. Drizzle olive oil over each one and season to taste with salt and plenty of black pepper. (The common wisdom is that mescciuà should be eaten hot in winter and lukewarm in spring, though some La Spezians claim that it should always be lukewarm.)

Gran Pistau

Like mescciuà, this is a hearty, filling dish, eaten mostly in winter. Similar in consistency to mescciuà (though without the softness of the beans and chickpeas), but more flavourful (thanks to the leeks), it is particularly associated in the western entroterra with *Deneàa,* a local name for Christmas Day (from the Latin *dies natalis,* birth day). I was introduced to gran pistau by the proprietor of Bordighera's La Via Romana restaurant, Romolo Giordano, who has made a study of this regional speciality – and who took me to Mara Allavena's excellent mountain trattoria, Osteria del Portico in Castelvittorio, for a definitive version of the dish. Though pork in some form is commonly added to gran pistau, Allavena doesn't put any meat in hers. "In Pigna," she sniffs, as if talking about some exotic foreign port (Pigna is about two miles from Castelvittorio), "they put in a pig's foot! This makes it much too fatty." She has also learned that by soaking the wheat for eight hours, she can create an authentic-tasting gran pistau without going through the "pistau" part – the arduous crushing of the wheat with a mortar and pestle. This is Allavena's recipe (though she cooks the wheatberries much longer).

to serve 4

225 g/8 oz	raw wheatberries
	White part of 2 leeks, washed very thoroughly and minced
	Extra-virgin olive oil
1.1 litres/2 pints	beef stock
	Salt*
¼ teaspoon	cayenne pepper or hot paprika
	Freshly grated Parmigiano-Reggiano

Soak the wheatberries in water to cover for 8 hours.

To prepare gran pistau, cook leeks in oil over low heat in a large saucepan for 20–30 minutes or until translucent and tender. Drain and add wheatberries, then add beef stock, salt to taste, and cayenne pepper. Cook, uncovered, over the lowest possible heat for 2½–3 hours or until wheatberries are tender. If liquid is almost evaporated, add a small amount of water as necessary. Finished dish should be very densely soupy, not too liquid but not dry. Serve with Parmigiano-Reggiano to be added to taste at the table.

> *Allavena uses stock made from bouillon cubes, which are already salted, and so doesn't add more salt.

Testaroli

I hesitate to give a recipe for this dish at all. Testelli, the special clay dishes in which testaroli should be made, are still produced, on a modest artisanal scale, in the village of Isciolli, near Ne in the Val Graveglia, inland from Chiavari. Some home cooks and a few home-style restaurants in the province of La Spezia use them to continue to turn out testaroli in something approximating the traditional manner. If this ancient method of cooking has survived this long, even as a curiosity, it seems a pity to encourage its demise by promulgating an alternative method of making testaroli – in a non-stick frying pan, for instance, as one book recommends. But testaroli are such an unusual treat that I've ultimately decided to offer this method of making them as a poor substitute for the authentic eastern Ligurian procedure – on the grounds that it provides at least a hint of what this uncommon almost-pasta dish is like, and might encourage the more dedicated reader to seek out the real thing in Liguria itself.

to serve 4

---

475 g/17 oz	**flour**
2	**pinches of salt**
	Extra-virgin olive oil

Sift flour and salt together, then gradually pour in about 850 ml/1½ pints water, stirring constantly with a wooden spoon to form a smooth, fluid batter, similar in consistency to crêpe batter.

Very lightly oil a griddle or large cast-iron pan and heat to medium-hot. Pour batter from a pitcher or a large spoon to form 1 or more pancake-like circles, 13-15 cm/5-6 inches in diameter and 6-3 mm/¼ to ⅛ inch thick. If making more than 1 at a time, do not let circles touch. Lower heat, cover (use a large concave pan lid if working on a griddle) and cook for about 3 minutes. (Surface may brown slightly but should not darken.) Turn over and cook for another 3 minutes, then drain on paper towels. Repeat the process until all the batter is used up.

To serve, plunge testaroli briefly into boiling, salted water, then remove, shake off excess moisture, and serve whole or cut into thick strips or wedges, dressed with pesto (see page 63) or simply with oil and freshly grated Parmigiano-Reggiano or pecorino Sardo. Testaroli may be made several hours ahead of time and refrigerated, well covered, until used.

POLENTA AND RICE

*Chi se contenta, qualunque pasto o l'è bon,
anche a polenta. (If you're happy, even
polenta tastes good.)*
— GENOESE PROVERB

*As a gift of heaven, [rice] shows the care of
the gods for mankind.*
— MAGUELONNE TOUSSAINT-SAMAT,
HISTORY OF FOOD

Cornmeal and rice are minority grains on the Riviera. Both are certainly eaten frequently enough in the region – cornmeal is especially popular in the western entroterra and the arrière-pays – but neither has an ancient history here, and neither is essential to the local cuisine.

Corn was cultivated in the Veneto as early as 1530 and reached the Po Valley and Friuli by the early 1600s. That it may have arrived in the region from the east, not directly from the Americas, is suggested by the fact that the Italian name for it is *granturco* – Turkish grain – while the original Tuscan name was *dura di siria,* Syrian sorghum. (The Genoese call it simply *o granun,* the large grain.) Though corn was used mostly for animal fodder until the nineteenth century, a recipe for cornmeal polenta first appeared in 1773, in a book published in Naples. Even earlier, in the 1760s, Smollett reported that around Nice there was "a good deal of Meliga, or Turkish wheat, which is what we call Indian corn . . . [whose] grain goes by the name *polenta,* and makes excellent hasty-pudding, being very nourishing, and counted an admirable pectoral [i.e., specific for the chest]." And in 1781, according to Bernard Duplessy, Abbé Expilly wrote that "The inhabitants of Nice eat large quantities of noodles made with large corn *[gros maïs]* or Turkish wheat." (I have unfortunately been unable to turn up an eighteenth-century Niçois recipe for cornmeal pasta.) If the Niçois were eating it that early, almost certainly the Ligurians were too.

I say "cornmeal polenta" in the previous paragraph, incidentally, because it is important to remember that there were other kinds. There was polenta – under that name – made from fava flour and buckwheat flour, among other things, long before "Turkish grain" made its appearance in Italy. Polenta noire, as the Niçois call the buckwheat variety (which indeed takes on a blackish colour) was eaten regularly until recent years in the arrière-pays, where it was the traditional ration of army conscripts.

The technique of making risotto probably came into Liguria from across the mountains, from Piedmont, but rice itself came up from the south, arriving in Liguria perhaps as early as 1400 from North Africa by way of Sicily. It quickly became a profitable item of trade for the Genoese, though it never threatened to push wheat – which is to say pasta – off local tables. Rice was known in Nice at least by the sixteenth century, and the Niçois quickly adopted and adapted risotto, and started putting rice in their stuffed vegetables and soups.

Risotto is popular in Genoa and vicinity today, as it is in most parts of Italy, especially in the north. But it is not in any sense a Ligurian speciality. Paolo Lingua, in observing that risotto with seafood sauce is currently particularly popular in the region's better restaurants, stresses that it is nonetheless a recent invention – and suggests that it is perhaps a conscious imitation of Spain's paella (which happens to employ a very similar variety of short-grain rice). More typically in Genoa, rice was baked in the oven with assorted meats in a kind of casserole called riso arrosto or riso al forno, or eaten as a kind of thick soup, with milk. This latter dish notwithstanding, there is a curious old Genoese expression, "dâ u risu cu-a natta," "to give rice with cream" – meaning to reprimand someone or make a disconcerting observation. According to folklorist Maria Luisa Rosciano Bertoldi, the phrase came about because Genoese sailors had encountered, in Portugal, a dish of rice cooked with cream that they found particularly disagreeable.

One part of Liguria that does have several original rice dishes is the Valle Argentina. One of these is a relative of riso arrosto, a sort of sausage-and-rice casserole, eaten during Carnival, called rezegùn. (The name, which dates from the sixteenth century, refers to the nearby mountain of Resegone, whose eleven little peaks the irregular top of the dish is said to recall.) Another is a curiosity from Molini di Triora called bernardun de pulènta, which is nothing other than a mixture of two parts polenta and one part cooked rice, mixed with chopped spring onions and baked.

"Enchained Polenta"
Polenta Incatenata

In most polenta-eating parts of Italy, the cornmeal is cooked simply in water, with nothing more than salt and perhaps olive oil or butter added. Additional flavour is lent simply by a dusting of cheese or by a sauce or accompaniment of some more complex kind – meat or tomato sauce spooned over it, say, or grilled quail or some such on the side. Along the Riviera, however, polenta is sometimes cooked with other ingredients stirred right in; like nearly every other edible thing in the region, that is, polenta is "stuffed." In the hills above Nice, for instance, there is a dish of polenta generously spiked with tiny boiled broccoli florets. And in the Lunigiana, polenta becomes "enchained" with white beans and kale or cabbage. There is a slightly more elaborate dish in the area, called frascadèi, which includes chopped-up bits of bacon and mortadella as well as vegetables, but I prefer this version – preferably with something meaty immediately adjacent.

to serve 4

175 g/6 oz	dried white beans (preferably cannellini or fagioli di Spagna)

	Salt
6	leaves kale, julienned
125 ml/4 fl oz	extra-virgin olive oil
350 g/12 oz	cornmeal
	Freshly grated Parmigiano-Reggiano

Soak beans overnight in a large bowl of warm water. Drain and place in a saucepan with 1.7 litres/3 pints water. Cover pan, bring to a boil, then reduce heat and let beans simmer until they are barely tender, ½ to 1 hour, depending on age and size of beans.

Salt beans generously, then add kale and oil to the pan and stir in well. Cook for about 10 minutes, then add polenta to the pan by scooping up a handful at a time and scattering it in, while stirring with a wooden spoon. When all the polenta has been added, raise heat slightly and cook for about 30 minutes, stirring constantly. Polenta should be very thick and come easily away from the side of the pan.

Adjust salt if necessary and serve with plenty of grated Parmigiano.

Polenta with Oranges

Polénta e Aanso

This simple but unusual dessert comes from Gianfranco Cricca's *Antiche ricette di Castelnuovo Magra*. The oranges are a reminder that the bustling port of La Spezia, 15 or 20 miles away from Castelnuovo, was once a conduit for exotic fruits and spices from other climes.

to serve 6

	Salt
350 g/12 oz	cornmeal
	Sugar
6	medium Seville or blood oranges, peeled and thinly sliced, with seeds removed
	Extra-virgin olive oil

Bring 1.7 litres/3 pints salted water to a boil, then reduce heat to simmer. Slowly add polenta to the saucepan by scooping up a handful at a time and scattering it in, while stirring with a wooden spoon. When all the polenta has been

added, raise heat slightly and cook for about 30 minutes, stirring constantly. Polenta should be very thick and come easily away from the side of the pan.

Spoon polenta evenly into six dishes. Dust lightly with sugar, then top with orange slices, arranged so that they overlap. Drizzle a little olive oil over the oranges, and, if the oranges aren't very sweet, add more sugar. Serve warm.

Buckwheat Polenta Casserole

Mataúfi de Skandéla

This is another unusual recipe from *Antiche ricette di Castelnuovo Magra* – one of the precornmeal polentas now almost vanished from the Riviera. The curious name, in the dialect of Castelnuovo, means simply a polenta of buckwheat.

to serve 4–6

1	onion, finely chopped
2	garlic cloves, minced
1	celery stalk, finely chopped
½	carrot, finely chopped
3	sprigs Italian flat-leaf parsley, minced
8–10	basil leaves, chopped
	Extra-virgin olive oil
	Pinch of nutmeg
3–4	ripe tomatoes, skinned, seeded, and chopped
	Salt
225 ml/8 fl oz	beef or chicken stock
450 g/1 lb	buckwheat flour
	Freshly grated Parmigiano-Reggiano

Cook onion, garlic, celery, carrot, parsley, and basil in olive oil over a low heat for 20–30 minutes, or until ingredients are very tender. Add nutmeg, then stir in tomatoes. Add salt to taste and cook for 5 minutes longer, then add stock. Stir well and continue cooking for 5–10 minutes, or until liquid has reduced and sauce is thick. Set aside off heat.

Bring 2.3 litres/4 pints salted water to a boil, then reduce heat to simmer. Slowly add buckwheat to the saucepan, as for polenta, by scooping up a handful at a time and scattering it in, while stirring with a wooden spoon. When all the buckwheat has been added, raise heat slightly and cook for about 30 minutes, stirring constantly until it begins to come away from the sides of the pan.

Preheat oven to 190°C/375°F/Gas Mark 5.

Lightly oil a round, deep 30-35 cm/12-14 inch baking dish, then cover the bottom with a layer of buckwheat polenta about 2 cm/¾ inch thick. Spread a thin layer of sauce over it, then cover generously with Parmigiano. Repeat the process until all ingredients are used up, ending with a layer of buckwheat polenta. Bake for 20 minutes. Serve hot, as an accompaniment to game or other rich meat dishes.

Polenta Baked with Rice

Bernardun de Pulènta

Just plain bernardun (without the "de pulènta") is a flat, baked, torta-like construction made from a simple unleavened dough into which onions or spring onions, a herb or two, and sometimes grated courgettes or other shredded vegetables are mixed; often there is cheese melted on top. Sandro Oddo, who lives in the famous old witchhunt town of Triora, in the mountains above Sanremo, and who knows as much about the food and folkways of the valleys of the far western entroterra as anyone, considers it a very subtle dish – one of the little masterpieces of his region's cooking. But what of bernardun de pulènta? When I noticed a reference to it one day, I immediately called Oddo to ask what it was. To my astonishment, he had never heard of it – but he investigated further, and discovered that it was an old speciality of his neighbouring village, Molini di Triora. He even found me the recipe – and it turned out to be simple, hearty, plain Ligurian mountain peasant fare par excellence.

to serve 4

	Salt
450 g/1 lb	cornmeal
225 g/8 oz	short-grain rice
5–6	spring onions, trimmed and finely chopped
	Extra-virgin olive oil

Bring 2.3 litres/4 pints salted water to a boil, then reduce heat to simmer. Slowly add polenta to the pot by scooping up a handful at a time and scattering it in, while stirring with a wooden spoon. When all the polenta has been added, raise heat slightly and cook for about 30 minutes, stirring constantly. Meanwhile,

place rice and 1.4 litres/2½ pints salted water in a saucepan, cover, bring to a boil, then reduce heat to low and allow to steam for 10 minutes.

While rice and polenta are cooking, preheat oven to190°C/375°F/Gas Mark 5.

Mix polenta, rice, and spring onions together well in a very lightly oiled baking dish. Season to taste with salt and a few drops of additional oil, then bake for 45 minutes.

Baked Rice with Meats

Riso Arrosto

Some sources suggest that this dish was originally a Genoese way to use up rice already cooked for risotto. Perhaps such rice was mixed with other ingredients and quickly reheated, but I find it doubtful that the resulting dish much resembled this well-loved classic of Genoa and the eastern entroterra – not least because cooked rice would probably have become unpleasantly soggy and sticky if treated this way.

to serve 4

15 g/½ oz	dried porcini mushrooms
1	onion, finely chopped
175 g/6 oz	mild Italian sausage, removed from casings and finely chopped
	Extra-virgin olive oil
175 g/6 oz	short-grain rice
2	artichokes
115 g/4 oz	shelled peas
1 litre/1¾ pints	beef or veal stock
125 ml/4 fl oz	tocco (see page 103) or other meat sauce
50 g/2 oz	Parmigiano-Reggiano, grated
	Salt
	Freshly ground black pepper

Soak mushrooms in 3 changes of warm (not hot) water, for a total of about 15 minutes.

Meanwhile, cook onion and sausage in oil in a large, ovenproof pot over low heat for about 10 minutes. Add rice and stir well so that grains are well coated with oil. When mushrooms are ready, finely chop them, add to pot, and continue cooking.

Cut stems off artichokes. Pull off tough outer leaves by hand, and trim off more layers of leaves with a sharp knife until only tender ones remain. Scoop out and discard the chokes, chop artichokes into small pieces, then add to pot.

Preheat oven to 230°C/450°F/Gas Mark 8.

Add peas and stock to pot, and stir ingredients well. Continue cooking, covered, for about 10 minutes, then stir in tocco, Parmigiano, and salt and pepper to taste. Bake for 10 minutes, or until liquid is absorbed and rice forms a light golden-brown crust.

Rice with Greens
Riso col Preboggion

The greens used for this speciality of the Genoese entroterra – also called simply riso con erbe, rice with herbs – should be at least partially bitter. Some recipes call for a spoonful or two of pesto to be stirred into the rice just before the dish is served; this certainly doesn't hurt, but I like the purer flavour of just the greens and rice, with some Parmigiano added for sweetness.

to serve 4

225 g/8 oz	Swiss chard
½	small head radicchio, julienned
3	flat-leaf parsley sprigs, minced
225 g/8 oz	other assorted greens (borage, curly endive, escarole, dandelion greens, mustard greens, etc.), julienned
	Salt
225 g/8 oz	short-grain rice
	Freshly grated Parmigiano-Reggiano

Trim stalks from chard, reserving them for another use, then cut into a very fine chiffonade. Add chard, radicchio, parsley, and other greens to 1 litre/1¾ pints of salted water. Bring to a boil, then lower heat and simmer for 20 minutes.

Add rice, stir well, then cover and continue cooking for 15–20 minutes or until rice is done. Adjust seasoning. (Stir in 1 or 2 tablespoons pesto at this point if you so desire.) Serve with plenty of Parmigiano.

BREAD, FOCACCIA, AND PISSALADIÈRE

A chi ha famme o pan o ghe pâ lasagne.
(To the hungry, bread tastes like lasagna.)
— GENOESE PROVERB

Metti toa, metti u pan, che i amixi i
vegneàn. (Set the table and put out the
bread and your friends will arrive.)
— ONEGLIESE PROVERB

Pasta had such great early success in Genoa, suggests Paolo Lingua in *La cucina dei genovesi,* and focaccia became such an important substitute for bread, because the bread of the region itself was frankly never very good. Sea air, says Lingua, is the enemy of rising dough: The resultant loaves tend to be moist and gummy; the crust resists crispness.

This may have been the case historically, but I've certainly had good bread in Genoa and elsewhere on the Riviera in recent years, as well as in other towns along the Mediterranean; perhaps modern technology has learned how to counteract the effects of the ambient humidity. Nonetheless, one does have the feeling that, given the choice between bread and pasta, the people of the coastal Riviera would vote for the latter by a large margin – especially if they could keep their focaccia in the bargain.

In the interior, far from the sea air, on the other hand, there is a good deal of nostalgia for the good, old-fashioned, home-style bread of earlier times. Home-*style* is the proper term: The truth is that, whatever romantic notions we may have today about the culinary folkways of the Mediterranean, genuinely home-baked bread has always been comparatively rare in the region. Housewives may have mixed up and worked the bread dough themselves, but it was nearly always baked in communal ovens. Fuel was too precious for every individual to build a fire (especially for only a loaf or two), and efficient bread ovens were too hot, and thus too dangerous, for home kitchens.

There was also a strong element of community involved; communal ovens were meeting places as well as bakeries. Several years ago, in the periodical called *A Vaštéra* – dedicated to the culture and language of the Tera Brigasca, a mountainous region that encompasses the far upper right-hand corner of the Niçois backcountry (including the town of La Brigue) and a portion of the western entroterra stretching from near Triora to the edge of Piedmont – a local woman named Graziella Dolla published a recollection of the bread-baking in her native village. When she was growing up in the 1950s and '60s, she writes, the perfume of bread baking in the communal oven "inundated the town, and our neighbours would come to see if it had been done properly, while we children would try for a bit of crust or some of the little doughnut-shaped biscuits that had been cooked [along with it]. . . . This wasn't a daily event, but was a rite, a festa."

As Dolla describes the process, "A mamma would leave a branch in the oven to 'reserve' it for one of the following days. The day before she was to bake, the father gathered wood in the forest; the same night, the mother made the starter [lëvoüra], with warm water and raw dough from the previous week which had been left to acidify. A bit of this was added to water and flour and allowed to rest overnight in a cauldron near the hearth. By morning it had risen so much that it sometimes overflowed. Then it was used to make dough with more flour and salted water. This was allowed to rise for three more hours, and taken to the oven – which had been lit three hours earlier. The oven temperature was controlled with the cover of the door, and if it got too hot, a pan of water was put in." The results, she says, were remarkable.

Bread of this kind is much romanticized today. Another issue of A Vaštéra published a poetic tribute to it by one Antonio Crespi, a peasant from the village of Ceriana, above Sanremo. It reads in part: "It is hot like the heart of a young girl / of 16 years, and it never goes stale. . . . / It is always fresh and flavourful / and smells beautifully of wheat, / a wheat sowed by hand on our lands, / crushed, brought to the mill on our shoulders, / made into dough on the table, / browned on the oven floor, / blessed with fresh water and a bit of salt, / white inside, and outside the colour of gold."

One communal bakery that still functions in the arrière-pays, at least once a year, is the "four ancestral" (ancestral oven) in the village of Châteauneuf-Villevieille. In late September every year, for the town's annual Fête du Pain, townspeople execute a token harvest of wheat growing nearby, thresh it, grind it at an old water-driven mill, and then help to make the dough to be baked in the oven. This kind of cooperative effort was once a frequent, if not quite a daily, event in such villages.

Today, commercial bakeries have taken the place of communal ovens. Some of these, happily, still use wood-burning ovens and produce excellent bread. Pieve di Teco, high above Imperia, for instance, is famous for its whole-grain bread, which is dense, crusty, and slightly smoky in flavour. The best bread I've encountered in Liguria, though, is the well-known pane di Triora, made only in the historic village of Triora itself. The typical Triora loaf is round and shallow, like a flattened dome; its crust is very even in texture, and a warm, almost honey brown in colour. The interior is dense and crumby, almost like a kind of dried-out cake, and it is absolutely delicious. It also lasts a long time: I've brought loaves back to the States and nibbled on them happily for a week. Bakers in other towns have tried to reproduce pane di Triora without success; perhaps it's a matter of the mineral content of the local water, or the effects of the altitude and climate on the dough, or the flavour of the wood, or the design of the local ovens – or, more probably, a combination of all these.

On the rare occasions when bread was baked at home, usually at isolated farmhouses without ready access to communal ovens, it was often cooked under a *testo,* a bell-shaped cover made of terra cotta or cast iron, suspended over an open kitchen fire by a cord. Don Sandro Lagomarsini, the pastor of the little church in Cassego, an isolated village in the eastern entroterra, remembers talking to one old local woman who used to bake bread that way as late as the 1960s. The bread was good, she recalled, but the smoke made everything in the kitchen black, and hurt her eyes.

Focaccia (fûgassa or figassa in Genoese), which is flat, slightly raised bread, similar to undressed (or lightly dressed) pizza crust, is known all over Italy, but is particularly popular (and well made) in Liguria. Unlike daily bread, focaccia could be baked at home, on flat stones kept hot behind the family hearth. (The word *focaccia* comes from *focus,* Latin for hearth.) Today, of course, focaccia, like other bread, is made mostly in commercial bakeries – but its cooking time is short and it is often turned out all day instead of just in the mornings. Plain or with subtle added flavourings, it is widely appreciated as a snack throughout the region; it is Ligurian fast food.

The focaccia of Recco is particularly famous – both the conventional kind and a very particular variety called focaccia col formaggio – focaccia with cheese. This does not resemble other focaccia in appearance: It is made with two thin sheets of unleavened dough, enclosing molten white cheese. Though it is often said to have been invented around World War I by a local trattoria owner, it can in fact be dated back thousands of years. Franco Solari of Ca' Peo in Leivi called my attention to a passage in *De Re Rustica* by Marco Porcio Catone, or Cato the Elder (234–149 B.C.), in which he writes, "Scriblitam sic facito. In balteo tractes caseo ad eumdem modum facito" – "This is how you make scribilita. Enclose between sheets [of dough] slices of cheese." The dish was called scribilita (or scribillare, or conscribillare), adds the work's Italian translator, "because one makes on top of it certain marks that resemble writing."

Pissaladière is often described as "the Niçois pizza." That's not necessarily inaccurate, since both are essentially flat rounds or rectangles of bread dough, topped with various ingredients and baked in a hot oven – and both were probably invented to use up scraps of leftover bread dough. But there are important differences, which begin with their respective names: The term *pizza* is now generally believed to be Germanic in origin (the Germanic Goths, remember, overran much of Italy in the fifth century A.D.), perhaps deriving from the Old High German *bizzo,* meaning "bite" or "bit." Pissaladière (pissaladiera in Niçois), on the other hand, takes its name from the fermented anchovy sauce called pissala or pissalat, which in turn is a contraction of the Niçois words *pèi salat,* or salted fish. Pissala, or at least anchovies, are thus basic to pissaladière – as they are not to pizza.

There are other differences: Pissaladière is never topped with tomatoes, which are all but essential to pizza; sweet, long-cooked onions, rarely if ever found on pizza, are de rigueur for pissaladière. Pissaladière is always inset with Niçois olives, but never, ever, topped with cheese. (The Niçois poet Victor Rocca, in his 1930 poem "La Pissaladière," describes the speciality in part as a "Poème du Terroir, synthèse douce et fière, / Qui mêle, sous un ciel triomphalement sec, / L'oignon blanc du Berbère et l'olive du Grec" – a "Poem of the Land, a sweet and proud synthesis, / Which joins, beneath a triumphantly dry sky, / The white onion of the Berber and the olive of the Greek.")

On the Italian side of the border, the distinction between pizza and what is locally called pisciadéla (or pissadella), piscialàndrea, sardenàira, or pizza al'Andrea, among other things, is somewhat less clear. This is basically a pissaladière, with anchovies or pissala – under its western Ligurian name, machetto – but also with the tomatoes forbidden to its Niçois counterpart. The Andrea in question, incidentally, is the great sixteenth-century Genoese admiral Andrea Doria, and it is often said that this was his favourite dish – though it is unlikely that Doria ever heard of, much less tasted, a tomato.

The Last Baker of
St. Étienne-de-Tinée

The communal oven in the attractive mountain town of St. Étienne-de-Tinée, about 60 miles northwest of Nice, was built in 1707, and functioned continuously until 1950. (The old bakery now houses the local Musée des Traditions.) Traditionally, the bread was rye, with a bit of precious white flour mixed in; white bread was baked only on special occasions – for weddings, for instance. In times of "grande misère," when even rye flour was unavailable, bread was sometimes made with the dried, ground-up fruit of the hawthorn bush *(aubépine)*. Étienne Gibellin, the town's last traditional baker, was interviewed in 1980 for a local oral history. This is an edited excerpt of his responses:

"I became the baker when I was thirty-five, and worked for thirty years. Near the end, I was making hardly any bread. I was baking once or twice a week, that's all – whereas before, I baked three or four times a day, making ninety loaves each time. The bread baked for two hours. But it depended: When the oven was really hot, it was done in an hour and a half. You needed a lot of wood. The oven had to be white-hot. The best wood was larch. Pine was bad wood, too fat. It would drip onto the stones and when you swept out the oven, it wouldn't budge. I don't know what kind of stone we used, but it was a special kind that could 'suffer' without breaking. There was no variety in the shapes of the bread. It was all large, round loaves. I stopped because there was no more wheat, and because the people, one after another, stopped making bread [for me to bake]."

Focaccia

Focaccia appears in almost every part of Italy. The Ligurians seem to have a special gift for it, however. They also seem to have more variations on the basic theme than other Italians. Simple focaccia of the sort described below, sometimes with even more olive oil added – so that it almost drips out when you pick up a piece – is particularly appreciated for breakfast along the Riviera di Ponente. But there are numerous refinements, both on the coast and in the mountains. There is focaccia with broken pieces of black olives worked into the dough or with whole black or green ones pressed lightly into the surface. There is focaccia made with white wine instead of water. One variety of focaccia has grated Parmigiano or pecorino mixed into the dough. Some has rosemary or sage either mixed into the dough or sprinkled on top. This is a basic recipe, worked out by trial and error, which yields a reasonably Ligurian-tasting basic version – moister and thinner than most focaccia made here, it should be noted.

to serve 4–6

	Salt
	Flour
10 g/¼ oz	active dry yeast
	Extra-virgin olive oil

Mix 1 tablespoon salt into 275 g/10 oz flour in a bowl. Dissolve yeast in about 225 ml/8 fl oz warm water and let stand for about 5 minutes, then stir in 125 ml/4 fl oz oil. Add yeast mixture to flour and stir in well with a wooden spoon, adding more water if necessary, until ingredients are well mixed.

Turn dough out onto a floured work surface. Coat hands with flour, then knead dough for several minutes until it has a smooth, firm, elastic character.

Form dough into a ball and place in a lightly oiled bowl covered by a towel. Place in a warm place and allow dough to rise for 1½–2 hours, or refrigerate and allow to rise for 6–8 hours.

Turn dough out onto a floured work surface again and shape roughly into a flat disc or a rectangle with your hands and a rolling pin. Place in a lightly oiled round or rectangular baking dish, make regular rows of slight indentations across the entire surface with your finger or the end of a wooden spoon, then cover with a towel and allow to sit for another hour at room temperature.

Preheat oven to 230°C/450°F/Gas Mark 8. Brush top of focaccia lightly with olive oil and season with more salt, then bake in middle of oven for

20–25 minutes or until crust has turned golden-brown. Serve warm or at room temperature, cut into wedges or squares.

Recco-Style Focaccia with Cheese
Focaccia col Formaggio

On our way from Genoa to Recco one afternoon, my friend Diego Moreno, an agricultural historian at the University of Genoa, suggested that we drive over the mountains instead of along the sea. He wanted to show me something, he said. As we wound up a precipitous little road above Nervi, he pointed out the hillscapes to me. "You see how everything is bare near the top? There was a very interesting division of agriculture here for many centuries. The lower reaches of the hills were privately owned, and planted with olive trees. Above about 350 or 400 meters, though, the land was common, and was used for grazing cows. We have carbon-dated samples of fossilized fodder here and found that this was so at least back to the Bronze Age. Because the land was nothing but grasses for so long, even today trees are very slow to take root and the hilltops remain almost empty." As we descended toward Recco, he delivered the punch line: "Now perhaps you will understand why the people of this region invented focaccia col formaggio: Unlike most other regions, they had olive oil and cow's milk side-by-side."

Though its precursor dates back to Roman times, focaccio col formaggio in the modern sense may indeed be traced to the area around Recco. It was known here for centuries, but traditionally (for reasons no one remembers) eaten only at funerals and on the Day of the Dead. In the early years of this century, it was apparently revived as a more frequent pleasure by one Emanuela, or Manuelina, Capurro – who owned a trattoria in Recco, on the west side of the Portofino Peninsula.

Rumour has it that Mussolini was fond of her creation, and, whether for that reason or not, her establishment was destroyed near the end of World War II. In 1960, Capurro's granddaughter opened a new place, dubbed Manuelina in her honour, and members of the family still run it today. The menu at Manuelina is long and the food is mostly pretty good, but focaccia col formaggio remains the undisputed star attraction. It is superb: a flood of free-flowing, pleasantly sour stracchino cheese, which becomes slightly grainy as it cools, between sheets of rich, salty dough that tastes faintly of the wood-burning oven. It is widely imitated today from Genoa to the Cinque Terre, but Manuelina's remains the best version I've sampled. Just to set the record straight, however, a restaurant just down the street from Manuelina, Ö Vittorio, has a sign out front advertising its own focaccia col formaggio as an "anticha specialità," or ancient speciality – perhaps with the Romans in mind. The following is based on Manuelina's "official" recipe.

to serve 4

	Salt
	Flour
450 g/1 lb	**stracchino or a good melting cheese***
	Extra-virgin olive oil

Mix 1 tablespoon salt into 275 g/10 oz flour in a bowl. Stir in 225 ml/8 fl oz warm water and 3 tablespoons oil with a wooden spoon, adding more water if necessary, until ingredients are well mixed.

Turn dough out onto a floured work surface. Coat hands with flour, then knead dough for several minutes until it obtains a smooth, firm, elastic character.

Form dough into two balls and roll each one out as thinly as possible into discs, transferring to a floured surface when done. Place 1 dough sheet carefully in a lightly oiled pizza or paella pan. Thinly slice or coarsely grate cheese, then spread it out on the dough sheet to cover the surface to within about 2 cm/¾ inch of the edge. Carefully place the other sheet on top of the cheese and press it down lightly. Do not crimp the edges.

Preheat oven to 230°C/450°F/Gas Mark 8. Drizzle olive oil and season with a bit more salt, then bake in middle of oven for about 25 minutes or until crust has turned golden-brown. Serve immediately, cut into wedges or squares.

*On special occasions, Manuelina uses a local cheese called simply formagetta, "little cheese," but stracchino is the everyday ingredient.

Pissaladière

Though pissaladière made with pastry dough is something of a fashion in France, the real thing should be made from bread dough. Jacques Médecin – who, of course, has strong opinions on the matter – adds that one should be suspicious of the pissaladières sold at sidewalk stands and in "drugstores" in Nice, where, he says scornfully, "the onions seem to have been applied with tweezers." According to Médecin, a good pissaladière, such as one might buy in the markets of Nice, is covered with a layer of onions fully half as thick as the tart's rather thick crust.

to serve 4–6

	Salt
	Flour
10 g/¼ oz	active dry yeast
	Extra-virgin olive oil
1.25-1.5 kg/2½-3 lb	white or yellow onions, very thinly sliced
	Freshly ground black pepper
	Bouquet garni of 2 sprigs each thyme and marjoram and 1 sprig rosemary, tied together with kitchen string
50 g/2 oz	Niçoise olives
12	anchovy fillets

Make a dough as for focaccia (see page 172), using the same quantities and techniques, but let dough rise only once, for about 1 hour at room temperature.

As dough is rising, add onions to 3 or 4 tablespoons oil in a large heavy sauté pan over very low heat. Season generously with salt and pepper, add bouquet garni, and cover pan to let onions steam for about 45 minutes, stirring occasionally. They should not brown but should cook down to a very tender marmalade-like consistency.

When dough has risen, turn it out onto a floured work surface again and shape roughly into a flat disc with your hands and a rolling pin. Place in a lightly oiled pizza or paella pan, then cover with a tea towel and allow to sit for another 30 minutes at room temperature.

Preheat oven to 230°C/450°F/Gas Mark 8. Spread onion mixture over top of dough, patting it down evenly. Arrange olives and anchovy fillets on top of onions in an attractive pattern. Season lightly with more black pepper, then bake in middle of oven for 15–20 minutes or until crust has browned. Serve warm or at room temperature, cut into wedges.

NOTE: To make pisciadéla (sardenàira), follow the directions above, but stir the chopped flesh of 900 g/2 lb skinned, seeded, very ripe tomatoes into the onions. After cooking for 40 minutes, uncover pan, and cook for 5–10 minutes longer, or until liquid from tomatoes has evaporated.

TORTE AND TOURTES

In our valleys . . . women . . . had to . . .
prepare, very quickly (because they worked
hard with the men), a meal that was varied
. . . , used only a handful of products,
and . . . could sustain the body for
punishing work. From these exigencies
were born, in particular, tourtes.

— MAMÉ CLAIRETTE, QUOTED IN
CUISINE TRADITIONNELLE EN PAYS
NIÇOIS BY BERNARD DUPLESSY

One hazy spring day I drove up into the western entroterra to Triora, to watch Adriana and Anna Saldo make a torta – which is basically a large, thin-crusted, savoury pie. Adriana and Anna are the mother and aunt, respectively, of my friend Sandro Oddo, who studies the culture and cuisine of the region and runs the town's little ethnographic museum (which is partially devoted to the famous witch trials held here in the late sixteenth century). On an earlier visit here, I had learned from Oddo's wife, Erica, that there were still women in the area who cooked torte [the plural of torta] the traditional way, outdoors, both over and under an open fire. This I had to see – and the Oddos were kind enough to make the necessary arrangements for my next visit.

We started in the Oddos' apartment, above a food shop in a terraced modern building just outside the old town. On the kitchen counter sat a big, old, well-blackened iron pan about 4.5 cm/18 inches in diameter with a sheet of dough laid into it – dough made of only flour, water, and a little oil (no eggs or salt), almost translucent but durable enough to be stretched to cover the pan without tearing. Onto the dough, Adriana dumped a big bowl of chopped raw potatoes, Swiss chard, parsley, and onion, all mixed up with eggs, crumbled fresh tuma (fresh sheep's-milk cheese, about the consistency of fresh mozzarella), and plenty of salt. She spread it out evenly with a wooden spoon, tamping it down a bit. Next, Anna rolled a second sheet of dough around a rolling pin and then, starting on the side nearest to her, unfurled it over the filling. She then patted it down lightly, pressed the edges of the sheets together, and trimmed and lightly crimped the dough. Adriana pierced the top sheet with a fork, and olive oil was drizzled across the top.

Then we took a little walk, outside and up the hill in back of the apartment to a small terraced garden area, Adriana carrying the torta pan and Anna carrying an empty pan that could have been its twin. In the garden, the women had earlier laid a fire of dried-out vine cuttings beneath a low cast-iron trivet. The torta was positioned on the trivet, then the empty pan was turned upside down over the full one, to form a dome-like lid. More vine cuttings were piled on top of the lid, and both fires were lit. We stood around, dodging waves of smoke that drifted first in one direction, then the other, for about 25 minutes. Then Anna announced that the torta was done. "You can smell it," she said – and indeed you could.

We trooped back inside with the pan, cut the torta into wedges, and ate it with little glasses of light red wine. It was undeniably a rustic dish – the dough was slightly chewy, and slightly burnt – but the filling had cooked perfectly, and it was very good and very satisfying. "In the old days," Oddo told me as we ate, "people made torte like this every day, using whatever vegetables were in season and plentiful – artichokes, potatoes, courgettes, cabbage, anything. Pasta, on the other hand, was considered a special treat. Today, it is the reverse. Torte are a rarity."

They are becoming more so. Until 1994, Triora held an annual torta contest every July in the Piazza della Chiesa, at which all the best cooks in town brought their torte to be tasted and judged. In 1995, the event was cancelled for good. "For the past few years," Erica Oddo told me, "only two women entered torte, so it wasn't much of a competition."

The idea of enclosing filling in two or more layers of dough to form a kind of pie is ancient – dating from Mesopotamia, according to some sources. The Egyptians, the Greeks, and the Romans all ate torte of a sort. (According to the *Grande enciclopedia illustrata della gastronomia,* the word derives from the late Latin *tortus,* past participle of the verb *torquere,* to fold or twist, presumably referring to the way the dough is sealed. This is also the root of the legal term *tort,* a wrongful act, and the French adjective *tort,* meaning simply "wrong.") In more recent times, torte figured prominently in the sophisticated cooking of the courts of Naples and in classic French cuisine – though they temporarily lost favour at the formal French table around the time of Carême (1784–1833), being considered too common.

Torte – called tourtes in the arrière-pays – are basic to the gastronomy of the Riviera, in both sweet and savoury forms. The first dish ever identified in print as Genoese was, as noted earlier, a torta – appearing in Mestre Robert's Catalan-language *Libre del coch* in 1520. More than two centuries earlier, though, in the *Libro per cuoco* (written c. 1300 by "Anonimo Veneziano," the Anonymous Venetian), there appears a recipe for torta lavagnexe – that is, from Lavagna, a town just east of Portofino, between Chiavari and Sestri Levante – made with chicken, mussels, bacon, eggs, cheese, sage, and parsley, flavoured with saffron.

The appeal of torte or tourtes to the thrifty, often impoverished peoples of the Riviera is obvious: Because they are made with thin sheets of dough (usually only two per dish), they use little precious flour – especially compared with the quantity required to make pasta or bread. They can also be filled with almost anything available – not just vegetables (including potatoes), but also rice and other grains (I've had torta di polenta in the western entroterra, and Salvatore Marchesi has an eastern Ligurian recipe for torta di farro – i.e., spelt), wild herbs, various kinds of lowly seafood (torte filled with fresh anchovies were once popular on the Riviera di Levante), eggs and cheese, and of course many kinds of fruit. They could also be baked in communal ovens, alongside or, more commonly, after the daily bread.

The queen of torte, the ultimate expression of the dish, is another of Genoa's emblematic specialities: torta pasqualina, or Eastertide torta. The torta pasqualina is a grand, plump pie, filled with layers of Swiss chard (or occasionally artichokes), onions, eggs, cheese (preferably prescinsêua), marjoram, and a little minced garlic. A traditional torta pasqualina always had thirty-three layers of dough – ten underneath the vegetables and twenty-three on top – one for each of the years of Christ's life. This, though, is almost impossible to find today. According to author-politician Paolo Emilio Taviani, when Nietzsche was living on the Piazza Portello in Genoa, he thought it worthwhile to spend an entire afternoon learning how to prepare a torta pasqualina from his landlady.

Two Basic Pastry Recipes for Torte and Tourtes

As a general rule, the torta pastry of Liguria is made with olive oil, while that of Nice is sometimes made with butter and even eggs. A recipe for each appears on page 179. The quantity given is sufficient for one 35-45 cm/14-18 inch round torta or tourte; leftover dough or scraps may be cut into pasta shapes and boiled or deep-fried. A secret I hesitate to reveal is that a pretty decent (and light and crisp) torte can also be constructed with ready made phyllo dough – using at least three layers on the bottom and two or three on top. For some reason this blatant inauthenticity doesn't bother me as much as the use of wonton wrappers for ravioli – maybe because phyllo dough is at least Mediterranean in origin. Torte/tourtes may be filled with almost any vegetable – including spinach, cabbage, artichokes, favas, and preboggion-style mixtures of greens, besides those mentioned in the following pages.

(1.)   For a standard Ligurian-style torta dough, sift 250 g/9 oz flour and 1 teaspoon salt into a bowl. With a fork or a small whisk, slowly beat in 3 tablespoons extra-virgin olive oil and then about 225 ml/8 fl oz water – enough to make a smooth, elastic dough. Shape dough into 2 balls, cover with a damp cloth, and refrigerate for 2 hours. Roll out both balls as thinly as possible on a floured work surface.

(2.)   For a richer, flakier dough, sift 275 g/10 oz flour into a bowl with a teaspoon of salt. Beat 2 large eggs lightly in another bowl, then stir them into flour with a fork. Stir in 225 g/8 oz unsalted butter at room temperature, continuing to mix with a fork until a crumbly mixture is formed. Turn dough out onto a floured work surface and knead several times, then roll out as thinly as possible on a floured work surface.

Mushroom Torta

Torta di Funghi

Silvio Torre offers this recipe, which I've altered very slightly, in his book on Savonese gastronomy, *Su e giù per boschi tra vigne e oliveti*. It was a speciality, he writes, of his great-grandmother, Nannina, who cooked for Paolo Boselli, president of the Italian Council of Ministers during World War I. Torre notes that this is a thin torta, and that it should be eaten "subito calda, calda" – immediately, hot, hot.

to serve 4–6

Extra-virgin olive oil
1   recipe torta dough No. 1 (see above)
1   recipe funghi a funghetto (see page 264)

Lightly oil a round baking dish (or pizza or paella pan) 35-45 cm/14-18 inches in diameter, and lay 1 pastry sheet down evenly in it.

Preheat oven to 190°C/375°F/Gas Mark 5.

Drain mushrooms in a colander for 10 minutes (reserve liquid for sauce or stock), then spread them out on pastry shell evenly, tamping them down lightly. Place second pastry sheet over them, pressing it down lightly with your fingers.

Crimp the edges of the sheets together and trim off excess. Drizzle olive oil over top of torta, then bake for 30 minutes or until crust is lightly browned and begins to come away from sides of dish or pan.

Chard and Potato Torta

Torta Verde

This is my version of the all-purpose torta cooked for me by Adriana and Anna Oddo at Sandro and Erica Oddo's place in Triora.

to serve 6

1	onion, finely chopped
2	large baking potatoes, peeled and cut into pieces about 12 mm × 2.5 cm/½ × 1 inch
8	large leaves Swiss chard, stalks and ribs removed, finely chopped
4	flat-leaf parsley sprigs, minced
4	large eggs, lightly beaten
175-225 g/6-8 oz	fresh pecorino or mild feta cheese, crumbled
	Salt
	Extra-virgin olive oil
1	recipe torta dough No. 1 (see page 179)

Mix onion, potato, chard, and parsley together in a bowl. Stir in eggs and cheese, and salt generously.

Lightly oil a round baking dish (or pizza or paella pan) 35-45 cm/14-18 inches in diameter, and lay 1 pastry sheet down evenly in it.

Preheat oven to 190°C/375°F/Gas Mark 5.

Spread potato mixture out on pastry shell evenly, tamping down lightly. Place second pastry sheet over it, pressing it down lightly with your fingers. Crimp the edges of the sheets together and trim off excess. Prick crust in several places with a fork. Drizzle olive oil over top of torta, then bake for 45 minutes to 1 hour, until crust is browned and begins to come away from sides of dish or pan.

Puréed Potato Torta
Pasta de Patata

At Osteria del Portico, in the western Ligurian mountain village of Castelvittorio, the local elementary-school kids – about ten of them – file in every day for lunch, with their teacher, shortly before 1 P.M. On the occasions when I've been there to see them, they've been high-spirited but well-behaved – and I can't help thinking that they get a kick out of eating in a real restaurant every day, surrounded by grown-ups, waited on by owner-chef Mara Allavena herself. They take pot-luck, basically eating whatever Allavena has plenty of. Sometimes it's one of her famous torte, called *paste* in the local idiom, which she makes with one oversized sheet of dough instead of two, stretching it inward so that the top crust is pleated, with a tiny hole in the middle where the edges of the sheet meet. This might be a pasta di polenta, made with cornmeal, onions, spinach, and wild fennel leaves, or a slightly simpler but no less savoury pasta de patata. (On special occasions, Allavena makes up the torta, then carries it on a large wooden paddle to bake at the communal oven nearby.) This recipe is based on Allavena's potato torta, and on a recipe for a similar dish given to me by Sandro Oddo in Triora.

to serve 6

6	medium-sized baking potatoes, well scrubbed
	Salt
1	large egg
2 tablespoons	grated Parmigiano-Reggiano
50 g/2 oz	fresh prescinsêua (see page 124) or ricotta
225 ml/8 fl oz	milk
25 g/1 oz	unsalted butter
	Salt and freshly ground black pepper
1	recipe torta dough No. 1 or No. 2 (see page 179)

Cook *potatoes unpeeled* in a large saucepan of salted water until done (20–30 minutes, depending on their size).

Preheat oven to 190°C/375°F/Gas Mark 5.

When potatoes are cooked, remove from water, cool slightly, then peel and place in a mixing bowl. Crush potatoes with a masher or fork, then mix in egg, cheeses, 175 ml/6 fl oz of milk, butter, and plenty of salt and pepper. Continue mixing until a smooth, moist paste is formed, adding rest of milk as necessary.

Make torta as in previous recipe and bake 30–40 minutes, or until lightly browned.

Eastertide Torta

Torta Pasqualina

Salvatore Marchese believes that this definitively Genoese torta dates from the fourteenth century; Paolo Lingua, whose history is usually better, cites a document indicating that it was well known by the sixteenth – and suggests that it was fashioned on the model of the fifteenth- and sixteenth-century torta mantovana (that is, the Mantua-style torta). It was originally known simply as *torta di giæe* in Genoa – Swiss chard torta – and apparently gained its more familiar name simply because it had become a part of the traditional Easter menu (along with stuffed lettuce leaves and roasted baby lamb or kid). There is a version made with artichokes, but chard is more traditional. If the ingredients are mixed together instead of layered, this becomes, strictly speaking, a torta cappuccina, or Capuchine torta. Lingua notes that, although the ingredients are modest, it is essential that they be of the highest quality. "The pasqualina," he warns, "is not the food of the miser."

to serve 6

1	double recipe of torta dough No. 1 or No. 2 (see page 179)
1.5 kg/3 lb	Swiss chard
	Salt
	Extra-virgin olive oil
225 g/8 oz	prescinsêua (see page 124) or ricotta
115 g/4 oz	Parmigiano-Reggiano, grated
1	small onion, very finely chopped
	Leaves from 3–4 sprigs marjoram
3	flat-leaf parsley sprigs, minced
6	small hard-cooked eggs, peeled

Divide dough into 7 or 8 small balls, then roll each one out as thinly as possible on a floured work surface. As sheets are finished, stack them, with a damp tea towel in between the layers, finishing with a damp tea towel on top.

Trim stalks from chard, reserving them for another use, then cut into a very fine chiffonade and blanch for 5 minutes in another saucepan of boiling, salted water. Drain and set aside.

Lightly oil a round baking dish (or pizza or paella pan) 35-45 cm/14-18 inches in diameter, and lay 1 pastry sheet down evenly in it. Brush very lightly with oil, then lay another sheet on top. Repeat until there are 4 or 5 layers (depending on whether you have 7 or 8 sheets; you'll need 3 for the top).

Spread a thin layer of about half the chard over the pastry. On top of this, carefully spread the prescinsêua. Mix about ¾ of the Parmigiano plus the onion, marjoram, and parsley into the remaining chard and spread this mixture over the cheese, season generously with salt, then tap down lightly.

Preheat oven to 190°C/375°F/Gas Mark 5.

With the back of a deep spoon, make 6 indentations in chard mixture in a circular pattern. Place 1 egg in each indentation and dust them with the remaining Parmigiano.

Place another pastry sheet over the filling, pressing it down lightly with your fingers, then repeat the process described above with the remaining 2 sheets. Crimp the edges of the sheets together and trim off excess. Prick crust in several places with a fork. Drizzle olive oil over top of torta, then bake for 45 minutes to 1 hour, or until crust is browned and begins to come away from sides of dish or pan.

Serve at room temperature.

Sweet Swiss Chard Torte
Tourte de Blettes

All over the Mediterranean, from Catalonia to the Peloponnesus, greens are cooked with pine nuts and raisins as a vegetable dish – a device that has always seemed quite medieval to me, but one whose effects I like very much. In Nice, the same idea is taken one step further: Swiss chard, with raisins and pine nuts mixed in, is sweetened, bound with egg, and baked in a pastry shell. The result is an unusual but strangely appealing dessert. The recipe is adapted from one used at Chez Barale in Nice.

to serve 8

4	large eggs and yolk of 1 large egg
275 g/10 oz	flour
225 g/8 oz	sugar
225 g/8 oz	unsalted butter, at room temperature
	Salt

900 g/2 lb	Swiss chard
75 g/3 oz	golden raisins
	Marc or grappa
40 g/1½ oz	pine nuts
50 g/2 oz	freshly grated Parmigiano-Reggiano
	Extra-virgin olive oil
2	large golden delicious apples, peeled, cored, and sliced 3mm/⅛ inch thick (optional)

Beat 2 of the eggs and set aside. Sift flour and half the sugar into a mixing bowl, then stir in beaten eggs, butter, and a pinch of salt with a fork until a crumbly mixture is formed. Turn out dough onto a floured work surface and knead several times. Shape dough into a ball, cover with a damp cloth, and refrigerate for 2 hours.

Remove stalks and ribs from chard and reserve for another use. Steam chard leaves for about 15 minutes in a small quantity of salted water, then drain, cool under a cold tap, and squeeze out as much moisture as possible. Finely chop chard and set aside.

Preheat oven to 190°C/375°F/Gas Mark 5. Beat remaining 2 whole eggs and set aside. Place raisins in a small saucepan with enough marc or grappa to cover the bottom of the pan and cook for about 1 minute over medium heat. Allow to cool, then mix raisins and remaining liquid mix with chard, pine nuts, remaining sugar, beaten eggs, and cheese in a large bowl.

Lightly oil a round or rectangular baking dish 35-45 cm/14-18 inches in diameter. Divide dough into 2 balls, 1 about twice the size of the other, then roll both out on a floured work surface to a thickness of about 3 mm/⅛ inch. Line bottom and sides of baking dish with the larger piece and form it around the edges. Prick lightly with a fork and spoon in filling, smoothing it down gently so that it is of even thickness. If using apples, layer over the filling. Cover with remaining piece of dough and crimp edges of dough pieces together, trimming off the excess. Prick top of pastry with a fork. Lightly beat the egg yolk and brush it over the top of the pastry. Bake until crust is golden and pulls away from sides of pan, about 30 minutes.

Serve at room temperature or lightly chilled.

SOCCA AND FARINATA

Socca, socca, caouda qué bullié! (Socca,
socca, boiling hot!)

– STREET CRY OF OLD NIÇOIS
SOCCA VENDORS

Mangiàive [la farinata] cauda,
percòuse fréida a nu va ciù in cufin.
(Eat the farinata hot, because you can't
swallow it cold.)

– SANREMASCO SAYING

One of the rituals of market-going on the Cours Saleya in Nice is stopping for a paper cone of socca to nibble at while strolling past the rows of fruit and vegetables. There are two major purveyors – a pink-fronted open storefront on the north side of the promenade, which bakes large pans of socca continuously all morning, and a stand set up under one of the market awnings daily by Chez Thérèse, a take-out food shop a few blocks away in Vieux Nice, and supplied with fresh socca directly from there. This woman who sells socca here is a real market character, good-natured, ceaselessly joshing, known to all – and for this reason, more than for an appreciable difference in quality, I prefer her socca.

Socca is a thin, crumbly, unleavened crêpe-like thing made from chickpea (garbanzo) flour, olive oil, salt, and water. It is traditionally cooked in large, flat, straight-sided copper pans in wood-fueled ovens. Cut into irregular slices and dusted with black pepper (a spice of which the Niçois are particularly fond), it is sold not only in the market but at stands and shops and tiny restaurants all over Vieux Nice, and elsewhere in town.

Socca is the ultimate Niçois street food, particularly appreciated as a midmorning snack or *merenda*. In earlier times, says Jacques Médecin, it was the favourite between-meals food of construction workers around the city, and socca vendors would circulate through the streets of Nice pushing two-wheeled carts on which were mounted big zinc boxes containing pans of socca warmed by chafing-dishes – the lunch wagons of their time. In 1908, in an effort to "clean up" the city so that it didn't seem too rustic to tourists and winter residents from the north, the local government banned these socca carts. There was an enormous outcry from all sides, however, and the ban was quickly rescinded. (Modern traffic, among other factors, has long since removed them from the streets again.)

In *Cuisine traditionnelle en pays niçois,* Mamé Clairette proposes that socca is similar in form to that ancient bread called *tailloirs,* which served as a plate on which food was arrayed. After they consumed whatever meats or other foods were on top of these tailloirs, she adds, the rich threw them to the dogs, while the poor ate them themselves.

Nobody seems to know exactly where the name *socca* came from. It is tempting to link it with the Catalan verb *soccarar,* to singe or scorch, since socca inevitably blackens a bit around the edges when cooking (the soccarat is the highly prized burnt bottom crust of a paella) – but the Catalan presence in Nice was brief. Another possibility is that it derives from *sciocca,* the name given to a kind of leavened chickpea-flour bread once popular along the Riviera di Levante – a word that comes, in turn, from *sciocco,* meaning soft or flabby, which socca would have seemed in comparison with ordinary bread.

Whatever the source of the term, it seems likely – though you'd never get a Niçois to admit this – that socca came to Nice from Liguria, where the same sort of chickpea-flour preparation has long been well known. A Genoese government decree of 1447 specifically describes it, and forbids the use of inferior oil in its manufacture. Travelling gastronome Lieut.-Col. Newnham-Davis encountered it at the Giardino Italia on the Piazza Corvetto in Genoa in the early years of this century, under the name faina – and remarked that it "somewhat resembles Yorkshire pudding made with pease powder and oil."

Faina (usually rendered fainâ) is still the Genoese name for the thing, though it is more commonly known throughout Liguria as farinata. If socca's name is mysterious, the origin of farinata's is obvious, but peculiar. It comes, of course, from *farina* – but that word means specifically white flour, not chickpea flour at all. This usage is apparently simply a reflection of the dish's origins among the poor in or near Genoa – to whom all flour was chickpea flour because white flour, most of it imported, was prohibitively expensive. (Across the line from the Ligurian Lunigiana into Tuscany, the same thing is called, rather more logically, cecina, from the Italian word for chickpeas, *ceci.*) Around the once wealthy port of Savona, on the other hand, white flour was more easily obtainable – and that region traditionally makes a white-flour farinata. Perversely, this one is *not* called farinata but rather turtellassu – lacy torta.

Close similarities aside, farinata is approached somewhat differently in Liguria than socca is in Nice. Socca, as noted, is street food, often eaten in the morning. Farinata can be a snack in Liguria as well, but is rarely eaten by pedestrians; it's something to be consumed sitting down, at a table, or at least while leaning over a bar – and it is considered fit fare for a light dinner, a role socca is less often given in Nice. Another difference is that – leaving aside an occasional attempt by a serious chef to work socca into a more complex dish (Franck Cerutti has been known, for instance, to serve red mullet with socca crêpes and tapenade at his Don Camillo restaurant) – the Niçois eat socca plain, seasoned only with pepper. Farinata, on the other hand, is sometimes flavoured with herbs, spring onions, or thin-sliced onions or baby artichokes. In Lerici, on one occasion, I even encountered it topped with fried miniature fish of the sort called bianchetti (see page 207).

Still another difference is the seriousness with which Ligurians tend to take farinata. The Niçois appreciate socca and defend it as an ancient, nourishing, delicious, and (they are sure) definitively local creation – but they don't get religious about it. Ligurians do tend to get that way about farinata, talking about its communal preparation as an "ancient rite," and the eating of the thing itself as a "communion." In La Spezia, there is even a special name for the man who bakes farinata; elsewhere he is called a farinataio, but in La Spezia, he is a "sagrista" – a sacristan; a keeper, if you will, of the sacred (wood-burning) flame.

Socca/Farinata

Ligurian additions aside, socca and farinata are essentially the same thing, with regional differences based on such variables as the water used, the proportions of water to chickpea flour, the amount of salt and/or oil added, the variety of oil (some professional farinata bakers prefer rapeseed – to olive), the nature of the oven in which they are cooked, and the fuel used to cook them.

It is widely believed that neither socca nor farinata should ever be cooked at home. As Renzo Fregoso puts it on a cassette tape he narrates on the joint subjects of mescciuà and farinata, "Eat farinata at home, but bring it in from the outside." It is a dish, he explains, that needs to be made in large pans, in large portions, in big, hot ovens. To an extent, I think that's true. I can't imagine home-made socca or farinata ever tasting as good as that made by old pros in blackened copper pans in wood-burning ovens in Nice, Genoa, La Spezia, or wherever. But a reasonable approximation can certainly be achieved – a socca/farinata that will offer at least a hint of the real thing, and be quite enjoyable on its own.

The main trick is getting the batter to the proper thickness. When I bought some chickpea flour from a grocer in Vieux Nice one day, mentioning that I planned to try making socca according to Jacques Médecin's recipe, he smiled and said, "Be careful. There are two recipes for socca: Jacques Médecin's and everybody else's." The difference, it turns out, is that Médecin calls for 250 grams of chickpea flour to a half-litre of water (9 oz to 1 pint); the correct proportion, the grocer assured me, was 300 grams per half-litre (10 oz to 1 pint).

There turns out to be a great deal of disagreement as to this all-important ratio. Mamé Clairette in Bernard Duplessy's *Cuisine traditionnelle en pays niçois* agrees with Médecin: 250 grams of flour. Mireille Johnston in *The Cuisine of the Sun* calls for the equivalent of about 130 grams for just over a half-litre. Elizabeth Romer in her *Italian Pizza and Hearth Breads* agrees, as it were, with the Niçois grocer, calling for approximately 300 grams of flour for about half a litre of water in her farinata recipe. Paolo Lingua says about 167 grams in *La cucina dei genovese*. In *Codice della cucina ligure,* the cookbook published by the Genoese newspaper *Il Secolo XIX,* the figure is 150 grams – and so on. These differences aren't necessarily capricious: Some socca or farinata is thicker than others, intentionally, as a matter of taste; and cooks using a very hot oven might deliberately add a higher portion of water knowing it will evaporate more quickly. After much trial and error with my own gas oven, I must say I think something close to Jacques Médecin's proportion works best.

to serve 6

---

450 ml/16 fl oz	room-temperature water
250 g/9 oz	chickpea flour*
	Extra-virgin olive oil
1 tablespoon	salt
	Freshly and very finely ground black pepper

Place water in a bowl, then sift in flour a little at a time, whisking to obtain a smooth batter. Whisk in 125 ml/ 4 fl oz olive oil and salt. Set batter aside to rest for 1 hour.

Preheat grill, and preheat oven to 230°C/450°F/Gas Mark 8.

Oil a 30-35 cm/12-14 inch ovenproof cast-iron or paella pan, then pour in batter, shaking it gently for a few seconds so that batter settles evenly. Grill for 4 minutes, then place in the oven and bake for 6–8 minutes longer.

Cut into irregular slices and serve hot, dusted with pepper.

*Available at Middle Eastern, Asian and Greek food shops

NOTE: If desired, just before baking socca/farinata at 230°C/450°F/Gas Mark 8, scatter 1 tablespoon fresh rosemary leaves or 2 finely chopped spring onions over the top.

Chickpea-Flour "Fries"

Panisses

To many food lovers, the word *panisse* suggests only one thing: Alice Waters's seminal Berkeley restaurant, Chez Panisse – which might fairly be called the birthplace of contemporary American cooking. Waters named her establishment, in turn, after the kindly sail maker in Marcel Pagnol's *Fanny* trilogy. Bernard Duplessy's Mamé Clairette says that Panisse was a noble name in Avignon in medieval times. If this is so, how it may have come to be applied to these delicious little fritters I cannot begin to guess. Although panisses are strongly associated with Nice, they are also well known along the western Ligurian coast – where they are called panisse or panizzie (or, in Savona, which seems to go its own way in matters of naming chickpea-flour preparations, *fette,* which simply means slices). I've heard rumours that, somewhere along the coast, panizzie are not fried but eaten in their initial cooked and solidified form, dressed with olive oil, lemon juice, and salt and pepper – but I've never run across this presentation in real life. Waverley Root reports still another preparation: "[I]f [farinata] is allowed to cool, is cut into lozenge-shaped pieces, soaked in olive oil with chopped onions, doused with mushroom sauce and grated cheese, and put back into the oven to develop a crust, it becomes paniccia or (the popular term) panissa." It sounds good, but it's not a presentation I've ever run across or heard about elsewhere.

to serve 4

	Extra-virgin olive oil
250 g/9 oz	chickpea flour
850 ml/1½ pints	water, at room temperature
	Corn, or grapeseed oil
	Salt and freshly ground black pepper

Lightly oil 6–8 saucers and set aside.

Mix flour and water* to make a batter. Cook batter in a large, heavy saucepan over medium heat, stirring constantly for 10–15 minutes or until mixture thickens. Remove from heat and continue stirring until very smooth. Pour immediately into saucers, filling them to their rims. Set aside and allow to cool and solidify for 30 minutes.

Gently slide solidified batter forms off saucers and cut into lengths roughly 2.5 × 7 cm/1 × 3 inches. Heat 2.5 cm/1 inch oil in a heavy saucepan over high heat. When very hot but not smoking, fry panisses in batches, without crowding, until golden-brown, about 5–7 minutes. Drain on paper towels and sprinkle with salt and pepper. Serve immediately or keep warm in a low oven.

> *Jacques Médecin makes his panisses with boiling water, and several other recipes call for warm water at the least – but I find that it's easier to obtain a smooth batter with water at room temperature.

Chickpea-Flour Croquettes
Cuculli

Like panisses, cuculli ("little darlings" or "chubby little ones" in Genoese slang) are basically fried chickpea-flour batter – the main difference being that cuculli are leavened, and thus lighter.

to serve 6

10 g/¼ oz	active dry yeast
250 g/9 oz	chickpea flour
850 ml/1½ pints	water, at room temperature
	Salt
	Leaves from 2–3 sprigs marjoram
	Pure olive oil

Dissolve yeast in 2 tablespoons warm water.

Make a batter of flour, water, a pinch of salt, marjoram, and dissolved yeast, whisking ingredients together well until very smooth. Set aside for 20 minutes.

Heat 2.5 cm/1 inch oil in a heavy saucepan over high heat. When very hot but not smoking, place tablespoons full of batter in pan, in batches, and fry until cuculli puff up and turn golden-brown, about 5–7 minutes. Drain on paper towels, sprinkle with salt, and serve.

FRITTELLE

*Ascemmellòu cómme o friscièû cacciòu a
eûio freido. (Stupid like a fritter tossed into
cold oil.)*

— GENOESE EXPRESSION

There is probably no single aspect of the Mediterranean diet – the real one –
that surprises us more than the fact that fried food is an essential part of it. This is
true above all in the Andalusia region of Spain (whose cooks are said to be able to
deep-fry the sea spray, so delicate is their hand) and – our concern for present
purposes – along the Riviera.

Frying is quick, and thus fuel efficient; it is physically an excellent way to
prepare food because, along with boiling, it is the only method that applies heat
evenly from all sides; and it can have the effect of bulking up food, increasing it in
size and caloric value – yet another way to extend the region's often meagre
culinary resources.

What mostly gets consigned to seething oil along the Riviera, besides fish
(especially the smaller ones), are fritters – frittelle in Italian, friscieu in Genoese,
beignets in French, and bignéta in Niçois. These are basically fried anything. The
simplest frittelle are simply strips of dough, leavened or not, plunged into oil and
dusted after cooking with salt or sugar. Others are more like little fried cakes,
filled with raisins, candied fruit, or just plenty of sugar and grated orange peel.
Some frittelle have herbs added, and plain herbs themselves – especially sage and
borage leaves – become frittelle, too. So do slices of fruit, squash blossoms, acacia
flowers (eaten on the Feast of St. John, June 23, in the Menton region), vegetables
of every kind (including cauliflower and cardoons as well as more expected ones),
cheese, various meats and organ meats, and puréed stockfish or salt cod, among
other items. One source even mentions a curiosity of the Riviera di Levante, in
which lemon leaves are dipped in chestnut-flour batter and fried; the leaves
themselves are not eaten, but the crust, impregnated with lemon flavour, is scraped
off with the teeth.

Scattered around Genoa's *centro storico,* or historic medieval core, and under
the arcades facing the port, are a number of little take-out food shops – sometimes
called *friggitorie,* or "fry places" – selling an assortment of frittelle, as well as
things like farinata and various tortas. The big day for fritters in the city is the

Feast of San Giuseppe (St. Joseph), March 19. On this day in 1684, the French navy bombarded Genoa – and for some reason, ever since, tradition-minded locals have celebrated the event by eating a surfeit of frittelle. In other parts of Liguria, fritters are associated with Carnival, or with the week before Easter.

Frittelle (and beignet) batter is usually made with eggs, sometimes with additional egg whites added – though a risen yeast batter may be employed instead. In earlier times in Nice, white wine, and even sometimes marc, known locally as branda, was used instead of water (I think wine is superb for the purpose). Colette Bourrier-Reynaud gives a formula using beer and melted butter (!) in her usually quite traditionally minded *Les recettes de Réparate,* and several Niçois sources mention that, in that region, beignets were often fried not in olive oil but in lard or bacon fat – another Mediterranean surprise.

Fried Dough
Frittelle

Vernazza is the jewel of the fabled Cinque Terre, a picture-book village built around the only natural port on this stretch of coastline – a small one, admittedly, but memorably picturesque. Precisely because of this port, Vernazza was colonized by the Genoese in the tenth century, and as a result became the most important of the five towns. Bohun Lynch reports in 1928 that his Italian friend Giovanni considered Vernazza worth seeing "if only to visit the dirtiest village in the world."

The years must have been kind to it, because today it fairly sparkles. Beautiful old houses crowd around the modest waterfront – simple, graceful structures, glowing warmly in assorted shades of yellow, pink, terra-cotta, and other vivid hues. A Genoese castle (now containing a restaurant with a great view) rises high atop the plump promontory that forms one side of the port, and more fortifications command a hill behind the town. From the end of the promontory, a modern breakwater hooks out to close half the port's mouth. On the other side of the port stands an attractive Ligurian church, dedicated to Santa Margherita di Antiochia. The square that gives onto the port is full of restaurant tables and fishing boats, and always filled with the buzz of conversation in assorted languages. I am particularly fond of two of these – Gianni Franzi and Gambero Rosso, at both of which the food is fresh, straightforward, and unfailingly savoury. And Gambero Rosso serves, as complimentary hors d'oeuvres, the best plain frittelle – they call it pane fritto, fried bread – I have yet encountered. This recipe, simplicity itself, is an adaptation of theirs.

to serve 6

	Salt
200 g/7 oz	flour
10 g/¼ oz	active dry yeast
	Vegetable oil
	Leaves from 2 sprigs rosemary

Mix a pinch of salt into flour in a bowl. Dissolve yeast in 125 ml/4 fl oz warm water and let stand for about 5 minutes, then stir into flour, mixing well with a wooden spoon and adding more water if necessary, until a smooth, pliable dough is formed. Let batter stand for 20 minutes.

Roll out dough as thinly as possible on a floured board, then cut into long, thin strips, as if you were making fettuccine. Cut strips into pieces 6-7.5 cm/2½–3 inches long.

Fill a deep cast-iron frying pan or other deep, heavy pan with about 5 cm/2 inches of oil and heat to about 190°C/375°F/Gas Mark 5, or use a deep fryer, and fry dough pieces in batches until light golden-brown. Drain on paper towels, sprinkle generously with salt and rosemary leaves, and serve at once. (Frittelle are best hot, okay warm, and not very good at room temperature.)

Fritto Misto

This is, strictly speaking, more a Piedmontese dish than a Ligurian one. It is, however, something one encounters not infrequently in the entroterra – where the border between Liguria and Piedmont is, anyway, often more cartographical than cultural or linguistic. I found a superb fritto misto, for example, at a homey trattoria called Del Pippo da Ugo (a name that means something like Ugo's Pippo Place) in the town of Neirone, six or eight miles inland from Recco. Da Ugo is one of those typical Ligurian mountain-town establishments where seafood is but a rumour, and the cooking is based instead around mushrooms, game, rabbit, meat and organ meats, and pasta – and fritto misto is one of the house specialities. This recipe is inspired by the restaurant's version of the dish.

to serve 6

225 g/8 oz	veal sweetbreads
450 g/1 lb	chicken livers, cleaned and halved
6	chicken thighs, boned and quartered lengthways
450 g/1 lb	veal scaloppine, medium thin, cut into strips about 2.5 × 5 cm/1 × 2 inches
225 g/8 oz	courgettes cut into 12 mm/½-inch slices
2	long, slender aubergines trimmed and cut into 12 mm/½-inch slices
6	large mushroom caps, halved
2	apples, peeled, cored, and sliced into thin rings
12	amarettini biscuits
12	large sage leaves
200-275 g/7-10 oz	flour
	Corn, or grapeseed oil
4	large eggs, beaten
175-225 g/6-8 oz	breadcrumbs
	Salt
12	lemon wedges

Plunge sweetbreads into a small saucepan of boiling water, cook for about 2 minutes, then drain and place in a bowl of cold water. Carefully pick the skin off the sweetbreads and cut them into pieces about 2.5 × 5 cm/1 × 2 inches.

Gently toss sweetbreads, chicken livers, chicken thighs, scaloppine pieces, courgettes, aubergines, mushroom caps, apple slices, amarettini, and sage leaves together in a large bowl with flour, then remove the ingredients individually, shake off excess flour, and place on a large platter.

Fill a deep cast-iron frying pan or other deep, heavy pan with about 5 cm/2 inches of oil and heat to about 190°C/375°F, or use a deep fryer. Dip ingredients individually in beaten egg, roll in breadcrumbs, then fry in batches (do not crowd oil so that ingredients stick together) until light golden-brown.*

Drain ingredients on paper towels, salt generously, and transfer to a serving platter, placing newly cooked ingredients on top of those already done to keep them warm. Serve at once, garnished with lemon wedges.

*Keep at least 4 cm/1½ inches of oil in pan at all times, adding more between batches (and allowing it time to heat up sufficiently) if necessary. Skim bits of dark brown flour out of oil to avoid imparting a burnt taste to ingredients. Work as quickly as possible, using 2 or 3 frying pans simultaneously and enlisting the help of a friend if you have room at the stove.

NOTE: Other possible ingredients for fritto misto include calf's liver, calf's brains, frogs' legs, tiny meatballs, artichoke hearts, roasted chestnuts, parboiled potatoes, courgette blossoms, and borage leaves.

Fried Dough with Sage

Skabèi a la Sarbia

This is a recipe adapted from Gianfranco Cricca's *Antiche ricette di Castelnuovo Magra,* a collection of old recipes from the corner of Liguria best known for its fried foods.

to serve 4–6

	Salt
200 g/7 oz	flour
90 g/3½ oz	buckwheat flour
20–30	sage leaves, julienned
10 g/¼ oz	active dry yeast
	Corn, or grapeseed oil

Mix 1 tablespoon salt into regular and buckwheat flour in a bowl. Mix in sage leaves. Dissolve yeast in about 450 ml/16 fl oz warm water and let stand for about 5 minutes, then stir into flour, mixing well with a wooden spoon and adding more water if necessary, until a smooth, pliable dough is formed.

Form dough into a ball and place in a lightly oiled bowl covered by a tea towel. Place in a warm place and allow to rise for 1½–2 hours, or refrigerate and allow to rise for 6–8 hours.

Roll dough out on a floured work surface to a thickness of about 8 mm/⅓ inch, then cut into strips about 2.5 cm/1 inch and 7 cm/3 inches long, or into "fantasy" shapes.

Fill a deep cast-iron frying pan or other deep, heavy pan with about 5 cm/2 inches of oil and heat to about 190°C/375°F, or use a deep fryer, and fry dough pieces in batches until light golden-brown. Drain on paper towels, salt generously, and serve at once.

Three Basic Batters for Frying

There is a surprising amount of variation between the all-purpose batters recommended for beignets and frittelle by various chefs and home cooks in Nice and Liguria – and a number of specific kinds of fritters have slightly different recipes of their own. Here are three approaches to an all-purpose one. One or the other of them can be used for virtually any kind of vegetable, fruit, or small fish or cut-up meat you might want to try frying.

(1.)   According to Franck Cerutti at Don Camillo in Nice, the traditional local recipe for beignet batter – which practically nobody uses anymore – calls for 175 g/6 oz flour, 225 ml/8 fl oz water, 1 egg, a few sprigs of minced parsley, and a clove or 2 (to taste) of minced garlic. All the ingredients are mixed together thoroughly, and the batter is used at once. This batter is suitable only for savoury fritters, obviously. It is also quite thick, and thus better for such solid foodstuffs as courgette or aubergine slices than for more delicate ones, like squash blossoms.

(2.)   In their *Les Recettes de la table niçoise,* Raymond Armisen and André Martin propose a much lighter but more complicated batter: Mix together 250 g/9 oz flour, 1 litre/ 1¾ pints water or milk, 1 tablespoon olive oil, 2 egg yolks, a pinch of salt, and a pinch of dry yeast. Let the mixture sit for 2½ hours, then beat 2 egg whites separately and stir them into the batter. This recipe produces a light, almost tempura-style coating on fried food. Try it with squash blossoms, or for a lighter batter on sliced aubergines or courgettes, apples, or onion rings.

(3.)   The simplest batter of all, which I use for little fried fish (i.e., anchovies), sage or borage leaves, and other items with a certain amount of exterior texture (to help the batter cling), is simply 50 g/2 oz flour – or very slightly more – mixed very thoroughly with 225 ml/8 fl oz dry white wine.

Fried Squash Blossoms
Fleurs de Courgette Frites

The most beautiful squash blossoms I've seen on the Riviera were in Ventimiglia, the first town in Liguria across the French border. Named for a Ligurian tribe called the Intemelii, who established a pre-Roman settlement nearby between 400 and 300 B.C., Ventimiglia has an attractive old quarter, on a hill above the Roia or Roya River – but most visitors pass through only the modern town below, perhaps stopping to shop or eat, and perhaps to visit the Ventimiglia market, just off the main street. Occupying a large, rectangular concrete pavilion, particularly drab-looking when it's closed (afternoons and all day Sunday), this market certainly can't compete with the Cours Saleya for looks or charm. But even the Niçois, who cross the border frequently, admit that it is full of treasures.

Strolling through the place one late June, for instance, I found, among other things, the curiously ridged, heart-shaped, pale-red-and-green tomatoes called cuore di bue; fat heads of radicchio both red and green; fresh capers and fresh chickpeas (both rarities); bundles of deep purple asparagus; fat pea pods; tiny red and yellow plums; and veritable cascades of courgette and pumpkin blossoms. These were not the twee little flowers attached to baby courgettes that our own "gourmet" markets sell. They came large and larger, with delicate rococo egg-yolk-yellow tracery against pale green – and they never were attached to squash: The blossoms used for stuffing and frying here are the male ones, which don't produce fruit, and they somehow seem to remain slightly crisper and sweeter because of it. If Ventimiglia had the best blossoms in their natural state, though, Nice has my favourite fried ones – specifically, those made by Jean Giusti at La Merenda. This is his recipe.

to serve 8

50 g/2 oz	flour
	Salt
450 ml/16 fl oz	water
1 tablespoon	extra-virgin olive oil
1	large egg, lightly beaten
16	large or 32 small squash or courgette blossoms
	Corn, or grapeseed oil
1	garlic clove, minced
2–3	sprigs flat-leaf parsley, finely chopped

Combine flour and about 1 teaspoon salt in a mixing bowl and stir in water, then oil and egg.

Gently open blossoms and remove pistils, then wash carefully, inside and out, and pat dry with paper towels.

Heat about 4 cm/1½ inches vegetable oil in a large heavy frying pan until hot but not smoking.

Stir garlic and parsley into batter, then dip flowers into it, coating them thoroughly. Shake off excess batter, and fry in small batches for about 1 minute or until golden, turning as needed. Remove with slotted spoon as done and drain on paper towels. Dust lightly with salt and serve.

Fried Raisin Pastries

Frittelle all'Uvette

In giving this recipe – under its Genoese name, friscieu co-o zebibbo – in his amusing and informative collection of definitive Ligurian recipes, *Mandilli de sœa,* Franco Accame points out that the Genoese word for fritters, *friscieu,* is "onomatopeia par excellence, rendering instantly the idea of dough sizzling in smoking oil." He also notes that, on the great frittelle-eating day of the Feast of St. Joseph (San Giuseppe), these particular frittelle figure in a kind of practical joke traditionally played by Genoese carpenters, whose patron saint Joseph is. It seems that the men gather for a meal, at which huge platters of frescieu co-o zebibbo are presented. One of the fritters, out of the many, is filled with cotton wool. The carpenter who bites into it, says Accame, "has only to buy drinks for the crowd."

to serve 6

10 g/¼ oz	active dry yeast
	Sugar
300 g/11 oz	flour
125 ml/4 fl oz	full fat milk
3	large eggs
	Grated peel of 1 lemon
	Salt
150 g/6 oz	sultanas
	Corn, or grapeseed oil

Dissolve yeast in 2 tablespoons warm water. Mix 225 g/8 oz sugar with flour, then stir in dissolved yeast, milk, eggs, lemon peel, and a pinch of salt, and mix very well to form a firm but supple dough. Cover with a tea towel and allow to rise for 3 hours in a warm place.

Work in raisins so that they are well distributed in dough.

Fill a deep cast-iron frying pan or other deep, heavy pan with about 5 cm/2 inches of oil and heat to about 140°C/275°F, or use a deep fryer; form dough into elongated spheres about the size of eggs, then fry them in batches until light golden-brown. Drain on paper towels, dust generously with sugar, and serve at once.

Opposite: Rice with Greens

Part 3
From
the Sea

FISH AND SHELLFISH

Pesci! Pesci chi vuole? / Triglie, acciughe,
soglióle. / Pesci! Pesci chi toglie? / Triglie,
acciughine, soglie. (Fish! Fish, who wants
it? / Mullet, anchovies, big sole. / Fish!
Fish, who takes it? / Mullet, little
anchovies, sole.)

– "La Pescatrice di Bordighera"
(popular song, c. 1880)

Dickens called Camogli "the saltiest, roughest, most piratical little place that ever was seen." Sean O'Faolain, about 100 years later, thought it had "a beautiful restless vivacity." I found it raucous but basically good-natured rather than rough or restless, one Sunday morning in May not long ago, when I joined the crowds in the Camogli's Piazza Colombo for the town's annual Sagra del Pesce, or Fish Festival.

Camogli, on the eastern flank of the Portofino Peninsula about a dozen miles from Genoa, is one of the prettier towns on the eastern Ligurian coast, with clusters of tall, narrow buildings in shades of yellow, beige, and terra-cotta rising above a long waterfront promenade lined with caffès, boutiques (nothing too chic), and foccaccia and gelato shops. One section of the promenade borders a stone beach; the other hugs the port, in which fishing boats (called *gozzi*) often seem to outnumber yachts, and fishermen clump ashore carrying damp nets and baskets of fish.

Camogli was once famous for its *tonnara* or tuna-fishing fleet, which at one point is said to have brought in three catches a day – and fishing in general has long been a vital (if small) industry here. It even gives the town, by extension, its very name – at least according to one theory: Camogli, it is said, is a contraction of the Genoese *cà de mogee,* or "house of wives" – a reference to the fact that the men of Camogli were usually out on their boats, leaving their spouses alone at home. (A local sailor's song says "Passòu u munte de Purtufin, / Addíu muggé che sun fantin" – "Beyond the cape of Portofino, / Good-bye, wife; I'm a bachelor.") (Other theories derive the town's name from *cà a muggi,* piled-up houses, or from Camulo, the Etruscan Mars – the latter a distinct possibility, since the earliest written reference to the town, in the eleventh century, calls it Vila Camuli.)

The Sagra del Pesce is officially part of a religious celebration, the Festa di

Santo Fortunato Martire, held annually in honour of Camogli's patron saint, an event which begins with the burning of wooden pyres on the beach and a fireworks show on Saturday night, and then continues with a benediction offered after Mass in the basilica of Santa Maria Assunta on Sunday morning. What draws literally thousands of visitors from Genoa and elsewhere in the region, though, is a midday fish fry of heroic proportions sponsored by the Cooperativa Pescatori Camogli. At the edge of the piazza, set on a shelf of planks extending out over the water, an immense pan – four metres (about 12 feet) in diameter, with a 20-foot-long handle sticking out into the air – bubbles with oil over a large gas fire. (The oil is not olive but a vegetable one of no specified origin called Friol, whose manufacturer helps sponsor the sagra.) Behind the pan, fishermen deliver Styrofoam boxes of glistening fresh little fish – large sardines, or something similar. Assembly-line volunteers from the fisherman's cooperative dredge them in flour, plunge them into the oil, fry them to a perfect medium brown, dump them onto paper-covered tables to drain, scoop them into white plastic boxes bearing the Friol label, scatter them with salt and stick lemon wedges and paper napkins into each box, and then hand them to waiting celebrants.

That's us: a jam or maybe a scrum of people, the vast majority Italian (and more or less local), mostly acting like schoolkids despite the fact that some of them were obviously grandmothers and grandfathers – pushing, rubbing, tweaking friends' ears or anonymously tapping shoulders, shouting, making dirty jokes. The gulls, meanwhile, circle hopefully overhead, drawn by the smell, driven back by the smoke. Purists deride Camogli's Sagra del Pesce as a tourist lure and nothing more, and indeed it is a recent creation, dating only from 1952. But it seems genuinely popular, in the original sense of the word – drawing hordes of people who seem to have come for no other reason than to have fun and eat a bit of fried fresh fish. That fish, when I finally get my portion, incidentally, is sublime, and serves as a savoury reminder – in this era when everything piscatorial, at least in the United Kingdom, seems to get either grilled or seared (or served raw) – what a very good method frying is for cooking fish.

Historically, as noted earlier, the Genoese preferred preserved fish – dried or salted – to fresh. Salted tuna, called tonnina, was particularly important. What fresh fish they did eat was often from fresh water – for instance, sturgeon, perch, or trout, all of which were considered more delicate than ocean fish. As also noted earlier, there was another reason that fresh fish from the Mediterranean was not consumed more often on the Riviera in earlier times: Not all that much of it was caught, due both to the poverty of Ligurian fishing waters and to the often difficult sailing conditions here. (These conditions might explain the curious Genoese proverb, curious because of Genoa's reputation for trans-oceanic trade and exploration, that advises, "Lodá o mâ ma stanni a câ" – "Praise the sea but stay home.")

Unlike Provence and Catalonia (among other Mediterranean locales), then, Liguria has no real traditional seafood cuisine. Not counting stockfish or salt cod dishes and some treatments of anchovies as antipasto, the only multi-ingredient preparations of seafood essential to the Genoese culinary repertoire are ciuppin (fish soup), burrida (fish stew), and possibly seppie in zimino (cuttlefish cooked with Swiss chard, onions, and tomatoes). Cappon magro is an essential, and includes fish, but fish is a comparatively minor part of the dish. Virtually everything else tends to be very simple, very plain, cooked by frying or roasting, seasoned with not much more than salt and perhaps a herb or two (oregano is common with fish in La Spezia, for example). The Genoese reluctance to do much to fish is suggested by the proverb "Chi in sciö pescio ghe mette o limon, ò o l'è cûneo, ò l'è ûn belinon" – "He who puts lemon on his fish is either a jerk or a fool." This is said because lemon is thought to mask lack of freshness in fish.

There was quite a to-do about a modern Ligurian seafood recipe some years ago – one with no apparent connection to traditional local cooking. This was scampi as served at the now-defunct Da Ü Batti in Portofino. This popular restaurant was famous for the dish, and for the fact that the proprietor had once asked Prince Rainier and Grace Kelly (who may well have come to sample it) to wait their turn for a table like everybody else. Proprietor Battista Costa's scampi recipe was top secret. According to Mauro Vincenti, my Roman restaurateur friend in Los Angeles, there was a contest among local gastronomes in Portofino every year in which the object was to duplicate it exactly; no one ever did.

I tried the dish once myself in the late 1980s, shortly before Da Ü Batti closed. It was quite good – little curled-up scampi tails, very fresh, cloaked in a rather rich, salty sauce that reminded me, generically, of "continental" chafing-dish cookery. An edition of the *Guida d'Italia* from the early 1980s listed scampi cooked with a raspberry distillate as one of the Batti's specialities – but I don't think that was the same dish. (If I had entered the scampi contest myself, I might have started with clarified butter and sherry and gone from there.) Since Batti's death and the demise of his Portofino restaurant, his widow, Ida, and son, Gian, have continued to make the scampi and other Batti specialities at a new establishment, called Da Ö Battj (an alternate dialect spelling of the name) in nearby Santa Margherita. They did not respond to my request for the recipe, and to the best of my knowledge have not revealed it to this day.

There are sceptics who tell you that virtually no seafood in the markets of Genoa is local and that most of it has probably been frozen (or is at least five days old) to boot; there are also optimists who believe that almost everything is local and caught that morning. The truth probably lies somewhere in between. In any case, I've seen the following items in the city's fishmongers' stalls, labelled as fresh and coming from Ligurian or neighbouring Tuscan waters: at least four kinds of bream (including red bream, called besûgu or bezügu in Genoese – a word that also means someone who is not very bright; as Maria Luisa Rosciano Bertoldi puts it drily in her *Guida ai detti genovesi e liguri,* "It would have been difficult for a bezügu type to have invented the radio or discovered penicillin"), hake, rascasse, mackerel, swordfish, tuna, bogue (whose wonderful Linnaean name is *Boops boops*), smooth hound *(palombo),* red mullet, sea bass (*Dicentrarchus labrax* or *Morone labrax,* called branzino or spigola in Italian and loasso in Genoese), conger eel, moray eel, octopus, curled octopus (moscardino), squid, cuttlefish, shrimp and scampi of various sizes, and mussels – not to mention the inevitable anchovies and sardines.

The Gulf of La Spezia is noted for its octopus and its cultivated shellfish. Octopus is particularly associated with Lerici and the coastal indentation known as the Gulf of the Poets – a name coined earlier this century by the playwright Sem Benelli (1877–1949), with perhaps more justification than is usual for such honourifics, since both Dante and Petrarch stopped here and mentioned Lerici in their verse, and Shelley drowned in a boating accident while staying there. Another literary figure, D. H. Lawrence, recounts a tale from Tellaro – a town not quite three miles south of Lerici – where the local church stands close to the water: One night, it seems, the citizenry was awakened by the frantic tolling of the church bell, the signal of an impending pirate raid. When they assembled at the church, however, they found a huge octopus, on the rocks below the belfry, pulling on the bell cord.

The waters off La Spezia itself – calm, comparatively full of plankton (for the Mediterranean), but not excessively salty – are perfect for mussel cultivation, and these bivalves are much appreciated and frequently eaten in the region. The Romans apparently raised seafood here as early as the first century A.D. – not just mussels but also oysters and the relatives of mussels called datteri or sea dates *(Lithophaga lithophaga),* for which the island of Palmaria, across the gulf from Lerici, was particularly famous. A millennium later, the Holy Roman Emperor Frederick Barbarossa (1123–1190) demanded shields filled with datteri as tribute from the lords of Vezzano, a town near La Spezia on the Magra River. Today they are endangered, and it is forbidden to harvest them – but the modern-day mussel industry, founded anew in the late nineteenth century, is thriving.

In Nice, in the Musée des Beaux-Arts, there is a display of sterling silver ex voto objects from the Trésor de la Confrérie de St. Pierre (the confraternity of Niçois fishermen) – thirty-three small, nicely detailed fish, all different. These are said to represent exactly the diverse species commonly taken in the waters off Nice in the seventeenth century. In the eighteenth century, Smollett found more than a dozen kinds of locally caught seafood in the city's markets. In 1976, Mireille Johnston wrote that 80 percent of the fish sold in Nice comes from the Atlantic, and the percentage is probably at least as high today. Not counting the deep-water tuna boats that sail out of Nice, there aren't more than six or eight fishermen now landing their catch here, and they mostly bring in red mullet, monkfish, turbot, forkbeard (mostelle or moustèla, a relative of whiting), shrimp, octopus, and squid – and not many of each.

Until the 1970s, fish was much more abundant between Nice and the Italian border than it is today. What made the difference was an engineering operation undertaken to divert the mouth of the Var River in order to facilitate the building of an extension to the Nice–Côte d'Azur airport. Now warm water and nutrients from the river flow westward, toward Antibes, not in the direction of Nice. The sea had its revenge on the airport: On October 16, 1979, two freak tidal waves hit Nice, sweeping cars out to sea, destroying boats, and engulfing the airport extension, still under construction. Nine workers were washed out to sea, and only two were saved. The unusual waves were apparently caused by an underwater landslide off Antibes, in turn triggered by masses of earth and debris carried into the bay by the Var, which had been flooded by heavy rains.

Small Fry

You see them in late winter and early spring in shallow Styrofoam boxes on little tables set up casually on the streets of Vieux Nice, or at the fish stalls at Genoa's Mercato Orientale. If you don't know what they are, they aren't particularly appetizing: They look like gelatinous masses of flat little worms, somewhere between pale white and translucent pearl in colour. These are poutines (in Nice) or bianchetti or gianchetti (in Liguria) – and they are one of the great subtle delicacies of the region.

Poutines are sardines and anchovies – and sometimes, so they say, red mullet, bream, and other more noble fish – in their larval or just-hatched state. They are rarely more than a couple of inches long and are as thin as string; there are literally hundreds of them to the pound. They have a faint flavour of the sea, and sometimes a pleasant tang of salt, but are not particularly pronounced in taste. The Niçois once used them to make pissala; now they eat them mostly in omelettes, and sometimes fried up as beignets; in Liguria they are eaten fried or simply boiled and dressed with olive oil, lemon juice, salt, and pepper.

The Alpes-Maritimes, whose capital is Nice, is the only département in France where it is legal to fish for poutines; elsewhere, they must be left to mature. According to Alan Davidson in his authoritative *Mediterranean Seafood,* this is because, even after it became part of France in 1860, the region continued to function under the fishery regulations of Sardinia, where taking these tiny creatures is allowed. According to another story, the Empress Josephine granted the dispensation somewhat earlier (she died in 1814) to the fishermen of Nice, because she considered them her friends.

The law says that poutines may be fished in the Alpes-Maritimes for a period of only thirty days, beginning in mid-February each year (this limit does not appear to be taken very seriously), and no French boat may take more than 100 kilos per season. The regulations for bianchetti in Liguria are somewhat more relaxed, and the season runs officially longer, from January to May, and sometimes again from August to October.

Two stylistic if not ichthyological relatives of poutines are gobies (*Aphyia minuta*), called nonnats in Nice and rossetti in Liguria, which rarely grow more than a couple of inches long even as adults (these are what the Spanish call chanquetes); and tiny atherines or sand smelts (various species of *Atherina*), called melets in Nice and latterini in Liguria. These are generally eaten in the same ways as poutines – though Henri Heyraud, in his *La Cuisine à Nice* (1909), offers a recipe for salade monégasque that includes nonnats, chopped tomatoes, quartered artichokes, black olives, and potatoes, seasoned with oil, lemon juice, salt, pepper, mustard, and crushed anchovies.

That travelling bon vivant Lieut.-Col. Newnham-Davis ate nonnats in the early 1900s, when he asked M. Fleury, manager of the restaurant at the Hôtel de Paris in Monte Carlo, to prepare him a dinner with "as much local colour introduced into it as possible." One of the hors d'oeuvres, he reports in *The Gourmet's Guide to Europe,* was a friture de nonnats – which Newnham-Davis describes as "the small fry of the bay, smaller far than whitebait, and . . . delicious to eat." He adds, though, that "They are perhaps more suitable for breakfast than for a dinner of ceremony."

Mosciame and Bottarga

One morning ten or twelve years ago, browsing through the open-air fish market in Cádiz, the ancient port city on the tip of Andalusian Spain, I noticed a man selling paper cones filled with irregular small pieces of something dark and leathery, vaguely resembling beef jerky – something to eat, obviously, but I had no idea what. Of course, I had to try it, and it turned out to be mojama, which might be called *fish* jerky – chewy, salty bits of sun-dried something or other, strong but ultimately quite addictive.

Half a dozen years later, at a little seaside restaurant in the Cinque Terre, I was served an antipasto of thinly sliced dried fish dressed with olive oil and oregano, again salty, but rather delicate. This, I was told, was mosciame (or mosciamme or musciame). It was obviously a more refined Ligurian version of mojama (both names derive from the Arabic *mushammas,* exposed to the sun) – fish prosciutto, say, instead of fish jerky.

Both are simply fish cut into pieces, salted, and then dried in the open air and sun. Genoese ships used to have special shelves or baskets attached to their masts in which mosciame – once an essential part of the Genoese Lenten diet – could be made; more recently, fishermen would dry fish on the overturned hulls of their boats between voyages. I suspect that much of what is eaten today in Liguria is produced commercially, and not on the hulls of boats – but in any case, it is eaten simply, either as I had it or in a straightforward salad.

The fish most often used for mosciame in Italy today is tuna. When I asked the owner of the restaurant in the Cinque Terre what kind of fish I was eating, however, he smiled, made a show of looking around, and then said, "You're not from Greenpeace?" When I assured him that I wasn't, he whispered one word to me: "delfino" – dolphin. This, it turns out, was the fish, or rather mammal, traditionally used to prepare the delicacy. Today, of course, it is illegal – and I must say that, based on my sole experience of it and on numerous subsequent tastes of mosciame made from tuna, I'm not at all sure that it's any better than the more common version anyway.

Bottarga (bottaega or bottarega in Genoese) is another seafood speciality much appreciated in Liguria. This is not dried fish but rather dried fish roe – frequently from tuna but preferably (and this time completely legally) from muggine, which is grey mullet. The traditional way of making bottarga is to soak the egg sacs overnight in water, dry them thoroughly, salt them, and press them, weighted down, between two wooden slabs. They are kept like this for three days in a dry, well ventilated place, then a string is passed through the sacs at their thickest part and they are hung for fifteen days more to dry. Something close to this method was described by Platina in the fifteenth century. Today there are doubtless quicker, more contemporary ways of processing the sacs.

Like mosciame, bottarga is served thinly sliced, sometimes with tomatoes (I once had it with thinly sliced oranges instead, at a restaurant in Sardinia; delicious), or shaved onto pasta. In a shop in Bordighera, I recently found little urn-shaped jars of bottarga in powder form, for use on pasta, but I didn't like it very much.

Two Ways to Fry Fish

If your fish are small and very fresh, there is probably not a better way to cook them than frying. Dusted in flour or coated in a light batter and submerged in hot oil, fish cooks quickly and evenly, remaining perfectly moist; the slight crust formed on its exterior provides a perfect counterpoint to its juicy flesh; and a little salt and lemon juice – the only accoutrements needed – accent its flavour deftly without competing with it. When Bohun Lynch encountered fried sardines for the first time in Noli in the 1920s – fresh ones, of course, "not putative pilchard-fry extracted with much thumb-cutting, curses, and stupidity out of a small, flat, expensive tin" – he wrote that "only one word adequately sums them up, a word of my childhood, but none the worse for that – scrumptious." I agree.

(**1.**) Choose small whole fish if possible: small sole (or rex or lemon sole), sand dabs, butterfish, red mullet, perch, etc. If using larger fish, cut them crosswise into thin "steaks" without removing the bone. (The smaller the fish or fish steak, the less likely it will be to break up when you remove it from the fat.) Allow about 350 g/12 oz bone-in fish per person for a main course, about 150 g/5 oz per person for an appetizer. (An assortment of fried small fish, usually with small squid added, becomes a fritto misto mare.) Fill a deep cast-iron frying pan or other deep, heavy pan with about 5 cm/2 inches of oil and heat to about 190°C/375°F, or use a deep fryer. Rinse fish and pat dry, then dredge in flour and fry in small batches until light golden-brown. Drain on paper towels, salt generously, and serve with lemon wedges.

(**2.**) *La vera cuciniera genovese* gives a slightly fancier alternative to simply dredging the fish in flour. Instead, mince 1 garlic clove and 3–4 flat-leaf parsley sprigs per 450 g/1 lb of fish and stir them into beaten eggs (about 2 per 450 g/1 lb of fish). Prepare oil and rinse and dry fish as above, dip into egg mixture, then dredge in breadcrumbs and fry. Serve as above.

Ciuppin

Cioppino, the tomato-rich fish stew of the San Francisco Italian community, obviously derives its name, if not its form, from this classic Genoese fish soup (whose name is, in turn, simply a corruption of the Genoese word *sûppin*, meaning "little soup"). The obvious major difference between the two is that cioppino is typically full of fish and shellfish – a stew concocted with the typical exuberant abundance of Italian-American immigrant cuisine – while ciuppin is a straightforward puréed or sieved soup, not dissimilar to the basic soupe de poisson found all over Provence, though with more texture left to it. Ciuppin is particularly popular just east of Genoa, between Chiavari and Sestri Levante. It is almost universally considered, incidentally, that the proper accompaniment for both ciuppin and buridda is young, fresh red wine – a Rossese di Dolceacqua from western Liguria, for instance, or a Dolcetto from neighbouring Piedmont.

to serve 6

2	onions, finely chopped
1	celery stalk, finely chopped
1	carrot, diced
2	garlic cloves, minced
4	flat-leaf parsley sprigs, minced
	Extra-virgin olive oil
4	anchovy fillets, chopped
4	large ripe tomatoes, skinned, seeded, and chopped
350 ml/12 fl oz	Ligurian Vermentino or other dry white wine
1.5 kg/3 lb	hake, cod, halibut, or other flavourful ocean fish, skin and bones removed, cut into large pieces
	Salt and freshly ground black pepper
6	slices grilled or toasted country-style bread

Cook onions, celery, carrot, garlic, and parsley in a heavy saucepan or casserole in olive oil over low heat until onions are soft and translucent, about 15 minutes. Add anchovies and tomatoes and continue cooking about 10 minutes longer.

Add wine, turn heat to high, and cook for about 5 minutes, stirring constantly. Reduce heat to low again, add fish and 450-675 ml/16-24 fl oz hot water, and cook for 20 minutes, uncovered, until fish is tender and liquid has reduced slightly.

Pass ingredients through a food mill, or process briefly in a food processor, then return to pan and season to taste with salt and pepper. Cook over low heat for about 5 minutes longer. Soup should be neither watery nor too thick; if necessary, cook slightly longer to reduce liquid further or add a few additional spoonfuls of hot water to dilute to proper consistency.

Serve over bread slices.

Buridda

Also known as pesce in tocchetto (literally fish in pieces), buridda is similar to ciuppin, except that it is not puréed or sieved. Buridda – which shares an obvious kinship with the Provençal fish stew called bourride – was standard shipboard fare for hundreds of years in and around Genoa, and the osterie clustered around that city's massive port specialized in it until well into this century. Despite attempts by Genoese gastronomic writers to give the word *buridda* an Arabic etymology, it might very well come from the Spanish *podrida,* meaning rotten, as in "olla podrida" – literally "rotten pot," the name of a Spanish meat and vegetable stew. The original buridda was made with stockfish – which suggests that it might be a very old dish, predating the development of the Genoese taste for fresh fish – and is still sometimes made that way in the entroterra.

to serve 6

25 g/1 oz	dried porcini mushrooms
2	onions, finely chopped
1	celery stalk, finely chopped
1	carrot, diced
2	garlic cloves, minced
4	flat-leaf parsley sprigs, minced
	Extra-virgin olive oil
4	anchovy fillets, chopped
4	large ripe tomatoes, skinned, seeded, and chopped
350 ml/12 fl oz	Ligurian Vermentino or other dry white wine
225 g/8oz	cleaned squid
450 g/1 lb	hake, cod, halibut, or other flavourful ocean fish, cut into large pieces
450 g/1 lb	saltwater eel or conger (if possible) or monkfish, cut into large pieces
	Salt and freshly ground black pepper

Soak mushrooms in 3 changes of warm (not hot) water, for a total of about 15 minutes. Set aside in final change of water.

Meanwhile, cook onions, celery, carrot, garlic, and parsley in a heavy saucepan or casserole in olive oil over low heat until onions are soft and translucent, about 15 minutes. Add anchovies and tomatoes and continue cooking about 10 minutes longer.

Add wine, turn heat to high, and cook for about 5 minutes, stirring constantly. Reduce heat to low again. Add squid and other seafood to the pan, then strain in mushroom water. Chop mushrooms and add them, season to taste with salt and pepper, then cook, uncovered, for about 45 minutes.

Fresh Anchovies in Tomato Sauce

Bagnun

Also known as zuppa di acciughe (anchovy soup), this speciality of the Golfo di Tigullio, between the Portofino Peninsula and the promontory beyond Riva Trigoso, and especially of Chiavari and Sestri Levante, is said to have been invented by fishermen in the late nineteenth century – during the time of, as Paolo Lingua puts it, "the aggressive advance of the tomato." It was cooked up at dawn on little charcoal stoves, on the beach or the dock, as the nets dried after a night's work. Riva Trigoso itself helps keep the dish alive by celebrating an annual Sagra del Bagnun every July. There is absolutely no point in making bagnun, incidentally, if you don't use fresh anchovies or sardines – preferably anchovies. Though these are hardly supermarket staples, they can be found sometimes (or special-ordered) at good fish markets, especially in Italian, Spanish, Portuguese, or Greek neighbourhoods.

to serve 4

2	cloves garlic, minced
½	onion, finely chopped
4	flat-leaf parsley sprigs, finely chopped
	Extra-virgin olive oil
450 g/1 lb	ripe tomatoes, skinned, seeded, and chopped
	Salt and freshly ground black pepper
350 ml/12 fl oz	Ligurian Vermentino or other dry white wine

900 g/2 lb	whole fresh anchovies or sardines, rinsed, cleaned, with heads removed
4	ship's biscuits (gallette marinare) or
4	pieces country-style bread, toasted

Cook garlic, onion, and parsley in olive oil over a low heat for 15–20 minutes, or until onion is very tender and translucent. Add tomatoes, stir well, and continue cooking for about 10 minutes. Season to taste with salt and pepper, then add white wine.

Raise heat slightly and add anchovies or sardines. Cook without stirring for about 15 minutes. Place 1 gallette or 1 piece toasted bread in each of 4 large, shallow bowls, and spoon anchovies and sauce over them.

Stuffed Squid
Totani Pin

One of the real successes of Genoa's 1992 Columbus quin-centennial celebrations – perhaps the only lasting one – was the renovation and enlargement of the city's aquarium. Now one of the largest such institutions in the world, it occupies a long ship-grey structure in the heart of the port (it looks as if it might steam off to sea itself at any moment), holds four million litres of water, and displays more than a thousand sea creatures. Through its numerous multi-lingual placards, charts, and audiovisual aids, it is also a veritable reservoir of fascinating information about the oceans of the world, the legend and lore of sea creatures and ships alike, and the culture of the Mediterranean.

Among the disparate facts I learned while strolling past its tanks:

- The Mediterranean used to be ringed with vast oak forests (there are remnants in Sardinia and North Africa), later cut for firewood and timber and to clear fields for agriculture; with the trees gone, fertile topsoil washed away, grazing sheeps and goats prevented new forestation, and the now ubiquitous scrub-like maquis grew instead.
- Ships were originally christened with animal blood, so the animal's spirit would protect the vessel; later, wine (that eternal

symbol of blood) was substituted, and this evolved into today's traditional champagne.

- The octopus has been called the most intelligent of the invertebrates.
- Pliny had a theory that species of fish caught together in nets were allies, and those never caught together were at war.
- Julius Caesar once served 6,000 morays at a single victory banquet.
- Much of the Mediterranean floor is covered with *Posidonia oceanica,* or sea olive, a highly developed plant bearing both fruits and flowers, which functions as a marine habitat, oxygenates the water and adds organic materials to it, and, through its roots and rhizomes, protects the sea floor from erosion. Today, unfortunately, the sea olive beds are threatened by pollution, by the construction of ports and piers, and by the introduction into the Mediterranean, through the Suez Canal, of competing sea plants.

I had occasion to express my appreciation of the Genoa aquarium one evening when I met its then-director, Andrea Rossi, at a potluck dinner at the home of my friends Giorgio Bergami and Maria Deidda. Rossi, who is now in charge of the historic old section of Genoa's port, is an accomplished cook – seafood, hardly surprisingly, is his speciality – and he had brought one of his favourite dishes: totani pin, as it is known in Genoese. I translate this here as "stuffed squid," but the totano is not exactly squid; it's a similar creature, of a different genus, whose English name is apparently "flying squid" (it is said to be able to propel itself out of the water and into the air). It has shorter, fatter rear fins than a squid, set farther back on the body, and thicker tentacles – but is very similar to squid in flavour and texture. As prepared by Rossi, filled with a simple stuffing and then cut into rounds, it was delicious and even elegant in a rustic, portside sort of way. This is his recipe, which works perfectly well with regular old sea-bound squid.

to serve 4

4	large squid (about 15 cm/6 inches long and 7.5 cm/3 inches wide), or 8 or 12 smaller ones, depending on size
1	garlic clove, minced

4	flat-leaf parsley sprigs, minced
	Leaves from 3–4 sprigs marjoram or oregano
50 g/2 oz	Parmigiano-Reggiano, grated
1	large slice country-style bread, crusts trimmed, soaked in milk
2	large eggs, lightly beaten
	Salt and freshly ground black pepper
	Extra-virgin olive oil
350 g/12 oz	ripe tomatoes, skinned, seeded, and chopped
75 g/3 oz	pine nuts

Clean the squid well, then cut off tentacles and chop them finely. Mix tentacles in a bowl with garlic, parsley, marjoram, and Parmigiano. Lightly squeeze moisture out of bread, tear into little pieces, and add to mixture. Stir in eggs, season with salt and pepper, and amalgamate well.

Stuff squid bodies with mixture, closing the open end securely with toothpicks, or sew shut with a large needle and kitchen string. Cook stuffed squid in olive oil in a large heavy frying pan over medium heat, turning several times, until lightly browned on all sides. Add tomatoes and 225 ml/8 fl oz water to pan, cover, and cook for 30 minutes. Remove cover, add pine nuts, and continue cooking for 10–15 minutes or until sauce is thick.

Remove squid from sauce and cut into slices about 2.5 cm/1 inch thick. Distribute evenly between 4 plates. Season tomato sauce to taste with salt and pepper, spoon over squid slices, and serve hot. The slices and sauce can also be served at room temperature.

Tuna "on the Slate"

Tonno in sciä Ciappa

For some reason, we usually think of tuna as being a fish of the great oceans, the Atlantic and the Pacific. But tuna of several species is plentiful in the Mediterranean, including the famed bluefin and albacore (though the similarly esteemed yellowfin is absent) – and, as seafood authority Alan Davidson puts it, "The tuna fisheries in the Mediterranean are of considerable commercial importance and great antiquity." Because tuna is a great export item, however, relatively long-lasting and much in demand all over the world, it is not much eaten on the Riviera – except in the form of the sun-dried tuna flesh called mosciame and the salted, dried tuna roe sacs called bottarga (see box, page 209).

Franco Accame does offer one traditional fresh tuna recipe, however, in his *Mandilli de sæa*. Tonno in sciä ciappa, literally tuna on the slate, is tuna seared directly on a thin piece of slate heated over an open fire. Accame recalls that this method of preparing food seemed the height of sophistication during the outdoor summer parties of his youth. Even without a heated piece of slate – even indoors, with a griddle or a large frying pan standing in – I like this way of cooking tuna. It's simple and savoury – and a reminder that "charred rare ahi" isn't the only manifestation of fresh tuna worth eating.

to serve 4

4	tuna steaks, 150-225 g/5-8 oz each
	Extra-virgin olive oil
	Fresh breadcrumbs
	Salt and freshly ground black pepper
1	lemon, quartered
4	flat-leaf parsley sprigs, minced

Heat a large, dry cast-iron or non-stick frying pan or a griddle over high heat for 2–3 minutes, then reduce heat to medium.

Rub tuna steaks well with olive oil, then dredge on both sides in breadcrumbs.

Place steaks carefully in heated pan or on griddle. Season tops generously with salt and pepper. Cook for 2–3 minutes, then turn. Season cooked side with salt and pepper to taste. Continue cooking, without turning again, for 4–6 minutes (or longer if necessary, depending on thickness of tuna) until tuna is just cooked through.*

After placing steaks on plates, squeeze ¼ lemon over each and scatter them with parsley.

*Tuna is never served rare or even pink in traditional Italian cooking.

Trout Cannelloni

Cannellonis de Truite

One spring afternoon, having spent the day in the Ligurian mountain town of Triora, not far from the French border, I decided to try driving to La Brigue the hard way. La Brigue is an historic mountain town in the arrière-pays, about 50 miles from Nice. Named for the Brigiani, the last of the Ligurian tribes to submit to Rome, it earned a certain fame in earlier times for its lavender, honey, and wool, and even for wine – though no trace of this now remains.

I had planned to visit La Brigue in search of several local dishes – notably the gnocchi-like sugelli and the leek-and-potato-filled tourte brigasque for which the town is known – and it seemed to me from looking at my map that instead of returning to the coast and taking the good road up into French territory from Ventimiglia, I might essay a very small and winding road that seemed to lead to La Brigue through Realdo (a hamlet just northwest of Triora) and over the Col de Sanson. My friends in Triora recommended against this itinerary when I mentioned it: I was driving a nice big Renault Safrane, a terrific car but not exactly designed for mountain paths, and anyway, they said, parts of the road might have been washed out. I decided to risk it and was rewarded with a beautiful, bumpy ride over a broad path scattered with stones, badly rutted, seriously muddy, that led up and down hill and dale over what I later learned was officially called the Route de l'Amitié or Strada dell'Amicizia, the road of friendship.

Arriving safely – the Safrane performed admirably – I found an attractive old settlement, made mostly of time-burnished stone, beneath a sheer rock facing, its lower reaches dense with shrubs and low trees and illuminated by mimosa, its higher portions bare. Garden plots, planted heavily with potatoes, stretched along a small irrigation canal, partially shaded by weeping willows and by cherry, peach, and fig trees, plane trees, and acacias. I checked into my hotel, rested a bit, and then walked a few blocks to the homey little Auberge St. Martin, where I couldn't resist sampling a dish I hadn't expected: delicate, opulent cannelloni filled with fresh trout from one of the local streams that feed into the Roya River. For reasons of his own, the proprietor of the Auberge subsequently refused to share his recipe with me – but I've worked out what I think is a pretty good version of the dish.

to serve 6

8	rainbow trout, cleaned (about 225 g/8 oz each)
1	large sprig fresh tarragon
1	large sprig fresh oregano or marjoram
1	bay leaf
1	celery stalk
3	shallots, minced
1	garlic clove, minced
	Unsalted butter
450 ml/16 fl oz	cream
18	cannelloni wrappers or 18 sheets of mandilli de sæa pasta (see page 69)
50 g/ 2 oz	fresh ricotta

Place the trout, herbs, and celery in a large saucepan with water to cover over high heat. Bring to the point of a boil, but do not boil; reduce heat and simmer, uncovered, for 15 minutes. Carefully remove trout and set aside to cool, reserving water in the pan but discarding herbs and celery.

Cook shallots and garlic in a large saucepan in about 2 tablespoons butter over low heat until soft, about 5 minutes.

Meanwhile, when trout has cooled, cut off and discard heads and tails, peel off skin, then fillet and thoroughly bone. Flake fish into shallot mixture. Add 125 ml/4 fl oz cream and mash with a fork to form a thick, slightly chunky paste.

Preheat oven to 200°C/400°F/Gas Mark 6.

Return reserved water to a boil, then cook cannelloni wrappers or pasta sheets in batches for about 3 minutes, removing them carefully with a slotted spoon and draining them on clean tea towels. (Do not use paper towels.)

Spread a small amount of trout mixture along one side of each wrapper or sheet, covering no more than a third of its surface and keeping mixture about 12 mm/ ½ inch from each end of the pasta, then carefully roll each one into the shape of a tube, starting from the fish side. As the cannellonis are filled, place them, seam side down and side by side, in a generously buttered baking dish just large enough to hold them.

Heat remaining cream in a small saucepan (do not boil), then stir in ricotta until it dissolves. Spoon over cannellonis and bake for 10–12 minutes, or until filling is heated through and tops are lightly browned.

Fresh Cod with Anchovy Vinaigrette

Morue Fraîche à la Vinaigrette du Pissala

Pissala, the Niçois anchovy sauce, is often identified as a descendent of the famous garum, or fermented fish sauce, of the Romans. At Don Camillo in Nice, chef Franck Cerutti makes his own pissala and uses it in a way dreamed of by neither Romans nor the Niçois of a more traditional bent. (The fish he specifies is called morue fraîche, incidentally, to distinguish it from morue salée, or salt cod.) This is an adaptation of his recipe, made with anchovy fillets instead of pissala.

to serve 6

2 tablespoons	sherry vinegar
	Extra-virgin olive oil
12	oil-packed anchovy fillets, finely chopped
6	flat-leaf parsley sprigs, finely chopped
	Salt and freshly ground black pepper
900 g/2 lb	white potatoes, scrubbed but not peeled
1.5 kg/3 lb	fresh cod fillets, skin on, cut into 6 pieces

At least 2 hours before cooking cod, make vinaigrette by whisking together vinegar, 125 ml/4 fl oz olive oil, anchovies, and about half the parsley. Season to taste with salt and pepper and set aside.

Cook potatoes in a large saucepan of salted water over high heat until tender, about 15–20 minutes. Drain and cool slightly. Slip skins off. Mash with a fork or a potato masher, leaving plenty of lumps, and gradually drizzle in about 4 tablespoons olive oil. Season to taste with salt and pepper and set aside, keeping warm.

Brush fish with oil and cook, skin side down, in a large, lightly oiled cast-iron frying pan over medium heat for 5 minutes. Reduce heat to low and continue cooking for about 25 minutes. Cover pan and cook for 3 minutes longer.

To serve, divide vinaigrette evenly between 6 plates, then place 1 piece of cod atop each pool of vinaigrette. Add a spoonful of potatoes to each plate and garnish with remaining parsley.

Clams with Broccoli and Potatoes

Palourdes avec Broccoli et Pommes de Terre

This is another of Niçois chef Franck Cerutti's innovations. As he puts it, "It's not traditional, but it could be" – which could be said of much of his food.

to serve 4

3–4 dozen	small clams
	Salt
	Individual florets from 1 or 2 small pieces broccoli (10–12 florets in all)
2	medium white potatoes, peeled and cubed
2	garlic cloves, peeled
	Extra-virgin olive oil
225 ml/8 fl oz	dry white wine
2	flat-leaf parsley sprigs, minced
	Juice of ½ lemon

Scrub clamshells with a small brush under running water. Place clams in a large bowl or stockpot and cover with cold water. Shake bowl or pot gently, then let clams stand for at least 1 hour, shaking once or twice more during that time.

While clams are soaking, blanch broccoli florets in boiling salted water, then drain (but do not rinse) and set aside. In another pan of boiling, salted water, cook potatoes for about 10 minutes, then also drain and set these aside, too, again not rinsing them.

Cook garlic cloves slowly in olive oil in a large heavy frying pan for about 10 minutes, then discard. Add clams to oil, cover the pan, and cook over high heat for 2 minutes, shaking pan gently. Add wine and cook 2 minutes more or until clams open. Uncover pan and remove clams with a slotted spoon and transfer to a bowl. (Discard any clams that have not opened.) Add 2–3 tablespoons olive oil, parsley, and lemon juice to pan and cook for a minute or so, stirring constantly. Reduce heat to medium, add broccoli, potatoes, and clams, and cook for 2–3 minutes longer until sauce is emulsified. Salt to taste.

STOCKFISH

I païsi de mâ i cunusce tütti u stuchefissu.
(The cities of the sea all know stockfish.)

– LUCETTO RAMELLA, *RICETTE*
TRADIZIONALI DELLA
LIGURIA: LA CUCINA
ONEGLIESE

Stockfish is in these people.

– PINO SOLA, GENOESE
RESTAURATEUR

On the rocky shores of the Lofoten Islands, an archipelago in the northwestern Norwegian region of Nordland, 600 miles or so from Oslo, stand thousands of wooden structures – open frameworks, like the skeletons of small houses – either tall A-frames whose sides are crosshatched with joists and crossbars or structures with four A-frame corners themselves supporting rows of crossbars. For about three months every year, from late February to late May, these structures are hung with fish, most of it cod *(Gadus morhua)*. Caught in the icy waters of the Norwegian Sea, the cod is cleaned and decapitated on shipboard, then landed here, tied in pairs by the tail, and slung over the crossbars to dry in the cold, dry, constant wind. This is how one of the most important food products used on the Riviera, 1,700 miles or so to the southeast, has been made for centuries – a food product so basic to the cuisine that its importance is almost heraldic.

With the possible exception of anchovies, the plentiful food fish of the poor, the single variety of seafood consumed most frequently in Liguria and Nice in earlier centuries – and quite possibly in our own day as well – is precisely this Norwegian air-dried cod, which is called stockfish in English, estocafic in Niçois, stoccofisso or pesce stocco in Italian, and stocchefisciu or simply stocche in Genoese. All these names derive from the Middle Dutch word *stokvisch,* or stick fish, and if you've ever seen stockfish, you'll know why it's called that: It is as firm as wood; the only way to cut it is with a saw.

The Sagas of the twelfth century mention fishing shanties built in the Lofotens by King Øystein (1089–1122), but stockfish was being made in Scandinavia even earlier, perhaps by the late tenth century. Jarle Sanden, director of the Romsdal Museum in Molde, Norway, who is a specialist in the history of the cod industry, tells me that it was being shipped to England as early as A.D. 900. Somewhat later, Erik the Red and his son, Leif Eriksson, are said to have provisioned their voyages of exploration with it, and indeed it was the perfect sailors' food: light in weight (about eleven pounds of fresh fish reduce down to just over two pounds when dried), highly resistant to spoilage (at least 70 percent of the cod's moisture is removed by drying), and nutritious, being very high in protein (79 grams per 100 grams of weight) and rich in B vitamins and calcium. And though the old Norwegians wouldn't have known this, or cared if they did, stockfish is also high in now trendy omega-3 fish oil.

It may be no accident that the greatest seafarers of the medieval world – the Vikings and later the Portuguese and the Genoese – all had access to and a taste for dried cod: It both helped fuel their voyages and provided impetus for them. Alan Davidson goes so far as to suggest that "there are grounds for thinking that the European colonization of North America was prompted to a large extent by the existence of large stocks of cod on that side of the Atlantic." Indeed, on maps from the sixteenth century, an embryonic North American continent is sometimes labelled "Bacculearum" – "Land of the Cod."

Not everybody likes stockfish, it must be said. Unlike salt cod, which can be confused with fresh fish when properly desalted, stockfish remains somewhat chewy in texture even after proper preparation, with a distinctive, almost earthy flavour and an unmistakable aroma. The Norwegians themselves eat comparatively little of it, and most of that is in the form of lutefisk – which is stockfish soaked in lye to render it gelatinous, a quality the Norwegians like.

The Genoese and the Niçois, who eat it a great deal, tend to marry it, quite sensibly, with other foods of strong flavour – onions, garlic, tomatoes, olives, and such. But how and when and why did this Norwegian speciality become a staple on the Riviera? According to some sources, both Norway and Iceland started trading dried cod with France, Spain, and Portugal – in exchange for grain, tiles, and wine – as early as A.D. 1000. It wasn't until the formation of the Hanseatic League (whose capital was the Norwegian city of Bergen) and the subsequent decline of the Vikings in the thirteenth century, however, that stockfish exportation developed into a major commercial enterprise, with fishing and drying largely controlled by so-called "spit kings" – village headmen who owned the spits of land on which the cod were landed and hung.

Legend has it that the first Italians to sample stockfish were the Venetian sea captain Pietro Querini and his crew, who were blown up from the coast of Portugal by a raging storm in 1432 and tossed onto the island of Rost, the southernmost of the Lofotens. When stockfish first reached the Ligurian coast is not certain, though it is sometimes said (probably incorrectly) that Columbus, like Leif Eriksson before him, provisioned his ships with stockfish on his voyages of discovery – and even that, as a young man, Columbus traded briefly in stockfish.

At the latest, it was being imported into Genoa and consumed there by the mid-sixteenth century. The historian and geographer Giambattista Ramusio (1485–1557) describes a product called *socfisi,* which is "dried by the winds and the sun, and because it's a fish of little moisture, becomes hard as wood." And Genoese archives show that in 1586, a ship from the Danish port of Ålborg unloaded 16,877 dried fish in the city, with a value of 3,100 Genoese lire.

Though it was certainly known before then, the official entry of stockfish into Italian cuisine came in 1570, with the publication of what was to become the most famous of early Italian gastronomic texts, the *Opera di M. Bartolomeo Scappi, cuoco secreto di Papa Pio V.* Scappi writes incorrectly that stockfish came originally from Spain, recommends soaking it for about eight hours in warm water, and then offers several recipes "Per cuocere Merluccie secche in più modi" – "to cook dried cod in more ways." One method is to flour and fry it, then serve it with orange sauce and pepper, and mustard on the side; another was to make a "pottaggio" of stockfish with oil, white wine, verjuice (the acidic juice of unripe grapes), ground almonds, herbs, pepper, cinnamon, and cloves ("because this fish loves spices").

In their definitive *Stoccafisso e baccalà,* Vicenzo Buonassisi and Silvio Torre hypothesize that the sudden popularity of stockfish in Italy might have been inspired by the Council of Trent (1545–1563). The council had a fish problem: As a part of its revision of Church law, it had promulgated stricter regulations for fasting and abstinence (from meat) among the faithful; the only acceptable high-protein substitute for meat was fish – but there was a shortage of ocean fish along the coast (for reasons discussed earlier), and neither freshwater nor saltwater fish could be shipped any great distance in the interior. But one of the participants in the council, it seems, was a Swede named Olof Mansoon – italicized as Olao Magno – later to be named bishop of Uppsala, and Buonassisi and Torre suspect that he might have proposed stockfish to the council as a possible solution to the problem. Being easily transported and stored, that is, stockfish could stand in for meat (and fresh fish), thus easing the burden of the faithful and increasing compliance with the new laws.

Whether Magno deserves the credit or not, religious exigencies are indeed one good reason for the great popularity of preserved fish in the Catholic countries along the Mediterranean (and eastern Atlantic) coast – a popularity that sometimes surprises observers from other regions or religious traditions. The avoidance of meat during prescribed periods, remember, was serious business for Catholics in earlier times. In pre-Reformation England, eating meat on Friday was a crime punishable by death. Even as late as 1765, Smollett remarked – while sailing in western Liguria and observing the assiduousness with which the crew observed Catholic dietary laws – that "a murderer, adulterer, or [sodomite], will obtain easy absolution from the church, and even find favour with society; but a man who eats a pidgeon [sic] on a Saturday, without express licence, is avoided and abhorred, as a monster of reprobation."

By the time of Smollett, Venice and Genoa had become major stockfish ports – as had Marseilles and, to a lesser extent, Nice and its neighbour, Villefranche. The everyday diet in Liguria in the eighteenth century, say Buonassisi and Torre, was stockfish, chestnuts, and greens. By the 1820s, according to Genoese historian Giovanni Rebora, over three million pounds of stockfish a year were being imported through Savona, Finale, Loano, Alassio, and Oneglia. On the other side of the border, a typical Niçois meal in the mid-nineteenth century, wrote G. Boréa in "De la puissance stomacale des anciens niçois," might include "stocafic ben ounch e autre stocafic en un autra moda" – "a dish of stockfish with plenty of oil and another stockfish in another style."

The surprise about stockfish today – given the liberalization of Catholic dietary laws, the waning strength of orthodox Catholicism, the easy accessibility of fresh fish, and the trend (even in Italy) toward ever faster and more convenient food – is that it remains immensely popular in Liguria and Nice. While it is no longer essential to the local diet, it is still widely appreciated and enjoyed – for its flavour and texture, nowadays, instead of just its nutritional or religious values.

Norway currently produces something like ten million pounds of stockfish annually, about four-fifths of the total (with most of the rest coming from Iceland). With the possible exception of North Sea oil, it is the country's principal export. "It's a paradox," says Peter Gati, U.S. representative for the Norwegian Seafood Export Council. "In Norway we consider ourselves to be a modern industrial country, but our main export is a product that's been made the same way for a thousand years."

Italy imports at least 90 percent of Norway's stockfish, with the vast majority going to Liguria, Venice, Naples, and portions of Sicily. There are twenty-two grades of stockfish sold worldwide, and the tradition was to name them after the ports that were their best customers. To this day, the finest grades are sometimes labelled "Genoa 1" and "Genoa 2." In Liguria itself, the best stockfish is called *ragno* – a term said to come from the name of a famous Norwegian stockfish exporter, Ragnor or Ragnar. (Another theory says that, because the fish is thin

and webs of bones show through the skin, it is thought to suggest a spider –
ragno in Italian.)

Something like 800 pounds of ragno are shipped directly from Norway to the
attractive old town of Badalucco (founded 1340), in the western Ligurian
entroterra, every September for that municipality's annual Festival du Stocafissu.
The festival dates only from 1970, but Badalucco's association with stockfish dates
back to the 1600s, when – tradition has it – it was able to resist a ferocious
Saracen siege by virtue of the supplies of stockfish stored within its walls.

The event is in two parts: a private dinner for local bigwigs and invited guests
on Saturday night on the long, narrow Piazza Duomo; and a popular feed the
following morning on the much larger Piazza Marconi, including music, speeches,
and food. The culinary centrepiece on both occasions is the dish called either
stocafissu a Baücôgna or stocafi a-a Bahaücögna (Badalucco-style stockfish, in
either case). One of many courses at the Saturday night dinner, it is offered to one
and all on Sunday for 10,000 lire – about £4.00 – with a plastic cup of fresh, dark
red wine on the side.

This is a fascinating dish, first of all because it is innocent of all the post-
Columbian foodstuffs usually cooked with stockfish (i.e., potatoes, tomatoes,
peppers); instead it uses onions, garlic, pine nuts, dried mushrooms, white wine,
and a few other minor ingredients. If the recipe isn't genuinely medieval – and
locals swear that it is – then it certainly could be. It is fascinating, too, because the
stockfish is cooked on a bed of its own bones (which themselves become edible).
And it is quite delicious.

In Nice, stockfish appears most often in the form of estocaficada, arguably the
most typical and essential of all Niçois dishes. This is a hearty stockfish stew made
with tomatoes, potatoes, onions, garlic, olives, sweet peppers, herbs, and, ideally,
the innards or *boyaux* of the stockfish. There is even a civic association, nearly a
century old, called l'Estocaficada; the membership includes local politicians,
businessmen, clergymen, and artists, and the group meets regularly to both
consume the dish and sing its praises. (The "Chancellor for Life" of the group as
I write this goes by the wonderfully medieval-sounding name of Ménica Paeta.)

The Niçois have even written extravagant poems in honour of stockfish.
Gusta Sauvan's 1914 "Istoria de l'estocafic," for instance, proposes that Eve
tempted Adam not with an apple but with "un estocafic ben coundit" (well
sauced), and that what kept the Roman citizenry in line was not "panem et
circences" (bread and circuses) but "panem et stocafic." In 1838, the most
famous Niçois poet, Giausé Rosalindo Rancher (1785–1843), wrote a veritable
ode to stockfish, and specifically to a particular preparation of it, called

"L'Estocafic a la branlada" or "Stockfish Brandade." Of this wondrous stockfish purée, he wrote: "Recrea lou palat, ciarma coura s'avala, / Fassil à degerir, laugier à l'estomac, / Vou laïssa un souon tranquil prolongar su l'amac" – "Treat for the palate, caresse for the throat, / Easy to digest, flatterer of the stomach, / It will let you sleep peacefully for a long time underneath the arbor." No one ever said that about sole Véronique.

Dealing with Stockfish

Stockfish is not exactly commonly available in British shops – but it can be found here if you're willing to look, primarily in Italian, Caribbean and West African markets. The question, of course, is what to do with it once you've got hold of some.

Unlike salt cod, which requires no more than a few days of soaking in several changes of water to leach out its salt, stockfish needs to be completely reconstituted. There are several theories on how this may best be accomplished. The fourteenth-century *Ménagier de Paris* gives perhaps the earliest instruction for rendering it edible: "When one desires to consume it," says the text, "it must be beaten for a full hour with a hammer of wood, then put to soak in warm water for fully 12 hours or more, then cooked and skimmed well like beef." In our own century, Escoffier recommended simply leaving it for three days in running water. His approximate contemporary, J.-B. Reboul, thinks it sufficient to soak it for "at least four days in a large quantity of water, changing it twice a day." Franck Cerutti swears he knew an old man in the arrière-pays who put his stockfish in the overhead cistern of his toilet – the perfect solution, thought the old-timer, since there water would automatically be changed with every flush, but his water bill would be no higher than usual. (He did admit, Cerutti added, that his bathroom became unusually fragrant.)

In my own admittedly limited experience of preparing stockfish, I've never found it necessary to pound the thing with a mallet – though some chefs apparently still do this (if not quite for an hour). One tool that does come in handy is a saw, if you happen to buy stockfish in pieces too large for the cooking pot. There is literally no other way to cut it. Fortunately, however, it is usually sold in manageable lengths.

My own first experience with stockfish started with a pretty piece of ragno I bought one afternoon, a day before returning to the United States, at La Bottegadi Angelamaria, the extraordinary little boutique filled with the entroterra's bounty in Molini di Triora. The going price at the time was about 55,000 lire per kilo – roughly £10 a pound. For about half that sum, I obtained a hunk about five inches long, three inches across, and barely an inch thick. It seemed to me to weigh about as much as a similarly sized piece of balsa wood might have but was much firmer.

Back home, I couldn't figure out a convenient way to leave it in running water, so I decided to try simply soaking it, with water changes four or five times a day. I placed it in a large bowl filled with water almost to the rim, which I set on a shelf (near a window) in the kitchen. After about 12 hours, it began to plump up a bit. The next day it was still plumper, and had whitened noticeably from its original brown-grey hue; it remained as hard as wood, however. On the third day, there was a certain give to the flesh – it was more like hard rubber than wood – and it was again a bit whiter and thicker. It continued to develop in that way, but every day now the water was milky when I went to change it, and the smell was increasingly stronger. By the eighth or ninth day, the water was full of oily, scale-like bits of something every time I went to change it, and by the tenth day, it was obviously time to cook the stockfish – which I did to good effect, using it as the basis for a sort of improvised estocaficada.

The next time I prepared stockfish, I soaked it for only a week, but – at the suggestion of food and wine scholar Darrell Corti – I increased its absorption of water by gently bending or flexing it once a day in my hands. That worked fine. Be forewarned: However you soak the stockfish, it will reek as it softens and swells. Keeping it in the refrigerator helps a bit, but doesn't suppress the odour entirely. Colette Bourrier-Reynaud gives very good advice in *Les recettes de Réparate*: Ideally, for the process, she writes, "You need an isolated room, well ventilated, with running water, which you can abandon to the stockfish for eight days. . . . If by chance you have a pond at the bottom of the garden, that would do very well."

Salt Cod

Salt cod – called baccalà in both Italian and Genoese, morue in French, and merlussa in Niçois (though, confusingly, the Italian word *merluzzo* refers to hake, a different fish altogether) – begins as exactly the same kind of fish that stockfish does, and is taken in the same waters, by the same fishermen or their near neighbours. The only difference is in the way the fish is processed. Both are cleaned and decapitated; stockfish is then hung by the tail, whole, to begin drying; salt cod is split open lengthways and layered with salt.

Stockfish is older than salt cod by at least a couple of hundred years, simply because there was little salt produced in the Scandinavian countries. It wasn't until the salt trade between northern and southern Europe became established in the twelfth and thirteenth centuries that salt was available in northern Europe in commercial quantity. Once the trade began, as Maguelonne Toussaint-Samat puts it in *History of Food,* "Salt-producing and salt-consuming countries . . . exercised a kind of mutual blackmail. . . . [T]he whole trade was an economic network linking nations."

Some nations, of course, were more intimately linked than others. As a generalization, and with exceptions on both sides, it can be said that Spain eats salt cod and Italy eats stockfish. Southern France eats both salt cod and stockfish, with the latter taking over from the former somewhere around the Camargue – about where bullfighting disappears and whitewashed buildings begin to give way to those painted in Savoyard pastels. (The one Italian region that does consume a considerable amount of salt cod, in addition to stockfish, is Sicily – which of course was once under Catalan-Aragonese,

Opposite: Marinated Salt Cod

which is to say "Spanish," rule. The many dishes *called* baccalà in the Veneto and the region of Friuli-Venezia Giulia are actually made with stockfish.)

One Ligurian salt cod recipe I find particularly appealing comes, not surprisingly, from the famously poor region of Castelnuovo Magra, east of La Spezia. This is a relative of the Catalan escabetx and related dishes.

Marinated Salt Cod (Bakalá Amainá)

To make enough for four as an appetizer, soak about 450 g/1 lb of salt cod (a single "middle" piece, if possible) in abundant water, in the refrigerator, for 48 hours, changing the water three or four times a day. When it's ready, remove any bones or thick skin and cut it into bite-sized pieces. Mince two cloves of garlic, two or three sprigs of flat-leaf parsley, and two or three tablespoons of rosemary leaves. Stir them into 125 ml/4 fl oz of olive oil, warm the mixture on a low flame for about five minutes, then stir in 225 ml/8 fl oz of good-quality white wine vinegar (*not* balsamic vinegar, for heaven's sake). Let the mixture simmer while you dredge salt cod pieces in flour and fry them in olive oil, in batches, until golden-brown. Skin, seed, and chop two ripe tomatoes, and place them and the salt cod in a bowl. Pour the warm vinegar mixture over them, adding more oil if necessary to cover the salt cod completely. Let the salt cod marinate, covered and at room temperature, for somewhere between 12 and 24 hours, then remove salt cod and tomatoes with a slotted spoon and serve plain on plates, or on a small bed of field greens. (Gianfranco Cricca, *Antiche ncette di Castelnuovo Magra*.)

Genoese-Style Stockfish

Stoccafisso alla Genovese

This classic dish – also called stoccafisso in umido (stockfish stew) and stoccafisso accomodato or, in Genoese, stocche accomodou ("convenient" stockfish) – is the basic Ligurian preparation of the fish. I first encountered it when my Genoese friend Giorgio Bergami took me to a hole-in-the-wall joint on the Molo in the port of Genoa, called Fratelli Ivaldi. The blackboard menu at this most basic of establishments offered not much more than trenette al pesto or with meat and tomato sauce, baked salt cod, roast veal with potatoes, and stockfish two ways – simply boiled with potatoes or in umido, with potatoes, olives, and pine nuts. I tried, and was seduced by the utter simplicity of, both – but I preferred the latter, finding that the olives, slightly ammoniated, accented the earthiness of the stockfish, and that the oily, powdery texture of the pine nuts was a perfect foil to the fish's chewy character. The overall effect was one of concentrated flavours, rich and unequivocal; if you like your food mild and sweet, this is not a dish for you – but I find it delicious, in a memorable, proto-Mediterranean way.

Some recipes for Genoese-style stockfish add many more ingredients – including carrots, celery, anchovies, and dried mushrooms. I prefer the dish in the simpler form in which I first encountered it, and this is my approximation of the way it was served by the Ivaldi brothers.

to serve 4

1	onion, finely chopped
1	garlic clove, minced
2	flat-leaf parsley sprigs, minced
	Extra-virgin olive oil
900 g/2 lb	soaked stockfish (see page 229), cut crosswise into 12 mm/½-inch pieces
6	potatoes, peeled, halved lengthways, and cut into 12 mm/½-inch slices
75 g/3 oz	pine nuts
450 ml/16 fl oz	Ligurian Vermentino or other dry white wine
	Salt
175 g/6 oz	Taggiasca or Niçoise olives*

*See third note, page 92.

Cook *onion, garlic,* and parsley in olive oil over low heat for about 20 minutes. Add stockfish, potatoes, and pine nuts. Stir well to coat ingredients with oil, adding more oil if necessary, then add wine and 225 ml/8 fl oz water, and salt to taste.

Cook uncovered over low heat for about 40 minutes, or until potatoes are cooked and liquid has reduced by at least a half. Stir in olives, cook for 5 minutes more, and serve.

Stockfish Brandade
Brandacujun

A speciality of San Remo, with obvious connections to the brandade of Provence on one side and the baccalà (which is to say stockfish) mantecato of the Veneto region on the other, this is stockfish for beginners – probably the most accessible of classic stockfish dishes, flavourful yet comforting in texture. Virtually the same thing is also eaten in Menton, under the name brandaminccian or brandaminchan – but there is, strangely, no real equivalent in Nice. The name comes from two San Remo dialect words that relate directly to how it is traditionally made: *branda,* meaning shaken, and *cujun,* meaning tired, because the dish is mixed and puréed by being shaken vigorously in a closed pot – so vigorously that the action is fatiguing. About the best brandacujun I've encountered is at Paolo e Barbara, my favourite San Remo restaurant. This is an adaptation of their recipe.

to serve 4

675 g/1½ lb	soaked stockfish (see page 229)
4	potatoes
3–4	flat-leaf parsley sprigs, minced
175 ml/6 fl oz	extra-virgin olive oil
	Juice of ½ lemon
	Salt
75 g/3 oz	Taggiasca or Niçoise olives, pitted

Cook *stockfish and* potatoes simultaneously in 2 saucepans of boiling salted water, for about 30 minutes. Drain both and allow to cool. Remove bones and skin from stockfish and shred coarsely with your fingers. Place in a wide, shallow pot or other container with a tight-fitting lid.

evaporated or been absorbed. At this point, the ingredients are crushed together vigorously with a large wooden dowel. More salt and oil are added if necessary. Stocafi a-a Bahaücögna is always washed down with red wine – preferably a local Rossese. "The real recipe," warns the Calendaiu de Bahaücu, "has secret ingredients. If you want to taste the 'verace stocafi,' come to Badalucco on the third Sunday of September."

Estocaficada

To say that estocaficada is a hearty dish is an understatement; it is a *strong* one – intense in texture, flavour, and aroma. The scent of it (like the scent of tripe) sometimes puts people off. Jacques Médecin acknowledges as much when he writes that "I know more than one person who, [initially] trusting the harsh reactions of his olfactory nerves, later gave in [to the dish] for the sake of peace and quiet, and then regretted not having discovered the joys of the supreme ragout earlier."

There are minor variations in recipes for this dish. Some are full of tomatoes, for instance, while others are flavoured only with a bit of tomato purée; some formulas call for a shot of marc and others don't. But the Niçois tend to be adamant on one matter: The boyaux or dried intestines of the fish should always be included. This imperative, obviously, is easier to observe for someone in Nice than for someone in, say, London or New York – and a perfectly good estocaficada can be made without innards. One other Niçois commonplace about the dish makes more practical sense away from Nice: As Colette Bourrier-Reynaud says, "Estocaficada is not a dish for two or three people. It is best eaten at large tables." She also notes that, while it is excellent the day of its preparation, "some like it even better reheated." As with most ragouts, indeed, a day in the refrigerator only seems to help it. This recipe is adapted from one given to me by Jean Giusti at La Merenda – whose estocaficada was probably the best I've ever had.

to serve 8

1.5 kg/3 lb	soaked stockfish (see page 229), cut into 6 approximately equal pieces
	Salt
125 ml/4 fl oz	extra-virgin olive oil
4	onions, coarsely chopped

Peel potatoes, crush with a fork, and add to stockfish. Add half the parsley and the oil, lemon juice, and plenty of salt. Cover container and, holding lid on tightly, shake vigorously in several directions for at least 5 minutes.

Serve at room temperature, garnished with olives and remaining parsley. (Serve with toast if desired.)

Stockfish Badalucco Style
Stocafi a-a Bahaücögna

"One simply cannot make this dish at home for a regular family," says stockfish expert Silvio Torre. "It's for a community event, or perhaps a very large family reunion." Two problems are the very long cooking time required and the sheer volume of stockfish required to obtain enough of the requisite stockfish bones. I've done a "mini" version a few times at home, and it's been reasonable enough in flavour, but it doesn't come close to the genuine article. I offer this sort-of recipe, then, more for information than for practical reasons – though the more adventurous among you may wish to take it on as a challenge. The particulars come partially from an official recipe published by the Pro Loco di Badalucco (more or less the chamber of commerce) in the 1992 edition of its annual Calendaiu de Bahaücu, or Badalucco Calendar, and partially from watching and talking with chef Francesco Ammirati as he prepared the dish under the arcades of the Piazza Duomo for the town's stockfish festival in 1994.

Place stockfish bones on the bottom of a huge cauldron, as insulation and a kind of rack for the stockfish. (When the dish is finished, these will be not only edible, but, in my opinion, the best part.) Cut the soaked stockfish into long pieces and stack it, as if it were firewood, leaving a hole in the centre of the pile. Into the hole, pour olive oil. Ladle a combination of white wine and water over the stockfish until it is more than covered. (Ammirati used veal stock; though this seemed like a refinement for our private dinner, Silvio Torre told me that the dish has probably been made this way by the wealthier local families for centuries.) To the liquid are added dried mushrooms, pine nuts, onions, pitted olives or olive paste, and salt. Hazelnuts, anchovies, and carrots are optional. The liquid is brought to a boil, then the heat is reduced, and the cauldron simmers, covered, for about 12 hours. When the cover is removed, the fish looks dark yellowish brown and rich, almost like kippered herring, and the liquid has

1	bouquet garni of 2 sprigs each flat-leaf parsley, thyme, and fennel, 1 bay leaf, and 1 sprig marjoram or oregano, tied together with kitchen string
8	cloves garlic, peeled and crushed
2	tomatoes, skinned, seeded, and chopped
1 tablespoon	tomato purée
2	red bell peppers, seeds and veins removed, chopped
1.5 kg/3 lb	potatoes, peeled and coarsely chopped
75 g/3 oz	Niçoise olives*

Place cod in a saucepan with enough salted water to barely cover. Add olive oil, onions, bouquet garni, garlic, tomatoes, and tomato purée. Bring to a boil, then reduce heat, cover, and simmer for 1 hour.

Add peppers and simmer for 1 hour longer, still covered, then add potatoes and olives. Raise heat to medium and cook, uncovered, for about 20 minutes, or until potatoes are soft and sauce is thick. (Add more water if sauce reduces too quickly.) Serve hot.

*See third note, page 92.

Part 4
From the
Back Country

CHESTNUTS

*A matin castagne, a megiudi pestümi, a
sèira castagnòn. (In the morning, chestnuts;
at midday, chestnut crumbs; in the evening,
dried chestnuts.)*

— TRIORESE SAYING

In earlier, harsher times, they say, when famine visited the backcountry of the
Riviera, villages that grew chestnut trees survived, while those that did not were
decimated. In the Ligurian entroterra, as elsewhere in northern Italy, the chestnut
was known as *l'albero del pane* – the bread tree – both because it provided the
common nourishment and because bread could literally be made from chestnut
flour. For many centuries, chestnuts were arguably the single most important
foodstuff in the entroterra and the arrière-pays – the daily fare. They were eaten
fresh, either boiled or roasted or stewed in milk or wine. Dried, they went into
soups, or were reconstituted by boiling in water with fennel flowers and salt (the
water blackens, and this yields a Genoese expression for a treacherous person or
affair, "cæu cumme l'ægua de ballettu" – dark like chestnut water), or were
popped plain into the mouth and chewed, like caramels. (The smoke-dried
chestnuts of earlier times were softer and sweeter than today's oven-dried variety –
which are not recommended for chewing.)

They were also, especially in Liguria, ground into flour – used not only to make
bread (usually in combination with white flour), but also for pasta and gnocchi
(see pages 67/128), as a polenta-like gruel to be eaten with fresh cheese, and as
porridge. Chestnut batter was also fried into frittelle and made into testaroli.

In addition, chestnut wood has long been used on the Riviera for tools, barrels,
and furniture, and between the sixteenth and nineteenth centuries, in the hills
behind Genoa, it was grown specifically to be turned into charcoal to fuel Genoese
ironworks. In the arrière-pays, where Isola is the chestnut capital, and towns like
Le Moulinet and Coaraze have annual celebrations of the tree and its fruit, there
was even a French government inquiry, in 1807, into the possibility of making
sugar from chestnuts – which apparently proved impractical. The chestnut does,
however, indirectly provide another sweetener, on both sides of the border:
chestnut honey. This is an unusual and quite delicious product, not very sweet at
all but rich and full-bodied, with a pleasant bitterness.

I learned about traditional Ligurian chestnut harvesting and processing in the Val di Vara, which stretches westward from Varese Ligure, inland from Sestri Levante in the eastern entroterra – a particularly poor and isolated region, in which l'albero del pane has always been particularly important. The chestnut harvest begins in the Val di Vara around mid-October and lasts for about two weeks. It is followed by a second harvest – of the dried chestnut leaves, which are used as winter bedding for cows. Processing chestnuts is labour intensive and, perforce, was always a community project. Ten or twelve pounds of chestnuts at a time were placed in heavy sacks, then the sacks were laid out on the ground and two people beat each one with chestnut-wood staffs to crack the shells – striking exactly forty blows (some say forty-two) apiece, it is said, for fewer won't do the job and more will crush the meat as well as the shells.

Next, the chestnuts were taken to a freestanding building called a *seccatoio,* or drying place (*seccàeso* in Genovese). Here they were spread out on an elevated alderwood grille, high above a slow fire of chestnut, alderwood, or dried heather roots, and smoke-dried for hours, as farmers and their friends and neighbours waited patiently, gossiping and eating. (That the process was frustratingly slow may be gleaned from the fact that the term for chestnut drying, *seccatura,* also means nuisance or tedium.)

After the chestnuts had dried, everyone gathered around to shell them and pick them over. The wormy or rotten ones were set aside for the pigs, and the rest either stored dry or sent to a mill to be turned into flour. According to a booklet called *Per Selve, per campi: La Vegetazione tra natura e storia,* published in Varese Ligure, there was also a method of conserving chestnuts for many months in fresh state – but, notes the text, "The secret . . . is one that some people know but nobody will reveal."

Chestnut trees grow both wild and cultivated in the Val di Vara. (The wild ones produce smaller fruit, it is said, but are more resistant to disease.) In one local village alone, Cassego, there were once seven mills grinding chestnut flour. Now there's only one in the whole region, on the road to Sestri Levante – and even that is temporarily closed as I write this, pending the imposition of updated hygiene regulations by the Italian government, at the prompting of the EEC.

The Val di Vara is the only major valley in the entroterra, east or west, that runs parallel to the sea rather than perpendicular to it – and it looks very different from the rest. Typically, the valleys are narrow, with steep, terraced walls. Here, the landscape is gentler, more rounded, with crops growing in high meadows instead of on near-vertical terraces. Pale-hued houses seemed glowingly illuminated against the still-green hills and the autumnal glow of the woods and orchards when I visited the region one day in late October. If there had been a few red barns and white church steeples, it could almost have been Connecticut or Pennsylvania.

I was there not just to learn about chestnuts but to attend Cassego's modest Sagra di Castagne, or Chestnut Festival. The event was inaugurated in 1975 by the village priest, Don Sandro Lagomarsini (see box, page 245). It draws a few visitors from Genoa and Sestri Levante – Lagomarsini is a well-known character, with friends in academic, political, and gastronomic circles all over eastern Liguria – but remains primarily a local affair. The festivities began, inevitably, with Mass at Don Sandro's little church. This is followed by a communal lunch, innocent of chestnuts, at the diocesan vacation house on a nearby hill. Here I sat down in a large hall, at a long table covered with a throwaway plastic red-and-white-checked tablecloth, and joined a group of about 150 celebrants in a hearty meal of polenta with meat sauce, roast veal with roasted potatoes, quail in a dark red wine sauce, good bread, unmarked bottles of local white wine, squares of delicious locally made cow's-milk cheese (which everyone ate with his hands), and then pieces of plain, dryish cake and mixed-fruit tart washed down with sparkling young red wine. After lunch, an accordionist began to play informally inside and a guitarist outside; a few youngsters danced, and a few played football in the parking lot, in the crisp but sunny afternoon; a few hard cases remained at the tables, finishing the wine; and the mayor gave an address in another room on the possibility of obtaining Common Market funds for the restoration of Cassego's church.

Then everyone decamped and reassembled in a vacant roadside area just downhill from the church. Here, literally thousands of chestnuts were boiling atop small, circular cast-iron stoves or being roasted in long-handled pans with perforated bottoms over bonfires of beechwood and chestnut. There was also a stand dispensing cheese, torte both sweet and salted, raw chestnuts, wine, and soft drinks. These cost money, but the chestnuts were free, and in generous supply, and Don Sandro walked back and forth through the crowd with boxes of them in his hands, as if to make sure that everybody got enough. The citizens of Cassego and their friends, meanwhile, just sort of stood around talking and nibbling and talking some more until the light had faded. Then they all went home.

Sagra Dolce Sagra

A *sagra* (from the Latin *sacra,* meaning holy things or sacred rites) is literally a dedication, as of a building, or the celebration of a patron saint's day – but in recent years it has come to mean also a kind of gastronomic festival devoted to a single dish or foodstuff. There are sagras all over Italy, but I would be very surprised indeed if any region boasted more per square mile, and per month, than Liguria. Sagras have become a kind of mania in the region, in fact; scarcely a town is without one, from well-known seaside resort communities like Camogli with its hectic, jam-packed Sagra del Pesce (see pages 202-203) to obscure little villages high in the mountains. Some towns – Sestri Levante, for instance – have two or three sagras a year.

Sagras almost invariably take place on a weekend, and involve a communal meal of some kind, served up (sometimes for free, sometimes at a modest price) in the town square. There is usually music attached, usually a Mass, and maybe fireworks and dancing in the evenings. Sometimes the sagra is attached to a civic holiday or (back to the term's original meaning) the feast of a town's patron saint – but just as often, its scheduling seems arbitrary.

Despite what local boosters sometimes like to maintain, such sagras are not an ancient tradition. Camogli's Fish Festival, vintage 1952, was probably the first one in the modern sense.

Sometimes sagras are devoted to a particular fruit or vegetable: Monterosso, in the Cinque Terre, has a Sagra del Limone (lemon) every May; Castelbianco pays tribute to cherries each June each year. Other sagras concentrate on a single dish. Riva Trigoso has a Sagra del Bagnun, featuring that local anchovy-and-tomato dish; one of Sestri's sagras is based on minestrone; San Colombano Certenoi has staked out polenta with braised goat as its speciality. There is even a Sagra dell'Asado, in Follo, in the eastern entroterra – asado being, in this case, Argentinian-style roasted meats, brought home by Ligurian emigrants who ventured to South America for work. (There is even a town near Varese called Buenos Aires.)

Sagras can be great fun – opportunities to taste authentic regional cooking in colourful, vibrant surroundings. They can also be lame tourist spectacles. Whatever they are, though, one thing is sure, however: there are too many of them. Things have got to the point that in May of 1994, a group of restaurateurs in the Savona region issued a public statement condemning sagras, on the grounds that they were costing them business. Who will pay for a decent meal, they asked, when they can have goat with polenta practically for free?

Don Sandro of Cassego

Cassego, a tiny hamlet in the upper reaches of the Val di Vara, a mile or two from the edge of Emilia-Romagna, was established by the Lombards in the thirteenth century. Because the Val di Vara runs approximately east-west instead of north-south, it offered no natural passageways between the interior and the sea. For that reason, the valley, and Cassego, remained isolated, more or less forgotten. Until the local priest, Don Angelo Bacigalupo, raised enough money and volunteers to build a road between the village and Varese in 1920, no road linked it with the outside world. Mail arrived on horseback, or on foot.

"Because this area was cut off for so long," says Don Sandro Lagomarsini, Bacigalupo's modern-day successor, "it remained completely autonomous. It produced its own food, clothing, building materials, everything, all with tools made at home in wintertime, when other work was impossible." The ingenuity of the local peasants was legendary: When a law was passed forbidding them to cut chestnut branches to feed their sheep, one farmer put his animals in a cage and raised it up with a rope so they could eat directly from the tree – which was not technically forbidden. Nonetheless, poverty here was intense, and the cuisine was poor – so much so that polenta, elsewhere considered the most basic of sustenance, was a treat eaten only on holidays. On the other hand, famine was almost nonexistent in the area, and the plague touched very few people here. "It was written," notes Lagomarsini, "that the mountains repopulate the cities."

Lagomarsini – his name identifies him as a member of one of the most important *parantelle*, or clans, in this part of

Liguria – is originally from Ameglia, below La Spezia, near the far southeastern tip of the region. He is proud of the fact that his grandfather helped build the fortifications in La Spezia, working with two oxen and an ass (to correct a disparity of weight between the oxen). A stocky, amiable, articulate man of fifty-five or so, Don Sandro has been pastor in Cassego since the mid-1960s, and in addition to safeguarding the spiritual health of his parishioners, he has worked tirelessly to preserve the area's unique local culture. He is very concerned, he says, with the transmission of knowledge from old to young, and to help the flow of information, he publishes mimeographed pamphlets on the region's folkways, flora and fauna, and the like – and maintains a little two-room museum of peasant life behind the church. Here he has collected well-worn examples of the implements and simple machines with which the village lived for centuries. Often, he says, he has missed prize examples. "Either some antique dealer has just come through and bought things for a few thousand lire, or people have just got tired of them and thrown them away."

Nonetheless, his collection is impressive. There are shoe lasts, wool-combing tools, harvesting implements, cheese-making tools. (The area of production for Parmigiano comes just to the top of the mountains beyond the village – you can see it in the distance – but here there's a problem. "There are apparently certain enzymes lacking in the milk," says Lagomarsini, "so the cheese tends to fall apart." Nonetheless, I bought a wheel of cow's-milk cheese here and found it pretty good and perfectly cohesive.)

There is also equipment for making wine and cider (and apple wine, called u vin de pumme), including wineskins made out of goat hide and tall, thin, vertical barrels made from hollowed-out chestnut trunks. And, incongruously, there is a huge, shiny conch shell. When I express surprise at its presence so deep in the entroterra, he picks it up and blows a deep, hollow, Polynesian tone with it. "Every house in the area used to have a *corno marino,* a seashell horn," he explains, "to call farmers in from the fields."

Dried Chestnut Soup

Bouillon de Châtaignes

When he was growing up in Lantosque, in the arrière-pays about 30 miles north of Nice, remembers Niçois chef Franck Cerutti, people dried chestnuts in their attics, lighting fires in the stoves below and letting smoke spill into the upstairs chambers – which had holes in the roofs that could be opened as vents. The attics of Lantosque, he recalls, were always black. This dish is Cerutti's refined version of a typical peasant soup of the arrière-pays. It is opulent, creamy, both salty and slightly sweet, and also very delicate: Start early, though. Dried chestnuts have to be soaked for 48 hours before cooking.

to serve 4

225 g/8 oz	dried chestnuts
1	celery stalk
½	bulb fennel
1	bay leaf
	Salt
225 ml/8 fl oz	double cream
2 tablespoons	unsalted butter
	Freshly ground black pepper
4 tablespoons	fresh ricotta
	Extra-virgin olive oil
	Coarse salt

Place chestnuts in a bowl of warm water for about 30 minutes to loosen their skins, then pull skins off with your fingers. Place chestnuts in a bowl of cold water and soak for 48 hours.

Drain chestnuts and transfer them to a saucepan. Add celery, fennel, and bay leaf, and enough salted water to cover all the ingredients. Bring pan to a boil, then reduce heat and simmer, covered, for 1½ hours. Remove celery, fennel, and bay leaf, then purée chestnuts with their cooking water in a food processor or blender, adding a bit more warm water if necessary to obtain a medium-thick but fluid soup.

Return soup to pan, stir in cream and butter, and season to taste with salt and pepper. Mash ricotta into soup. Ladle soup into wide, flat bowls, drizzle with olive oil, and scatter a few grains of coarse salt on top.

Chestnut-Flour Tart

Castagnaccio

Castagnaccio is known all over Liguria but is a particular speciality of the Savona region, where it was once cooked in old communal ovens around the countryside for such special occasions as the eve of the Day of the Dead and Easter eve. It was considered very nutritious and was also a typical schoolchild's snack. One writer has called it "the ultimate home-made confection, from its elementary flavours to the evocative aroma that impregnates the student's satchel." That odour is indeed unmistakable. Because the chestnuts it's made from are dried in smoke, chestnut flour has a lingering, smoky, almost bacony smell. As the flour gets older, this smell begins to change from evocative to unpleasant. Chestnut flour is a perishable commodity and within months turns sourly acidic and comes alive with vermin. Fortunately, no reputable grocer will sell it once it's past its prime.

Castagnaccio is a curious thing, part tart, part pudding. Some people find it unpleasantly gummy, and it is certainly an acquired taste. I wasn't terribly fond of it myself at first, but I've come to enjoy its earthy, but sugarless, sweetness. In addition to the ingredients listed below, some recipes call for fennel seeds, some call for rosemary, but none calls for sugar. In the Lunigiana, where it is also known as pattona, castagnaccio is made with only chestnut flour, oil, water, and salt, and then smeared, after cooking, with stracchino or some other cheese, or even served with salami or sausage. A sparkling white wine is said to be the ideal accompaniment. I adapted this recipe from one found on a package of chestnut flour I bought in Ventimiglia.

to serve 8–10

450 g/1 lb	chestnut flour
1.7 litres/3 pints	milk
75 g/3 oz	pine nuts
150 g/6 oz	sultanas
	Grated peel of 1 lemon
2 teaspoons	salt
	Extra-virgin olive oil

Preheat oven to 190°C/375°F/Gas Mark 5.

Sift chestnut flour into a mixing bowl, then pour in milk, in a slow, steady stream, stirring constantly with a wooden spoon. Stir in pine nuts, raisins, lemon peel, and salt.

Lightly oil a shallow round baking dish or pan (a paella pan works perfectly), then bake for about 50 minutes. Allow to cool to room temperature before cutting into wedges to serve.

OLIVES AND THEIR OIL

The olive is the Mediterranean symbol par
excellence. Its branches signify peace,
honour and victory, protecting supplicants
and ambassadors.

– PLACARD AT THE MUSEO
DELL'OLIVO, ONEGLIA

Sensa euriu e sensa paiela non se peu frize.
(Without oil and a pan you can't fry.)

– BORDIGOTTO PROVERB

The Riviera is olive country. The hills are covered with olive trees; olives themselves are added to stews, sautés, pastas, and savoury pastries, or eaten by themselves after curing with salt, olive oil, and some combination of fennel flowers, cloves, lemon peel, and thyme or other herbs. Olive oil, of course, illuminates nearly every local dish today (if not historically), and seems the very lubrication of the Ligurian and Niçois kitchens – and, at its best, it is excellent oil, mild and sweet but with true olive flavour.

Olive trees were almost certainly cultivated, and olive oil produced, along the Riviera in Roman times – and perhaps as early as the sixth century B.C., according to one authority – but the first document referring specifically to olei-culture in the region is a deed dated June 5, A.D. 774, in which one Carlo Magno cedes to Guinibaldo, Abbot of Bobbio, in the zone of Bracco, a farm with olive trees. By about A.D. 1000, olive groves were well established in the hills and valleys near the coast, and by the time of the Crusades, in the twelfth and thirteenth centuries, olive oil had become an important commercial product for Genoa, and was being shipped all over the Mediterranean in special containers – bell-shaped, with handles and spiggots – called *barili*.

At about this time, Benedictine monks at their monastery in Taggia, a few miles northeast of San Remo, introduced a new variety of olive to the region. One tradition has it that they imported it directly from the Holy Land; but they were themselves originally from Montecassino, and it seems more likely that they brought it with them from Tuscany – or even bred it in Liguria. Small and dark, with a mild but distinct flavour, this Benedictine olive came to be known as the Taggiasca – and is today the most important variety, by far, in Liguria, both as an eating olive and for oil.

Other olives grown in the region, though very much in the minority, include the Colombaia, Pignola or Pignua (very small, not much bigger than the pine nuts it's named after, and perhaps just a miniaturized clone of Taggiasca), Murtine (similar in size to the Taggiasca), Olivastro, and Frantoio (from which the Taggiasca may have been cloned). Another variety sometimes mentioned is Lavagnina, but this is simply an eastern Ligurian name for Taggiasca. On the French side of the border, the only olive seen in any quantity is the Niçoise, called the Cailleté or Cailleter in the interior (as in Provence) – similar in appearance to the Taggiasca.

The Taggiasca thrives in the mild climate of the Riviera, especially in the barely fertile, calcareous soil on the terraced mountainsides of the inland valleys. Though the quantity of oil produced in the region was never great, the quality was recognized early as being particularly fine. In 1615, for instance, one Gerardo Basso wrote to the Spanish authorities in Milan that the valley of Oneglia was now yielding oil "as perfect as any produced in all of Italy." By the early nineteenth century, oil was being shipped from Laigueglia to as far away as England, Holland, Denmark, and Russia. In his *Viaggio nella Liguria marittima*, published in 1834, the Piedmontese writer Davide Bertolotti appraised the local oils as being "of perfect quality . . . the most delicate and delicious in the world for their lightness [and] the combination of their sweetness and their olive flavour, through which they entice the palate in a pleasant manner, and do not sting."

But olive cultivation ebbed and flowed along the Riviera. In 1709, a great freeze destroyed or severely damaged virtually all the olive trees along the Mediterranean coast, from Catalonia into Tuscany. More freezes followed in 1739, 1792, and 1794. In the region of Nice, where the olive tree had been known proudly as *l'arbre-seigneur de Comté* – the lord-tree of the County – whole groves had to be replanted; in Liguria, however, some of the trees survived the weather and eventually reflowered. The French started buying oil from their Italian neighbours, and for a time, until Niçois trees were again producing, olives became western Liguria's most important crop. The 1870s, says Silvio Torre, were the golden age of Ligurian olive oil.

It didn't last. An English observer in 1898 reported that olive cultivation was decreasing on the Côte d'Azur and the Riviera di Ponente, with olive trees being replaced by vines in the region of Nice and by roses around San Remo, Menton, and Ospedaletti. Another crisis was precipitated by World War I: Competition from cheap southern Italian olive oil, and from seed oils from various parts of the peninsula, had brought olive prices down in Liguria, and as many as 600,000 olive trees were sacrificed as fuel for the war effort and to run the trains.

The international financial crisis of 1929 had its effect, too. Oil exports from Imperia in 1933 were half what they'd been in 1929. Another Englishman noted matter-of-factly, in 1931, that "now that carnations and stocks have occupied the terraces in the place of the olive trees, the manufacture of oil has diminished, and pure olive oil, without adulteration of cotton and nut oil, is rarely found." (A literary footnote: One tireless champion of Ligurian olei-culture was the botanist Mario Calvino, father of Italo. Born in San Remo, where he became the curator of the local botanical garden, he was a passionate amateur of olive and flower growing, and would spend his Sundays, in the 1930s, travelling from village square to village square in the entroterra, improvising *comizi*, or assemblies, on the subject of modern agriculture and promulgating up-to-the-moment practices of cultivation and pruning.)

Today the Ligurian olive oil industry is small but is growing in reputation, as more and more of its better examples become available around Europe and in the United States. The capital of the Ligurian olive oil industry is Imperia – which is not a city but an agglomeration of two cities, Porto Maurizio and Oneglia, on opposite banks of the Impero River, joined officially in 1923. Imperia is the headquarters for several large oil packagers and shippers, most notably Fratelli Carli (which maintains the superbly designed and richly furnished Museo dell'Olivo adjacent to its plant), Sasso, and Isnardi (which now owns the premium Ardoino brand, whose foil-wrapped bottles are available here).

It is also the centre of a major production area. In the mountain communes rising above the city, in the so-called Valli dell'Olivo, there are currently about 11,000 acres of olive trees under cultivation, and some 3,540 individual olive farmers – of whom 40 or 50 make oil and sell directly to the public. These valleys, with old red-roofed stone towns perched here and there, tend to be sparsely but evenly wooded, not just with olive trees but with holm oaks, chestnuts, and lindens, surrounded by dense green scrub interrupted here and there by bright yellow swatches of commercially grown mimosa.

It is the olive trees, though, that most indelibly define the landscape. Many of them are very tall and old, and sometimes gnarled and knotted. All of them glow with an eerie gray-green light. Olive trees always have a ghostly aspect: Jean Renoir once said that his father loved the olive tree because it was "a tree without a shadow"; Aldous Huxley described the trees as "numinous" (which means not just supernatural or mysterious but specifically, according to Webster, "filled with a sense of the presence of divinity"). The effect becomes dramatic when, as above Imperia, the trees range over whole hillsides and up the sides of mountains as far as the eye can see. And the dramatic turns almost chilling when you realize that most of the trees in the upper reaches of the valleys are literally ghosts – abandoned, because they are too difficult to tend.

The olive harvest traditionally began along the Riviera as early as the first days of October. ("A San Fransescu, öiu frescu," says a proverb in Oneglia – "On St. Francis Day [October 4], new oil.") These days, it is more likely to start in November or December, and to extend as late as May. One producer, Ardoino, makes an extraordinary oil from olives harvested very late, called biancardo – light but flavourful, clear in colour, and almost totally lacking in acidity. Smollett discovered the desirability of late-harvested olives in the hills above Nice in the eighteenth century: "Olives begin to ripen and drop in the beginning of November," he writes, "but some remain on the trees till February, and even till April, and these are counted the most valuable."

The harvest had just finished when I visited the little farm owned by Francesca Barnato and her father, Umberto, in San Damiano di Stellanello, in the hills above Andora, between Imperia and Alassio. Rust-red nets, strung by harvesters to catch the olives as they beat the trees with staffs, still hung beneath many of the trees. I noticed a hunched little old man walking alongside the road as I drove past. "He's eighty-five years old," Francesca told me, "and two years ago, he was dying in the hospital. I saw him just the other day up in a tree, on a rainy day, beating the highest branches."

Olives are measured in the region by the *misura* or *quarta,* equal to 12 kilos (about 26.5 pounds). Each misura yields between two and three litres of oil, depending on the ripeness of olives. In a good year, each tree yields about one and a half misure. The Barnato olive grove numbers about 1,700 trees, the vast majority of them Taggiasca, with about 1,100 currently in production; these produced about 3,000 litres of oil in 1993, the year before I visited. The oil is pressed just down the street at the local olive mill, called a *gumbo* or *gombo* in western Liguria. Here, Romano Rosso crushes the olives between grinding stones, sandwiches the resulting pulp between thick woven mats called *fiscoli* or *panelli,* presses it, then centrifuges it to remove the water it inevitably contains. The oil is then bottled, and the pits, dried and cracked, are used for fuel and as feed for cows and chickens. The Barnatos' oil is dark yellow-green, slightly cloudy, full-flavoured, and slightly more bitter than usual in the region, but not bad at all. Francesca's sister, Elisabetta Grow, sells it in America, from her home in Oklahoma.

My favourite Ligurian oil, however, is that produced by winemaker Marco Romagnoli. Formerly labelled Castello di Perinaldo, this oil now simply bears Romagnoli's name. I first encountered it not in Liguria but at Don Camillo in Nice, where Franck Cerutti puts it on the tables. It is a particularly delicate oil, almost evanescent on the palate but at the same time possessed of a wonderful, intense olive flavour. "When I first tasted it," Cerutti told me, "I had the impression that they had simply squeezed the juice from olives." I know just what he meant – and I later found an echo of his assessment in an issue of *Les Annales du Comté de Nice* from 1936, in which Paul Canastrier described an unnamed Niçois oil as being "sweet, lightly fruity, perfumed, [and giving] the impression of pressing in the mouth fat black olives, perfectly ripe."

Good oil from the Niçois region is harder to find. Cerutti has recently discovered a very delicate, nutty example made just northeast of the city in La Trinité by one Yves Lessatini – but this is an exception. The oil sold by farmers on the place Pierre-Gautier, off the Marché des Fleurs on the Cours Saleya, is highly variable in quality – sometimes rich and flavourful in a rustic sort of way and sometimes rough and dirty tasting. Two shops on the Rue St. François-de-Paule (which extends westward from the Cours Saleya), the famous old Alziari and the newer Maison des Caracoles, sell oil, both in tins and/or bottles and straight out of large metal tanks – but the former's is of unspecified origin (and almost certainly not from around Nice) and the latter's, which is somewhat better, is from Opio, across the Var near Grasse. (Both shops are worth visiting, in any case, for their high-quality local products of other sorts.)

There is one oil from the arrière-pays that I'm dying to try, however: that of Malaussène, about 30 miles northwest of Nice, near the wine town of Villars-sur-Var. Here, in 1994, the communal oil mill, which had gone unused for more than thirty years, was revived. Inhabitants of the village, including a clutch of schoolchildren, gathered around as it creaked into life for the first time since the mid-1960s, and then celebrated the occasion with an old-style snack that was once always eaten after the year's first pressing – brissauda, which is simply grilled bread rubbed with garlic and topped with anchovies and lots of just-pressed oil. The rehabilitation of the mill was inspired by a TV documentary about the village; a retired miller and his wife who lived nearby saw the program and decided on the spot to revive the mill, with the assistance of the local government. Even if the oil turns out to be rough and dirty tasting, how could I resist?

❖ ❖ ❖

Niçois "Caviar"
Fachoira

What is the single indispensable ingredient of tapenade? Olives, most people would say, since tapenade is a purée of olives (above all) and other ingredients – and in practical terms, that's right. But etymologically, the answer is capers, since the word *tapenade* itself comes from *tapeno* – Provençal for that flavourful greenish bud. I don't know that there's any real difference between the tapenade of Provence and the fachoira (or fachouìra) of Nice – Jacques Médecin says the Niçois version is "légèrement différent," but he doesn't say how – but I do like the fact that the name of the thing is more straightforward: *Fachoira* does not mean caper; it derives from the Provençal adjective *fachouiro*, meaning prepared or preserved olives (probably derived in turn from *facho*, the past participle of *faire*, to do or make, and *óulivo*, olive). I will leave it to more advanced students of the linguistic sciences to explain how *fachouiro* has also come to mean both a cheese-drying tray and a troublesome woman. This recipe is adapted from Médecin's.

to serve 6–8

450 g/1 lb	pitted Niçoise olives, minced
1	garlic clove, peeled and minced
2 tablespoons	anchovy paste
2 tablespoons	large Niçois or Spanish capers, minced
4	basil leaves, minced (optional)
	Extra-virgin olive oil
	Freshly ground black pepper

Combine olives, garlic, anchovy paste, capers, and basil (if desired) in a bowl and mash them together well with a fork. Drizzle in oil, mixing it well, until mixture has the consistency of a thick paste. Pepper to taste and serve on small rounds of toasted bread or crackers.

❖ ❖ ❖

Rabbit with Olives

Coniglio con Olive

With slight variations, this dish exists all over Liguria and around Nice – a natural combination of two plentiful regional ingredients. San Remo claims a version of its own, under the name coniggio a-a sanremasca, and something very similar is known in other parts of the region as coniggio a-a carlonn-a, meaning rabbit in a careless or haphazard style. This name may well have been applied to the dish precisely because it can be made with many combinations of ingredients; as long as the rabbit and the olives are present, that is, the other particulars may not matter too much. Here's a version with a bit of everything.

to serve 4

1 × 1.25-1.5 kg/2½-3 lb	rabbit, cut into 8 pieces
1	onion, finely chopped
2	cloves garlic, minced
	Extra-virgin olive oil
3	sage leaves, minced
2–3	sprigs of thyme, whole
2	small sprigs of rosemary, whole
75 g/3 oz	pine nuts
2 tablespoons	capers, drained
450 ml/16 fl oz	Ligurian Vermentino or other dry white wine
30–40	Niçoise or Taggiasca olives, pitted
	Salt

Fry rabbit, onion, and garlic in a large frying pan in olive oil over medium-high heat, turning rabbit frequently until it browns on all sides. Add sage, whole thyme and rosemary sprigs, pine nuts, and capers. Lower heat and cook ingredients together for 2–3 minutes, then add wine, cover, raise heat, and bring to a boil. Immediately lower heat to a simmer and cook, covered, for 30 minutes. Add olives and salt to taste and continue cooking, still covered, for 10 minutes more.

WILD GAME, MUSHROOMS, AND SNAILS

A sciensa a ven dâ montagna.
(Science comes from the mountains.)

– GENOESE PROVERB

The backcountry of the Riviera – the entroterra of Liguria and the arrière-pays behind Nice – is one of the northern Mediterranean's great secrets. All but unknown to the holiday makers who crowd the coast and the gastronomes who flock to the wine and truffle towns of Piedmont practically next door, this mountainous interior is dramatically beautiful, full of charming little hill towns, and almost totally unspoiled by industry – once you get past the suburban lower reaches of many of the valleys, anyway.

My first experience of the entroterra came in the early 1980s, when I turned up into the hills near Albenga, following a restaurant guide's recommendation of a restaurant called La Baita, located in Gazzo, a hamlet attached to the village of Borghetto d'Arroscia. I quickly left the towering concrete pylons of the autostrada and the bustle of the coastal roads behind; I quickly passed by the hillside apartment blocks, the batteries of commercial greenhouses, the warehouses and furniture outlets. Within a mile or two of the sea, I was suddenly surrounded by hills thick with olive and chestnut trees and beeches, framed by steep, green-cloaked cliffs. Higher up, the olives and chestnuts disappeared, and pines and spruce trees filled the landscape, covering the ever-higher hills defining narrow cuts and passes as they receded off into the distance on either side of the tortuous river valley far below. Here and there stood a Savoyard church, seemingly alone, its pastel hues improbably vivid against the deep, uniform green that surrounded it.

Gazzo turned out to be a nondescript agglomeration of mostly postwar buildings. But La Baita was a delight – one of those places where a set, and seemingly endless, progression of delicious, hearty dishes comes forth until the diner begs for mercy. In this case, the theme was mushrooms, which the proprietor-chef, Augusto Ferrari, picks and then dries or preserves (in oil or vinegar, with attendant herbs and spices) in wide variety for use the year around; he also makes his own wine, olive oil, bread, sausage, and liqueurs. His cooking is simple but sure, and my first repast at his hands included among its dozen-plus courses – if I remember correctly – a mushroom-studded terrine, several kinds of marinated mushrooms, sausage with polenta, pasta with mushrooms, snails with garlic and parsley, roast veal with mushrooms, and a mushroom-shaped ice cream mould for dessert.

Mushrooms are a major culinary resource in the entroterra, and only slightly less so in the arrière-pays. Liguria especially, in autumn, is a mushroom hunter's paradise – quite possibly the richest part of Italy from a mycological point of view. Especially abundant are porcini (*Boletus edulis,* ceps), galletti (*Cantharellus cibarius,* or chanterelles), and ovoli or funghi imperiale (*Amanita caesarea,* or Caesar's amanita, called boaei in Genoese – possibly the most delicious mushroom of all). There are also said to be black truffles, the real thing, around Manie, just inland between Noli and Finale Ligure, but I've never encountered them.

Porcini and ovoli are also known in the region as "blacks" and "reds," respectively, as in a bawdy old street cry of Genoese mushroom sellers: "Ghe l'ho neigri e rosci! Donne, boggighile e balle a vostro maio!" – "There are blacks and reds! Women, cook them for your husband and turn him on!" In the Val di Vara, in eastern Liguria, where porcini are called servette, the mushrooms are so appreciated that peasants there distinguish between at least four kinds: funghi di faggio, white and elongated, which grow under beech trees; funghi di castagno, dark, with thick stems, and found under chestnut trees; funghi di posto, which grow in established mushroom beds; and funghi da freddo, which appear in autumn, and are sometimes even found under the snow.

Dried porcini are indispensable to Genoese cooking. Nearly every sauce or stew seems to employ them – just a few, for depth of flavour. (It's part of Ligurian mushroom lore that in 1867, a wealthy Genoese admirer of Gioacchino Rossini sent the composer, in Paris, a case of dried porcini from Varese Ligure; they were much appreciated.) Because fresh porcini are so highly valued, however, local mushrooms rarely are converted to this use; most of the dried porcini sold in Liguria today are said to come from Slovenia or Bulgaria.

In Nice and vicinity, the favoured mushroom is the sanguin *(Lactarius delicosus* or *sanguifluus)* – the milk-cap or bleeding milk-cap – which is typically cooked with garlic, white wine, and herbs, or boiled in vinegar and then preserved in olive oil. The Mentonnais traditionally cook sanguins with tomatoes, onions, and chipolata sausages.

Wild game is somewhat less important than mushrooms in the region – probably simply because, woods and hills notwithstanding, this is not particularly fertile hunting ground. Small birds (thrushes, starlings, warblers, and such) and wild rabbits are the usual take; wild boar, deer, and chamois (a goat-like mountain antelope) are considerably more scarce. In Colette Bourrier-Reynaud's *Les Recettes de Réparate,* a woman named Paulette Grec, from the hamlet of Le Gabre de Bonson, just west of Plan-du-Var, reveals that when grain harvesters were working in the fields some distance from their villages, they'd typically spend the night in situ and eat whatever they could catch – often squirrel, which they cooked like rabbit, in tomato sauce. "I can tell you," Grec adds, "that it was a treat."

One wild creature that is considerably more plentiful is the snail. Snails were once an almost daily "meat" in some portions of the interior; where there were vineyards and lettuce patches, there were snails, munching through the leaves with ancient slowness, easy to pluck and purge and cook. Known as lumache in Italian, lûmasse in Genoese, and bagiöi, gï, gélli, and scaragöi, among other things, in various Ligurian dialects, they were stewed long, with herbs (especially mint), red wine, and sometimes vinegar, and often served with potatoes or rice. In the entroterra behind Oneglia, snails were also used medicinally, as a specific for toothache – crushed, dusted with flour, and made into a compress to be pressed against the cheek. In Nice, where they are called cantaréou (which always makes me think that they're expected to sing), they were typically stewed with tomato sauce.

Today, local snails are comparatively rare. With so many farms abandoned, it is said, there is no longer sufficient cultivation to support them – though Savonese winemaker Domenico Boiga, whose specialities include a white called Lumassina, or little snail, says that it's pollution that has all but killed them off. In any case, most snails eaten in Liguria today come from the other side of the mountains, from Piedmont.

Interior Importance

Because of their small size and their relative physical isolation, it is easy to forget how significant some of the old towns of the interior once were, and how vital to trade between the Riviera and Piedmont (which is to say between the Mediterranean and northern Europe) were the rough-hewn passes that cleave through these steep, narrow valleys.

Pieve di Teco, for instance, was a major trade capital, standing at the spot where several of the "salt roads" between Piedmont and the Riviera converged. (Along these routes, the Genoese sent oil, salt, and dried and salted fish north and got flour, cheese, and red wine in return.) It was also an important and much-contested military outpost defending Genoa against the Piedmontese. Seborga, built around a palace constructed by Benedictine monks from the Île de Lerins in 959, minted its own coins, and the local abbot held the title of prince. Triora was such a thriving town that it boasted ten churches and five castles. The villages of Bordighera, Borghetto San Nicolò, Camporosso, San Biagio, Sasso, Soldano, Vallebona, and Vallecrosià actually combined themselves into a tiny republic, called the Otto Luoghi or Eight Villages, in the late seventeenth century. Peille was an honoured stopping place for the popes of the fourteenth century, every time they journeyed between Avignon and Rome. Tende and La Brigue were both, at various times, capitals of their own small states. And so much business was done in Saorge, a prosperous trading village on another of the main routes between Piedmont and the sea, that some twenty-two notaries hung out their shingles there in the first half of the seventeenth century alone.

Duck Leg Daube

Daube de Cuisse de Canard

The conventional Niçois daube, like its Provençal cousin, is made with beef; there is also a version made with lamb. But virtually any kind of meat may be cooked in this manner – G. Boréa in his famous essay "De la puissance stomacale des anciens niçois," published in *Nice Historique* in 1945, mentions a recipe for turkey daube dating back to 1688 – and wild duck, among other things, makes for a splendid dish. This recipe is from Franck Cerutti, chef-owner of Don Camillo in Nice.

to serve 6

10	duck legs, from wild ducks if possible
	Extra-virgin olive oil
	Unsalted butter
2	carrots, diced
2	onions, finely chopped
4	shallots, finely chopped
2	celery stalks, diced
1 tablespoon	flour
1	bottle red Côte-de-Provence or other dry red wine
	Leaves from 2–3 sprigs fresh thyme
	Leaves from 1 sprig fresh rosemary
2	bay leaves
6	juniper berries
	Salt and freshly ground black pepper
1 tablespoon	jus de veau (optional; see page 102)

Cut the duck legs in two lengthways (around the bone), then cook them slowly in a large heavy saucepan , in batches, in plenty of oil and butter; turn frequently until legs are lightly browned on all sides.

Return all duck pieces to the pan, add carrots, onions, shallots, and celery, increase heat, and cook for about 5 minutes, stirring frequently.

Turn ingredients out of the pan into a colander and allow to drain for 5–10 minutes. Place ingredients in a large terra-cotta or glass baking dish that can be covered. Sprinkle flour over ingredients, and stir once or twice until it disappears. Add wine, thyme, rosemary, bay leaves, juniper berries, and salt and pepper to taste. Cover tightly and cook over slow heat, without lifting lid, for 2 hours.

When daube is done, stir in jus de veau if desired. Serve 3 leg pieces per person (with 2 pieces left over), accompanied by polenta or by gnocchi tossed with butter and Parmigiano-Reggiano.

Marinated Boar

Sanglier en Marinade

This is a variation on a recipe from the Niçois backcountry, originally for marinated haunch of chamois, appearing in Colette Bourrier-Reynaud's *Les Recettes de Réparate*. In the absence of wild boar, it can also be made successfully with tame pork.

to serve 6

1	bottle Syrah, Mourvèdre, or other full-bodied Provençal-style red wine
4	garlic cloves, peeled and crushed
3–4	sprigs of thyme
2	bay leaves
2	onions, thinly sliced and separated into rings
10–12	black peppercorns
	Salt
1× 1.25-1.5 kg/2½-3 lb	piece wild boar (shoulder or haunch) or pork
	Extra-virgin olive oil
2 tablespoons	flour

Pour wine into a deep bowl or baking dish large enough to hold boar or pork in 1 piece. Add garlic, thyme, bay leaves, onions, and peppercorns, and stir once.

Salt wild boar or pork thoroughly, then place in marinade. Cover and allow to marinate, at room temperature, for about 12 hours (for wild boar) or 24 hours (for pork), turning several times.

Remove meat from marinade, reserving liquid. Blot meat dry with paper towels, then cook for about 15 minutes in olive oil over medium heat in a large pan that can be covered, turning several times so that it browns evenly on all sides.

Sprinkle cooked meat with flour, then pour marinade into pan. Bring liquid to a boil, reduce heat, cover, and cook for about 1 hour. Remove pan from heat and let sit, covered, overnight, turning meat once.

Return liquid to a boil and cook, covered, for 2 hours longer. Adjust seasoning if necessary. To serve, cut or pull meat from bone and spoon sauce and onions over it. Accompany with boiled potatoes or noodles or gnocchi dressed with butter, Parmigiano-Reggiano, and parsley.

Hunter's Wife's-Style Chicken

Pollastro a-a Caccieuia

I'm using the Genoese name of this dish simply to avoid calling it by its more familiar moniker, pollo alla cacciatora or "chicken cacciatore" – which suggests a candle-in-the-Chianti-bottle cliché of chicken stewed with all the usual "Italian" vegetables. What is this preparation's connection with the hunt? Until the postwar years, chicken in Liguria (as in most other parts of Europe) was reserved for special occasions; it was much too valuable, for the eggs it produced, to be eaten casually. It was thus almost exclusively the centrepiece of family banquets and holiday repasts. But a tradition did grow up that hunters, on the eve of their hunt, would order up a chicken cooked in a simple sauce as fuel for the coming chase – thus the name. The temptation is always to make dishes like this more complicated than they need to be, and pollo alla cacciatora is sometimes made with bell peppers, celery, carrots, garlic, even salt pork or ham. I think this simpler recipe is best, however – as long as you remember the secret ingredient: Use *very good* chicken, free-range if possible.

to serve 4

2	onions, chopped
	Extra-virgin olive oil
1 × 900 g-1.5 kg/2-3 lb	fryer, cut into small pieces (bone in)
225 ml/8 fl oz	Ligurian Vermentino or other dry white wine
450 g/1 lb	tomatoes, skinned, seeded, and chopped, or 1 × 450 g/ 1 lb tin tomatoes, chopped
1	bay leaf
	Salt
225 ml/8 fl oz	strong chicken stock

Fry onions over medium-high heat in a large heavy frying pan in olive oil for about 5 minutes, then add chicken pieces. Continue frying, turning several times so that they brown on all sides.

Add wine and continue cooking until it evaporates, then add tomatoes, bay leaf, and salt to taste, reduce heat to low, and cook, partially covered, for 45 minutes, adding more stock if liquid evaporates.

Serve with boiled potatoes or rice.

"Mushroomed" Mushrooms
Funghi a Funghetto

This simple, classic Ligurian method of cooking fresh mushrooms, native to the entroterra above Recco, is usually reserved for porcini, but it works well with other similarly meaty ones more readily available in this country (for instance, portobellos, shiitakes, or matsutakes), and even with ordinary white or brown mushrooms. Some recipes call for tomatoes, but they seem superfluous to me; some recipes call for parsley instead of oregano or marjoram, but I like the herbal earthiness the latter impart.

to serve 6

675-900 g/1½–2 lb	fresh porcini or other meaty mushrooms
3	garlic cloves, minced
	Leaves from 3–4 sprigs of fresh oregano or marjoram
	Extra-virgin olive oil
	Salt

Clean mushrooms thoroughly with a damp cloth and cut into slices about 6 mm/¼ inch thick. Set aside.

Cook garlic and oregano in olive oil in a large saucepan over low heat for about 5 minutes, then add mushrooms, stirring them so that they are well coated in oil. Season to taste with salt, then continue cooking, uncovered, stirring occasionally, for about 30 minutes or until mixture has lost its excess liquid but is not completely dried out. Serve as an appetizer or side dish, or as a sauce for pasta or rice.

Raw Porcini Salad
Insalata di Porcini Crudi

I don't know that this salad is necessarily typical of the Riviera, but I can't resist including it here, both because I think it's so good, and because I've encountered it in restaurants at both ends of my subject area – in a refined interpretation (with a mousse of porcini at its core) at Don Camillo in Nice and in a straightforward version, similar to that given here, at Il Pozzo in Monterosso Mare in the Cinque Terre, an establishment where wild mushrooms are something of a speciality, which is unusual on the Ligurian seaside.

to serve 4

450 g/1 lb	fresh porcini (ceps)
	Extra-virgin olive oil
	Juice of ½ lemon
	Flaked sea salt (gros sel)
115 g/4 oz	Parmigiano-Reggiano in 1 piece
2	flat-leaf parsley sprigs, minced

Clean mushrooms thoroughly with a damp cloth and, using a mandoline or very sharp knife, slice lengthways as thinly as possible.

Divide porcini slices evenly between 4 plates, arranging them in overlapping layers. Drizzle with olive oil and lemon juice and season lightly with salt.

Again using a mandoline or very sharp knife, shave Parmigiano into pieces as thin as possible. Scatter them over the mushrooms. Drizzle more oil over the cheese, scatter with parsley, and season again with salt.

Mushrooms and Potatoes
Funghi e Patate

Mushrooms and potatoes have a natural affinity, and are cooked together in many cuisines. In Liguria, the favoured variety for this dish is the ovolo, Caesar's amanita – but I like it equally well with porcini, which are easier to obtain in this country. Anyway, it was with porcini that this preparation was first described to me some years ago by Luigi Miroli at his Da Puny in Portofino. He used the dish as an example of the simplicity and, above all, frugality of Ligurian cuisine, pointing out that, after long cooking, the two main ingredients blended into one another so thoroughly that it was difficult to tell them apart; the mushroom's volume was thus doubled, on the cheap.

to serve 4

450 g/1 lb	fresh porcini
2	cloves garlic, minced
1	small bunch flat-leaf parsley, minced
	Extra-virgin olive oil
450 g/1 lb	potatoes, peeled and very thinly sliced
	Salt

Preheat oven to 180°C/350°F/Gas Mark 4.

Clean mushrooms thoroughly with a damp cloth and carefully remove stems, taking care not to damage the caps.

Chop stems very fine and mix with garlic and parsley.

Generously oil the bottom and sides of a wide, shallow baking dish with a tight-fitting cover. Arrange potatoes in overlapping layers on the bottom of the dish, salting each layer generously. Sprinkle half the parsley mixture on top of potatoes, then arrange mushroom caps over it in a single layer. Salt the mushroom caps, then sprinkle remaining parsley mixture over top.

Seal baking dish with foil, then cover and bake for 1 hour.

Snails in the Style of Molini di Triora
Lumache alla Molinasca

The Sagra della Lumaca or snail festival held every September in Molini di Triora, in the western entroterra, was inaugurated in 1959 by a group of snail-loving local citizens. Molini takes its snails seriously – a large, handsome ceramic one decorates a wall in the centre of town, and a tourist brochure published there describes Molini as "città delle lumache" – and this is the official civic recipe, as given to me by Angelamaria Zucchetto, whose food shop is the social and gastronomic centre of the town.

to serve 4

---

450 ml/16 fl oz	extra-virgin olive oil
900 g/2 lb	snails in shells, fresh if possible, well cleaned
6	cloves garlic, lightly crushed
1	onion, sliced
1	bay leaf
1	sprig rosemary
2	large sprigs thyme
1	bottle Ligurian Rossese or Ormeasco or other light, dry red wine
	Salt and freshly ground black pepper
1 litre/1¾ pints	strong beef stock
2 tablespoons	red wine vinegar
50 g/2 oz	fresh breadcrumbs
3	flat-leaf parsley sprigs, minced
10–12	mint leaves, minced

Heat oil over medium heat in a large heavy casserole or Dutch oven for about 5 minutes. Add snails, garlic, onion, bay leaf, rosemary, and thyme. Cook over medium heat, stirring well, for about 20 minutes, then add wine and season to taste with salt and pepper.

Continue cooking over medium heat until wine has evaporated, then add beef stock. Lower heat and simmer, uncovered, for 1 hour.

Stir vinegar into breadcrumbs, then stir breadcrumbs, parsley, and mint leaves into stock.

Serve with crusty bread, escargot forks or long toothpicks to pick the snails from their shells, and a soup spoon for the broth.

....

Part 5

Desserts
and
Confections

....

DESSERTS AND CONFECTIONS

*Ligurian pastry takes off from different
forms of sweet bread which are less
desserts than coffee cakes, ideal with
breakfast.*

– WAVERLEY ROOT,
THE FOOD OF ITALY

*Si l'on te parle choux à la crème,
frangipane, meringues, sabayon, sorbets,
régale-t'en à l'occasion, mais n'imagine pas
manger niçois. (If one offers you cream
puffs, almond-cake, meringues, sabayon,
sorbets, avail yourself of the opportunity,
but don't think that you're eating Niçois.)*

– MAMÉ CLAIRETTE IN CUISINE
TRADITIONNELLE EN PAYS
NIÇOIS BY BERNARD DUPLESSY

Nice and its neighbours east of the Var share with Provence the Christmas tradition of *les treize desserts* – the thirteen desserts. An essential part of the classic regional Christmas Eve repast for centuries, the desserts are thirteen in honour of Christ and his twelve apostles. Do not, however, picture a groaning board laden with a baker's dozen of complex delicacies. The thirteen desserts are mostly fruit (both dried and fresh) and nuts. According to Jean et Danièle Lorenzi in their *Cuisine monégasque/Cüjina de Munégu,* the catalogue of treats in Monaco went like this: grapes, apples, pears, and then *trei sacumi* (three fruits that one cracks – i.e., walnuts, hazelnuts, and almonds), *trei secumi* (three dried fruits: figs, raisins, and apricots), *dui agrumi* (two citrus fruits: oranges and tangerines), and *dui fritumi* (two fried pastries: i.e., beignets). Elsewhere, the thirteen items might include pomegranates, winter melon, dates, chestnuts, quince paste, candied fruits, nougat, or a fougasse perfumed with orange water, studded with pralines and sweet almonds, and dusted with fine sugar, among other things.

Though there are certainly more elaborate desserts than mere fruit and nuts along the Riviera, the truth is that the region doesn't devote a lot of attention to its sweets. There is little in Liguria or Nice to compare, for example, with the opulent Moorish-inspired egg-yolk confections and sugary ice creams of Sicily and

Naples or the delicate Austrian-accented pastries of the Alto Adige. There is no single dessert from the region that has achieved the worldwide popularity of the Veneto's inevitable tiramisù or even of the biscotti of Tuscany.

One reason for this is simply the local passion for fruit both fresh and preserved. In Nice, notes Jacques Médecin, "la frucha," fruit, is literally another word for dessert – and "it was the production of our gardens which constituted for the most part the endings of Niçois meals." Another reason is the region's poverty. Flour was needed for bread and pasta; there wasn't enough to go around for cakes – and if there had been, there would have been little sugar or cream to enhance them.

What both Nice and Liguria do well, in great variety, are small fried and baked pastries and biscuits of various shapes and sizes, most of them made from little more than flour, water, sugar, oil or butter, and sometimes eggs. Besides these, plus some variations on the theme of fried cream or milk, a few simple fruit or nut tarts, and several sweet interpretations of ravioli, the most famous Ligurian desserts are the holiday pandolce of Genoa (that city's simplified version of panettone; see page 278); a rather curious preparation of wine-poached peaches stuffed with a paste made from candied fruit and the nuts of the peaches themselves (prised from inside the split-open kernels; the facile modern version tosses the kernels and crushes a few almonds instead); and a moist, biretta-shaped pastry-shop creation filled with dense zabione and frosted with marzipan, called sacripantina – the name means "little bully" in Italian – said to have been invented in the nineteenth century by a Genoese pasticceria called Preti. (Under the name Vëgia Zena, or Old Genoa, the cake is a speciality today of Fratelli Klainguti, an historic 1828-vintage Genoese pastry and ice-cream shop on the Piazza Soziglia.)

Nice's most original dessert is certainly tourte de blettes, a pie of Swiss chard with apples, raisins, and pine nuts (see page 183); its simplest is grata-quéca, the Niçois granita. There are also, since this is France, some fruit tarts and more elaborate, not specifically indigenous specialities – and Médecin has the wit to include, in his *La Cuisine du comté de Nice,* three culinary immigrants, which he says have become widely accepted in Nice: English Christmas pudding (which his grandmother called *ploum-pudding*), Russian Easter cake, and *la tarte de courge rouge* – which readers might know better as pumpkin pie.

Romanengo

Dried and candied fruits, nougats (called by their Spanish name, torrone, in Italy), and other preserved sweets are highly appreciated on the Riviera – perhaps nowhere more than in Genoa, where they have long been enjoyed not only for their flavour but also because they satisfied the local frugality (fruits abundant in their season wouldn't spoil or go to waste if they were preserved) and lent themselves neatly to exportation.

A veritable temple of frutti canditi, torrone, and the like, founded in 1780, thrives in the city to this day. This is the shop called the Confetteria Pietro Romanengo fu Stefano, on the Via Soziglia. (There are two other, smaller branches – shrines rather than temples, if you will.) Using traditional methods and the finest raw materials from Liguria and abroad, Romanengo produces an astonishing array of delicacies, and its customers seem to spend hours, sometimes, choosing individual items to be set, jewel-like, into its elegant gift boxes.

Romanengo's marrons glacés, flavoured with orange-flower water, are world famous. Its candied apricots, bananas, oranges, bitter cherries, quince, figs, strawberries, melon, pears, prunes, medlars, and other fruits are as good as such things get. (They do not look like waxwork, though. Little sugared oranges from Nervi, for instance, have rough edges and honeycombs of pith; they look like, and are, the real thing.)

Romanengo's chocolates are some of Italy's best (including liqueur-filled chocolate-covered cherries that redeem the cliché and a stunning assortment of chocolate Easter eggs). Then there are irresistible pralines (from almonds, pine nuts, and pistachios), first-rate caramels and mint pastilles, excellent preserves (including a wonderful one made from the firm black

cherries called amarene), intensely flavoured fruit syrups (one
from rose petals), and even something called conserva di
manna – a sweet, white, honey-like substance produced by the
flowering ash tree, *Fraxinus ornus*. The Genoese, with little
justification, like to associate this conserve with the manna of
the Bible. (There are several substances known as manna, most
of them, including that of the ash, associated with scale insect
infestation – and it is impossible to know which one the Bible
referred to.) I wonder how many of the Genoese matrons and
young sweet-lovers who enjoy conserva di manna realise that,
Biblical or not, *Fraxinus ornus* is undeniably the source of the
baby laxative Mannitol – infamous in the '60s and '70s as a
substance with which cocaine was diluted for illegal sale.

Christmas in Menton

The traditional name for Christmas Eve in Menton is Cachafueg, literally fire-laying – after the old custom of lighting a huge dead tree in the main square during midnight Mass, at precisely the stroke of 12, when it was announced that the Christ Child had been born. The surrounding houses would be lit up with a red glow, and the people hurrying from church would cast long, dark shadows on the walls, lending the city what one writer has called "a truly Dantesque charm." Meanwhile, inside the houses, preparations for the post-Mass meal were taking place. In an issue of *Annales de Menton* published in 1954, the Mentonnais author Louis Ravalin, under the pen name Marcel Firpo, captures a moment in the process:

"The mistress of the house visits the *feniera* [attic], where, strung along ropes, hang bunches of dried white muscat grapes, packets of sorbs in vermillion hues, apples with shiny red cheeks attached to a rope by little threads tied to their stems; in the corner, white canvas sacks are full of walnuts, hazelnuts, and almonds; nearby is a large walnut chest where, cozily arranged on a bed of peach and bay leaves, figs taken from the drying screen are dusted with a frost of powdered sugar. And over all these beautiful and good things, jars filled to bursting with [olive] oil rest, undisturbed, showing an aspect as majestic as it is severe. You may come, Noël!"

Carnival Fritters

Beignets de Carnaval

These light, long fritters, also called ganses, were the definitive Niçois Carnival-time dessert. Jacques Médecin claims that in earlier times there was not a family in Nice that didn't serve them for Mardi Gras – sometimes even eating them in place of bread on the breakfast table that day. There are two kinds of beignets de carnaval: leavened and unleavened. These are the latter, which are obviously somewhat heavier, but which I prefer for their cake-like weight. The recipe comes from the 1909-vintage *La Cuisine à Nice* by chef Henri Heyraud, a well-known teacher at the Nice hotel school (École Hôtelier) and one-time director of the city's Restaurant du Palais de la Jetée-Promenade.

to make about 24 fritters

250 g/9 oz	plus 2 tablespoons flour
	Sugar
	Yolks of 2 large eggs
1 tablespoon	orange-flower water
1 pinch	salt
	Corn or oil for frying

Mix 250 g/9 oz flour, 175 g/6 oz sugar, egg yolks, orange-flower water, salt, and about 4 tablespoons water together to make a smooth, thick dough, similar in consistency to pasta dough. Form it into a ball and let it rest for ½ hour.

Dust a work surface and a rolling pin with remaining flour. Roll out dough to a thickness of about 12 mm/½ inch, then cut it into strips about 5 cm/2 inches long and 1 mm/½ inch wide. Roll these individually into long, narrow shapes about 2 mm/⅟₁₆ inch thick, then make small crosswise incisions down the length of each with a knife, being careful not to come more than about 12 mm/½ inch from edges.

Fill a deep cast-iron frying pan or other deep, heavy pan with about 5 cm/ 2 inches of oil and heat to about 190°C/375°F/Gas Mark 5, or use a deep fryer, and fry fritters in batches until light golden-brown. Drain on paper towels, dust generously with additional sugar, and serve at once.

Bugie

Traditionally served in Liguria with zabaione (see page 277), and also as a treat on Giovedì Grasso ("Fat Thursday," a sort of pre–Mardi Gras, five days earlier), these are a close relative of the leavened version of Nice's beignets de carnaval – little fritters shaped like hollow, puffed-up ravioli. Bugie (böxie in Genoese) literally means fibs, and one theory holds that they are called this because they are puffed up with their own importance, with nothing (inside) to back up their pretense.

to serve 4

250 g/9 oz	flour
1	large egg
2 teaspoons	orange-flower water
	Zest of ½ lemon
15 g/½ oz	dry yeast
175 g/6 oz	sugar
1 pinch	salt
	Corn oil for frying

Make a dough out of flour, egg, orange-flower water, lemon zest, yeast, 115 g/4 oz sugar, and salt, kneading it well until it is very smooth.

Roll out dough on a floured work surface with a floured rolling pin, then cut into strips to fit a pasta machine. Roll each strip through machine through setting No. 5 to form thin dough sheets. As each one is done, lay it out on a lightly floured work surface. Cut dough into square or round pieces, preferably with a deckle-edged ravioli cutter.

Fill a deep cast-iron frying pan or other deep, heavy pan with about 5 cm/2 inches of oil and heat to about 190°C/375°F/Gas Mark 5, or use a deep fryer, and fry fritters in batches until puffed up and light golden-brown. Drain on paper towels, dust generously with additional sugar, and serve at once.

Zabaione

Zabaione or zabaglione (the name may come from *sbaglione,* meaning a big mistake; dishes are often said to have been invented "mistakenly" in culinary folklore) is not a Ligurian creation. It may be Sicilian in origin, since one of its three ingredients, marsala, comes only from Sicily, and another, egg yolks, is typical of Moorish-inspired Sicilian pastries. Nonetheless, it is popular in the entroterra, and is especially famous at La Capanna da Bacì in the perched town of Apricale, due north of Bordighera in the western entroterra – another of those mountain osterie where the single fixed-price repast (sausages, stuffed vegetables, polenta, several pastas, grilled lamb or boar, etc., etc.) seems to go on forever. Here, strangely enough, this wine-spiked warm custard is served every afternoon at 3:30.

The story is that one day, in the 1960s, a bicyclist arrived at the inn at about that hour, greatly fatigued (you'll know why if you essay the steep, winding road that leads to Apricale), and asked for zabaione as a pick-me-up. The proprietor whipped one up, and liked the idea of this dish at this time of day so much that he decided to make a tradition of it. Today, food lovers from the coast and from other nearby hill towns often make an after-lunch excursion to Bacì for zabaione – which is always served now with the little fritters called bugie (see previous page). This is an approximation of Bacì's recipe.

to serve 4

6	large egg yolks
115 g/4 oz	sugar
175 ml/6 fl oz	Marsala*

Gently beat the egg yolks and sugar together until they form a pale yellow cream.

Stir in the Marsala well, then pour the mixture into the top of a double boiler over medium-high heat. Continue mixing the zabaione, slowly but steadily, for 5 minutes, then pour into 4 warm glass bowls. Serve warm, at room temperature, or lightly chilled.

*Pigato (see page 287) or another fragrant but dry white wine may be substituted for Marsala, but the resulting zabaione, obviously, won't be as sweet – unless you compensate by adding another few tablespoons of sugar.

Old-Style Genoese Panettone

Pandolce Antica Genova

A sort of bread-dough cake filled with raisins and candied fruits is eaten all over Italy, under such names as panettone, panforte, and panspeziale, depending on the region. The Genoese name, rendered in dialect as pandöçe, is the most direct: This really is sweet bread. The origins of pandolce and its relatives are very old. Some scholars trace a similar confection back to ancient Persia. In Genoa, pandolce's immediate ancestor was apparently a kind of dense raisin bread, known popularly if not exactly appealingly as pan de mangiä e spüä – bread to eat and spit (since the dried grapes inside still had pips). Both Martin Piaggio and another Genoese poet, Filippo Castello, wrote odes to pandolce; Piaggio's, as usual, was partly a recipe in verse ("lì ghe drento du çetron / do fenoggio, do vin bon, / pigneu freschi, e che zebibbo" – "inside there are citron / fennel seeds, good wine, / fresh pine nuts, and raisins").

Though a light, cake-like, leavened pandolce is now common in Genoa, the old way of making it was as a dense, unleavened loaf – very buttery and crumbly, and delightfully perfumed with vanilla and orange flower water. This is a pandolce in that style, based on the one prepared at Genoa's venerable Pasticceria Villa on the via Garibaldi.

to make 1 × 20 cm/8 inch pandolce

115 g/4 oz	unsalted butter
175 g/6 oz	sugar
1	egg
125 ml/4 fl oz	milk
4 teaspoons	orange flower water
2 teaspoons	vanilla extract
350 g/12 oz	flour
50 g/2 oz	currants
50 g/2 oz	sultanas
50 g/2 oz	candied orange peel, finely diced
50 g/2 oz	pine nuts
½ teaspoon	fennel seeds
¼ teaspoon	ground coriander

Preheat oven to 180°C/350°F/Gas Mark 4.

In a large bowl, work the butter and sugar together until well blended, then stir in egg until mixture is smooth.

Combine milk and orange flower water in a small saucepan and warm over low heat (do not boil), then stir into butter mixture. Add vanilla and stir. Work in flour, kneading dough for a minute or so until it becomes smooth and firm. (Add another tablespoon or two of flour if the dough seems too wet.) Add currants, sultanas, orange peel, pine nuts, fennel seeds, and coriander, working them in until they're well distributed in dough.

Shape dough into a disk about 16 cm/6 inches in diameter (it will spread as it bakes) and place on a lightly greased baking tray. Bake for 1 hour and 15 minutes, lowering temperature slightly if loaf browns too quickly. The finished pandolce should be a deep golden brown.

Monégasque Lemon Tart
Tarte au Citron

The filling for this unusual lemon tart comes from Jean and Danièle Lorenzi's *Cuisine monégasque/Cüjina de Munégu*. It is, they believe, a recipe from Monaco's old *ghetu* or Jewish ghetto, now long since disappeared.

to serve 6

150 g/5 oz	flour
2	large eggs
115 g/4 oz	plus 1 teaspoon unsalted butter, softened to room temperature
90-115 g/3-4 oz	almonds, brown skins removed
225 g/8 oz	sugar
	Juice of 8 large lemons (about 450 ml/16 fl oz)
	Zest of 1 lemon and 1 orange
25 g/1 oz	fresh breadcrumbs

Preheat oven to 200°C/400°F/Gas Mark 6.

Sift flour into a bowl. Beat eggs lightly in another bowl, then stir into flour with a fork. Stir in 115 g/4 oz butter, continuing to mix with a fork until a crumbly mixture is formed. Turn dough out onto a floured work surface and knead several times.

Lightly grease a 23 cm/9 inch pie dish with remaining butter, then press dough into dish evenly, shaping it up around the edges. Trim edges, then roll out leftover dough and cut it into several long, thin strips to decorate tart.

Crush almonds to a powder with a mortar and pestle or food processor. Stir sugar into lemon juice, dissolving it well, then mix in the ground almonds and lemon and orange zest. Stir in breadcrumbs and mix in thoroughly.

Line tart shell with wax paper and fill with dried beans or pie weights. Bake for 15 minutes.

Remove wax paper and weights from tart shell, allow to cool, then pour in lemon juice mixture, and crisscross remaining dough pieces on top of it. Reduce heat to 160°C/325°F/Gas Mark 3 and bake for 45 minutes.

All-Citrus Dessert

Dessert Tout Agrumes

This rather time-consuming but not overcomplicated dessert is made at Don Camillo in Nice by pastry chef Denise Gerbert – who happens to be owner-chef Franck Cerutti's mother-in-law. Not traditionally Niçois, this speciality is nonetheless refreshingly evocative of the many citrus trees that grow between Nice and Menton.

to serve 4

3	large eggs, separated
450 g/1 lb	sugar
1 tablespoon	powdered milk
450 ml/16 fl oz	fresh-squeezed orange or blood-orange juice
450 ml/16 fl oz	fresh-squeezed grapefruit juice
4 tablespoons	cream
¾ teaspoon	powdered gelatin
2	oranges or blood oranges
1	small grapefruit

Whisk egg yolks, 2 tablespoons sugar, and powdered milk together for about 2 minutes, until thick.

Mix 350 ml/12 fl oz each orange and grapefruit juice with cream in a saucepan and scald over high heat. Do not allow to boil.

Strain juice mixture into egg yolks and stir until very smooth. Transfer to the same saucepan and bring to a boil, whisking constantly. Boil for 2 minutes, continuing to whisk, then pour into a bowl. Stir in gelatin, dissolving it thoroughly. Cover bowl and set aside.

In small saucepan, dissolve 115 g/4 oz sugar thoroughly in 4 tablespoons water over medium heat, then raise heat and bring to a boil without stirring. Continue boiling until mixture reaches 130°C/250°F on a sugar thermometer.

Meanwhile, beat egg whites vigorously until stiff. Drizzle syrup over egg whites slowly, continuing to beat for about 5 minutes, until mixture has cooled completely. (It should be very stiff.)

Gently fold mixture into gelatin mixture and divide it between 2.6 litres/4½ pint soufflé or gratin dishes. Place in the freezer for 3–4 hours.

Combine remaining orange and grapefruit juice in a pan and stir in 150 g/5 oz sugar over low heat until sugar dissolves completely. Raise heat to high and bring mixture to a boil. Reduce heat immediately and continue cooking over low heat for several minutes, swirling the pan once or twice so that syrup colours evenly. When it reaches 160°C/325°F on a sugar thermometer, remove it from heat and set aside.

Cut peels from oranges and grapefruit in large pieces, scrape off pith, and cut remaining peel into a fine julienne. Separate oranges and grapefruit carefully into segments and set aside.

In a small saucepan, dissolve remaining sugar thoroughly in 225 ml/8 fl oz water over low heat, then raise heat and boil for 1 minute. Add orange and grapefruit zests and boil for 1 minute. Drain and set aside.

To serve, dip soufflé or gratin dishes into warm water and unmould gratins onto 4 dessert plates. Spoon orange sauce over them and decorate with orange and grapefruit segments and candied zests.

Walnut Cake with Honey and Ricotta
Gâteau aux Noix avec Miel et Ricotta

This is another delicious dessert from Denise Gerbert at Don Camillo in Nice, and again, while it's not traditional, it makes use of basic products of the region. In the original version, ricotta is replaced by brousse (see page 120).

to serve 4–6

6 tablespoons	unsalted butter, melted
225 g/8 oz	shelled walnuts, finely chopped
1 teaspoon	baking powder
350 g/12 oz	sugar
2 tablespoons	flour
	Whites of 5 large eggs
	Zest of 1 orange
125 ml/4 fl oz	fresh-squeezed orange juice
4 tablespoons	chestnut, orange-blossom, or other natural honey
225 g/8 oz	fresh ricotta

Preheat oven to 180°C/350°F/Gas Mark 4.

Grease a cake tin with a little of the butter and line the bottom with wax paper.

Mix remaining butter, walnuts, baking powder, 150 g/5 oz sugar, and flour together well in a bowl. Add approximately 2 egg whites and mix in thoroughly.

In another bowl, beat remaining egg whites until stiff, then add 75 g/3 oz sugar, a little at a time, beating it in well. Fold egg whites into walnut mixture, combining thoroughly. Pour batter into cake tin and bake for 30–40 minutes. Remove from oven and set aside to cool.

Meanwhile, in a small saucepan, dissolve 75 g/3 oz sugar thoroughly in 125 ml/4 fl oz water over low heat, then raise heat and boil for 1 minute. Add orange zest and boil for 1 minute. Drain and set aside.

Dissolve remaining sugar thoroughly in orange juice in a small, heavy saucepan over low heat. Raise heat to high and bring mixture to a boil. Reduce heat immediately and continue cooking over low heat for several minutes, swirling the pan once or twice so that syrup colours evenly. When it reaches 160°C/325°F on a sugar thermometer, remove it from heat and set aside.

Melt honey in a small saucepan over low heat.

To assemble, cut cooled cake into 4 or 6 pieces, and place pieces on dessert plates. Alongside each one, place a scoop of ricotta. Pour orange sauce over ricotta and drizzle honey over ricotta and cake. Decorate with additional orange zest if desired.

Part 6

The Wines
of the Riviera

LIGURIA

Ligurian wine has got some bad press, as it were, over the years. In the first century B.C., Diodorus Siculus wrote that the region was "inaccessible a Cerere e a Bacco" – inaccessible to Ceres and Bacchus (i.e., to grain and wine). Around the same time, the geographer Strabo reported that the libations of choice in the region were milk and a beverage made of rye (beer?), and that Ligurian wine was resinous, harsh, and meagre in quantity. Stopping on the edge of the Lunigiana on his way to Sarzana in 1581, Montaigne noted, "I was forced to drink new wines – they drink no others in these parts – which, with a certain kind of wood and the whites of eggs, are made so clear that they lack none of the colour of old wines; but they have an undefinable unnatural taste." As recently as 1980, in the quasi-official publication *Italian Wines & Spirits,* whose brief is to promote said products in the English-speaking world, the headline for an article on the wines of Liguria read, "Drink Them but Beware, They May Scratch."

The quantity is still meagre. Vines account for only about 5 percent of the agricultural plantings in Liguria, and the region produces less than one-half of 1 percent of Italy's total wine output – with only 3 or 4 percent of that classified and likely to be sold commercially outside the immediate region. As for quality, I think I can safely say that I've consumed as much Ligurian wine over the past few years as any non-Ligurian (and more than some Ligurians, too), and I must admit that one of them was quite possibly the worst wine I've ever tasted: It was yellow-brown in colour, smelled like Pino Silvestre bath oil, tasted like pitch mixed with a particularly flowery perfume, and finished with a nasty acidic bite; I was frankly afraid to drink it. But it was not commercial wine; it was something made by a farmer near Finale Ligure, served to me at dinner by a friend in Genoa whose table is considerably better than his wine cellar.

Apart from this one wine, I've enjoyed most of what I've encountered. At their worst, Ligurian wines are inoffensive – decent mouthwash to lubricate a meal. At their best, they're memorable. The better Pigatos of the western Riviera are complex, delightfully fruity, impressively aromatic white wines of admirable structure. The Vermentinos of both west and east, the latter especially, are often lean, crisp, pleasantly acidic whites, with an attractive lingering herbaceous flavour. The Rossese grape produces light, bright, fruity red wines, often full of charm, all along the Riviera di Ponente. In the Lunigiana, the almost-Tuscan reds, made mostly from Sangiovese, can attain extraordinary depth and richness. And though the dry wines of the Cinque Terre, these days, don't have much to recommend them (they are too little wine for too much money in my experience), the region's sweet or semi-sweet Sciacchetrà is unique and delicious.

The terraced vineyards that surround the towns of the Cinque Terre are almost vertical. Were it not for a dense skein of mortarless stone walls forming thousands upon thousands of narrow terraces – it is said that soil was brought here by ship and carried uphill by Roman slaves, and that the walls, taken together, stretch some 6,800 miles, almost twice the length of the Great Wall of China – neither vines nor anything else but scrub could grow here. Despite, or perhaps because of, the difficult conditions under which the grapes grow, the wines of the Cinque Terre have been famous since antiquity. By the thirteenth century, they were being shipped as far away as England and the Netherlands. Boccaccio sang their praises. Petrarch wrote of the region's "vines illuminated by the benevolent eye of the sun and most beloved by Bacchus." The popes drank them – and Dante condemned Pope Martin IV to purgatory for the sin of gluttony, for having eaten a surfeit of eels stewed in Vernaccia from Corniglia. (The very grape name Vernaccia, now used in many parts of Italy, may be a corruption of Vernazza.)

Early in this century, Lieut.-Col. Newnham-Davis wrote of discovering, in some cellars in Genoa, wines from the Cinque Terre "dating back sixty years or more." These were almost certainly examples of the region's celebrated Sciacchetrà. This is a passito-style wine, mildly sweet but not sugary, made from grapes dried on straw mats. The curious name (pronounced approximately "shock-eh-TRAW") is said to come from the Genoese verbs *sciaccâ,* to crush, and either *tiâ,* to pull – a reference to the fact that the grape skins were pulled out of the fermenting wine almost immediately – or *travasá,* to rack (which in wine terminology means to draw wine off its lees).

The wines of the Cinque Terre, both Sciacchetrà and dry whites, are extremely popular with tourists and are represented on better wine lists all over Liguria. How much longer such wines will be around, however, is uncertain. The old farmers are dying off, and their sons and daughters don't want to work this punishing land. ("They'd rather get a desk job in La Spezia and buy cheap Pinot Grigio from Friuli than break their backs out here to make their own wine," one local vintner told me sadly.) About 50 percent of the sparse agricultural land in the Cinque Terre has been abandoned since World War II; even the vineyards on the hills surrounding the region's wine cooperative have been forsaken.

For now, at least, the Cooperativa Agricola di Cinqueterre remains by far the largest wine producer in Liguria, turning out more than 20,000 cases a year – a generic Cinque Terre, three single-vineyard wines, a declassified bottling called Muretti, a Sciacchetrà, and a bit of spumante – from grapes supplied by more than 200 growers. All the wines are white, as are the majority of the vintages of the region, and are made mostly from a variety called Bosco, with the addition of some Albarola and Vermentino and a few straggles of minor local cultivars. (The cooperative also makes two grappas; there's very little grappa elsewhere in Liguria, except for a bit around Dolce Acqua, and a surprising amount in the Cinque Terre – most of it quite good, especially that made from Sciacchetrà.)

The single-vineyard offerings, which are sporadically available here, are Costa da Posa di Volastra, Costa de Sèra di Riomaggiore, and Costa de Campù di Manarola. Over the past few years, I've found them consistent in quality from one vintage to the next, clean, inoffensive, and pretty much indistinguishable from one another – though the Costa da Posa has perhaps a bit more flavour then the rest. At £3 or £3.50, they'd be good party wines; at £7.50 or £8.00, which is more what they're liable to cost, they're way out of their league.

The anonymous carafe wines you get in restaurants in the Cinque Terre are usually dark yellow, rather piney, and oxidized. (A waiter at Gianni Franzi in Vernazza confided to me years ago, "You order three bottles, and you'll get one that's good." If that.) One searches for something between these and the bland, if technologically correct, wines of the Cooperativa. The closest thing I've found is the wine made by Forlini Cappellini in Manarola – a clean, flavourful white with a generous bouquet, about 85 percent Bosco, from an assortment of tiny vineyard plots around the town. (I tasted several tank samples of the 1993 vintage, as yet unblended, and was surprised at how different they were.) Small quantities have been imported into Britain.

Alberto Cappellini and his wife, Germana Forlini, with Riccardo Arrigoni as consulting winemaker, also produce a little of red and some Sciacchetrà for their own use, and they were kind enough to let me taste both. The red, made from Canaiolo and a variety called Teta Vaca – local dialect for "cow's teat" (because it gives a lot of juice, Forlini explained) – was bright in colour and fizzy, with a not unattractive citrusy aroma. The Sciacchetrà was very good – about the colour of an old, caramelized whisky, with a dried-grape aroma, a nutty, faintly sour flavour, and a surprisingly dry finish. I don't know that the red would win many fans in the restaurants of Milan or London, but I think the Sciacchetrà could become a cult favourite, and I wish there were enough of it for the winery to sell commercially.

Riccardo Arrigoni makes his own wines in La Spezia, including a crisp, straightforward, but rather dull Cinque Terre called Giumin, and a Colli di Luni Vermentino, equally crisp but with more character. He also makes Sciacchetrà. A few days before I visited Forlini Cappellini, Franco Solari at the Ca' Peo restaurant in Leivi had given me a bottle of Sciacchetrà labelled only with a strip of tape reading "1986." Deep reddish-brown in colour and still languidly fermenting in the bottle, it had a distinct rancio character (that desirable sourness certain old brandies and sweet wines obtain) and a rich, full, woody flavour. When I described the wine to Arrigoni, he thought it may have been one he made and sold to Solari. And when I mentioned that Solari had suggested that Sciacchetràs like this take on something of the character of old Barolo, Arrigoni replied, "Well, I would say it's just the opposite – old Barolos take on the character of Sciacchetrà."

On the other side of Liguria, between Genoa and the French border, the grapes of choice are Vermentino and Pigato for white wine and Rossese for red. The best-known denominazione di origine controllata (DOC) or appellation for red wines specifically is Rossese di Dolce Acqua, or simply Dolce Acqua; the region's other DOC, Riviera Ligure di Ponente (with three subappellations, Albenganese, Finalese, and Riviera dei Fiori), encompasses Rossese from east of the Dolce Acqua region as well as the aforementioned whites and a few other minor red and white wines.

The origins of Rossese are a matter of some dispute. According to some sources, it is clearly a clone of Dolcetto, imported from the Piedmont region (which abuts Liguria); indeed, Dolcetto was widely planted in Liguria until the latter part of the nineteenth century. Winemakers around Dolce Acqua, on the other hand, seem to think that it must be French in origin, because vineyards growing it were traditionally trained in a French, not an Italian, style. If it is from France originally, that might explain why Napoleon, who encountered it while staying at the Doria castle in Dolce Acqua, particularly liked it and had some shipped back to Paris, where he served it to guests. Burton Anderson notes that Napoleon magnanimously offered to let local vintners call the wine by his name henceforth. "Few producers ever did," says Anderson. "Maybe they . . . had heard that the Emperor's palate was no match for his ego."

Vermentino may have originated in Spain, or on the island of Madeira, and is apparently related to Malvasia – though Malvasia, confusingly, seems to have come from Greece. In any case, it was being cultivated in Spain, Sardinia, and Corsica by 1100 or so, and is first recorded in Liguria around 1300. It has been estimated that there are as many as forty clones of the grape growing in Liguria today.

There is a romantic theory that Pigato comes from the Castelli Romani, outside Rome, and was first planted in Liguria by Caesar's legions. In fact, it is probably of Greek origin, and it has been growing in Liguria only since around 1600. Its name comes either from a dialect word, *pighe,* meaning stained or coloured – for the mottling on its skin – or from the Latin *pix,* pitch, in reference to the resin with which it might once have been flavoured.

Comparing their two principal white wine grapes, Ligurian winemakers (they *are* Italian, remember) like to say that Vermentino is feminine and Pigato masculine; a more useful differentiation might be to propose that Vermentino is somewhat more austere, often suggesting thyme, rosemary, and other herbs, while Pigato is rather more robust and more likely to recall apricots, peaches, or perhaps (say some tasters) mimosa.

Legendary Rossese was made in the 1960s and '70s by Emilio Croesi, onetime communist mayor of Perinaldo, and the owner of a famous vineyard in nearby Soldano called Vignetio Curli. Croesi, now deceased, kept the yield of his vines very low and made his wines, all 350 or 400 cases a year, by traditional methods. By all accounts, they were rich, well balanced, and intense in flavour and aroma. Franco Solari, the wine-conscious proprietor of Ca' Peo in Leivi, says that Croesi's wines were erratic – but that he recalls one bottle, brought to him as a gift by another Rossese producer, as the best Italian red of any kind he's ever tasted.

Silvio Viglietti, proprietor of the highly rated Palma in Alassio – who claims to have "discovered" Croesi (as does Pino Sola in Genoa) – told me that he said to him one day, "You're a communist, so why don't you start a cooperative and sell everybody's wines together?" Croesi replied, "Because mine is so much better." I keep hoping I'll run across a well-preserved old bottle of Croesi's wine in somebody's cellar, and that it will offer me at least a hint of its former quality – but so far that hasn't happened.

Today's Rossese, alas, often turns out to be anything but intense; much of it is light and ingenuous, sometimes with a candyish sweetness. Modern approaches to the grape vary, but there is now a great deal of experimenting going on in both vineyard and winery to try to improve the wine. I've tasted the results, and I have to say that I can't help feeling that a number of obviously skilled and intelligent winemakers are wasting their time trying to do something significant with what is fundamentally and irrevocably a minor grape. Paris-based wine importer and wine bar owner Tim Johnston, with whom I tasted a number of these wines, thinks perhaps that Rossese is picked too early – and that it might need to be grafted onto new rootstock for vigour.

Nonetheless, I have enjoyed some Rosseses. Some of the more promising efforts were made in the early 1990s in Perinaldo by Marco Romagnoli, under the Castello di Perinaldo label. Romagnoli – who once told me that he thought Rossese had the potential to be a great wine grape, as noble as nebbiolo – produced three different bottlings: a regular bottling and two single-vineyard ones, one called Brae and the other made from Croesi's old property, Curli. All three were rich in colour with suggestions of that barnyardy nose that good burgundies have, and a lot of fruit and spice on the palate – though these qualities tended to become obscured by too much time in new French oak. Romagnoli is no longer associated with Castello di Perinaldo, however. I haven't tasted anything his successor there may have produced – but Romagnoli now makes an attractive Vermentino under the Tenuta Giuncheo label, and has more Rossese in the works. (He also produces excellent olive oil; see page 250.)

The Cantina del Rossese, just outside Dolce Acqua, makes a sort of schizophrenic Rossese, wonderfully fragrant and fresh smelling but sort of candyish and earthy on the palate. Mandino Cane, with wine-making equipment located beneath peeling frescoes in a portion of a desanctified church in Dolce Acqua, makes light, clean, faintly cherry-flavoured Rossese, called simply Dolce Acqua (the best is a single-vineyard Vigneto Arcagna), that fairly blooms with food. (Winemaker Giobatta Cane, incidentally, has recently planted small experimental plots of Syrah and Viognier.)

In a beautifully equipped winery in the hamlet of Brunetti, above Camporosso, brothers Claudio and Paolo Rondelli make an acclaimed barrel-aged Rossese under the Terre Bianche label that seems to be getting better, and more concentrated, every year. (Their '94 was full of extract and delicious.) They also produce Vermentino and Pigato, and a blend of the two – oak tends to predominate in these wines – and maintain an exquisite little Agriturismo operation on their estate, welcoming paying guests to a simple ten-room inn with a magnificent view of the countryside and a pretty little dining room.

The Rosseses I liked the best in the Dolce Acqua region, as it turned out, were the least "technological": those made by Pippo Viale and his son Roberto in Soldano, in a winery that is basically a garage, equipped not with stainless steel but with three old tonneaux and lots of wicker-wrapped glass demijohns. Viale's wines, made from old vines, have a certain roughness to them, and are sometimes a bit raisiny, but they're full of character – and one of the older vintages I tasted, his '91, was quite remarkable, with a nose of cinnamon, pepper, and cloves, and a lusciously complex, earthy, fruity flavour.

Rossese and Vermentino are also made northeast of the Dolce Acqua region, up the Ligurian coast toward Genoa, and Pigato appears more regularly in this region. At Colle dei Bardellini on the outskirts of Imperia – a technologically advanced winery (must chiller, bacteriological filtration, cold stabilization, sterile bottling line, etc.) partly owned by Genoese restaurateur Pino Sola – the Pigato is pleasant, with a herbaceous nose and an astringent finish, and there is a light, supple Rossese. But Bardellini's best wine is its limited-bottling Vigna Ü Monte Vermentino, which has a nose of thyme and cedar and a dry, faintly grassy flavour. I find this to be seafood wine par excellence.

High in the mountains above Imperia, in Pieve di Teco, Tommaso and Angelo Lupi run a good-sized winery and négociant operation, producing or bottling, among other wines, a medium-bodied, moderately fruity regular Pigato and a richer, vaguely musky Pigato di Campochiesa called Le Petraie; decent Vermentino and Rossese; and an overly oaky Pigato-Vermentino blend called Vignamare.

Lupi has made something of a speciality, however, of a grape called Ormeasco – which is a clone of the Dolcetto of Piedmont, originally from the Piedmontese town of Ormea. Ormeasco is widely planted in the deep western entroterra; this is perhaps a legacy of the mayor of Pornassio, who ordered, in 1303, that it be cultivated in the region to the exclusion of other varieties, under pain of decapitation. Wines made from the grape are famously long-lived, though they rarely seem to have the deep concentration of pretty fruit that Piedmontese Dolcetto can achieve. Lupi, nonetheless, makes an attractive enough Ormeasco Superiore and an ambitious wood-aged version called Le Braje – as well as a dry but fruity Ormeasco rosé called Sciac-trà (from the same etymological roots as the Sciacchetrà of the Cinque Terre, and meaning the same thing, i.e., that the skins and juice are quickly separated).

Pigato achieves its apotheosis with Riccardo Bruna in Ranzo Borgo and Pippo Parodi in Bastia d'Albenga, both inland from the seaside town of Albenga. Bruna has his own small winery and also makes wine for the Capello family in Ortovero. Virginio Capello was a pioneer of fine Pigato. I met him one day, when he was ninety-two, sitting in his car outside Bruna's grocery store in Ranzo. "I planted only Pigato," he told me proudly, as if that were his testament. Then he added, "I drank too much of it" – with a near toothless grin that said he hadn't stopped yet. Bruna is married to Capello's only daughter, and produces a wonderful Pigato called Villa Torrachetta from vines around the Capello villa. Typically, it boasts immense perfume, plenty of body, ample fruit, ample acidity, and an attractive mild bitterness that throws all its other elements into perspective.

Pippo Parodi's Pigato, sold under the Cascina du Fèipu label (and occasionally seen here), isn't quite as rich and complex as Bruna's, but it is absolutely delicious, with a subtle bouquet and just a point of carbonation. In the best vintages, these are as good as any white wines in Italy – and are certainly more pleasant to drink than all those overblown oak-flavoured Chardonnays the Tuscans are so fond of. (Parodi is bottling an unfiltered Pigato for the Paolo e Barbera restaurant in San Remo, which I'm anxious to sample.)

At Podere Boiga, near Perti, on the inland edge of Finale Ligure, Domenico Boiga makes an acidic, bracingly greenish Vermentino and a surprisingly attractive Lumassina. This grape, which may be a clone of Trebbiano, can yield nastily acerbic, mouse-piss sorts of wines. Boiga's, however, while undeniably acidic, has a grassy, Muscadet-like authority and a wonderful bouquet, suggesting the wild scrub of the nearby hillsides. I would order it in a second to go with oysters or mussels – and I'd be very happy to encounter it on a hot summer day even without seafood.

There's a good Lumassina as well, grassy and lemony, at Vladimiro Galluzzo's handsome, almost California-style (and all-organic) Terre Rosse winery outside of Manie, also near Finale. Named for the luminously red earth that surrounds the winery, Terre Rosse also makes a superlative Vermentino, simultaneously rich and sharp, a subtly oaky Pigato-Vermentino blend called Banche, and credible Pigato and Rossese. The winery's triumph, however, is a passito, or sweet wine made from dried grapes, blended from 70 percent Pigato and 30 percent Vermentino – incredibly aromatic, luxuriously rich, and absolutely delicious.

In Quiliano, in the hills overlooking Savona, beneath a sign reading A Cantinna du Türcu, Innocenzo Turco makes minuscule quantities of Buzzetto and Granaccia – the latter something of a legend in Liguria and even up into Piedmont. Buzzetto from Quiliano is mentioned as early as 1200, and Silvio Torre speculates that it might have been the wine that Columbus drank. In fact, Buzzetto is the local name for Lumassina; the word comes from the Genoese büso, underripe or sour – and I have to admit that I find Turco's version, at least, to possess more sourness than charm. (Another local name for the grape is Mataosso, which would appear to mean "bone-killer.")

His Granaccia – the grape is of course the Garnacha of Spain and the Grenache of France – is another story. It is powerful stuff, dark, thick, bursting with flavour, and not a bit like any other red wine from Liguria. (It is also apparently long-lived; Turco told me that he has bottles dating back to 1902, and that they are still good. He didn't offer to prove it, alas.) In the '94 vintage, which was difficult throughout Liguria – many vintners lost nearly ripened grapes to rain and hail – he made only about 300 litres (400 bottles) of the wine. It was, however, pretty impressive stuff, big and rustic, with lots of alcohol and tannin, an immense amount of fruit, and a pronounced but not at all unpleasant overripe flavour. (This wine would have been quite a hit in California in the 1970s.) There are only three or four producers of Granaccia in Quiliano today, but Turco remains dedicated to the wine. "Granaccia is a Ligurian tradition," he says. "One must defend Ligurian traditions."

Other wines to look for on the Riviera di Ponente include the lemony, ever so slightly smoky Calleri Pigato di Albenga; Ettore Vio's faintly sparkling, complex Pigato dell'Albenganese; Feola Pigato dell'Albenganese, with lovely peach-like fruit and an enduring richness; Laura Aschero Vermentino, slightly lemony and slightly grapey, and well-balanced in a medium-light sort of way; full-bodied, flower-scented Vermentino from La Rocca di S. Nicolao; and Stefano Centa Lumassina, very soft and gentle but with a slight acidic back-bite.

Genoa has traditionally drunk other than Ligurian wines. Usually that means those of Piedmont, especially the reds. But the Genoese were also among the first in Italy to pay attention to port and sherry, and the trading vessels of the republic regularly brought wines from Puglia, Sicily, Sardinia, and Corsica into the city itself and its subject ports. (The Sea Rat in *Wind in the Willows* describes a sea voyage he made from Corsica to Alassio in a ship carrying wine. Upon arrival, he says, the casks are thrown overboard, tied together with ropes, and then floated into shore behind rowboats, forming a "long bobbing procession of casks, like a mile of porpoises.") Genoa's own wines are the light, mildly fruity, often slightly pétillant white vini da tavola called Coronata and Val Polcevera, both from the entroterra just above the city. They are made from Vermentino and a grape called Bianchetta Genovese – said to be the same as Piedmont's Arneis – and are pleasant enough, though I think you'd have to be a real Genoese patriot to order them when you could have a modest Vermentino or Pigato for the same price. (D'Annunzio once cracked that "Genoa is called 'Proud'; all proud men have a bad heart and all proud cities have a bad wine.")

There was once a famous wine made in Leivi, in the hills above Chiavari. Bartolomeo Paschetti mentions it in his *Del Conservar la sanità, et del vivere de genovese,* published in 1602. There are still vines on the site, and there is a project to make commercial wine from them again. For the time being, however, Chiavari's enological claim to fame is the Enoteca Bisson, in the town itself. The Enoteca is a full-scale wine shop, selling vintages from all over Italy, as well as a few wines from France, and (at least the last time I was there) one each from California, Australia, and Spain – plus a wide assortment of distilled drinks, cheese, biscuits and sweets, pasta, and the like. But in the back room there is a small but technologically sophisticated winery, from which flow a number of different wines. The best of these are a nouveau-style wine made from Ciliegiolo grapes with carbonic maceration; a woody, earthy Caratello (Albarola) with a flavour of honey and maybe figs; a passito called Acinarari, made from Bianchetta and a little Vermentino (dried for three months with a table fan), with a gingerbread nose and an appealing softness on the palate followed by a tannic bite; and a mild but perfectly drinkable Albarola frizzante, which, at 5,500 lire (about £2.00) a bottle, is almost certainly the cheapest bottle-fermented sparkling wine in the world.

Probably two-thirds of all Ligurian wine is made east of Genoa, mostly in the province of La Spezia – but apart from the vintages of the Cinque Terre, most of it is wine no one outside the immediate neighbourhood has ever heard of, or would be apt to drink. At least, that was the case until recently. Proposals to establish a DOC for the Riviera di Levante as a whole have been turned down repeatedly in the past, due largely to lobbying by producers in the Riviera di Ponente DOC, who fear that consumers would readily confuse the two appellations and that their own business (especially considering the comparative vastness of the Levante's production) would suffer as a result. In late 1993, however, the Italian government did grant a DOC to one section of the region, the hills above Levanto, on the northern end of the Cinque Terre. Vino di Levanto – white made from Bosco, Albarola, and Vermentino, and red made from Ciliegiolo and Sangiovese – has not, at this writing, had time to establish itself with any sort of identity in the marketplace, but it is a category to watch.

The next-youngest DOC in eastern Liguria, dating from 1989, is the Colli di Luni, north and east of La Spezia. This region boasts two of Liguria's best wineries – Ottaviano Lambruschi and La Colombiera, both in Castelnuovo Magro. Ottavio Lambruschi was a pioneer in the region. Now his son, Fabio, makes the wines: a citrusy, acidic, fragrant white, sometimes with the merest tingle of carbonation, from a blend of Vermentino, Trebbiano, and Albarola; a straight Vermentino with a damp-straw nose, a good measure of fruit, and a faint almond aftertaste; and a medium-dark, medium-rich, elegantly structured red composed of 60 percent Sangiovese, 30 percent Merlot, and 10 percent Canaiolo and Pollera Nera.

At La Colombiera, I found another attractive Vermentino, but, more important, what I believe are the best red wines of Liguria. Bottled under the name Terrizzo, these are blends of Sangiovese (65 to 70 percent), Merlot, Canaiolo, and

Ciliegiolo, and are so intense and complex that Pieralberto Ferro, who makes wines here for his father, Francesco, says people accused him of buying in Tuscan grapes when he first produced them. I tasted five vintages of the wine, and found them all to be intense, well-focused wines, dark in colour, with huge bouquets (already developed, even in the youngest case) and lovely, clean, complex flavours. I'd put them up against a good many of the high-profile vini da tavola from next-door Tuscany.

Charles Dickens on the
Wines of Genoa

"[Genoese wine merchants] often get wine at these suburban
Trattorie, from France and Spain and Portugal, which is
brought over by small captains in little trading-vessels. They
buy it at so much a bottle, without asking what it is, or caring
to remember if anybody tells them, and usually divide it into
two heaps; of which they label one Champagne, and the other
Madeira. The various opposite flavours, qualities, countries,
ages, and vintages that are comprised under these two general
heads is quite extraordinary. The most limited range is
probably from cool Gruel up to old Marsala, and down again
to apple Tea."

Walking the Five Lands

The touristic canard is that the towns of the Cinque Terre, long isolated from the rest of the eastern Ligurian coastline by steep cliffs, are still all but inaccessible. As recently as 1971, Waverley Root wrote that the five villages could be reached "only by boat (or on foot, if you are a mountain climber)." He was apparently unaware of the railway line that went through the Cinque Terre in the 1890s, connecting it to Sestri Levante and La Spezia. Today it is even possible to achieve all five towns by car – though the roads that lead between them are admittedly sometimes narrow and tortuous.

One advantage to driving is that it provides a close-up look at the hills above the villages – the steep terraces, the narrow ravines, the stands of olive trees, the little one-seat monorails now used by workers in the vineyards to transport boxes of grapes (and themselves) up and down the arduous inclines. There is also a more intimate, and more demanding, way to see the territory, however: by hiking the *sentieri,* or footpaths, that run along the cliffs from one village to the next, following routes first carved out many centuries, if not millennia, ago.

The shortest and easiest of the principal sentieri is the so-called Via dell'Amore or Road of Love, which connects Riomaggiore and Manarola, hugging the coastline alongside scrub-tufted cliffs and beneath dramatic rock outcroppings. The longest and most difficult one, which has no nickname, runs between Monterosso and Vernazza. When I decided to walk at least one segment of the sentieri myself one spring morning several years ago, I thought immediately of the Via dell'Amore. At the time, unfortunately, it was closed for repairs (a sign on a fence at the Riomaggiore end read, in

English, "Dangerous Path" – which I thought apposite for a road of love), so I took the latter instead. Starting just below the Porto Roca hotel, I set off on a deceptively friendly-looking downhill pathway, and soon found myself scrambling up and down hills, climbing and descending hundreds of steep steps (some of fragmented rock, some of poured concrete), and stepping cautiously along sections of path no more than two feet wide, with no guardrails or other barriers separating them from long drops into thorny bushes or worse.

It was a memorable experience. Between the towns, the landscape grows wild. Dense scrub in a hundred shades of green covers the rocks, accented liberally with the yellows, whites, reds, and pinks of wildflowers. The variety of flora is immense – gorse, arbutus, valerian, wild juniper, spurge, wild thyme, rosemary, lavender, wild orchids, narcissus, asphodel, bilberry trees, Aleppo pines, holm oaks, and more. Closer to the towns, on both ends of the path, the human landscape of the Cinque Terre becomes more evident: I passed tiny rough gardens with short, neat rows of lettuce and snarls of courgette vines; clusters of olive trees; gnarled vineyards, hugging the soil. Here and there was a farmer's shack, sometimes with a few chickens pecking the hard ground outside. In places the path was lined with old stone walls into which were set wooden doors that look as if they hadn't been opened in fifty years. I felt as if I had discovered a secret rural civilization, and in a way I had.

NICE AND VICINITY

*If for the women coffee was the principal
beverage, the men absorbed wine – not
only to stanch their thirst but above all as
one of the pleasures of life, seen even as a
social duty.*

– FRANCIS ZUNINO, "SOUVENIR
IMAGINAIRE ET DESCRIPTIF SUR
LE VIN EN PAYS MENTONNAIS"
IN *LA CUISINE MENTONNAISE*

*Viéi bouòsc, viéi vin, viéi amic.
(Old woods, old wine, old friends.)*

– NIÇOIS PROVERB

The region of Nice boasts one famous set of wines (red, white, and rosé), scarce and often superb, but from a troubled appellation; one pleasant wine from a region whose vintages were once renowned; and the rumor of a surprising number of minor wines that seem to exist today only in memory.

The famous one, of course, is Bellet. "Of all the [French] Riviera wines I have tasted," wrote Waverley Root, "I would rate Bellet at the top." In their *Les Recettes de la table niçoise,* Raymond Armisen and André Martin state categorically that the Bellet region, which is in the hills directly above Nice, cheek by jowl with its industrial suburbs, and is administratively part of the city, "is certainly the oldest vineyard region in France." Grapes were first planted there, they continue, by Phocean Greeks (the founders of Marseilles and of trade colonies all along this littoral) – which would have been around the fourth century B.C. The vineyards of Bordeaux, by way of comparison, are thought to date from the second century A.D. Archaeologists have found some support for Bellet's claim: Fossil evidence suggests that early vines here were pruned and trained according to Greek, not Roman, practices.

The region is a natural for viticulture: Its slopes are comparatively gentle but rise nearly 1,000 feet in elevation; there's plenty of sun (as many as 2,700 hours per year) and sufficient rain; and light winds almost always blow up through the valley of the Var, moderating the heat of summer and discouraging mould in cooler weather. Unfortunately, these very characteristics make it attractive for residential real estate as well, and vineyards in Bellet are so few and far between today that they sometimes seem all but invisible. (The so-called Route du Vin de Bellet, which passes hardly any vineyards at all, is surely one of the least attractive wine roads on the planet.) At one time, in the nineteenth century, as many as 1,000 hectares (almost 2,500 acres) were under vine in Bellet. Today there are officially 700 hectares (about 1,730 acres) approved for vines in the appellation, but at most 50 of these (about 125 acres) are currently planted. And the rest of the land isn't lying fallow; much of it is covered with houses and apartments, and so would be reclaimable for viticulture only through the most drastic measures.

Bellet was granted an appellation contrôlée by the French government in 1941. The mix of grapes approved for the appellation is unusual: The principal white wine grape variety, said to lend Bellet blanc its finesse and a certain scent of pears and lemons, is Rolle – sometimes described as a clone of Vermentino, though local vintners don't believe this. (In their favour, it must be said that in Liguria a distinction is made between Vermentino and what is there called Rollo.) There is also a small amount of Chardonnay, here spelled *Chardonnais,* plus a bit of a local clone of Roussanne and a few other odds and ends. For rosé and red, the most important grapes are two local varieties: Braquet (which is probably the Brachetto of Piedmont), thought to give the reds and rosés their distinctive dried-herb aroma and typical black cherry flavour, and Folle Noire – Fûella Nera or Fouòla Nègra in Niçois. Folle noire, which is apparently not related to the Folle Blanche of western France, is said to derive its name (literally "crazy black") from the capriciousness of its quality from year to year; at its best, it lends structure and a faint spiciness to red Bellet. Smaller percentages of the familiarly Provençal Grenache and Cinsault are also grown, and there are some remnants of an old local variety called Nigraù or Négrette de Nice (the largest producer in the region says that he has fully two plants of it).

There are ten producers in the Bellet appellation today, the largest and most famous being Château de Crémat and Château de Bellet. Both have made excellent wines in the past; Château de Crémat's reds, at least up to the 1989 vintage, were probably the region's best, and Château de Bellet is especially successful with its impeccable whites and rosés – the former wonderfully rich and intense and the latter surprisingly long-lived. The other producers, all of them small and several of them new, are Clot dòu Baile, Charles Augier, Clos St. Vincent, Domaine de la Source, Domaine du Fogolar, Jean Massa, Hermès (owned by noted sculptor Sascha Sosno), and S.I.C.A. Les Coteaux de Bellet – the last of these being an organization of five growers who, until 1994, had supplied grapes to Château de Crémat.

The problem with Bellet is that there is not enough of it. Though expensive

(Château de Bellet's best white and red, for instance, sell for around £18 a bottle retail in France), it is immensely popular on the Côte d'Azur, as well it might be – it can be excellent wine, with a character very much its own, and it has a pretty, easily remembered name. Because production is small, however, producers habitually sell out of their stocks almost immediately upon release, usually to presubscribed clients. (To the best of my knowledge, no wine shop or restaurant wine cellar, even at the grandest establishments, has more than one or two producers represented; there is no such thing as a definitive selection of Bellet.)

With customers clamouring for the wine, it is not exactly surprising that there have been abuses and misrepresentations in Bellet. In 1994, southern French wine circles were abuzz with the news that two well-known producers in the region – Régis Méasson of Domaine de Font-Bellet and, shockingly enough, Charles Bagnis of the esteemed Château de Crémat (a man whose family had long been powerful in the appellation) – had been forced to divest themselves of their enterprises.

Bellet producers, naturally enough, aren't anxious to publicise these scandals. When my friend Tim Johnson (a wine merchant and wine bar *patron* in Paris) and I tried to visit the region in the autumn of 1994, we had no luck at all. We attempted for a week to reach Ghislain de Charnacé, director of Château de Bellet and president of the Bellet producers' syndicate, but he did not return phone calls. There was no answer at Château de Crémat, or at Bagnis's private number. No one was home when we stopped by Collet de Bovis unannounced – and when we unavoidably arrived half an hour late for the one appointment we had made, at Jean Massa, Massa himself was knocking off work for the day and refused to see us. Combined with the fact that, as noted, vineyards in the area are all but invisible, this misadventure left us with the feeling that Bellet had become something of a ghost appellation.

When I returned a year later, things had changed. This time, de Charnacé was available, and invited me to his exquisite little château. *Bellet* is actually the name of his mother's family, de Charnacé told me, and he clearly feels proprietary about the appellation as a whole. "Yes, there are now ten producers here," he continued, "but three of them, Massa, Augier, and Dalmasso [of Domaine de la Source] are professional flower-growers who also make a little wine; the proprietor of Clos Saint Vincent owns a pizzeria; Fogolar is owned by a university professor who is a bit of a fantasist. And I make Sosno's wine here." Of Méasson and Bagnis, he added simply, "Font-Bellet is finished. And Bagnis left – *et pas par hasard* [and not by accident]."

De Charnacé is an amiable man, obviously serious about protecting and enhancing the reputation of Bellet. He is sponsoring research, for instance, to determine once and for all the relationship between Rolle and Vermentino, and also wants to find out whether Braquet and Brachetto really are the same grape. "I'm practically the only one with Braquet," he told me. "Others have almost none. I make the only rosé that is 100 percent Braquet. Sometimes another producer will tell me that he has one, too – and I say, look, I'm president of the syndicate; I've seen your paperwork, and I know exactly what you have. I'm extremely rigorous. One must be."

As we talked, I tasted his impressive 1993 Château de Bellet white, full of fruit, with a faint lemony acidity and an attractive mineral-like undertone; the crisp and subtle 1994 rosé; and a pre-release sample of de Charnacé's reserve red, Cuvée Baron G., from the '93 vintage – a wine both complex and delicate, with an aroma of Provençal herbs and a lightly woody roundness on the palate.

When I asked de Charnacé what other producers I should visit, he replied, "Well, Jean Massa's wines are the most 'original' " – so I tried again with Massa. Again, this time I was welcomed. "I make wine for my own pleasure," Massa informed me, almost as soon as I'd got out of my car. "I don't use a centrifuge. I don't filter my wines, but even after five years, they are clear." He held up a bottle of five-year-old white to prove his point, and clear it was. Then, in his ramshackle cellar – amidst bottles stashed in every nook, a miscellany of barrels and demijohns, and a few small stainless steel tanks standing not entirely upright – I tasted two of his whites – the '94, still in wood, which was rich and aromatic but defined by a Vermentino-like acidity, and the rather strange '93, more perfumey than aromatic, with a hint of oxidation on the palate; the '94 rosé, which was excellent, with a complex, slightly smoky flavour (if perhaps a bit too much wood); and finally, from stainless steel, the then-three-month-old '95 red, which was powerfully, deliciously fresh and grapey, very bright in both colour and flavour, and quite tannic. "Bellet used to be a *vin de l'année*," Massa noted, "and was always very young and fruity." Though I've liked some older red Bellets, I couldn't help wishing that a wine like this one, at this age, would find its way onto the market.

Then Massa, whose primary business is raising carnations in greenhouses covering a nearby hill, showed me the results of a Bellet tasting done for the *Gault/Millau* magazine, in which one of his reds received the highest score of any wine. "They ask for my secret," he told me. "There is no secret. I make wine as it should be made. The most important thing is that the grapes and wood are healthy. I use no insecticides, and a minimum of suphur. Alcohol is my product of conservation, and I pick very late, sometimes a month after the others. I take a big risk in picking late. If it rains, I lose thirty or forty percent of my harvest. . . ." His eyes twinkled. "If I get sun, I get the highest marks in *Gault/Millau*."

I visited one other Bellet producer, Clot dòu Baile, which was founded in 1981 by Jean-Noël Cambillau, a Frenchman of Catalan origin who had made wine on a large scale in Algeria before emigrating – like so many other "pied-noirs" – to the region of Nice. "There are only two real viticulteurs in Bellet," according to Ludovic Cambillau, who has run the estate since his father's death in 1989. "Myself and Ghislain de Charnacé." As I found when I tasted a number of vintages, new and old, he makes a bright, acidic, fruity white wine, 100 percent Rolle, that turns honeyed and cider-like with age; a rather lacquery rosé (mostly Braquet, with some Cinsault and Grenache) that grows more interesting after three or four years; and a light, peppery, cherry-scented red (80 percent Folle Noire, the rest Grenache) with a distinct aroma of carbonic maceration – a wine very different in style from the richer, more tannic reds his father made through the 1989 vintage. "Why try to make a bordeaux or a burgundy in Bellet?" he asks rhetorically. "I want to make a simple, elegant red, that's all."

Like Bellet, Villars-sur-Var – the Villarium Oppidum of the Romans – has been planted in vines since antiquity. It is said, in fact, that wines from the region were shipped to Rome in the first century or two A.D., where they were highly regarded. The Knights Templar extended vineyard plantings in the region in the eleventh and twelfth centuries, and in the fifteenth and sixteenth, the counts of Grimaldi, who then ruled the area, established regulations for the cultivation and production of wine. What came out of the region developed a reputation in southern France as Mass wine, which wasn't necessarily a compliment. In 1800, on the other hand, one Abbé Bonifassy reported that "The good wine of Villars was asked for all over Piedmont" – and it was Villars wine and not Bellet that was served at the official banquet in Nice celebrating the unification of the region Niçois with France in 1860.

Despite the area's long wine-making tradition, commercial viticulture around Villars-sur-Var died out early this century, victim of disease, a run of bad weather, and, as usual, the encroachment of urban civilization. It has slowly revived since then, however, and today there are about forty growers in the area – which is the only portion of the Côtes-de-Provence appellation within the département of the Alpes-Maritimes – and one wine producer, Clos St. Joseph.

Clos St. Joseph which is owned by Antoine and Cécile Sassi and dates from 1978 and produces fewer than 1,000 cases a year of red and white wine combined, from a mere 2 hectares (about 6 acres) of vines. The white is 75 percent Rolle, with the balance Ugni Blanc, Clairette, and a trace of what Marie calls "little unknown cépages." The red is made from Cinsault, Syrah, Mourvèdre, and Cabernet Sauvignon. The wines, frankly, are not extraordinary. The white is fresh and fruity but finishes abruptly and doesn't seem to have much regional character; the red is light and clean, with a lovely, faintly oaky aroma and some nice fruit, but again somewhat anonymous. Still, they are well enough made and perhaps will improve in future vintages – and they certainly have roots.

Wine was once made all over the eastern portion of the Côte d'Azur. In medieval times, noted Edward and Margaret Berry in *At the Western Gate of Italy*, La Brigue was famous for its wine. There was also some produced a little further to the south in Breil. Smollett writes, in the eighteenth century, that St. Laurent, on the west bank of the Var, was "famous for its Muscadine wines," and refers in another place to "the sweet wine of St. Laurent, counted equal to that of Frontignan." Mamé Clairette praises to Bernard Duplessy, in *Cuisine traditionnelle en pays niçois,* the strong red wine of La Gaude and the late-harvest dessert wine of St. Jeannet (both also just across the Var), and another wine made from grapes that tasted like raspberries. She adds that good wine was made, as well, on Mont Gros, on the northeastern side of the city. Raymond Armisen and André Martin mention a mixed hectare of Rolle, Clairette, Barbaroux, Chasselas, and Cinsault at St. Blaise, and three hectares of Rolle, Barbaroux, Clairette, and Braquet, producing "vin clair consommé dans le pays" ("plain wine consumed locally"), at the foot of the château in Roquette-sur-Var – both towns north of the Bellet appellation.

In his *Le Tour de France gastronomique,* published in 1926, Édouard Dulac mentions the wines of Menton, along with those of Bellet, La Gaude, and St. Jeannet, as "representing the region's vineyards on all good tables." In his "Souvenir imaginaire et descriptif sur le vin en pays mentonnais," published as one of several appendices to *La Cuisine mentonnaise,* Francis Zunino recalls with pleasure wines made around Menton from grapes with such names as Marunvern, Caillan Noir, Craveirou, Daourin, and "Le Daga de Madonna" – "The Madonna's Dagger" (or perhaps "My Lady's Dagger"). According to Ghislain de Charnacé, a group of enthusiasts has recently installed a small new planting of this last variety near Menton in order to preserve it from extinction.

There was also, Zunino remembers, a quantity of *branda* – the Niçois name for marc – "to kill germs" produced each year with the aid of an alembic still owned by one of the neighbours. Clos St. Joseph in Villars-sur-Var and several producers of Bellet have their grape pomace distilled into branda – Clot dòu Baile calls theirs marc de Bellet – for local sale; I particularly like the Clos St. Joseph, which is quite fiery but has a vivid raisiny flavour.

At least some local farmers almost certainly still make a bit of wine, and probably branda, for their own use, but their vines are now counted individually rather than in hectares. It is unlikely that any world-class vintages have been lost as a result of the disappearance of the region's miscellaneous little vineyards – but it does seem as if the local gastronomic bounty has been diminished. As Mamé Clairette notes of the "tourists" who bought up the land for vacation houses, "[They] ignored all the vines, but they liked our last wines a lot."

Tobias Smollett on the Wines of Nice

The people here are not so nice as the English in the management of their wine. It is kept in flacons, or large flasks, without corks, having a little oil at top. It is not deemed the worse for having been opened a day or two before; and they expose it to the hot sun, and all kinds of weather, without hesitation. . . . That which is made by the peasants, both red and white, is generally genuine: but the wine-merchants of Nice brew and balderdash. . . . When the grapes are of a bad, meagre kind, the wine dealers mix the juice with pigeons-dung or quick-lime, in order to give it a spirit which nature has denied; but this is a very mischievous adulteration."

Orange Wine
Vin d'Orange

This is not wine made from oranges, but rather wine macerated with them and spiked with higher alcohol. Beverages of this kind are typical of the Nice region – an old-style version made with raspberries was served in all the cafés on the Cours Saleya as late as the 1960s – and wine flavoured with citrus fruit is particularly popular in the citrus-growing neighbourhood of Menton. I got this recipe from an agrumiculteur named Albert Manguine, who farms near Gorbio in the arrière-pays, when I bought a little bag of his oranges amères (bitter oranges) at Menton's Fête du Citron one year. I've made it several times, using a variety of wines and alcohols, and I can assure you that good raw materials yield a much better product than mediocre ones do. The best version I ever made was based on Bonny Doon Vin Gris de Cigare (a Provençal-style rosé from California) and, improbably enough, St. George Marc de Gewürztraminer (an Alsatian-style eau-de-vie, also Californian) – and on Manguine's own oranges, which were small (about the size of large tangerines) and irregularly shaped, with thick, green-spotted skin. While the liquid ingredients may vary, bitter oranges are essential to the mix.

to make about 4½ bottles

4	bottles light, dry rosé or white wine (preferably Provençal)
450 ml/16 fl oz	marc or grappa
6	bitter oranges*
1	lemon
1	sweet orange or blood orange
1	whole vanilla bean
450 g/1 lb	sugar

Combine all ingredients in a large glass or plastic container (a 14 or 23 litres/ 3 or 5 gallon water bottle is ideal) and agitate it vigorously to dissolve sugar. Leave in a cool, dark place, with a lid set lightly on top (do not seal tightly) for 40 days, agitating gently once a day.

Using a funnel, strain into another large glass or plastic container, then line funnel with several layers of muslin and pour into well-washed and dried wine bottles. Seal with corks and chill. Wine may be enjoyed at once, or aged indefinitely in the refrigerator.

*See page 30.

Appendices

Restaurants

This is not a listing of the best restaurants of the Riviera, many of which have little connection with the region's indigenous cuisine, but rather a personal choice of eating places, great and small, excellent and good, that offer some representation of that cuisine, traditional or contemporary or both. (When calling restaurants in Italy from outside that country, omit the "0" from the area code.)

Western Liguria

❖ **Ai Torchi, via Annunziata 12, Frazione Finalborgo, Finale Ligure, 019/69/.05/.31.** Imaginative contemporary-style Ligurian cooking in a converted olive mill (torchi are presses) in a very pretty medieval stone town attached to the beach resort of Finale. Ricotta torta with summer truffles, lettuce stuffed with vegetable mousse, and swordfish with grilled aubergine and courgettes are typical offerings.

❖ **Da Tina, via Caduti Partigiani 3, Quiliano, 019/887.116.** The simplest of Ligurian home-cooking – basic pastas, including soupy pastae ceci, plain roasted veal, and other such fare, served in a warm, thoroughly non-touristic setting.

❖ **Degli Amici da Piombo, via Roma 16, Isolabona, 0184/20.81.24.** In a handsome little hill town with a beautiful fifteenth-century public fountain, this modest restaurant specialises in stockfish cooked in several traditional ways.

❖ **Gastone, piazza Garibaldi, Dolceacqua, 0184/20.65.77.** Superb traditional cooking with an occasional innovation. Marinated "tonno di coniglio" (rabbit tuna – rabbit marinated to resemble the fish) stuffed with herbs, ravioli with artichokes, and goat with local white beans are some of the specialities. Large selection of local wines.

❖ **Lanterna Blu (Da Tonino), borgo Marina, Porto Maurizio (Imperia), 0183/63.859.** Upscale mostly seafood restaurant, where the pleasures include delicious home-made swordfish bottarga, soup of bianchetti (miniature fish) with borage and courgettes, and a renowned nasello (hake) gratinéed with herbs and breadcrumbs.

❖ **La Baita, Località Gazzo, Borghetto d'Arroscia, 0183/31.083.** Mushrooms, mushrooms, and more mushrooms – pickled, oil-packed, and dried if it doesn't happen to be the season for fresh – as well as snails, game, and other typical products of the entroterra. Good, solid home-style cooking.

❖ **La Capanna da Bacì, Apricale, 0184/20.81.37.** A homey trattoria in a "perched" mountain village where the food just keeps coming – home-made sausages, marinated aubergines, fried artichoke hearts, torta di zucchini, chard omelette, sausage and polenta, ravioli with borage, puréed stockfish, pasta with pesto. . . . One asks not so much for the check as for mercy.

❖ **La Via Romana, via Romana 57, Bordighera, 0184/26.66.81.** Elegant dining, with some refined improvisations based on local dishes (corzetti with red mullet sauce, baby calamari sautéed with olives and white beans in Vermentino sauce, etc.) as well as other dishes that are not particularly Ligurian but are based on the best local products. Attractive Liberty-style decor and a good Ligurian wine list.

❖ **Locanda del Bricco Arcagna, Località Arcagna, Dolce Acqua, 0184/31.426.** Not a restaurant, but an Agriturismo operation adjacent to the pretty hillside Terre Bianche winery, offering rooms, horseback riding, and simple local-style cooking (for guests and by reservation) – pickled mushrooms, assorted pastas, rabbit with olives, etc. – and of course winery tours and tasting. For information, contact the Azienda Agrituristica Terre Bianche, Frazione Brunetti 19, 18033 Camporosso (Imperia), 0184/31.230.

❖ **Osteria del Portico, via Umberto I 6, Castelvittorio, 0184/241.352.** A genuinely engaging little place with an informal air and a small menu of local specialities – which in this part of the western entroterra means lots of torte, hearty pasta, and (in the winter, and on request) the positively medieval gran pistau, among other things.

❖ **Paolo e Barbara, via Roma 47, San Remo, 0184/53.16.53.** An essential. Owner-chef Paolo Masieri is perhaps the master of contemporary Ligurian cooking, serving some classic dishes (his brandacujun – stockfish brandade – is definitive) and some improvisations (fried pansotti stuffed with potatoes and Alpine cheese, gnocchetti with salsa marò and baby shrimp), always using the finest local ingredients. Plenty of well-chosen local wines. Reservations an absolute must in this small, attractive dining room.

❖ **Vino e Farinata, via Pia 15, Savona, no telephone.** As the name says, wine (including an eminently drinkable house rosé) and farinata – plus cima alla genovese, stuffed sardines, and a few other simple items in the most elementary of surroundings.

Genoa:

What follows is admittedly an idiosyncratic listing of Genoese eating places. I have not included any of the city's more celebrated restaurants (which, anyway, are easy enough for the visitor to find in the guidebooks), either because they're not very Genoese – the pleasant but indisputably Piedmontese-style St. Cyr, for example – or because they're not very good. In this latter category is one famous establishment, which I will not name, whose most salient attributes seem to be particularly high prices and a celebrity clientele; this restaurant, a critic from Turin once proposed, "is a place the rich Genoese go to eat in the style of the poor Genoese." In fact, many of the city's "poorer" restaurants serve better food. The most modest of these, several of which are included below, usually don't accept reservations or credit cards, and are unlikely to have English-language menus or English-speaking staff – but they're friendly enough, and worth braving if you want a flavour of the real Genoa.

❖ **Carletto, vico Tempo Buono 5, 010/290.476.** A small, no-nonsense trattoria in Genoa's old quarter, with lots of seafood, pasta, and seafood pasta on the blackboard menu. Very good bianchetti in season, clams in tomato broth, fried fish, and mandilli de sæa, among other things.

❖ **Fratelli Ivaldi, vico Palla 15, 010/298.255.** A modest working-class establishment in the port district, with not much more on the menu than a couple of pastas, a couple of stockfish dishes (boiled with potatoes or cooked with olives and pine nuts), and roast veal. Nothing gastronomic, but a good representation of real everyday Genoese cooking.

❖ **Ristorante Rina, Mura della Grazie 3, 010/207.990.** First-rate seafood and a good list of Genoese specialities are offered at this popular restaurant, founded as a simple osteria a century or so ago. Plain grilled fish is always delicious, and the minestrone, stuffed vegetables, trofie with pesto, and stoccafisso alla genovese are all highly respectable and admirably representative of local cooking.

❖ **Rivaro, via del Portello 16, 010/277.0054.** A warm restaurant with a nautical feeling to it and a very long menu offering plenty of Genoese dishes – among them pansotti, ravioli di borragine, lattughe ripiene, cima, and sacripantina. The cooking is above average, but not much more than that – and one dines, frustratingly, surrounded by an encyclopedia of grappas and whiskies, none of which seems to be available to diners.

❖ **Sâ Pesta, via Giustianini 16, 010/208.636.** An unassuming local institution, on the site of an ancient salt-vendor's shop (the name derives from *sale pestato*, ground salt), which has been serving farinata, minestrone, and assorted torte to the Genoese for generations. There is a counter in the front, selling these things to go; in the back are a few tables, as simple as can be.

❖ **Sola Enoteca Cucina e Vino, via Barabino 120, 010/594.513.** A bustling, informal restaurant and wine bar. Owner Pino Sola is a partner in the Colle dei Bardellini winery near Imperia, but stocks hundreds of other labels as well, Ligurian, other Italian, and international. The cooking is simple and agreeable, and mostly Genoese (stuffed lettuce in tomato sauce, superb polpettone, etc.).

Eastern Liguria

❖ **Albergo degli Amici, via Garibaldi 80, Varese Ligure, 0187/842.139.** An unglamorous provincial hotel serving honest, straightforward presentations of mostly Ligurian food – stuffed vegetables, pansotti with walnut sauce, tomaxelle, and the like. Wild mushrooms are something of a speciality in season.

❖ **Araldo, via Jacopo 24, Levanto, 0187/80.72.53.** Good food, inventive but simple, in a beautiful dining room with luxurious table settings. Fried baby rabbit cutlets with fried courgettes, pasta with red mullet and asparagus, and the local fried ravioli called gattafin are typical dishes.

❖ **Ca' Peo, strada Panoramica, Leivi, 0185/31.96.96.** Well worth the drive up into the hills above Chiavari. Franco and Melly Solari serve resolutely Ligurian food – local products shaped with local techniques and philosophies – but allow room for invention as well. The wine list is famous.

❖ **Da Caran, via Genova 1, La Spezia, 0187/703.777.** One of two old roadside osterie on the main road out of town, big and handsome, with a short menu of local specialities, including famous messciuà, testaroli with pesto, penne with scampi (a popular pasta hereabouts), stockfish with polenta, home-made sausage, and assorted torte (onion, leek, spinach).

❖ **Da Luchin, via Bighetti 53, Chiavari, 0185/301.063.** On one of Chiavari's famous arcaded streets, this old-style osteria, with its 1907-vintage wood-burning oven, is famous for farinata, but also offers such things as superb pasta with pesto (without beans and potatoes), cappon magro, stuffed sardines, and home-made desserts.

❖ **Da Puny, piazza Martiri dell'Olivetta 5, Portofino, 0185/26.90.37.** Glitzy and expensive, but also excellent, with many good seafood dishes (branzino with olives and bay leaves, stockfish crostini) and superb pasta (spaghetti with rucola or with pesto corto, for instance).

❖ **Del Pippo da Ugo, via alla Chiesa, Località Ognio, Neirone, 0185/93.45.44.** A simple, typical small-town trattoria. Old men of the village drink and watch TV in the bar in front, while in back, the kitchen sends out ample portions of stuffed vegetables, ravioli or pansotti, fritto misto, rabbit with olives, and other traditional fare, all very well made. Ask to see the "museum" of old cars, grappa bottles, corkscrews, etc.

❖ **Fiammenghilla Fieschi, via Pestella 6, Sestri Levante, 0185/481.041.** This beautiful dining room, in a portion of an old villa on a hill overlooking Sestri, is named for the deep oval dish traditionally used to serve cappon magro (fiammenghilla) and the local reigning noble family of earlier times (Fieschi). Though some traditional specialities are offered (the local anchovy-and-tomato dish called bagnun, for example), the cuisine is more inventive than traditional, though always with a Ligurian base. Courgette-stuffed ravioli with a sauce based on courgette blossoms is a typical creation.

❖ **Gambero Rosso, Vernazza (Cinque Terre), 0187/81.22.65.** A delightful place, with terrace, in this delightful town. Wonderful complementary frittelle – just fried dough, salted and scattered with rosemary, but addictively good; pasta and seafood are above average, and the house speciality in summer is tian Vernazza (slices of potato with fresh anchovies, tomatoes, and peas).

❖ **Giainni Franzi, via Visconti 2, Vernazza (Cinque Terre), 0187/812.228.** More solid local cooking – marinated anchovies, stuffed mussels, pasta with pesto or mussels, simply grilled seafood, and some standard veal dishes – served at tables spilling out almost to the edge of the port.

❖ **I Gabbiani, molo Italia, La Spezia, 0187/779.177.** A barge moored near the fishermen's section of this city's huge port, with a terrace surveying the Gulf of La Spezia. The cooking is basic, but the marinated anchovies, testaroli with pesto, and simply cooked fish dishes are just fine.

❖ **La Brinca, Località Campo di Ne, Ne, 185/337.480.** Simple, delicious back-country cooking from the eastern entroterra in a family-run trattoria. On the menu are such things as fried borage leaves, preboggion (the pansotti filling of mixed field greens, here served as a cooked vegetable with potatoes and black cabbage), chestnut-flour gnocchi, and "asado" of veal (long-cooked in the Argentinian manner, a heritage of emigrants to that continent returning to this region).

❖ **Manuelina, via Roma 300, Recco, 0185/75.364.** Famous for its irresistible focaccia col formaggio, but also a full-scale restaurant with a wide range of Ligurian and other Italian offerings. The cappon magro is very good. An informal offshoot, Focacceria della Manuelina, via Roma 278, serves a selection of antipasti and vegetable dishes, one or two pastas and main dishes, and of course focaccia col formaggio.

❖ **Marina Piccola, via Discovolo 38, Manarola (Cinque Terre), 0187/92.01.03.** Fresh local seafood, simply cooked, on a veranda under a sort of lean-to overlooking the sea. Just across the street, fishermen lower their tiny boats down the cliffs to the water with winches.

❖ **Negrao, via Genova 428, La Spezia, 0187/701.564.** The other La Spezian roadside osteria, with a menu similar to that at Caran. Knowledgeable locals say the messciuà is the best in town – and that Negrao is the only restaurant that still makes it entirely the old-fashioned way.

❖ **Vento Ariel, calata Porto, Camogli, 0185/771.080.** On this pretty fishing town's busy waterfront promenade. Classic trenette col pesto plus excellent seafood – including boiled bianchetti and rosetti, grilled fresh sardines, and assorted fried baby fish. In the afternoons, you can sometimes see fishermen bringing their catch straight from their boats to the restaurant door.

Nice

(Note: As of October 18, 1996, when France adopts a new telephone system, it will be necessary to add 4 – 04 within France – as a prefix to the numbers below.)

❖ **Barale, 39 rue Beaumont, 93.89.17.94.** A one-stop introduction to cuisine niçoise, offering a single fixed-price meal nightly, ranging from pissaladière and socca through salade niçoise to ravioli and tourte de blettes. Expect to sing for (or after) your supper – and be sure to ask to see the private museum of old farm implements and such.

❖ **Don Camillo, 5 rue des Ponchettes, 93.85.67.95.** The very paradigm of a contemporary regional French restaurant, full of the flavours (and products) of Nice and the arrière-pays. The menu changes frequently, and of course seasonally, and though owner-chef Franck Cerutti now toils most nights at Louis XV in Monte Carlo, the place remains family run, and Cerutti's sous-chef does him proud. Familial service, a small but good wine list, and delicious non-Niçois desserts by Cerutti's mother-in-law.

❖ **La Merenda, 4 rue de la Terrasse, no telephone.** Owners Jean and Christiane Giusti say they are retiring at the end of 1996 but have sold the place to a sympathetic patron who won't change a thing. That remains to be seen. Under the Giustis, this tiny local institution, open only Tuesday through Friday, serves straightforward Niçois fare of the highest order – pâtes au pistou, estocificada, stuffed sardines, tripes à la niçoise, a classic daube, and more. One can only hope that the same spirit (and skill) remains under the new owner – if there is one.

❖ **Le Safari, 1 cours Saleya, 93.80.18.44.** Big, busy, and surprisingly good, with lots of simply cooked fresh fish, assorted local specialities (petits farcis with mesclun, soupe au pistou, "merda de can," etc.), and the best pizza in town – more Italian than French in style, with a perfect thin crust always slightly black around the edges. Great for people-watching on the Cours Saleya.

❖ **Nissa Socca, 7 rue St.-Réparate, 93.80.18.35.** A tiny, popular pizza-and-socca emporium in Vieux Nice (good stuffed vegetables, too), with tiny chairs and tiny tables. The socca is impeccable. Fun for a quick lunch.

Just There

In his book *The Italian Riviera,* published in 1928, Bohun Lynch describes a superior Ligurian restaurateur – manager of an unnamed hotel in Albissola Capo and master of the dining room:

"Signor Pescetto himself is the officiating priest who observes a close ritual in the administration of his tasks. He is in the tradition of great landlords. Before every meal he invites you to inspect the uncooked food, and to say precisely what you would like, and how you would like it. From a dish of assorted fish that have just been brought in from the sea he will point out which are succulent, which he, if he were you, would avoid; which should be fried, and why; which should be treated in some other way. The same with a great piece of meat which, raw, looks even less inviting in the dubious joints of the Continent than it does in England. Indeed, you seldom see meat in recognizable joints at all. But Signor Pescetto inspires confidence. With the tip of his knife he indicates where the fillet is thickest and most juicy. 'You shall have a piece from just there.' "

Bibliographies

(Books I found particularly useful are marked with an asterisk.)

Food and Wine

The Riviera

Accame, Franco. *"Aia d'arzillo"*: *Guidatavola tipica della Liguria*. Genoa: City 2 Editrice, 1985.

— *"Mandilli de sæa"; 100 piatti della terra di Colombo e la loro storia*, 6th ed. Genoa: De Ferrari Editore, 1990. (*)

— *Mangiare e bere in Liguria e dintorni 94*. Genoa: De Ferrari Editore, 1993.

— *Mangiare e bere in Liguria e dintorni 95*. Genoa: De Ferrari Editore, 1994.

Armisen, Raymond, and André Martin. *Les Recettes de la table niçoise*. Strasbourg: Librairie Istra, 1972.

Arvo, Paola, and Gabriella Viganego. *Le tradizione gastronomica italiana: Liguria*. Milan: Edizione Sipiel, 1991.

Bagnasco, Nada Boccalatte, and Renzo Bagnasco. *La tavola ligure ovvero le ricette tradizionali per la cucina d'oggi*. Milan: Edi.Artes, 1991.

Beniscelli, Giannetto. *La Liguria del buon vino*. Genoa: Editore Siag, no date (c. 1978).

Bigotti, Antonio. *Liguria: Bella e golosa*. Savignone (Genoa): Edizioni Puntomercato, 1989.

Bini, Bruno. *Codice della cucina ligure*. Milan: S.E.P./Il Secolo XIX, 1990.

Boccardo, Piero, et al., eds. *Sapore di Liguria: arte e tradizione in cucina*. Genoa: Commune di Genova, Assessorato all'Artigianato/Assessorato alle Attività Culturali, 1985.

Bonino, Marialuisa. *Le autentiche ricette della cucina ligure (odor di basilico)*, 13th ed. Genoa: Erga Edizioni, 1993.

Bourrier-Reynaud, Colette, ed. *Les Recettes de Réparate: la cuisine de tradition en pays niçois*. Nice: Serre Éditeur, 1993. (*)

— *Le Vin de Villars sur Var*. Nice: Mairie de Villars-sur-Var, 1993.

Calzolari, Enrico, ed. *Gastronomia nella Lunigiana storica: L'ordinamento della brigata di cucina del vescovo-conte (1188); La carta dell'arte dei macellai in Sarzana (1269); La pesca dello storione nel Magra (1201)*. Lerici: Inst. Prof. Alberghiero di Stato "G. Casini," 1989.

Cricca, Gianfranco. *Antiche ricette di Castelnuovo Magra*. Castelnuovo Magra: Commune di Castelnuovo Magra, 1981.(*)

La cucina di Genova e della Liguria. Bologna: Valenti Editore, 1975.

Dellepiane, Gaspare. *La cucina di strettissimo magro: senza carne, uova e latticini*, new ed. Edited by Giulia Fulghesu. Milan: Ice Nero/Jaca Book, 1990. (Originally published 1880.) (*)

Duplessy, Bernard. *Cuisine traditionnelle en pays niçois*. Aix-en-Provence: Édisud, 1995. (*)

En viagé, lou pan d'anouno/Autrefois Le Pain de seigle à St. Étienne de Tineé, Auron e dans leurs hameaux, 2nd ed. St. Etienne-de-Tinée: L'Association des Stéphanois, 1992.

Escudier, Jean-Noël. *La Véritable cuisine provençale et niçoise*. Paris: Éditions Gallia, 1953.

Esther. *Cucina ligure: ricette della nonna*. Genoa: Francesco Pirella, 1988.

Gavotti, Giuseppe. *Cucina e vini di Liguria*, 2nd ed. Savona: Marco Sabatelli Editore, 1974.

Grimaldi, Gianni. *Liguria in bocca*. Palermo: La Nuova Edrisi, 1987.

Heyraud, Henri. *La Cuisine à Nice.* Antibes: Imprimerie E. Roux, 1909.

Johnston, Mireille. *The Cuisine of the Sun: Classical French Cooking from Nice and Provence.* New York: Random House, 1976.

Lingua, Paolo. *La cucina dei genovesi.* Padua: Franco Muzzio Editore, 1989. (*)

Lorenzi, Jean, and Danièle Lorenzi. *Cuisine monégasque/Cüjina de Munégu.* Monte Carlo (?): n.p., n.d. (but post-1967). (*)

Marchese, Salvatore. *La cucina ligure di Levante.* Padua: Franco Muzzio Editore, 1990.

Martini, Dario G., and Manuelli Ferrer. *Pesto e buridda,* 2nd ed. Savona: Sabatelli Editore, 1975.

Médecin, Jacques. *La Cuisine du comté de Nice.* Paris: Juillard, 1972. (*)

Muccioli, Maria Teresa, ed. *Zeffirino and His World.* Perugia: Edimond, 1994.

Oddo, Sandro. *Sügeli e bügaéli: la cucina tipica dell'alta valle argentina.* (Collana "Conoscere la Valle Argentina," Vol. III). Arma di Taggia: Pro Triora Editore, 1995. (*)

Olivesi-Lorenzi, Ginette. *La Cuisine mentonnaise/A Cousina dou païs mentounasc.* Menton: Société d'Art et d'Histoire du Mentonnaise, 1993. (*)

Petrucci, Vito Elio. *Cucini i santi.* Genoa: Francesco Pirella, 1995.

Ramella, Lucetto. *Ricette tradizionali della Liguria: la cucina onegliese.* Oneglia: Cav. A. Dominici Editore, 1983.

— *L'ulivo nel Ponente Ligure.* Oneglia: Cav. A. Dominici Editore, 1986.

Ratto, G. B., and Gio Ratto, figlio. *La cuciniera genovese.* Genoa: Pagano, 1863. (*)

Rossi, Emanuele. *La vera cuciniera genovese facile ed economica.* Sala Bolognese: Arnaldo Forni Editore, 1992. (Originally published 1865.) (*)

Rossi, Stefania. *I menú della tradizione lunigianese.* Lunigiana la Sera: Editoriale Città del Libro, 1990.

Schmuckher, Aidano. *Pesto e mortâ: Il grande libro della cucina ligure.* Genoa: Guido Mondani Editore, 1984.

"Il segreto della messciua/La farinata" (audiotape), after an idea by Sergio Fregoso; text and narration by Renzo Fregoso. La Spezia (?): Accademia Lunigianese di Scienze Giovanni Capellini/Il Secolo XIX Spezia, no date.

Sola, Pino. *Album di Liguria; Le ricette.* Genoa: SAGEP, 1993.

Torre, Silvio. *Su e giù per boschi tra vigne e oliveti: Alla ricerca del ristorante segreto.* Savona: Camera di Commercio Industria Artigianato e Agricoltura di Savona, 1987.

General

Anderson, Burton. *The Wine Atlas of Italy.* New York: Simon & Schuster, 1990.

Bergese, Nino. *Mangiare da re.* Milan: Giangiacomo Feltrinelli Editore, 1969.

Boni, Ada. *Italian Regional Cooking,* translated by Maria Langdale and Ursula Whyte. New York: Bonanza Books, 1969.

Buonassisi, Vicenzo, and Silvio Torre. *Stoccafisso e baccalà.* Milan: "Piccoli Piaceri," Idealibri, 1988.

Cerini Di Castegnate, Livio. *Il libro del baccalà.* Milan: Longanesi, 1986.

Conil, Jean. *Gastronomic Tour de France.* London: George Allen & Unwin, 1959.

Davidson, Alan. *Mediterranean Seafood,* 2nd ed. Middlesex: Penguin Books, 1987. (*)

— *North Atlantic Seafood.* New York: The Viking Press, 1979.

Dulac, Édouard. *Le Tour de France gastronomique.* Paris: Les Éditions de France, 1926.

Escoffier, Auguste. *Le Guide Culinaire,* translated by H. L. Cracknell and R. J. Kaufmann. New York: Mayflower Books, no date.

Gavotti, Erina. *Millericette,* 25th ed. Milan: Garzanti Editore, 1992.

Grande enciclopedia illustrata della gastronomia. Milan: Selezione dal Reader's Digest, 1990. (*)

Lang, Jenifer Harvey, ed. *Larousse Gastronomique,* New American Edition. New York: Crown Publishers, 1988.

Milioni, Stefano. *Columbus Menu: Italian Cuisine after the First Voyage of Christopher Columbus.* New York: Italian Trade Commission, 1992.

Montagné, Prosper. *Larousse Gastronomique,* First American Edition, edited by Charlotte Turgeon and Nina Froud. New York: Crown Publishers, 1961.

Newnham-Davis, Lieut.-Col. *The Gourmet's Guide to Europe,* 3rd ed. London: Grant Richards, 1911.

Pettini, Cav. Amedeo. *Ricettario Carli.* Oneglia: Editori Fratelli Carli, no date.

Rebora, Giovanni. *Colombo a tavola: Antologia di ricette d'epoca.* Savona: Ermes s.r.l. Editoria Comunicazione, 1992.

Reboul, J.-B. *La Cuisinière provençale,* 22nd ed. Marseilles: Éditions Tacussel, no date.

Romer, Elizabeth. *Italian Pizza and Hearth Breads.* New York: Clarkson N. Potter, 1987.

Root, Waverley. *Food.* New York: Simon & Schuster, 1980.

— *The Food of France.* New York: Alfred A. Knopf, 1970.

— *The Food of Italy.* New York: Atheneum, 1971. (*)

Torre, Silvio. *Colombo: Un nuovo mondo a tavola.* Milan: Idealibri, 1991.

Toussaint-Samat, Maguelonne. *History of Food,* translated by Anthea Bell. Cambridge, Mass., and Oxford: Blackwell Publishers, 1992.

Wechsberg, Joseph. *Blue Trout and Black Truffles.* New York: Alfred A. Knopf, 1966.

Language and Proverbs

Bertoldi, Maria Luisa Rosciano. *Guida ai detti genovesi e liguri.* Milan: Sugar Editore, 1970.

Compan, André. *Glossaire raisonné de la langue niçoise.* Nice: Éditions Tiranty, 1967. (*)

De Fourvières, Xavier. *Grammaire provençale,* rev. ed. Avignon: Aubanel, 1973.

— *Lou Pichot tresor: Dictionnaire provençal-français et français-provençal.* Avignon: Aubanel, 1975.

Dolcino, Michelangelo. *E parolle do gatto: Dizionario genovese-italiano di termini, insulti, locuzioni e proverbi assolutamente sconvenienti,* 6th ed. Genoa: Erga Edizioni, 1989.

Frisoni, Gaetano. *Dizionario Genovese-Italiano e Italiano-Genovese,* new edition of the 1910 original. Genoa: Nuova Editrice Genovese, 1989. (*)

Frolla, Louis. *Dictionnaire Monégasque-Français.* Monaco: Imprimerie National de Monaco, 1963.

Petrucci, Vito Elio. *Grammatica sgrammaticata della lingua genovese.* Genoa: SAGEP Editrice, 1984.

Raimondi, Piero. *Proverbi genovesi.* Firenze: Aldo Martello/Giunti Editore, 1975.

Schiaffino, Pro. *Parlar camallo: Usi e costumi nel porto di Genova.* Genoa: SAGEP Editrice, 1983.

History, Natural History, Agriculture, Travel, Etc.

Allbaugh, Leland G. *Crete: A Case Study of an Underdeveloped Area*. Princeton: Princeton University Press, 1953.

Amicucci, Ermanno. *Nizza e l'Italia*. Milan: Casa Editrice A. Mondadori, 1939.

Belgrano, L. T. *Della vita privata dei genovesi*, 2nd ed. Genoa: Tipografia del R. Instituto Sordo-Muti, 1875.

Bent, J. Theodore. *Genoa: How the Republic Rose and Fell*. London: C. Kegan Paul, 1881.

Bernardini, Enzo, and Giuseppe E. Bessone, eds. *Bordighera ieri*. Genoa: Comitato per Le Celebbrazione del 500^e Anniversario della Fondazione di Bordighera, 1971.

Bernardy, Amy A. *Liguria (Forme e colori di vita regionale italiana, volume secondo)*. Bologna: Nicola Zanichelli Editore, 1927.

Berry, Edward and Margaret. *At the Western Gate of Italy*. London: John Lane/The Bodley Head, 1931.

Blume, Mary. *Côte d'Azur: Inventing the French Riviera*. New York: Thames and Hudson, 1992.

Braudel, Fernand. *La Méditerranée et le monde méditerranéan à l'époque de Philippe II*, 2nd rev. ed. Paris: Librairie Armand Colin, 1966.

Calvini, Nilo. *Gli antichi statuti comunali di Badalucco*. Badalucco: Comune di Badalucco, 1994.

Calvini, Nilo, and Marco Cassini. *Apricale*. Imperia: Dominici Editore, 1991.

Camporosso: In mautürà de couse du nosciu paise. Torino: Amministrazione Communale Camporosso, 1985.

Caperan-Moreno, Louis. *Histoire de Menton*, 4th ed. Menton: Annales de la Société d'Art et d'Histoire du Mentonnais, 1993.

Caserio, Jean-Louis. *A Lambrusca de paigran/La Vigne vierge de grand-père*. Menton: Société d'Art et d'Histoire du Mentonnais, 1987.

Catone, Marco Porcio (Cato the Elder). *Opere di Marco Porcio Catone*, translated and annotated by Giuseppe Compagnoni. Venice: Tipografia di Giuseppe Antonelli Ed., 1846. (Written c. 200 B.C.)

"C.C." *Riviera Nature Notes: A Popular Account of the More Striking Plants and Animals of the Riviera and the Maritime Alps*. Manchester: The Labour Press, 1898.

Chabrol de Volvic, *Statistique des provinces de Savone, d'Oneille et d'Acqui*. Paris: 1824.

De Witte, Ysabel. *The Romance and Legend of the Riviera*. London: John Hamilton, no date.

Dickens, Charles. *American Notes* and *Pictures from Italy*. Oxford, New York: Oxford University Press, 1957. (Originally published 1842/1846.)

Donte, Vincenzo Guido, Giovanni Garibbo, and Paolo Stacchini, eds. *La provincia d'Imperia*. Imperia: Consiglio Provinciale dell'Economia Corporativa di Imperia, 1934.

Durante, Bartolomeo, and Andrea Eremita. *Guide di Dolceacqua e della Val Nervia*. Cavallermaggiore: Gribaudo Editore, 1991.

Lous Esteves e las plantos/Les Stéphanois et les plantes: les stéphanois racontent comment ils utilisaient et utilisent les plantes sauvages. St. Étienne de Tineé: L'Association des Stéphanois, 1987.

Ferraironi, Padre Francesco. *Cultura e tradizioni in alta valle argentina*, edited by Sandro Oddo. Arma di Taggia: Pro Triora Editore, 1991. (*)

Ferrando, Nelio e Ivana. *Natale a Genova: Il "Tondo" tradizionale*. Genoa: SAGEP Editrice, 1991.

Festa tradizione folclore nella terra di Varese Ligure. Lavagna: Museo Contadino di Cassego/Circolo Acli di Varese Ligure, 1986.

Genoa and the Two Rivieras, English ed. Bologna: Italcards Editions, no date.

Giardelli, Paolo. *Il cherchio del tempo: Le tradizioni popolari dei liguri.* Genoa: SAGEP Editrice, 1991.

Girani, Alberto. *Guida alle Cinque Terre.* Genoa: SAGEP Editrice, 1990.

Graves, Charles. *The Riviera Revisited.* London: Evans Brothers, 1948.

Hare, Augustus J. C. *Winter at Mentone.* London: Wertheim, Macintosh, & Hunt, c. 1862.

Hawthorne, Nathaniel. *The French and Italian Notebooks* (*The Complete Works of Nathaniel Hawthorne,* Vol. X). Boston and New York: Houghton, Mifflin and Company, 1899 (?).

Howarth, Patrick. *When the Riviera Was Ours.* London, Melbourne: Century, 1977.

James, Henry. *Italian Hours.* London: John Heinemann, 1909.

Ludwig, Emil. *The Mediterranean: Saga of a Sea,* translated by Barrows Mussey. New York and London: Whittlesey House, 1942.

Lynch, Bohun. *The Italian Riviera.* Garden City, N.Y.: Doubleday, Doran & Company, 1928.

Marcenaro, Giuseppe, ed. *Viaggio in Liguria.* Genoa: SAGEP Editrice, 1992.

Miscosi, Giulio. *I quartieri di Genova antica.* Genoa: Arti Grafiche R. Fabris, 1935.

Montaigne, Michel de. *The Complete Works of Montaigne,* translated by Donald M. Frame. Stanford: Stanford University Press, 1948.

Nobbio, Claudio. *Un paese di pietra (Apricale).* Apricale (?): Edizioni Casabianca, n. d.

Oddo, Sandro. *Bagiue: Le streghe di Triora; fantasia e realtà* (Collana "Conoscere la Valle Argentina," Vol. II). Ama di Taggia: Pro Triora Editore, 1994.

— *La medicina populare nell'alta Valle Argentina.* Triora: Pro Triora Editore, 1989.

O'Faolain, Sean. *A Summer in Italy.* New York: The Devin-Adair Co., 1950.

Paschetti, Bartolomeo. *Del conservar la sanità, et del vivere de genovese.* Genoa: 1602.

Per selve, per campi: La vegetazione tra natura e storia. Varese Ligure: Sala della Compagnia, 1991.

Pescio, Amadeo. *Terre e vita di Liguria.* Milan: Casa Editrice Luigi Trevisino, 1929(?).

Petrucci, Vito Elio. *Profumi e sapori di Liguria.* Genoa: Silvio Basile Editore, 1976. (*)

Piaggio, Martin. *Chittarin zeneize.* Genoa: Tip. del R. Instituto Sordo-Muti, 1881.

— *Raccolta delle migliori poesie, edite e inedite.* Genoa: Tipografia dei Fratelli Pagano, 1846.

Pigna e il suo territorio. Novara: Istituto Geografica De Agostini, 1988.

Ramella, Lucetto. *A Cengia (Saggio di folclore ponentino).* Oneglia: Collana Tradizioni Liguri/Cav. A. Dominici Editore, 1979.

Relatione dell'origine et successi della terra di Varese descritta dal r.p. Antonio Cesena l'anno 1558 (Estratto da "Studi e Documenti de Lunigiana," Vol. VI, 1982). La Spezia: Accademia Lunigianese di Scienze Giovanni Capellini, 1993.

Ricordel, Franck. *Menton et la Fête du Citron.* Nice: Serre Éditeur, 1993.

Sidro, Annie. *Carnaval à Nice.* Nice: Serre Éditeur, 1993. (Pamphlet.)

Smollett, Tobias. *Travels Through France and Italy,* edited by Frank Felsenstein. Oxford and New York: Oxford University Press, 1981. (*)

Tinè, Santo. *I primi agricoltori e lo sviluppo del commercio* (from the series *L'Uomo e la civiltà in Liguria*). Genoa: SAGEP Editrice, 1983.

Treves, Sir Frederick. *The Riviera of the Corniche Road.* London: Cassell and Company, 1921.

Ungar, Catherine, and Marcelle Viale Barosi. *Le Vieux Nice: Guide Touristique.* Le Cannet: Éditions AIO, 1988.

Le valli dell'olivo. Imperia: Comunità Montana dell'Olivo and Novaro: Istituto Geografico de Agostini, 1990.

Periodicals

Among the many periodicals, current and historical, that I consulted in doing research for this book, these were the most useful: *Les Annales du Comté de Nice* (Nice), various issues 1934–37; *Armanac Niçart/Nissart* (Nice) (somewhere between 1920 and 1928 the spelling of the second word changed), editions of 1903, 1907, 1908, 1909, 1914, 1930, 1932, and 1945 (which contains the oft-cited article "De la puissance stomacale des anciens niçois" by G. Boréa); *Annales de Menton* (Menton), various issues from 1954 and 1955; *Giornale de Bordighera/Journal de Bordighera* (Bordighera), 1933; *Italian Wines & Spirits* (Milan), various issues 1980–95; *Lou Sourgentin* (Nice), various issues 1987–95; *Nice Historique* (Nice), 1906; *R̂ Nì d'Áigüra* (Il Nido d'Aquila) (Genoa), January–June, 1991; *Ou Païs Mentounasc* (Bulletin de la Société d'Art et d'Histoire du Mentonnais) (Menton), various issues from 1986, 1989, 1991, 1992, and 1993; *Petits Propos Culinaires* (London), various issues 1981–90; *Rivista di Studi Liguri* (Bordighera), 1990–91; *Studi Genuensi* (Bordighera and Genova), 1992, #10; *A Vaštéra* (Šucartari de gènte brigašshe) (San Remo), various issues from 1990, 1991, and 1994; *A Vuxe da Cumpagnìa* (Imperia), September and December, 1989; and *A Vuxe de Cà de Puiö* (San Bartolomeo al Mare), December 1987.

I also gleaned much information from *Il Secolo XIX* and *Nice Matin,* which I read daily when I was in Genoa and Nice, respectively, and found occasional items of interest in various issues of *Liguria Magazine* (Genoa) between 1992 and 1996.

Index

C
Ca'Ertà restaurant (San
Bernardino), 156
Ca'Peo restaurant (Leivi), 43,
70, 110, 150, 169, 287,
288
Caesar, Julius, 216, 288
Cake, walnut, with honey and
ricotta, 281-2
Calleri Pigato di Albenga, 292
Calvino, Mario, 252
Cambillau, Jean-Noël, 302
Cambillau, Ludovic, 302
Canard, daube de cuisse de,
261
Canastrier, Paul, 32, 254
Cane, Giobatta, 289
Cannellonis de truite, 219-20
Cantina del Rossesse winery,
289
Capello, Virginio, 290
Cappellini, Alberto, 286
Cappon magro, 78-81, 87-8
Capponada, 80
Capra e fagioli, 105-6
Capurro, Emanuela, 173
Caratello, 293
Carciofi
agnello con olive e, 109-10
ravioli di, al profumo di
timo, 144-5
Carême (chef), 177
Carnaval, 22-3, 192
fritters, 275
Carré de Mercantour, 125
Cascina du Fèipu Pigato, 291
Caserio, Jean-Louis, 98
Casserole, buckwheat polenta,
163-4
Castagne, Sagra di (Cassego),
243
Castello di Perinaldo
olive oil, 254
Rossesse, 289
Castello, Filippo, 278
Catholic Church, xix, 79,
225-6
Cato the Elder, 169
"Caviar," Niçois, 255
Ceci
pasta e, 35-6
in zinimo, 34-5
Cerutti, Franck, xxii, 39-40,
42-3, 101-2, 125, 147-8,

187, 196, 221-2, 229, 248,
254, 261, 280
Charcuterie, 100
Charles II, Count of Provence
and Duc d'Anjou, 22
Charnacé, Ghislain de, 300-2
Château de Bellet winery, 299-
301
Château de Crémat winery,
299, 300
Cheese, 119-123
focaccia with, 173-4
four ways with, 125
prescinsêua, 124
Chestnut gnocchi with pine nut
sauce, 133-4
Chestnut(s), 240-7
flour tart, 249-50
soup, 248
Chèvre de Massoins, 125
Chez Barale restaurant (Nice),
2, 3, 183
Chez Panisse restaurant
(Berkeley), 189
Chez Thérèse restaurant (Nice),
185
Chicken
fried, 193-4
hunter's wife's–style, 263-4
Chickpea(s)
flour
croquettes, 190
"fries," 189-90
socca and farinata,
187-9
and pasta soup, 35-6
stewed, 34-5
Christmas
in Menton, 274
salad, 94
Çighêugna, A (Rapallo), 2-3
Cima alla Genovese, 117-8
fritta, 119
Circolo Astistico Tunnel
(Genoa), 112
Citron
Fête du (Menton), 31, 306
tarte au, 279-80
Citrus dessert, 280-1
Ciuppin, 212-3
Clairette, Mamé, 46n, 24, 65,
129, 186, 188-9, 303
Clams with broccoli and
potatoes, 222

Clos St. Joseph winery, 302-3
Clos St. Vincent winery, 300
Clot dóu Baile winery, 300-2
Cocteau, Jean, 49
Cod
dried, see Stockfish
fresh, with anchovy
vinaigrette, 221
salt, 232-3
marinated, 233
Colle dei Bardellini winery, 290
Colli di Luni Vermentino, 287
Columbus, Christopher, 28, 95,
225
quincentennial celebrations,
215
Condiggion, 90-1
Confetteria Pietro Ramanengo
fu Stefano (Genoa), 271
Confraternità del Pesto, 55, 58,
63
Conqueiro, Alvaro, 62
Constantine, Emperor, 58
Cookbooks, Genoese, 15-16
Cooperativa Agricola di
Cinqueterre winery, 286
Cooperativa Pescatori Camogli,
203
Copts, 58
Cornetti, 133
Cornmeal, 159-61
Corti, Darrell, 230
Costa, Battista, 204
Costa, Gian, 204
Costa, Ida, 204
Coward, Noël, 2
Courgettes
fleurs de, frites, 197-8
fried, 193-5
gratin, 47-8
ratatouille, 45-6
stuffed, Coaraze-style, 48-9
tian de, 47-8
Crespi, Antonio, 168
Cricca, Gianfranco, 51, 64, 66,
162, 195, 233
Croesi, Emilio, 288-9
Croquettes
chickpea flour, 190
potato and pine nut, 53
Crusades, 30
Cuculli, 190